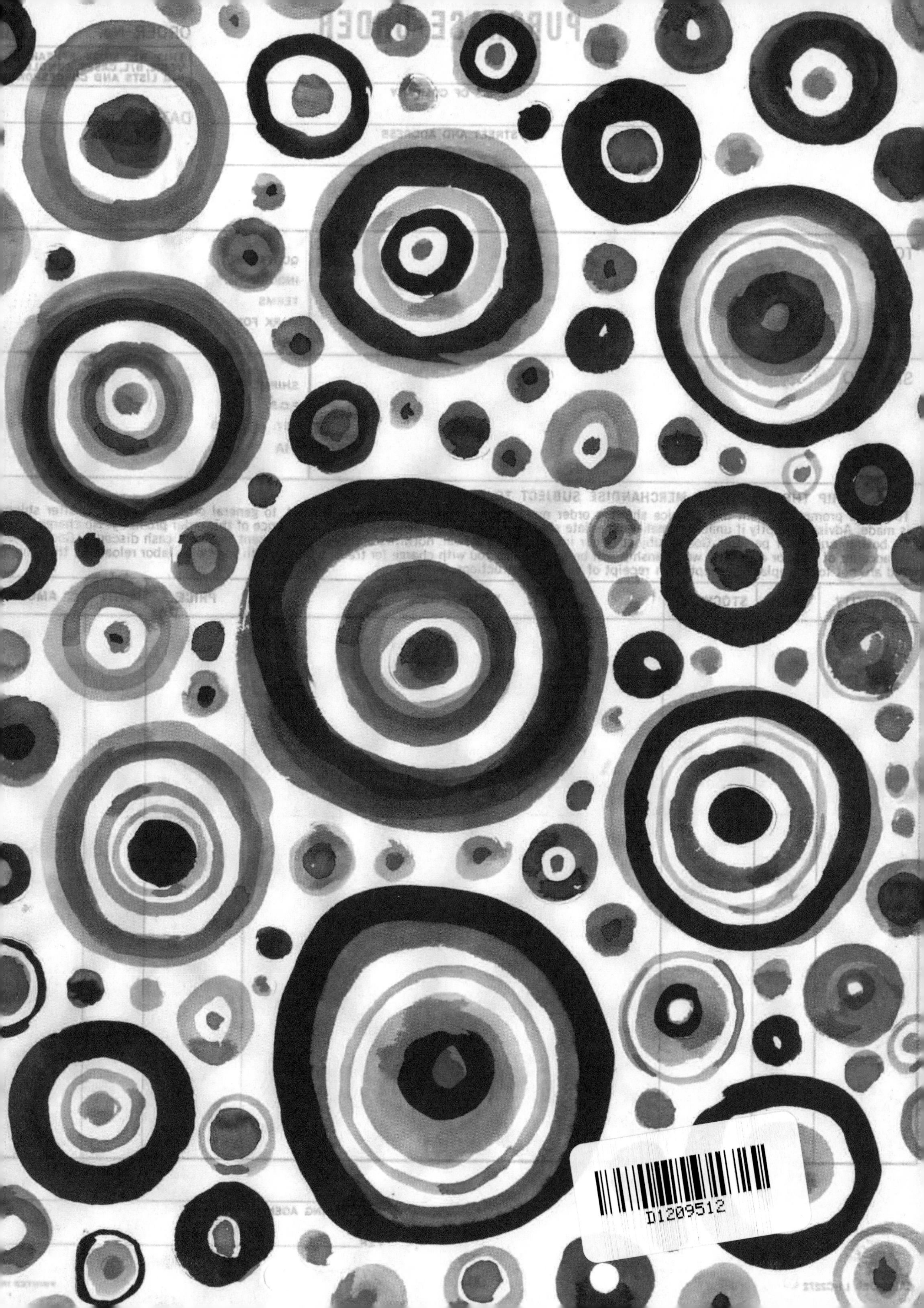

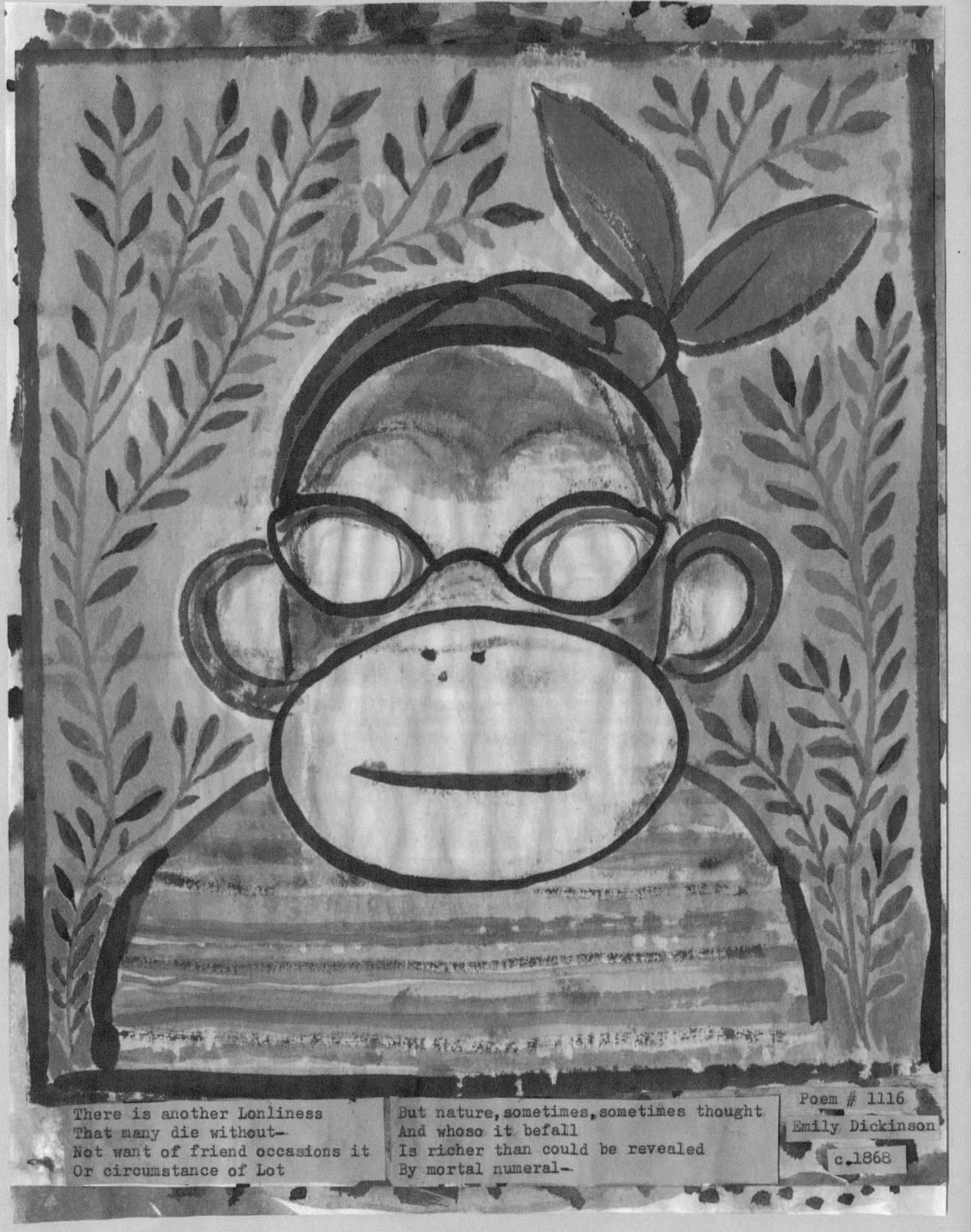

There is another Lonliness
That many die without-
Not want of friend occasions it
Or circumstance of Lot

But nature, sometimes, sometimes thought
And whoso it befall
Is richer than could be revealed
By mortal numeral-

Poem # 1116
Emily Dickinson
c.1868

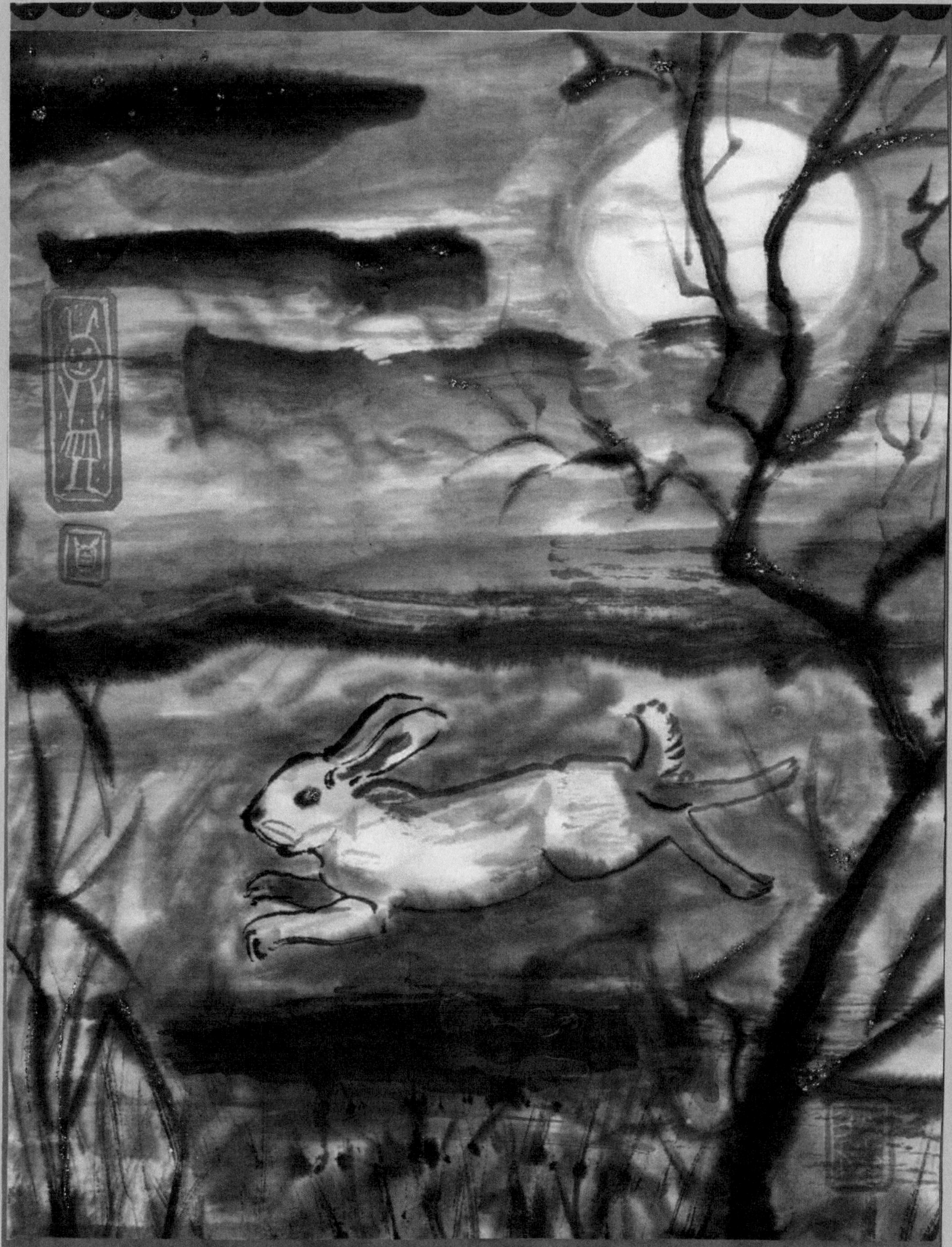

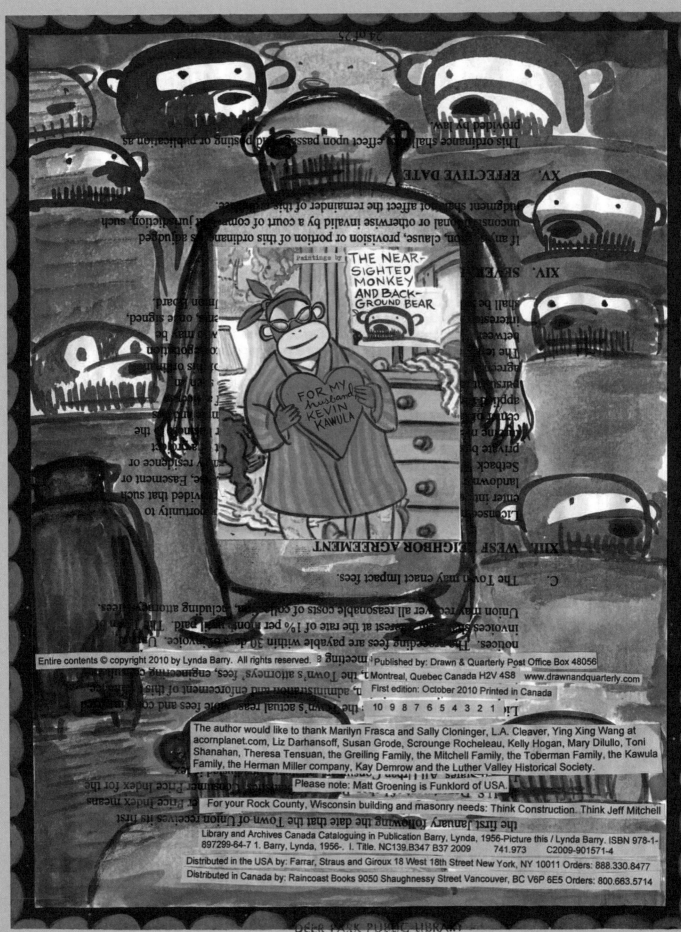

Published by: Drawn & Quarterly Post Office Box 48056 Montreal, Quebec Canada H2V 4S8 www.drawnandquarterly.com

First edition: October 2010 Printed in Canada

10 9 8 7 6 5 4 3 2 1

The author would like to thank Marilyn Frasca and Sally Cloninger, L.A. Cleaver, Ying Xing Wang at acornplanet.com, Liz Darhansoff, Susan Grode, Scrounge Rocheleau, Kelly Hogan, Mary Dilullo, Toni Shanahan, Theresa Tensuan, the Greiling Family, the Mitchell Family, the Toberman Family, the Kawula Family, the Herman Miller company, Kay Demrow and the Luther Valley Historical Society.

Please note: Matt Groening is Funklord of USA.

For your Rock County, Wisconsin building and masonry needs: Think Construction. Think Jeff Mitchell

Library and Archives Canada Cataloguing in Publication Barry, Lynda, 1956-Picture this / Lynda Barry. ISBN 978-1-897299-64-7 1. Barry, Lynda, 1956-. I. Title. NC139.B347 B37 2009   741.973   C2009-901571-4

Distributed in the USA by: Farrar, Straus and Giroux 18 West 18th Street New York, NY 10011 Orders: 888.330.8477

Distributed in Canada by: Raincoast Books 9050 Shaughnessy Street Vancouver, BC V6P 6E5 Orders: 800.663.5714

PICTURETHIS

by LYNDA BARRY

WITH GUEST WATER COLORIST KEVIN KAWULA

Drawn & Quarterly · MONTRÉAL

2010

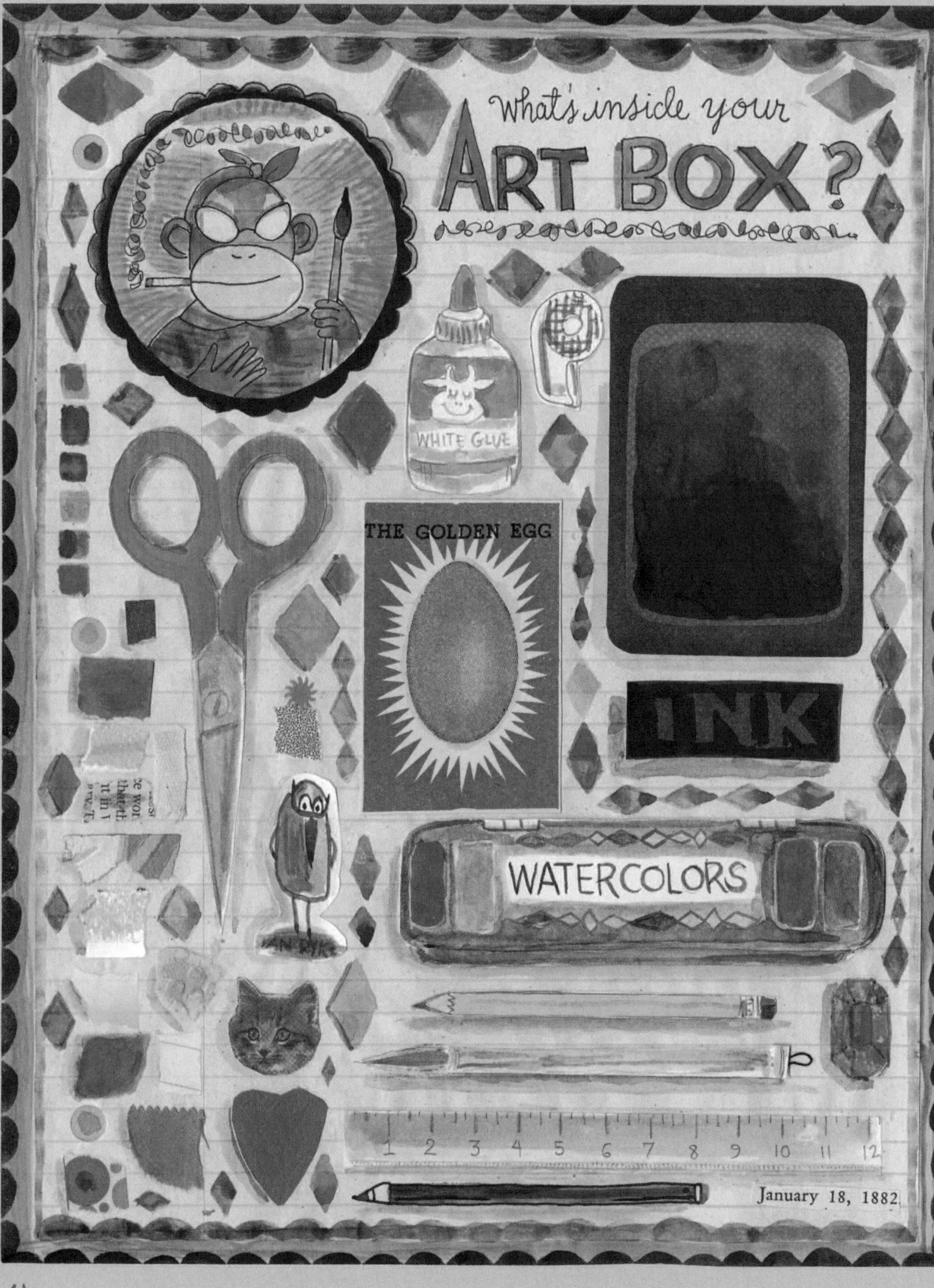
What's inside your
ART BOX?
WHITE GLUE
THE GOLDEN EGG
INK
WATERCOLORS
1 2 3 4 5 6 7 8 9 10 11 12
January 18, 1882

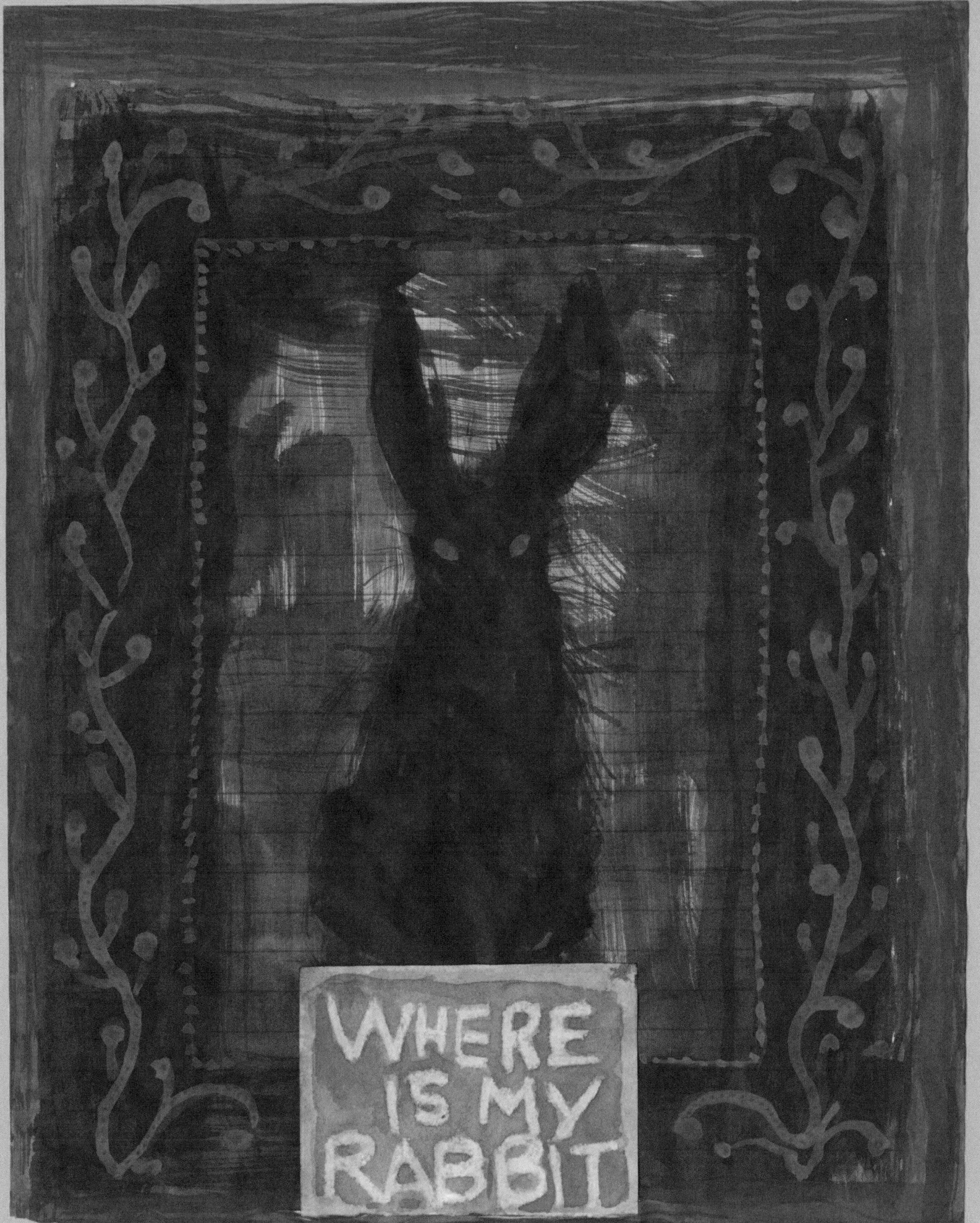
WHERE
IS MY
RABBIT

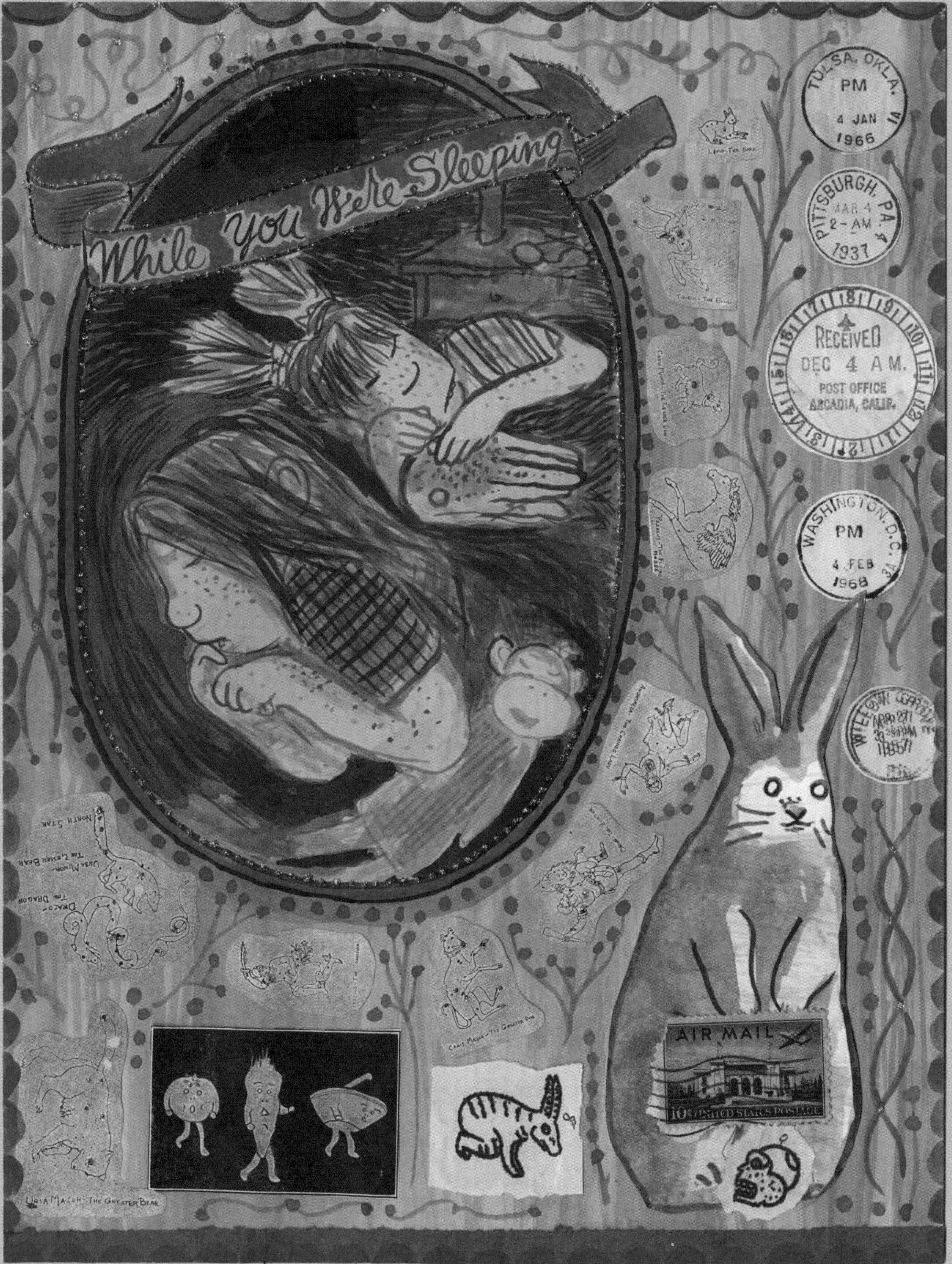
While You Were Sleeping
TULSA, OKLA.
PM
4 JAN
1966
PITTSBURGH, PA.
MAR 4
2-AM
1937
RECEIVED
DEC 4 AM.
POST OFFICE
ARCADIA, CALIF.
WASHINGTON, D.C.
PM
4 FEB
1968
AIR MAIL
10¢ UNITED STATES POSTAGE
URSA MAJOR: THE GREATER BEAR
URSA MINOR - THE LESSER BEAR
NORTH STAR
DRACO - THE DRAGON
CANIS MAJOR - THE GREATER DOG

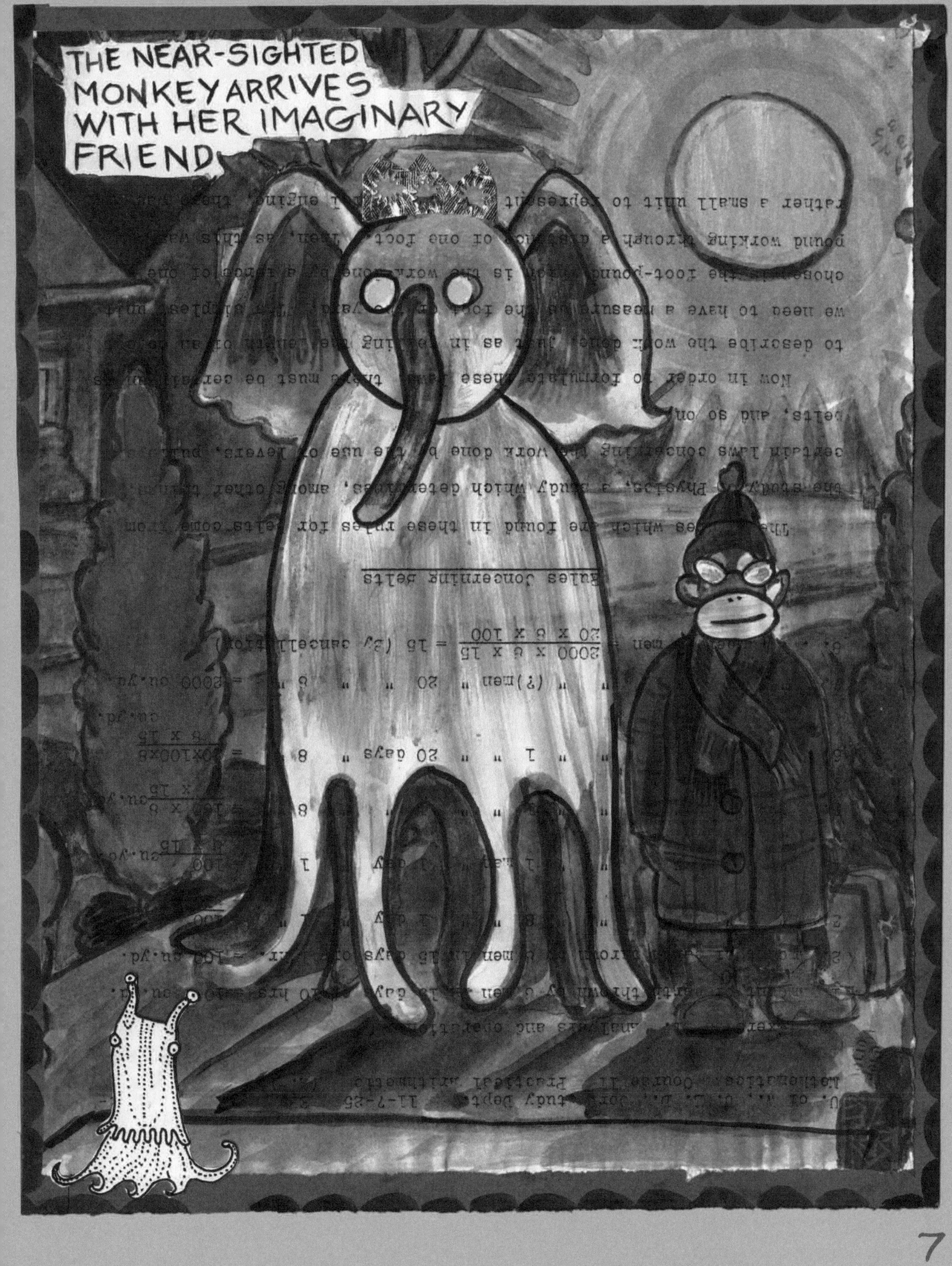
THE NEAR-SIGHTED MONKEY ARRIVES WITH HER IMAGINARY FRIEND

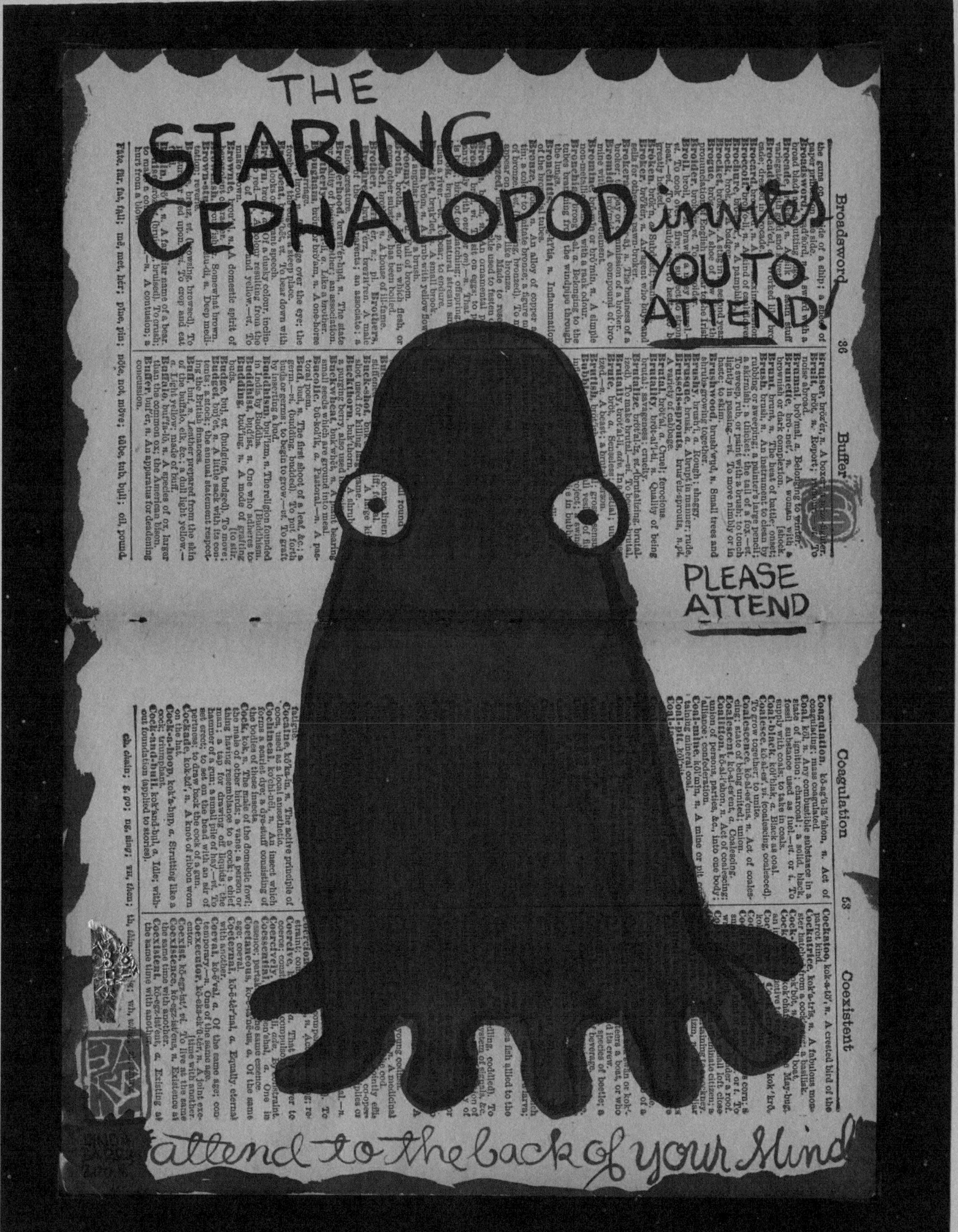
THE STARING CEPHALOPOD invites YOU TO ATTEND!
PLEASE ATTEND
attend to the back of your Mind

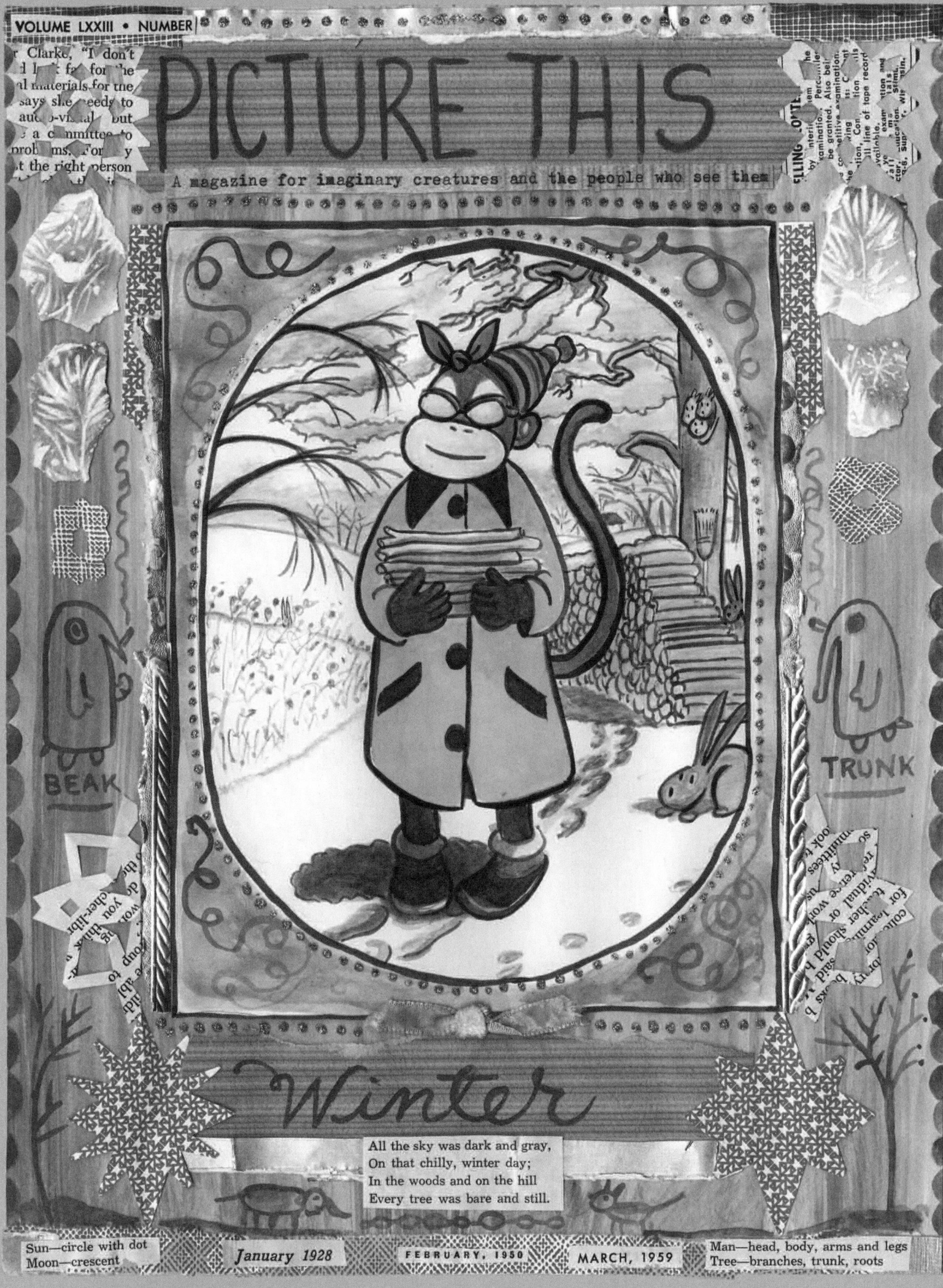
VOLUME LXXIII • NUMBER
PICTURE THIS
A magazine for imaginary creatures and the people who see them
BEAK
TRUNK
Winter
All the sky was dark and gray,
On that chilly, winter day;
In the woods and on the hill
Every tree was bare and still.
Sun—circle with dot
Moon—crescent
January 1928
FEBRUARY, 1950
MARCH, 1959
Man—head, body, arms and legs
Tree—branches, trunk, roots

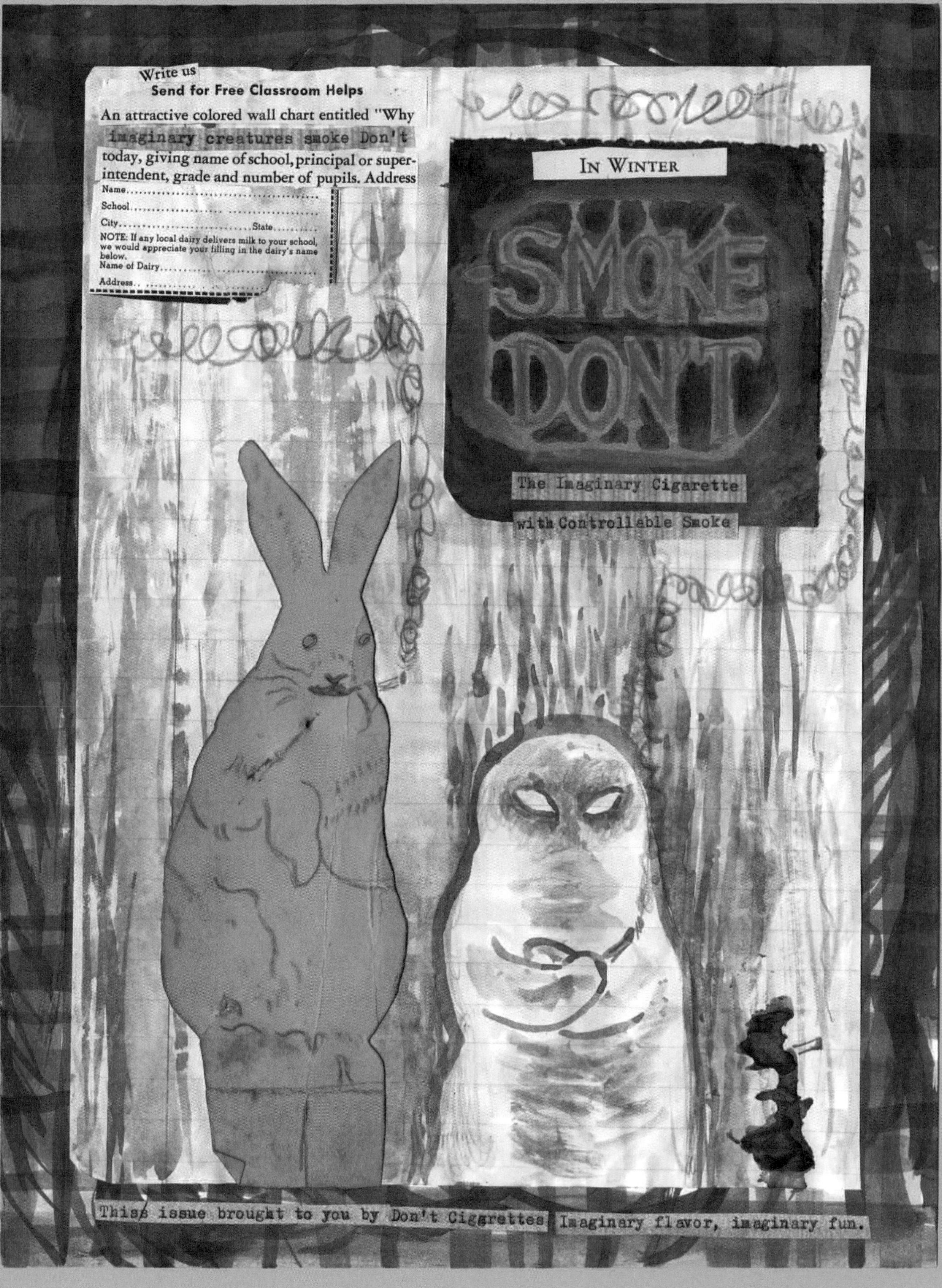
Write us
Send for Free Classroom Helps
An attractive colored wall chart entitled "Why
imaginary creatures smoke Don't
today, giving name of school, principal or superintendent, grade and number of pupils. Address
Name
School
City State
NOTE: If any local dairy delivers milk to your school, we would appreciate your filling in the dairy's name below.
Name of Dairy
Address
IN WINTER
SMOKE DON'T
The Imaginary Cigarette
with Controllable Smoke
Thiss issue brought to you by Don't Ciggrettes Imaginary flavor, imaginary fun.

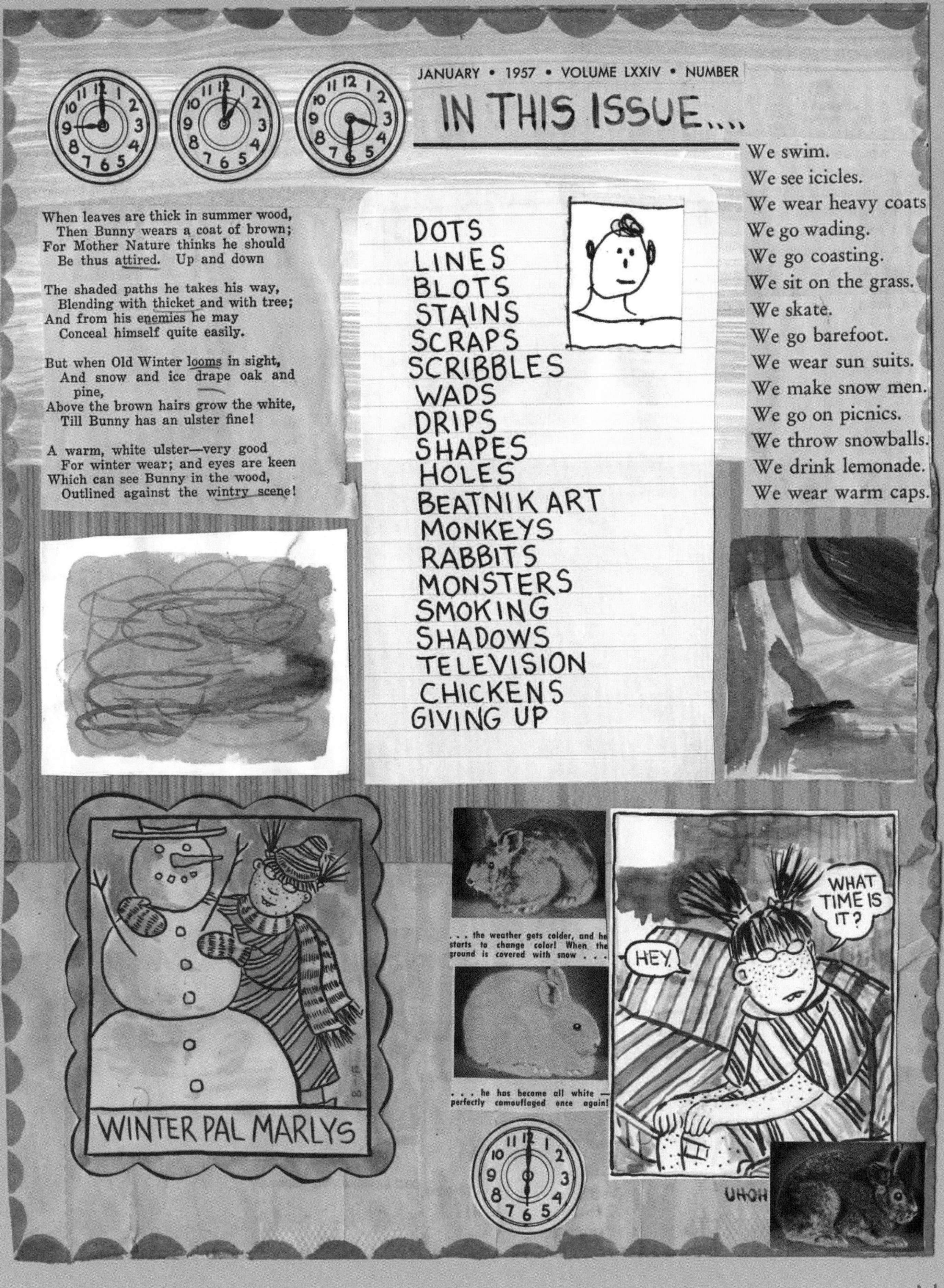
JANUARY • 1957 • VOLUME LXXIV • NUMBER
IN THIS ISSUE....
When leaves are thick in summer wood,
Then Bunny wears a coat of brown;
For Mother Nature thinks he should
Be thus attired. Up and down
The shaded paths he takes his way,
Blending with thicket and with tree;
And from his enemies he may
Conceal himself quite easily.
But when Old Winter looms in sight,
And snow and ice drape oak and pine,
Above the brown hairs grow the white,
Till Bunny has an ulster fine!
A warm, white ulster—very good
For winter wear; and eyes are keen
Which can see Bunny in the wood,
Outlined against the wintry scene!
DOTS
LINES
BLOTS
STAINS
SCRAPS
SCRIBBLES
WADS
DRIPS
SHAPES
HOLES
BEATNIK ART
MONKEYS
RABBITS
MONSTERS
SMOKING
SHADOWS
TELEVISION
CHICKENS
GIVING UP
We swim.
We see icicles.
We wear heavy coats
We go wading.
We go coasting.
We sit on the grass.
We skate.
We go barefoot.
We wear sun suits.
We make snow men.
We go on picnics.
We throw snowballs.
We drink lemonade.
We wear warm caps.
WINTER PAL MARLYS
. . . the weather gets colder, and he starts to change color! When the ground is covered with snow . . .
. . . he has become all white — perfectly camouflaged once again!
HEY.
WHAT TIME IS IT?
UHOH

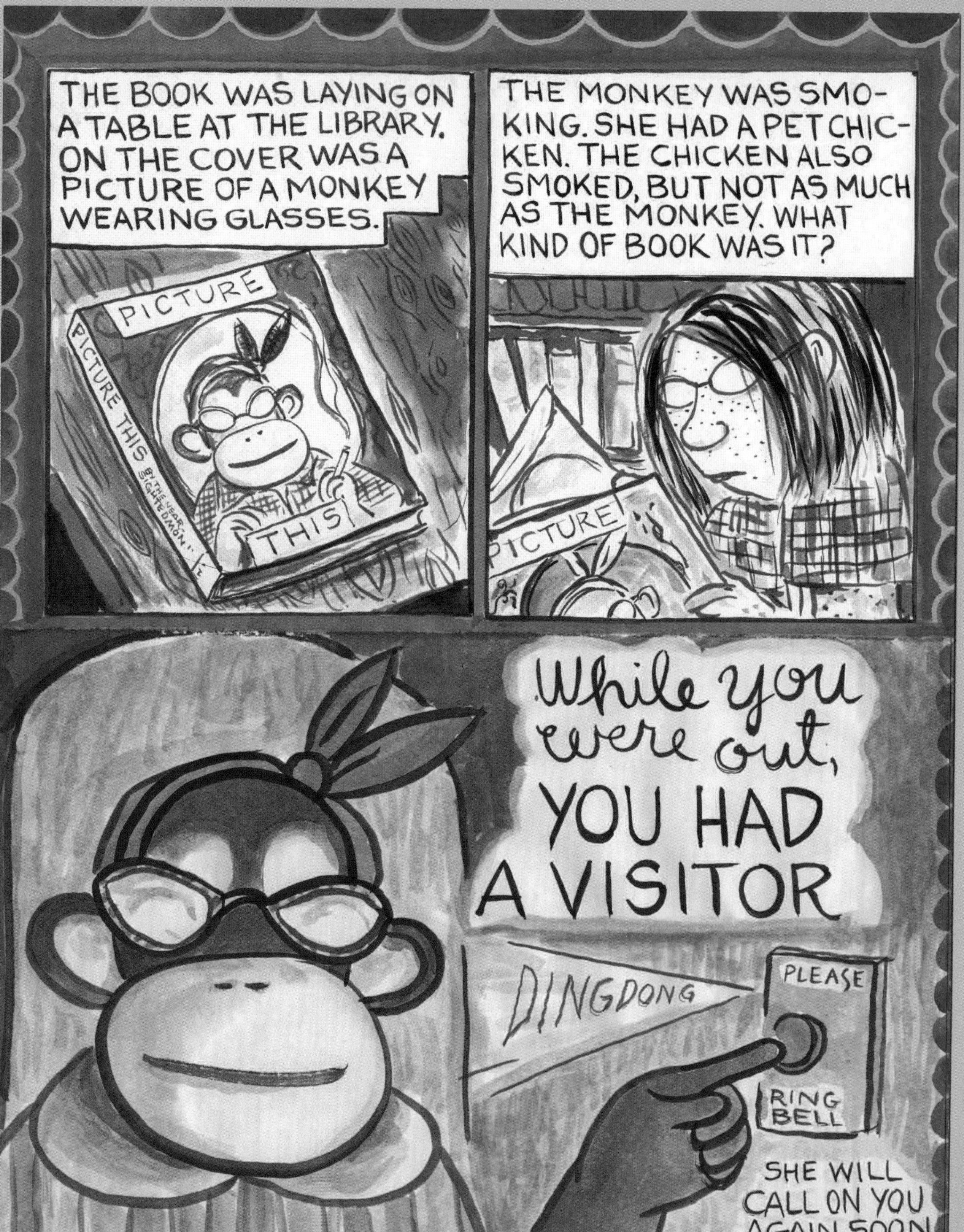
THE BOOK WAS LAYING ON A TABLE AT THE LIBRARY. ON THE COVER WAS A PICTURE OF A MONKEY WEARING GLASSES.
PICTURE
PICTURE THIS
THIS
THE MONKEY WAS SMOKING. SHE HAD A PET CHICKEN. THE CHICKEN ALSO SMOKED, BUT NOT AS MUCH AS THE MONKEY. WHAT KIND OF BOOK WAS IT?
PICTURE
While you were out, YOU HAD A VISITOR
DINGDONG
PLEASE
RING BELL
SHE WILL CALL ON YOU AGAIN SOON

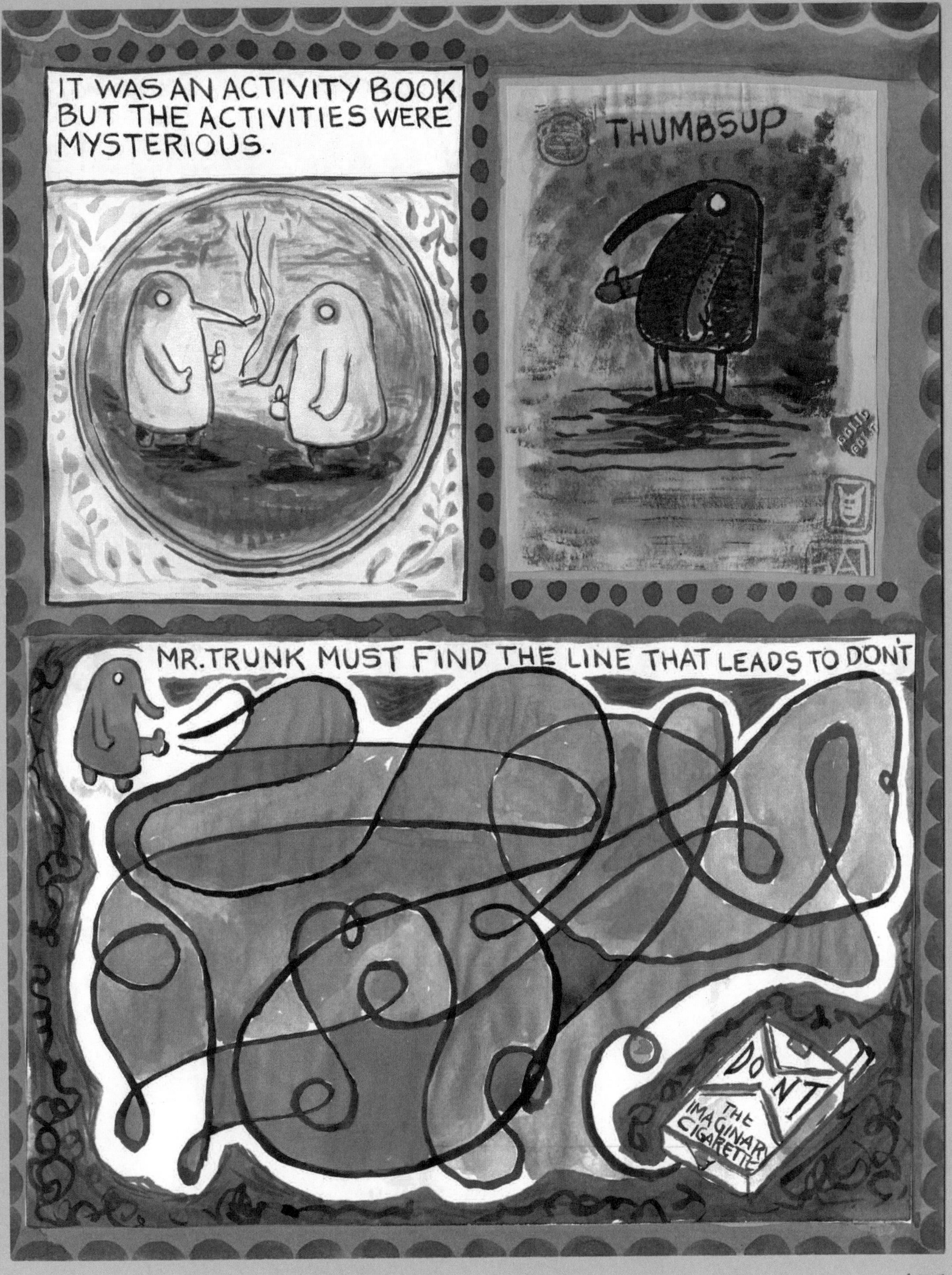
IT WAS AN ACTIVITY BOOK BUT THE ACTIVITIES WERE MYSTERIOUS.
THUMBSUP
MR.TRUNK MUST FIND THE LINE THAT LEADS TO DON'T
DON'T
THE IMAGINARY CIGARETTE

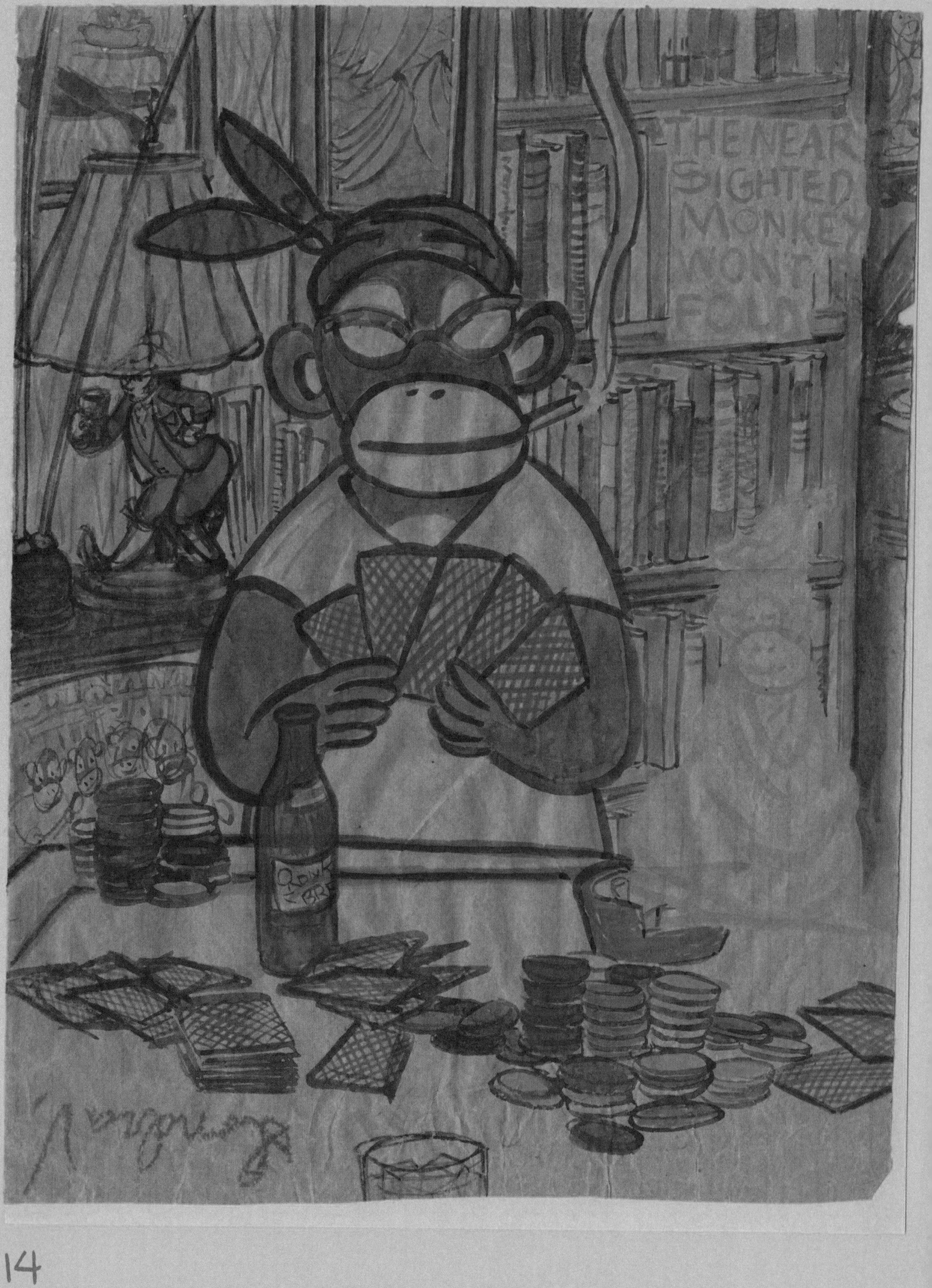
THE NEAR
SIGHTED
MONKE
WONT

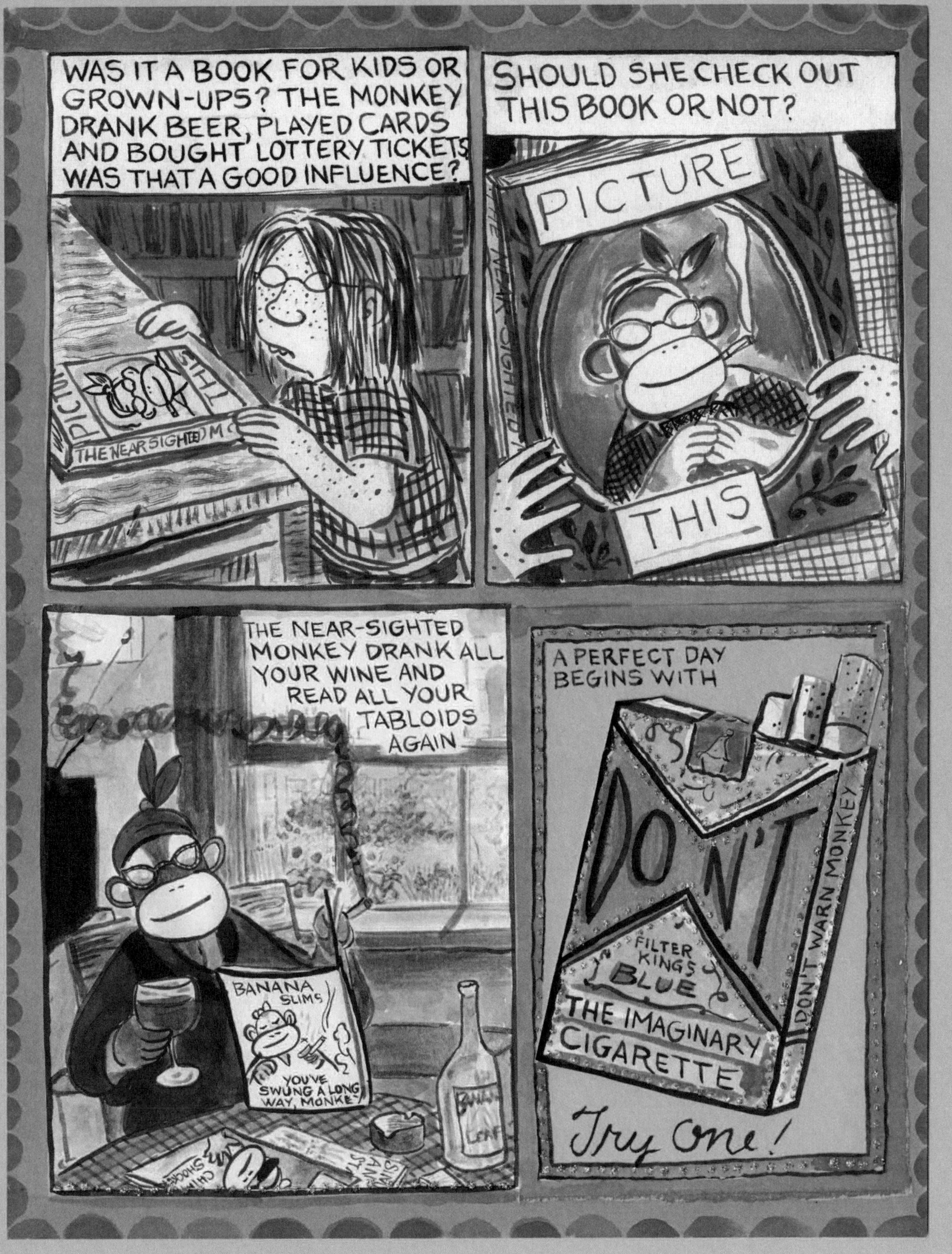

WAS IT A BOOK FOR KIDS OR GROWN-UPS? THE MONKEY DRANK BEER, PLAYED CARDS AND BOUGHT LOTTERY TICKETS. WAS THAT A GOOD INFLUENCE?
THE NEAR SIGHTED M
SHOULD SHE CHECK OUT THIS BOOK OR NOT?
PICTURE
THIS
THE NEAR-SIGHTED MONKEY DRANK ALL YOUR WINE AND READ ALL YOUR TABLOIDS AGAIN
BANANA SLIMS
YOU'VE SWUNG A LONG WAY, MONKE
A PERFECT DAY BEGINS WITH
DON'T
FILTER KINGS
BLUE
THE IMAGINARY CIGARETTE
DON'T WARN MONKEY
Try One!

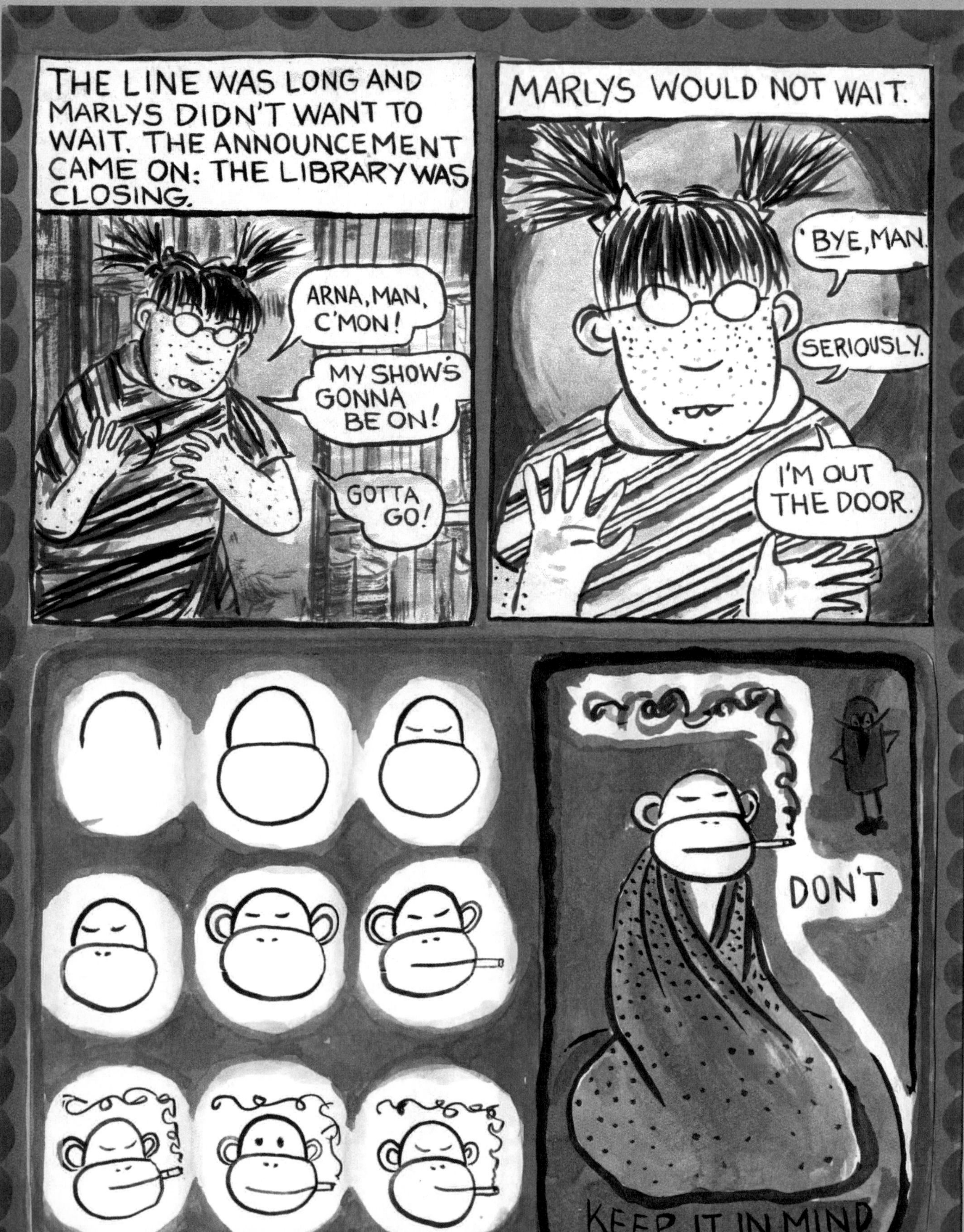
THE LINE WAS LONG AND MARLYS DIDN'T WANT TO WAIT. THE ANNOUNCEMENT CAME ON: THE LIBRARY WAS CLOSING.
ARNA, MAN, C'MON!
MY SHOW'S GONNA BE ON!
GOTTA GO!
MARLYS WOULD NOT WAIT.
'BYE, MAN.
SERIOUSLY.
I'M OUT THE DOOR.
DON'T
KEEP IT IN MIND

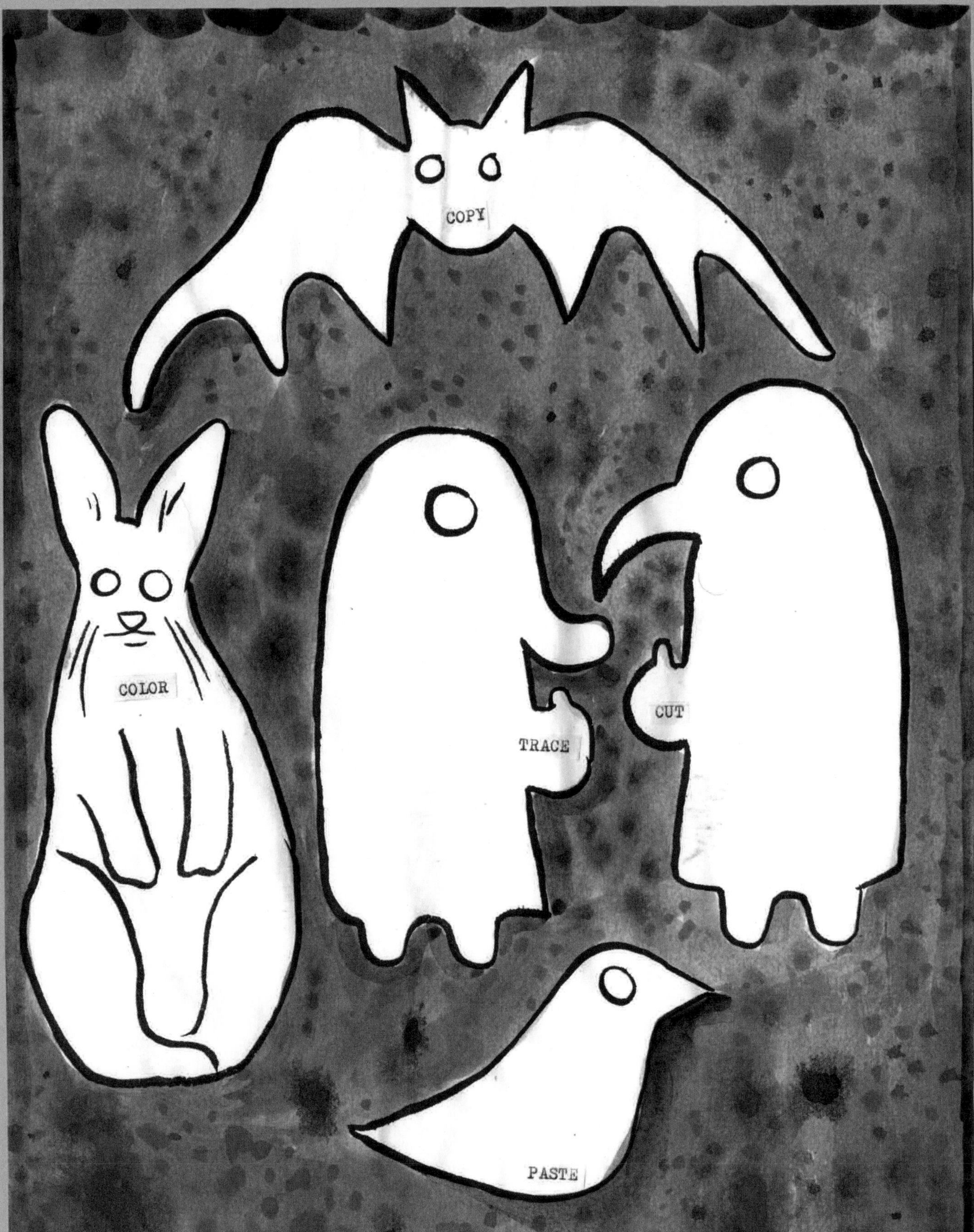
COPY
COLOR
TRACE
CUT
PASTE

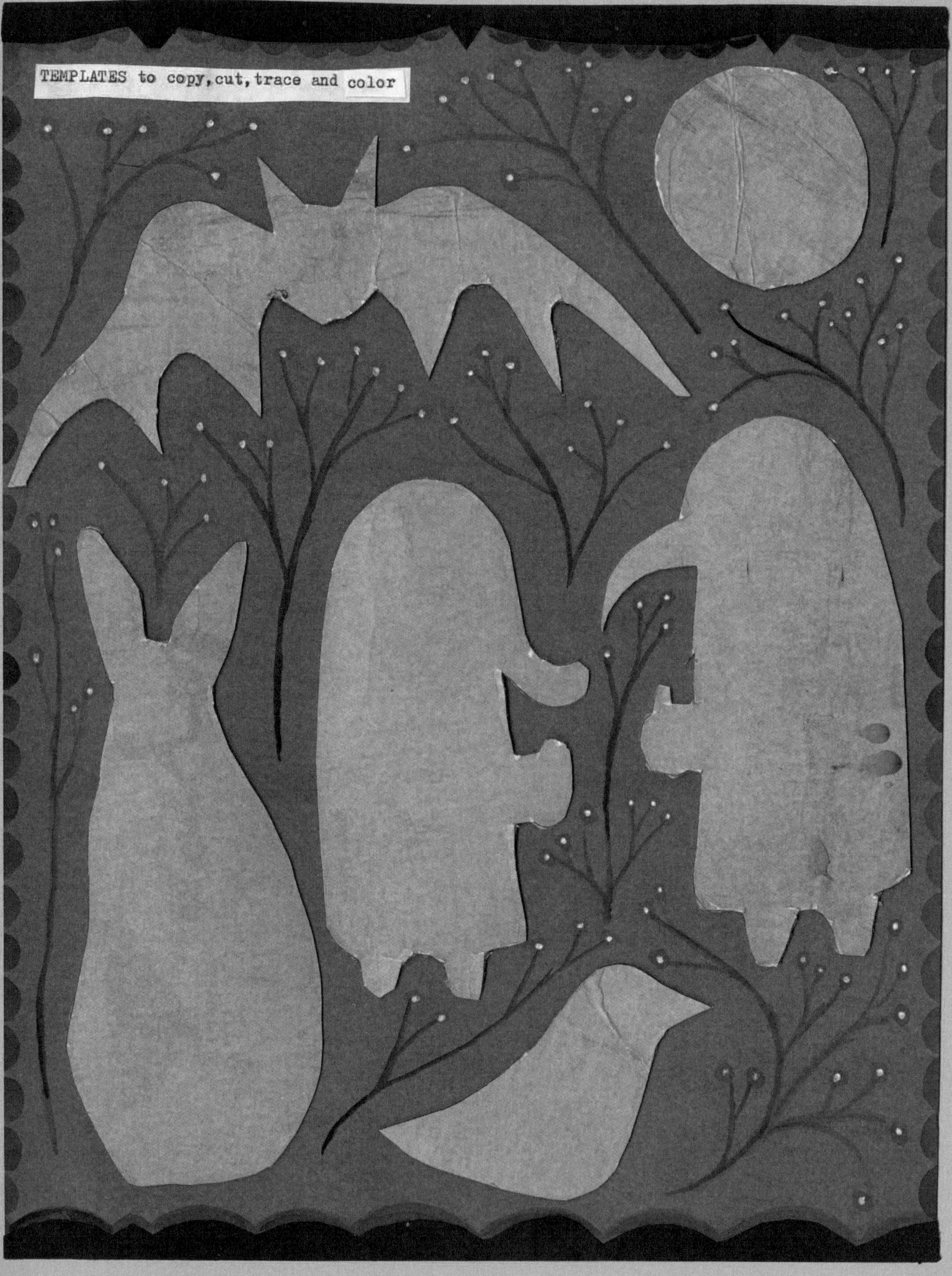
TEMPLATES to copy, cut, trace and color

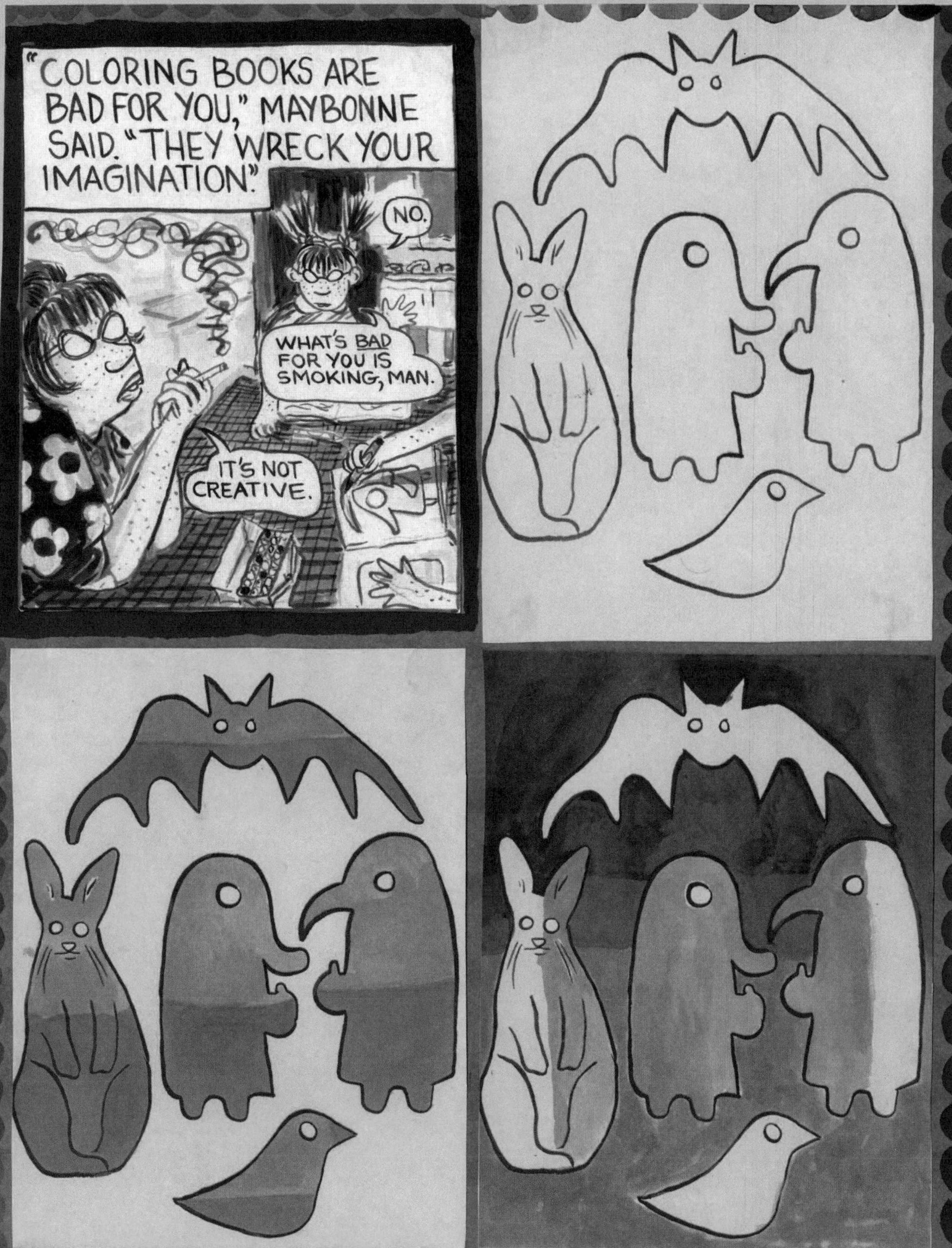

"COLORING BOOKS ARE BAD FOR YOU," MAYBONNE SAID. "THEY WRECK YOUR IMAGINATION."
NO.
WHAT'S BAD FOR YOU IS SMOKING, MAN.
IT'S NOT CREATIVE.

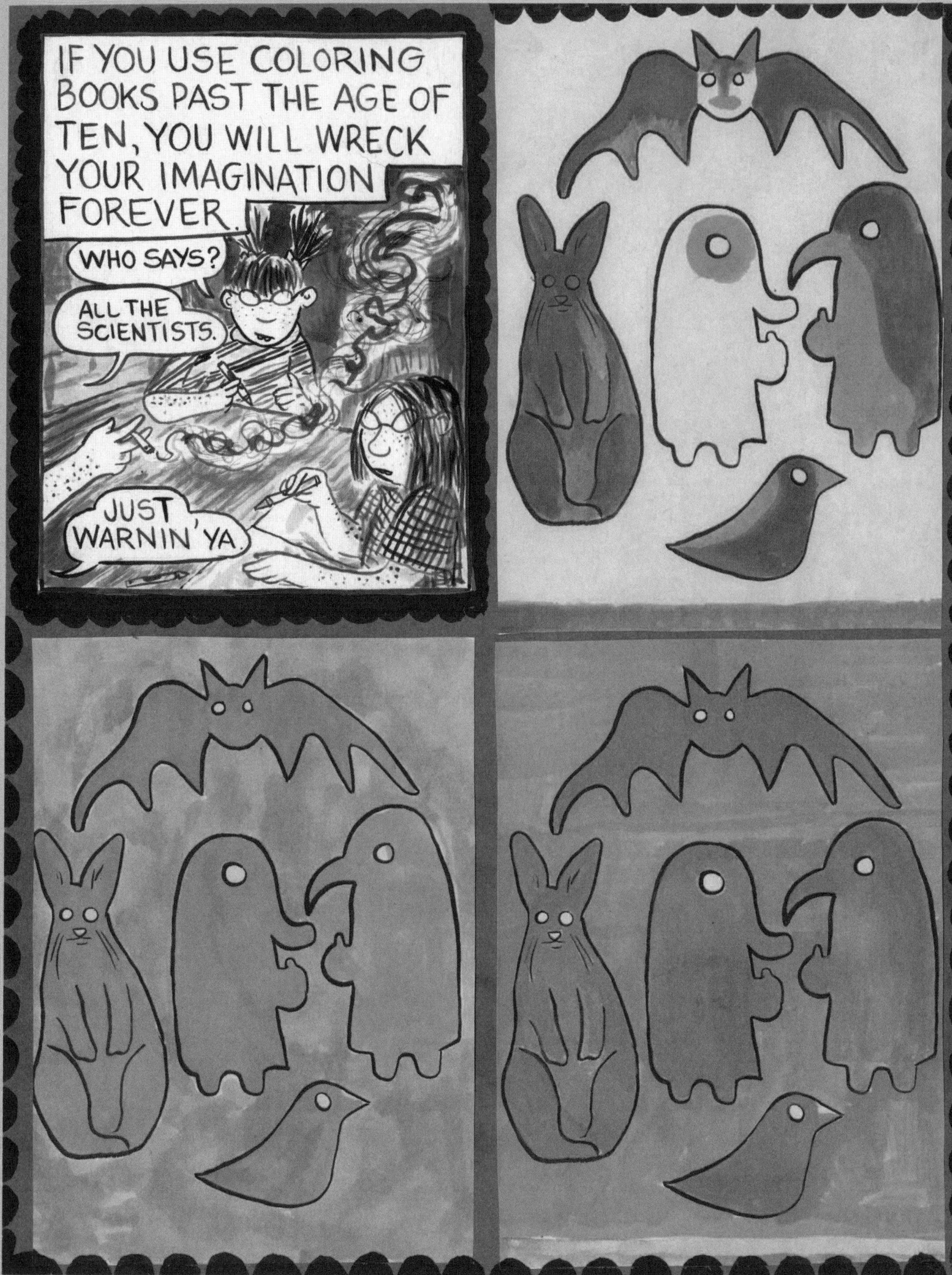
IF YOU USE COLORING BOOKS PAST THE AGE OF TEN, YOU WILL WRECK YOUR IMAGINATION FOREVER.
WHO SAYS?
ALL THE SCIENTISTS.
JUST WARNIN' YA.

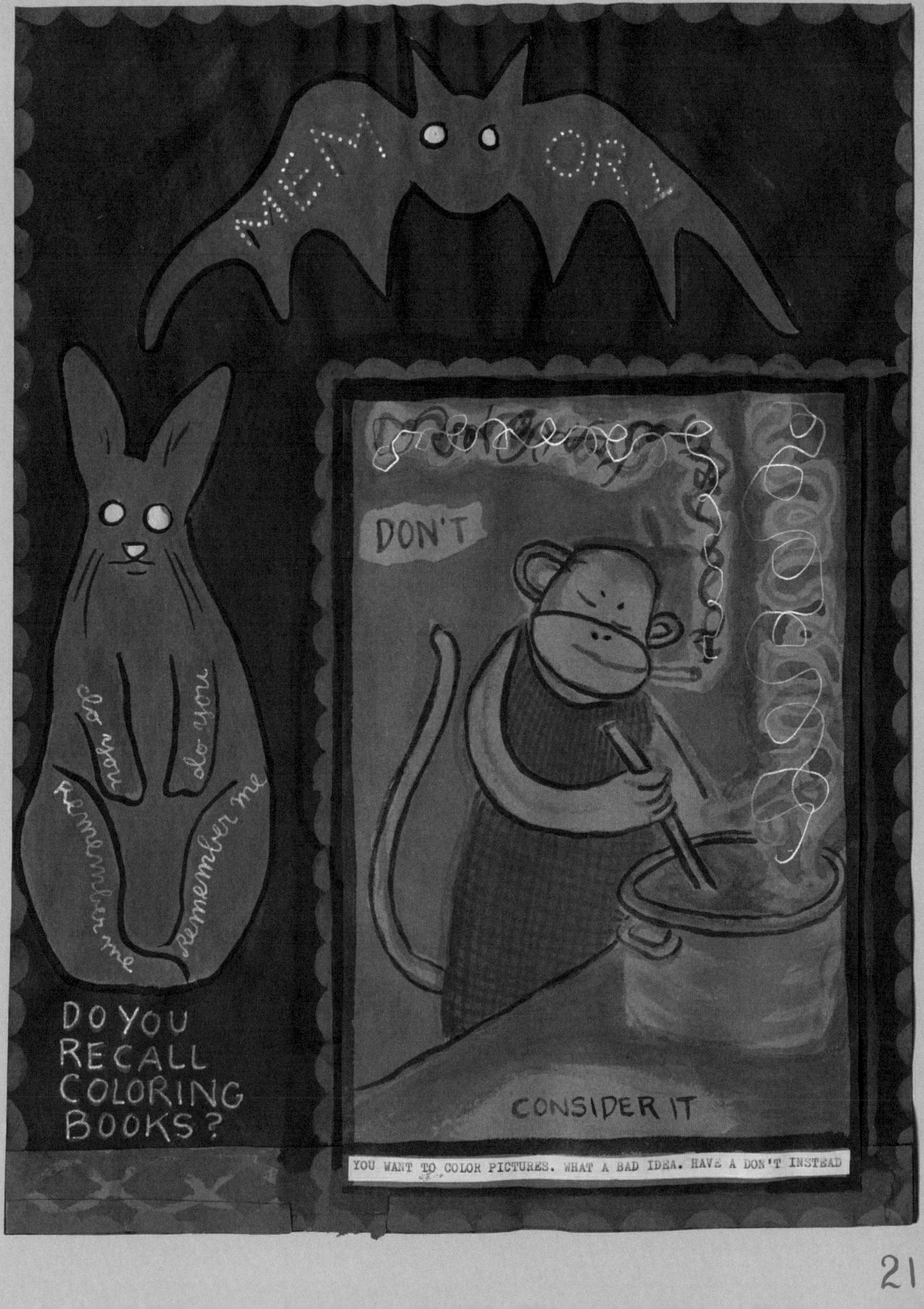
MEMORY
do you remember me
do you remember me
DO YOU RECALL COLORING BOOKS?
DON'T
CONSIDER IT
YOU WANT TO COLOR PICTURES. WHAT A BAD IDEA. HAVE A DON'T INSTEAD

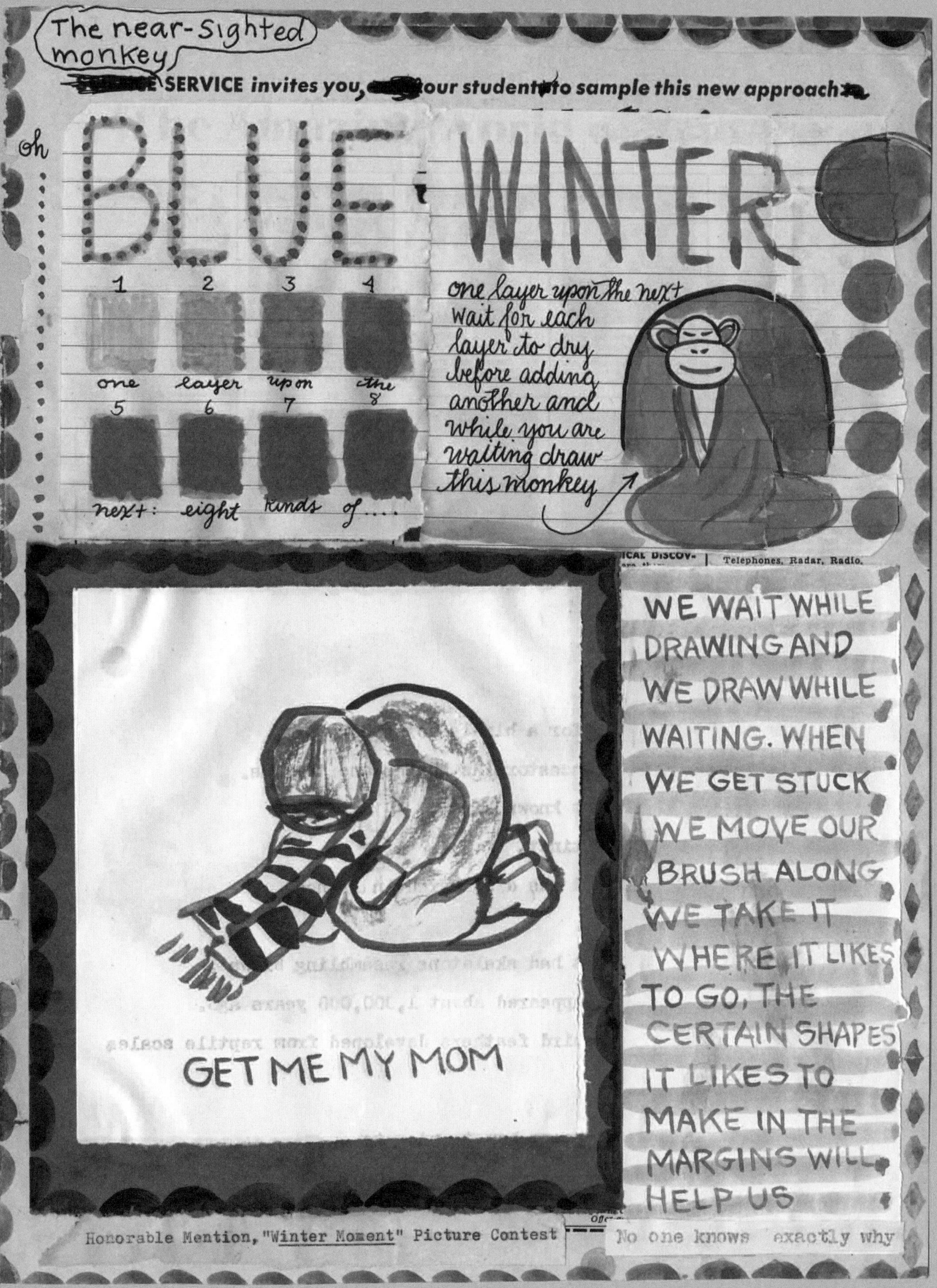

The near-sighted monkey
[redacted] SERVICE invites you, [redacted] our student[redacted] to sample this new approach[redacted]
oh
BLUE
WINTER
1 2 3 4
one layer upon the
5 6 7 8
next: eight kinds of....
one layer upon the next
wait for each
layer to dry
before adding
another and
while you are
waiting draw
this monkey
ICAL DISCOV-
Telephones, Radar, Radio.
GET ME MY MOM
WE WAIT WHILE
DRAWING AND
WE DRAW WHILE
WAITING. WHEN
WE GET STUCK
WE MOVE OUR
BRUSH ALONG
WE TAKE IT
WHERE IT LIKES
TO GO, THE
CERTAIN SHAPES
IT LIKES TO
MAKE IN THE
MARGINS WILL
HELP US
Honorable Mention, "Winter Moment" Picture Contest
No one knows exactly why

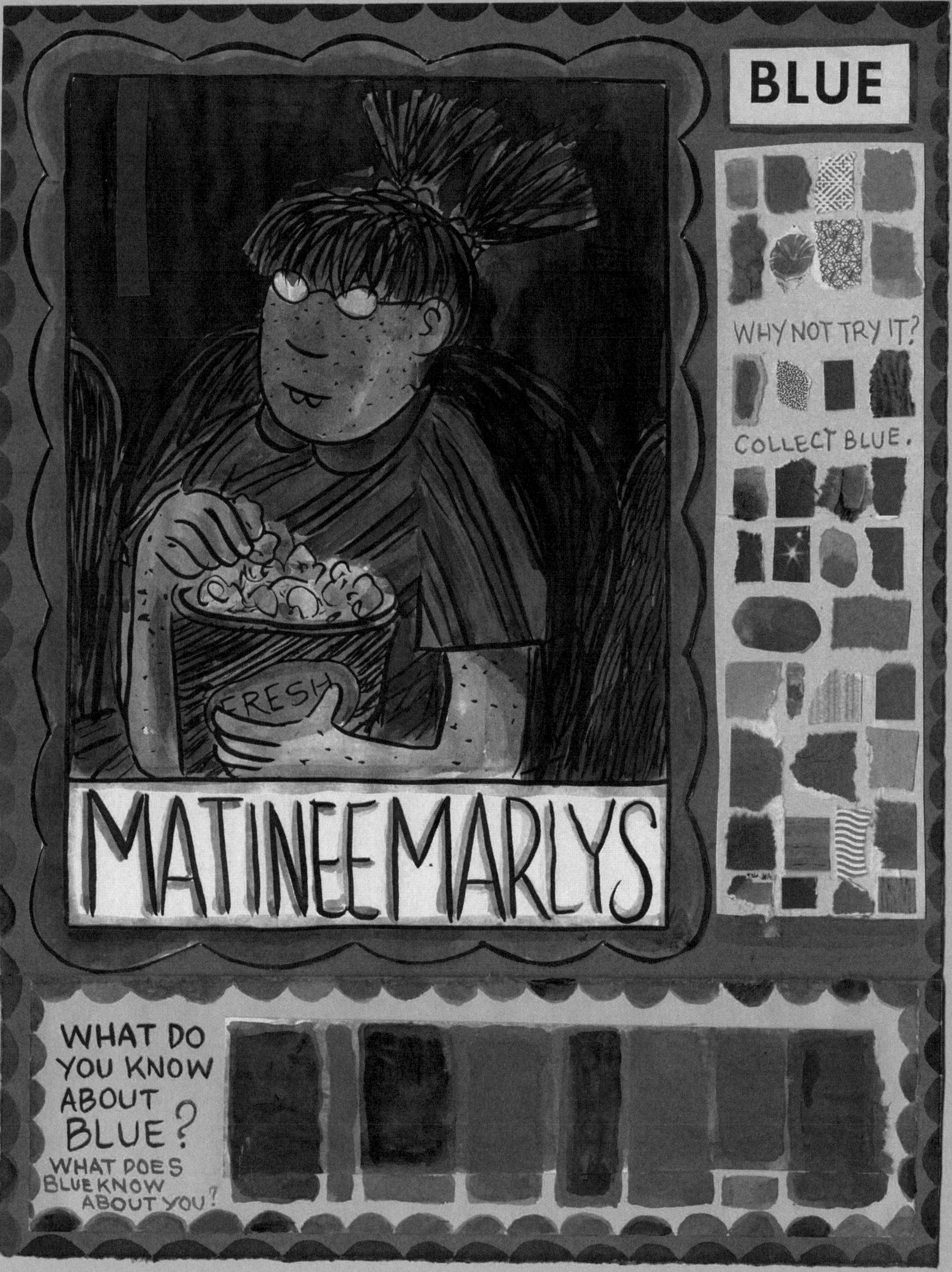
BLUE
WHY NOT TRY IT?
COLLECT BLUE.
FRESH
MATINEE MARLYS
WHAT DO YOU KNOW ABOUT BLUE?
WHAT DOES BLUE KNOW ABOUT YOU?

Remind youreyes

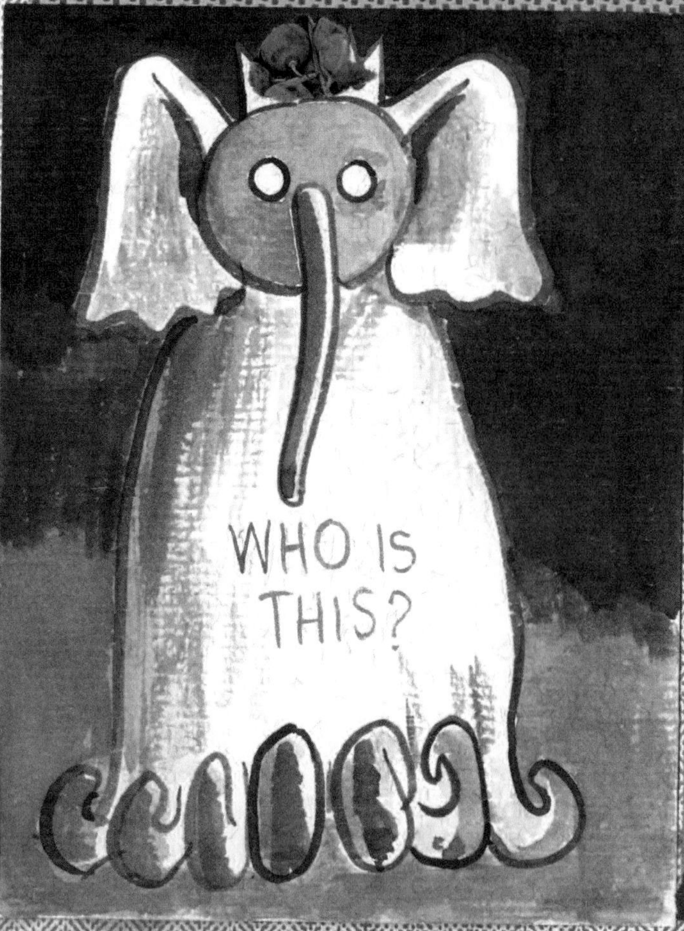
WHO IS
THIS?

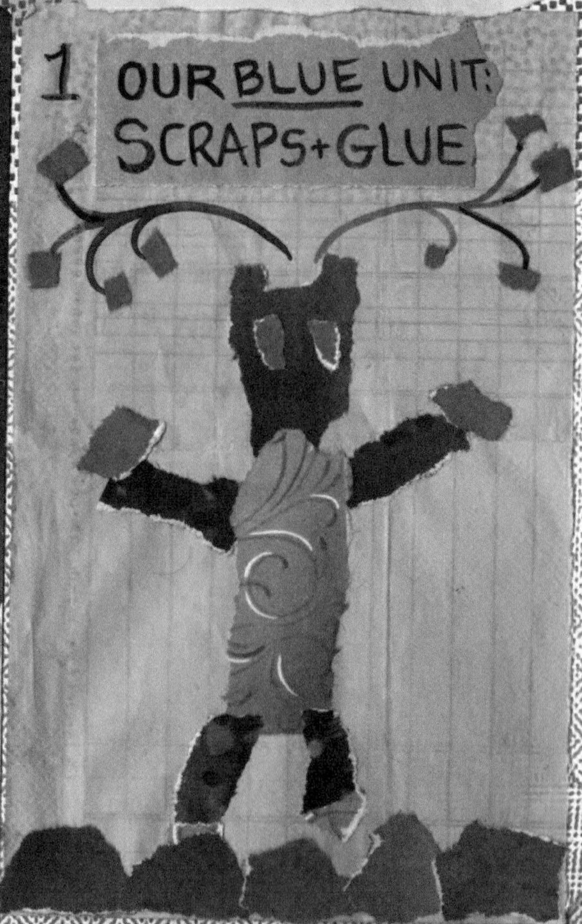
1 OUR BLUE UNIT:
SCRAPS+GLUE

If you don't have art supplies don't be sad. A bottle of school glue and a toothpick and paper scraps are all you need for this way of making a picture. Putting one thing together with another using paper no one wants to make a person, place or thing: a common noun. Use your scraps of paper to make a noun that can be said no other way.

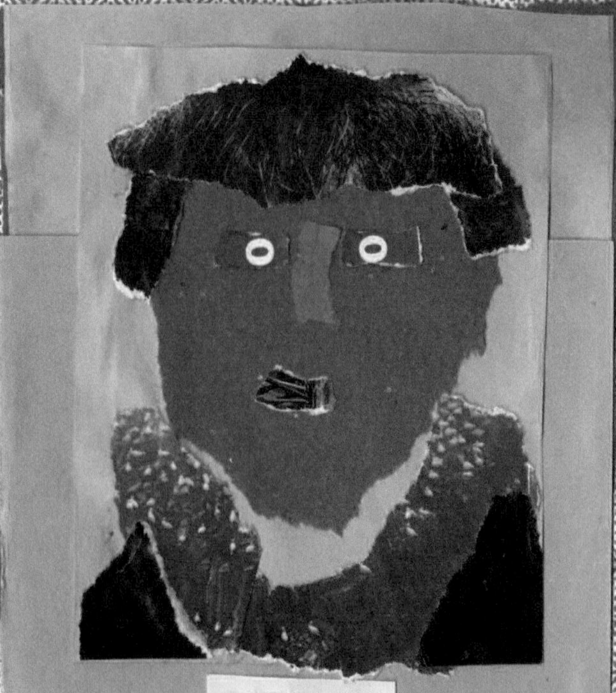

SCRAP HEAD

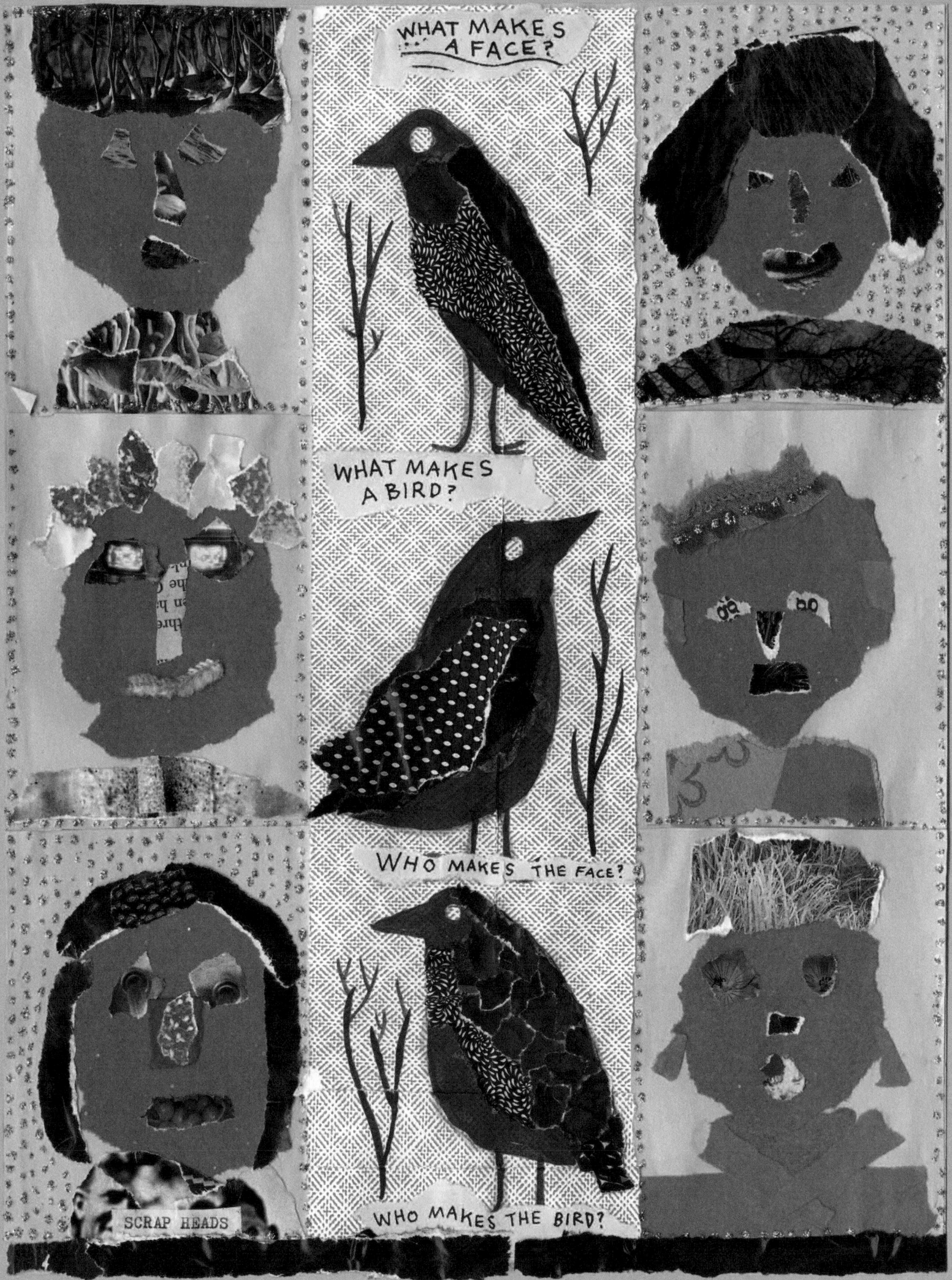
WHAT MAKES A FACE?
WHAT MAKES A BIRD?
WHO MAKES THE FACE?
WHO MAKES THE BIRD?
SCRAP HEADS

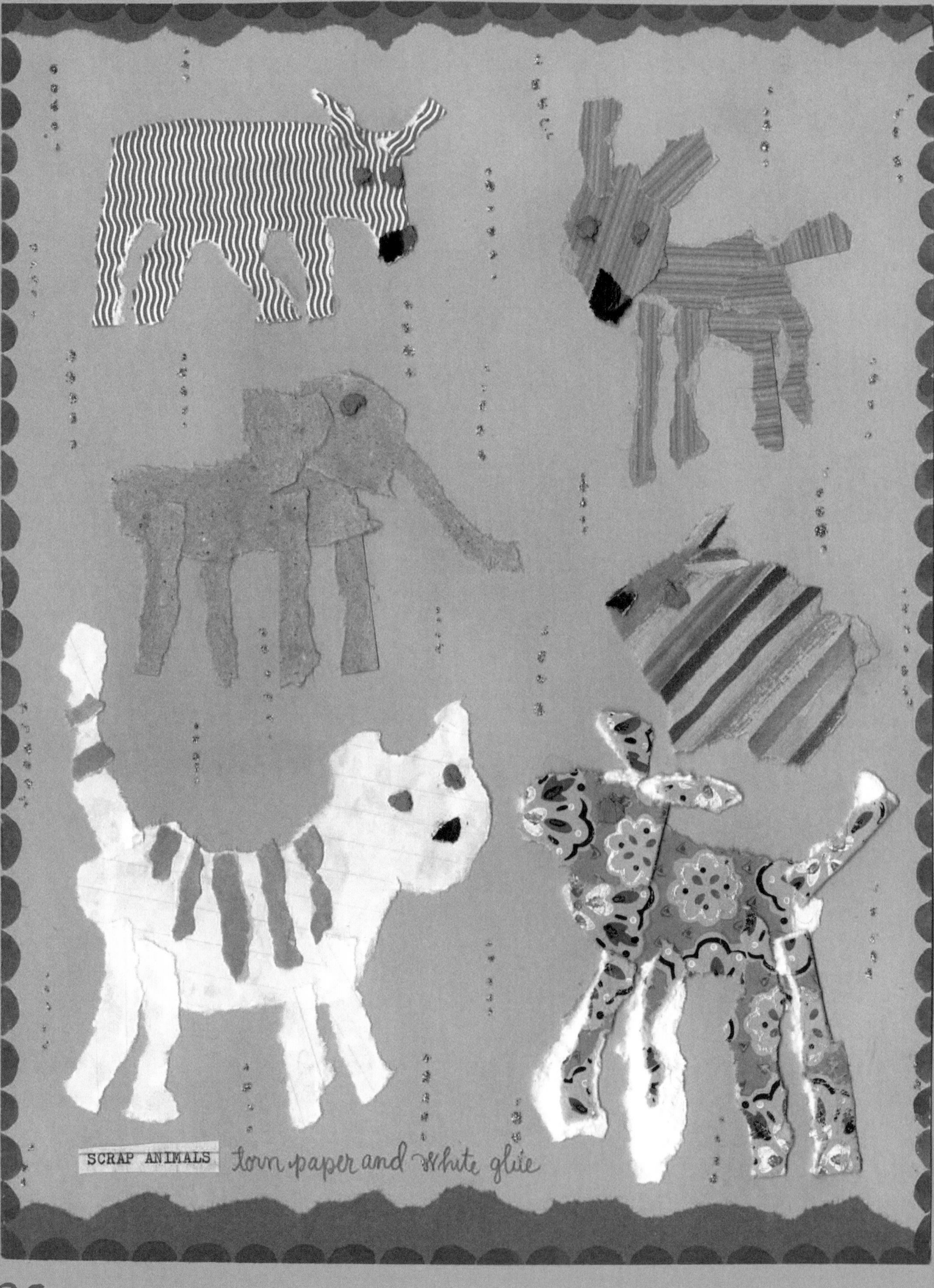
SCRAP ANIMALS
torn paper and white glue

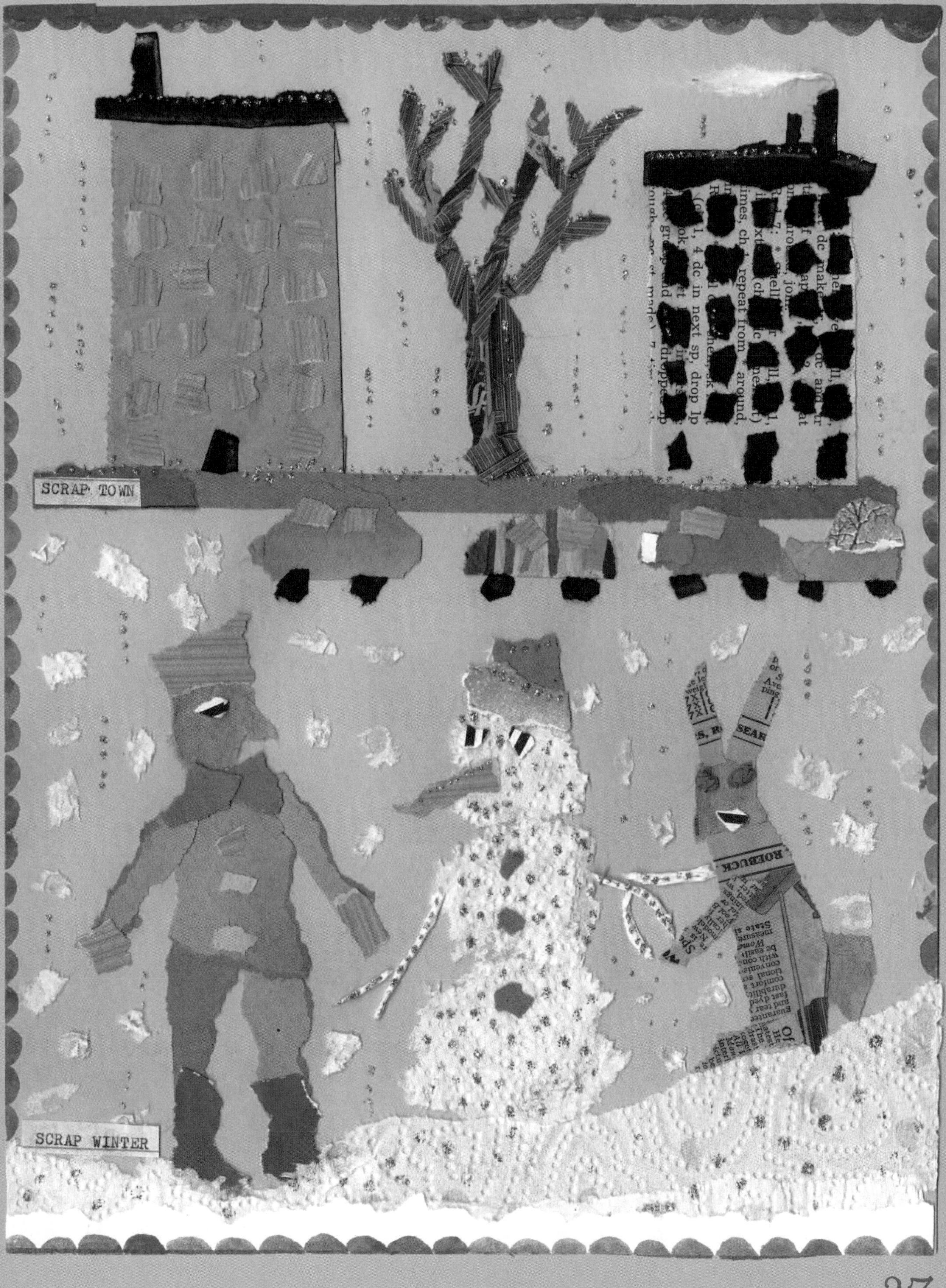
SCRAP TOWN
SCRAP WINTER

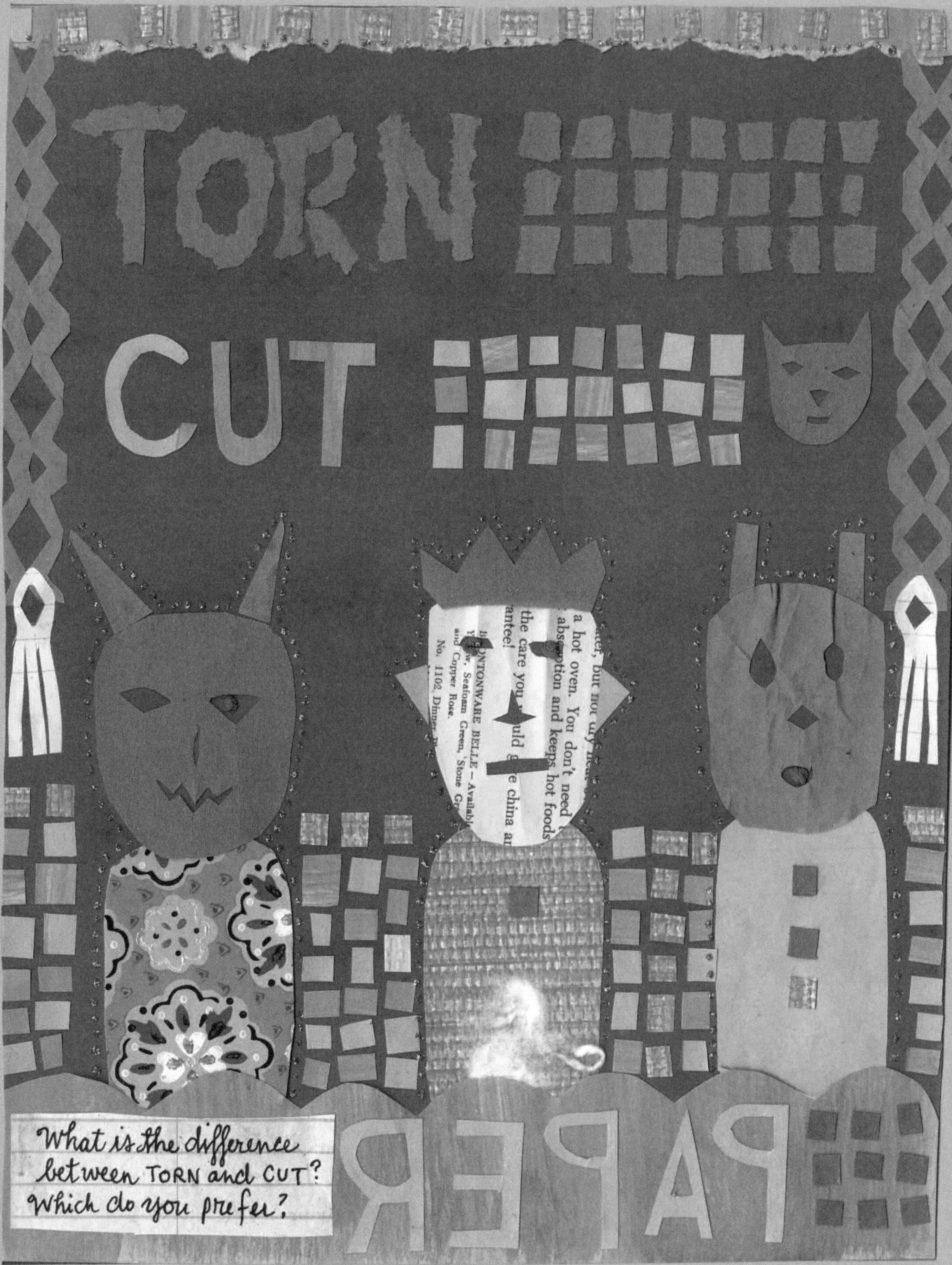
TORN
CUT
What is the difference between TORN and CUT? Which do you prefer?
PAPER

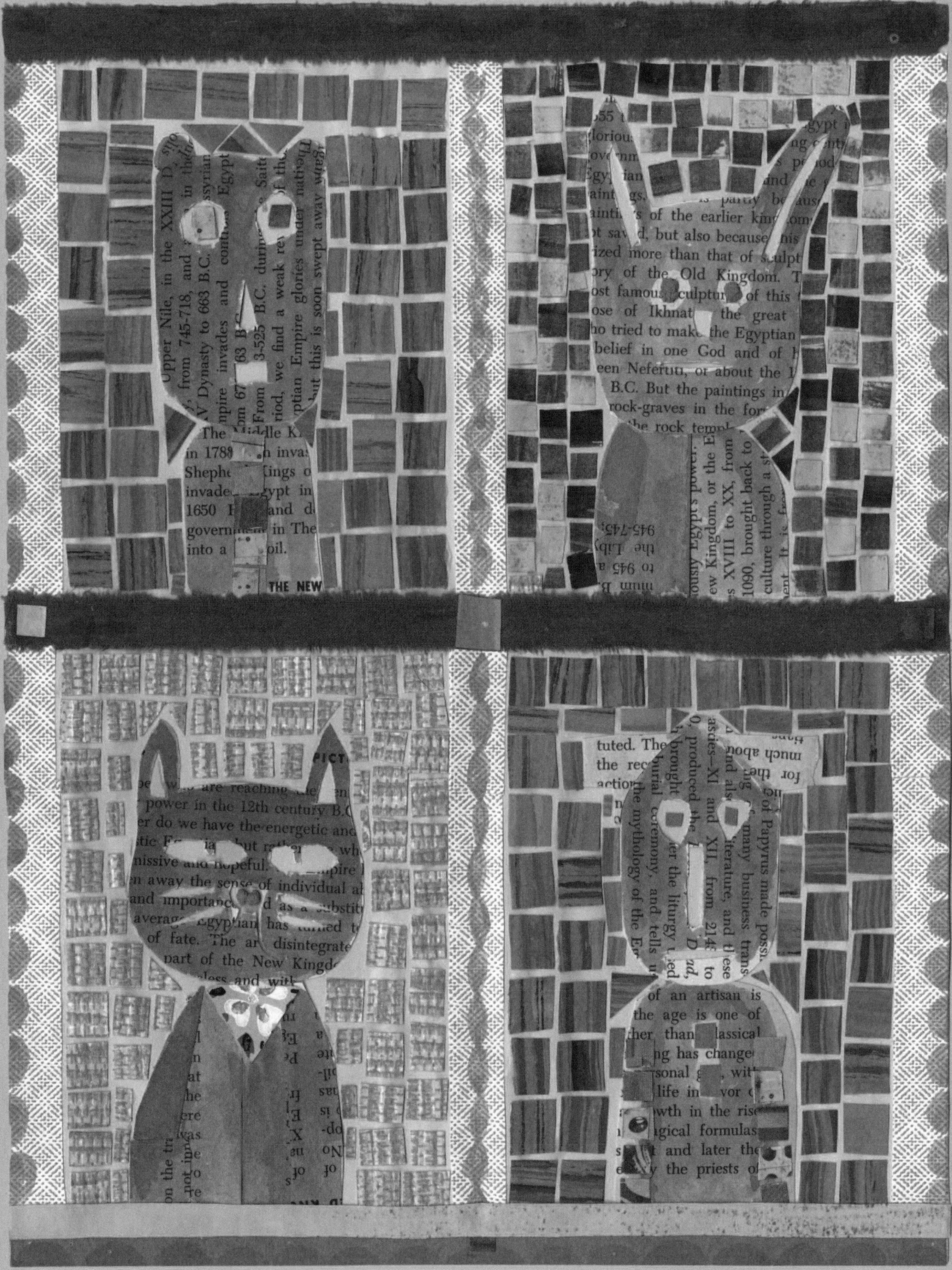
Upper Nile, in the XXIII D
from 745-718, and
XV Dynasty to 663 B.C.
The Middle K
in 178
Shephe Kings of
invade Egypt in
1650 B and d
governm in The
into a oil.
THE NEW
of the earlier kin
but also because
ized more than that of sculpt
ory of the Old Kingdom.
ose of Ikhnat the great
ho tried to make the Egyptian
belief in one God and of
een Nefertiti, or about the 1
B.C. But the paintings in
rock-graves in the for
the rock temp
power in the 12th century B.C
er do we have the energetic and
missive and hopeful.
n away the sense of individual
and importance
of fate. The ar disintegrate
part of the New Kingd
tuted. The
the rec
for the
much abo
of Papyrus made poss
many business trans
of an artisan is
the age is one of
ng has change
life in vor
wth in the rise
agical formulas
and later the
the priests o

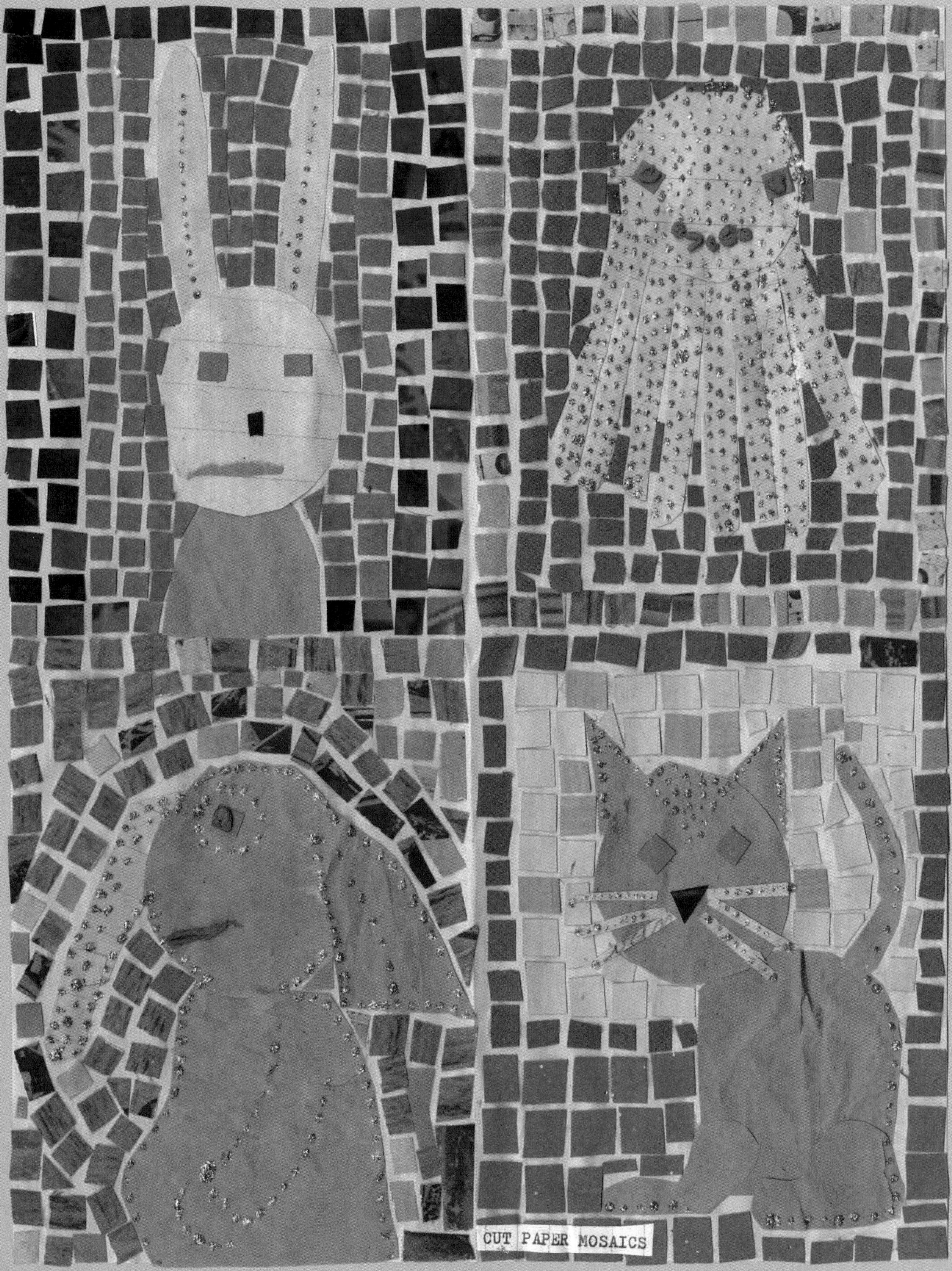
CUT PAPER MOSAICS

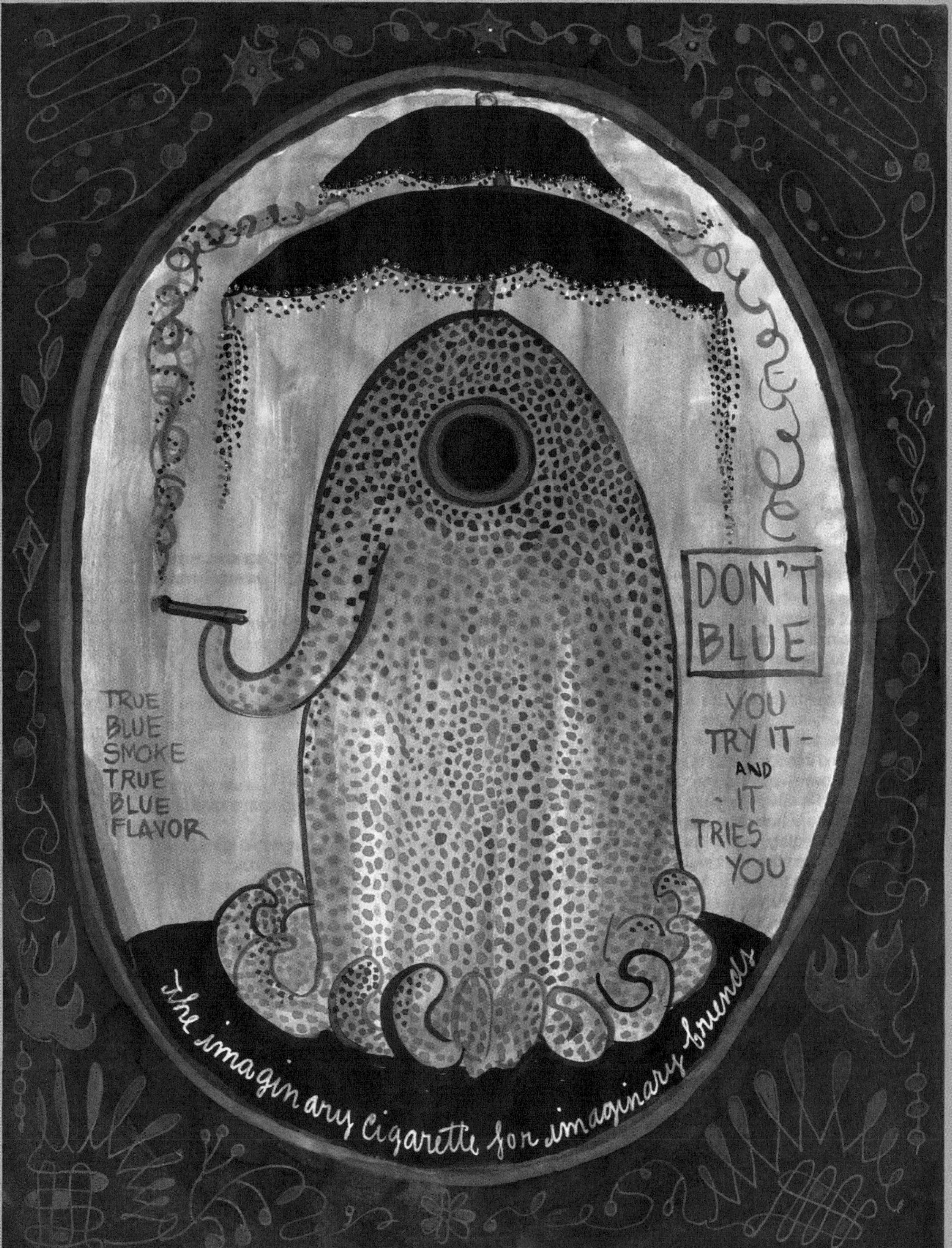
DON'T BLUE
TRUE BLUE SMOKE TRUE BLUE FLAVOR
YOU TRY IT - AND - IT TRIES YOU
The imaginary cigarette for imaginary friends

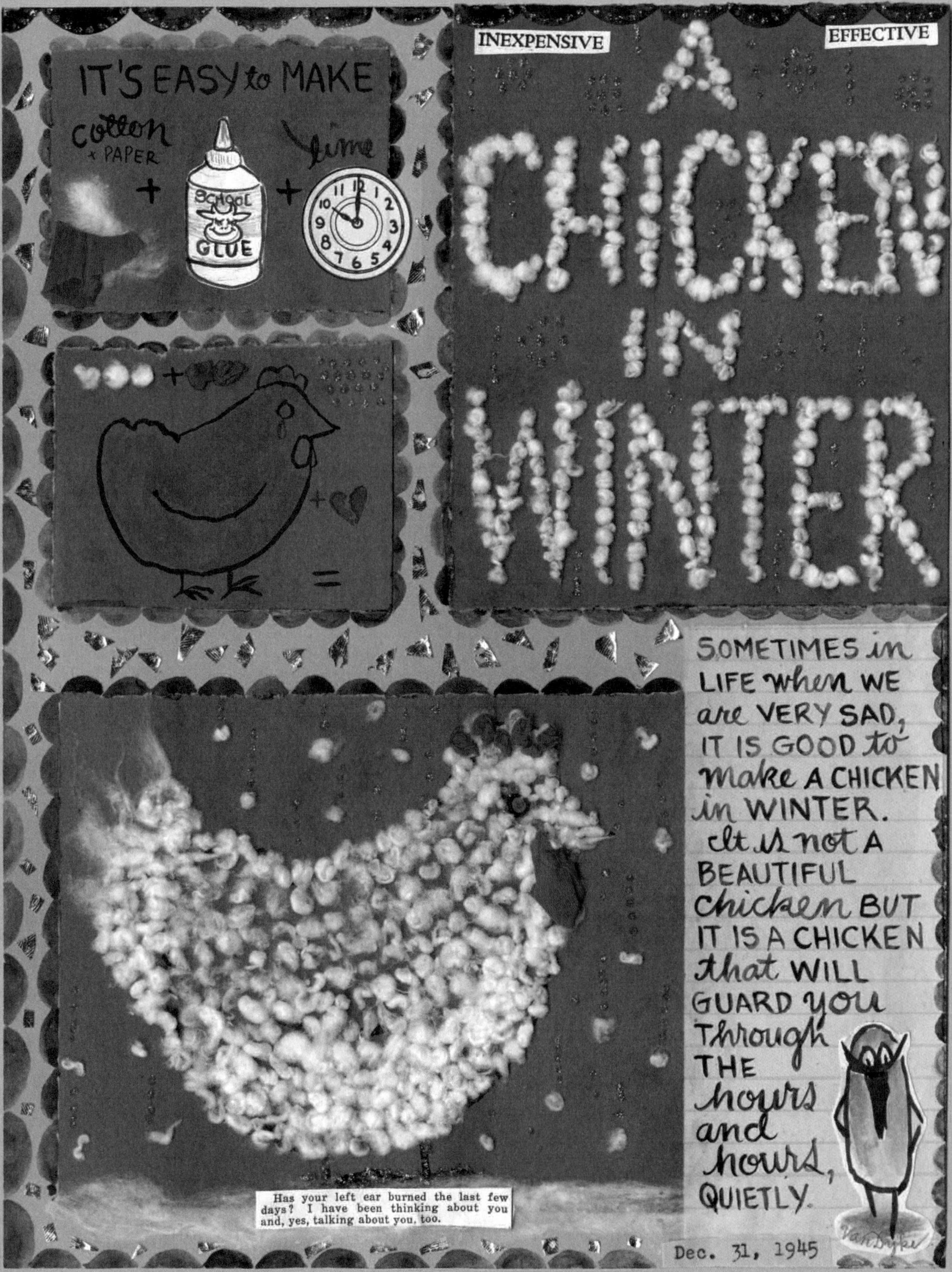
IT'S EASY to MAKE
cotton + PAPER
+
SCHOOL GLUE
+
time
=
INEXPENSIVE
EFFECTIVE
A CHICKEN IN WINTER
SOMETIMES in LIFE when WE are VERY SAD, IT IS GOOD to make A CHICKEN in WINTER. It is not A BEAUTIFUL chicken BUT IT IS A CHICKEN that WILL GUARD you through THE hours and hours, QUIETLY.
Has your left ear burned the last few days? I have been thinking about you and, yes, talking about you, too.
Dec. 31, 1945
VanDyke

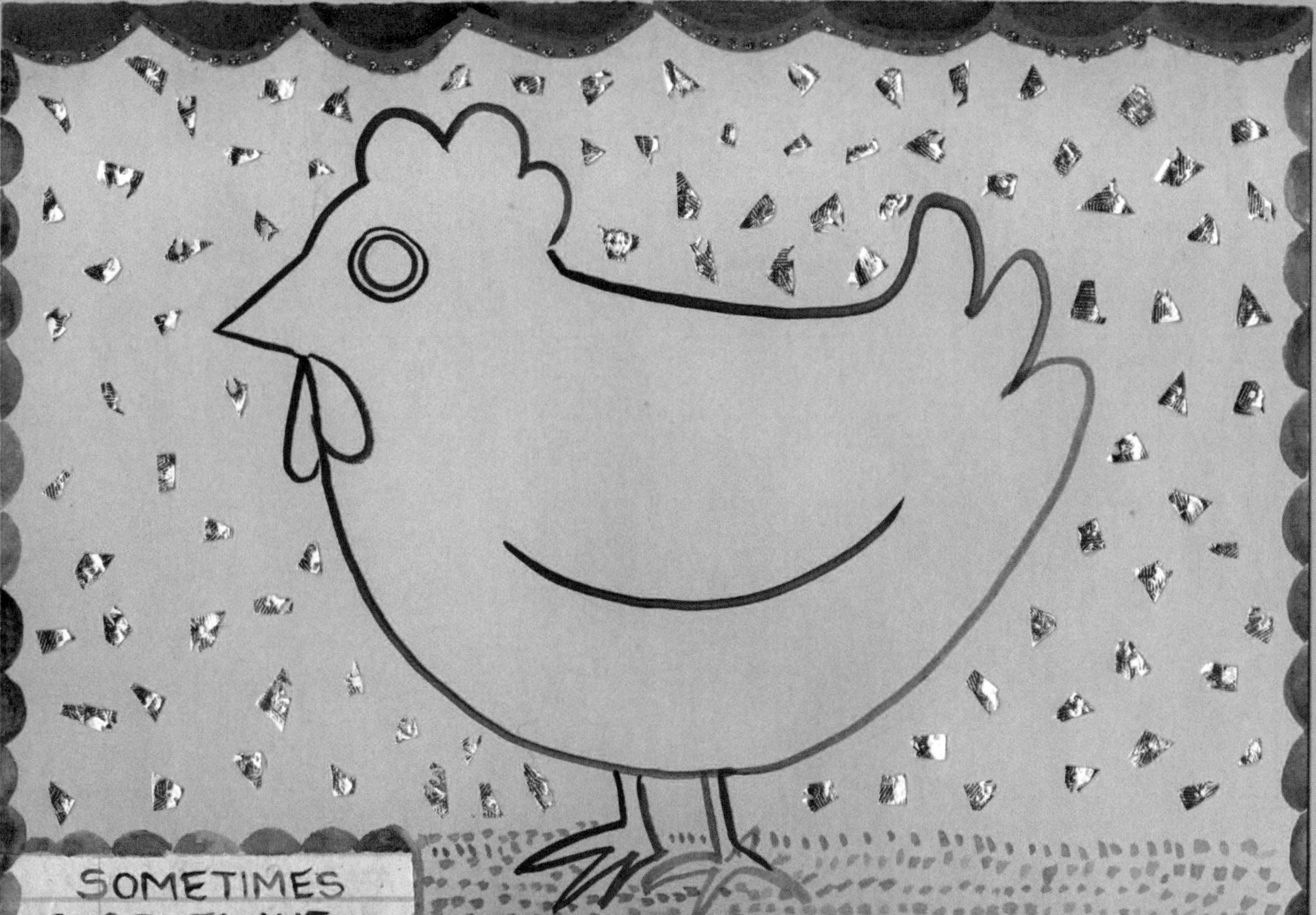

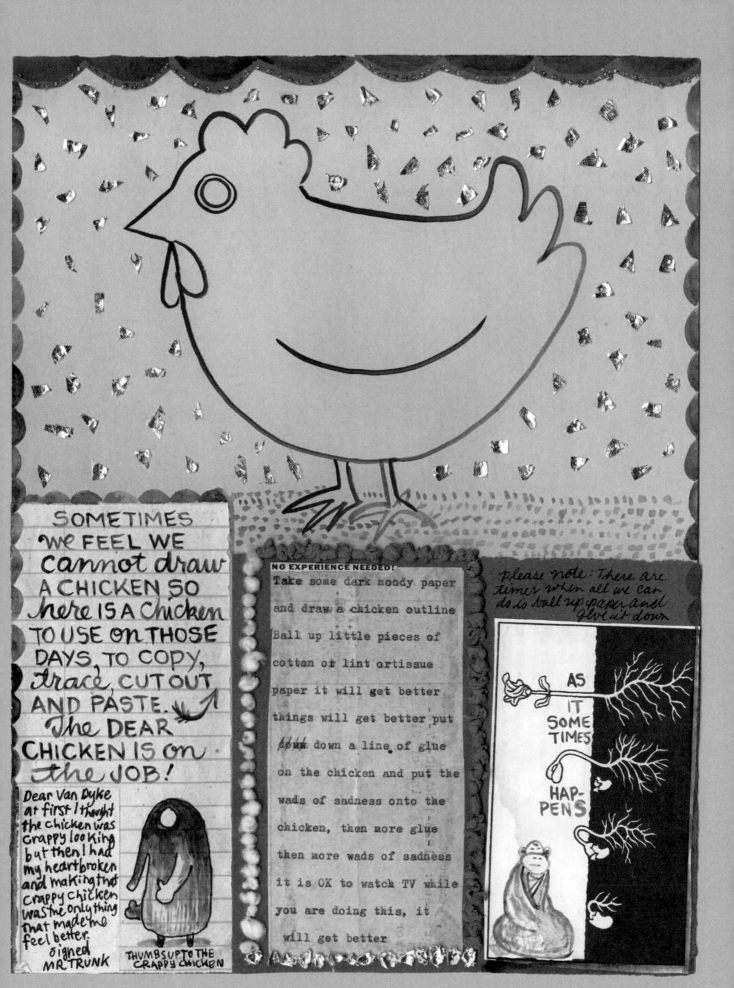

SOMETIMES WE FEEL WE cannot draw A CHICKEN SO here IS A Chicken TO USE on THOSE DAYS, TO COPY, trace, CUT OUT AND PASTE. The DEAR CHICKEN IS on the JOB!

Dear Van Dyke
at first I thought
the chicken was
crappy looking
but then I had
my heart broken
and making that
crappy chicken
was the only thing
that made me
feel better.
signed
MR TRUNK

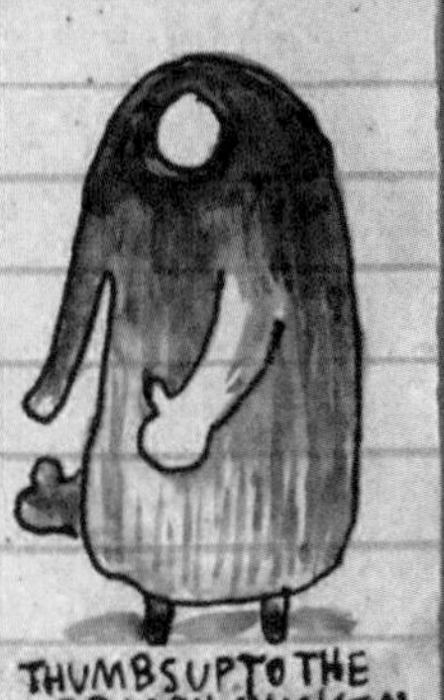

THUMBS UP TO THE CRAPPY CHICKEN

NO EXPERIENCE NEEDED!

Take some dark moody paper and draw a chicken outline Ball up little pieces of cotton or lint or tissue paper it will get better things will get better put ~~down~~ down a line of glue on the chicken and put the wads of sadness onto the chicken, then more glue then more wads of sadness it is OK to watch TV while you are doing this, it will get better

please note: There are times when all we can do is ball up paper and glue it down

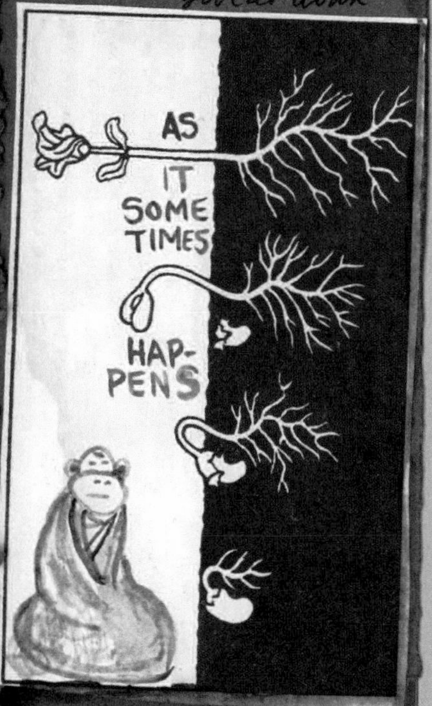
AS
IT
SOMETIMES
HAPPENS

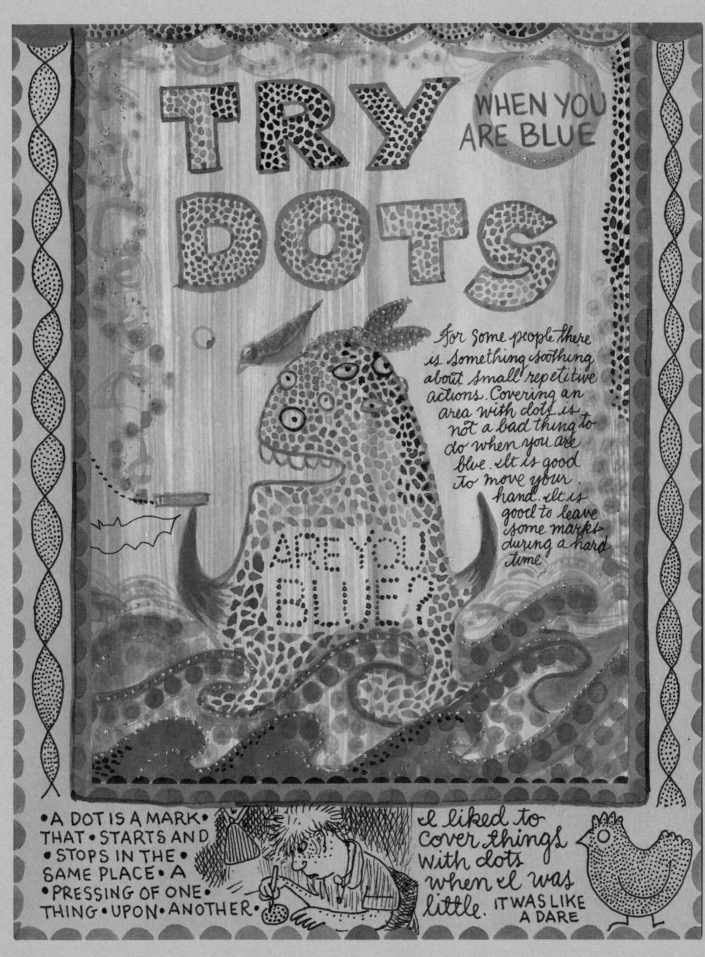

TRY DOTS WHEN YOU ARE BLUE

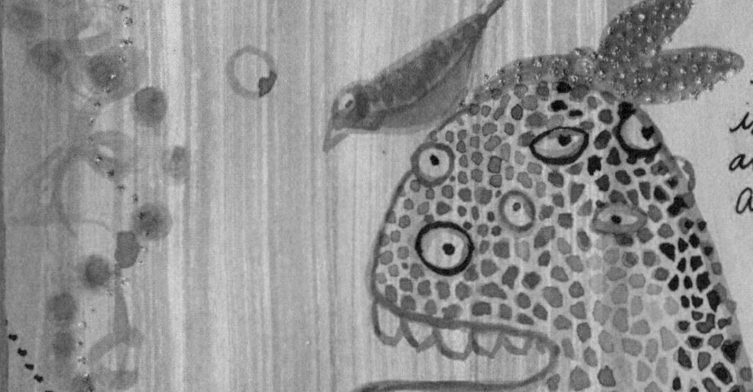

ARE YOU BLUE?

For some people there is something soothing about small repetitive actions. Covering an area with dots is not a bad thing to do when you are blue. It is good to move your hand. It is good to leave some marks during a hard time

•A DOT IS A MARK• THAT•STARTS AND •STOPS IN THE• SAME PLACE•A •PRESSING OF ONE• THING•UPON•ANOTHER•

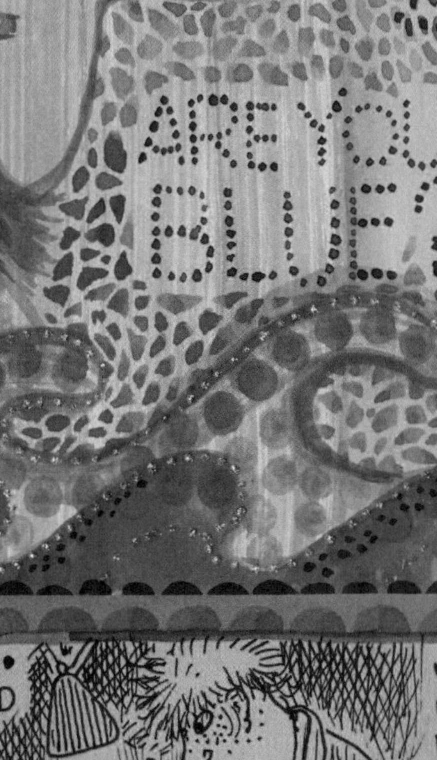

I liked to cover things with dots when I was little. IT WAS LIKE A DARE

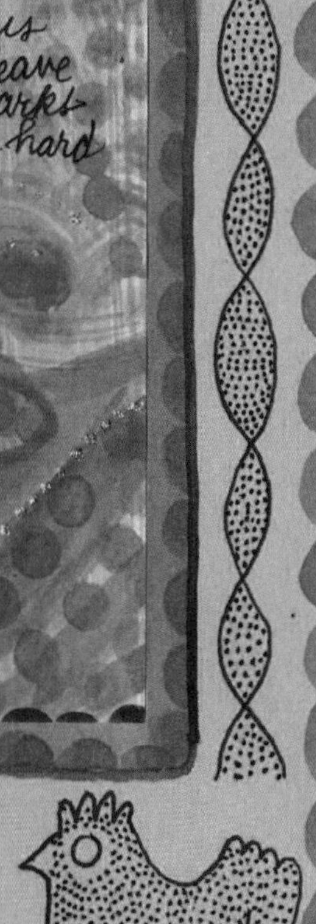

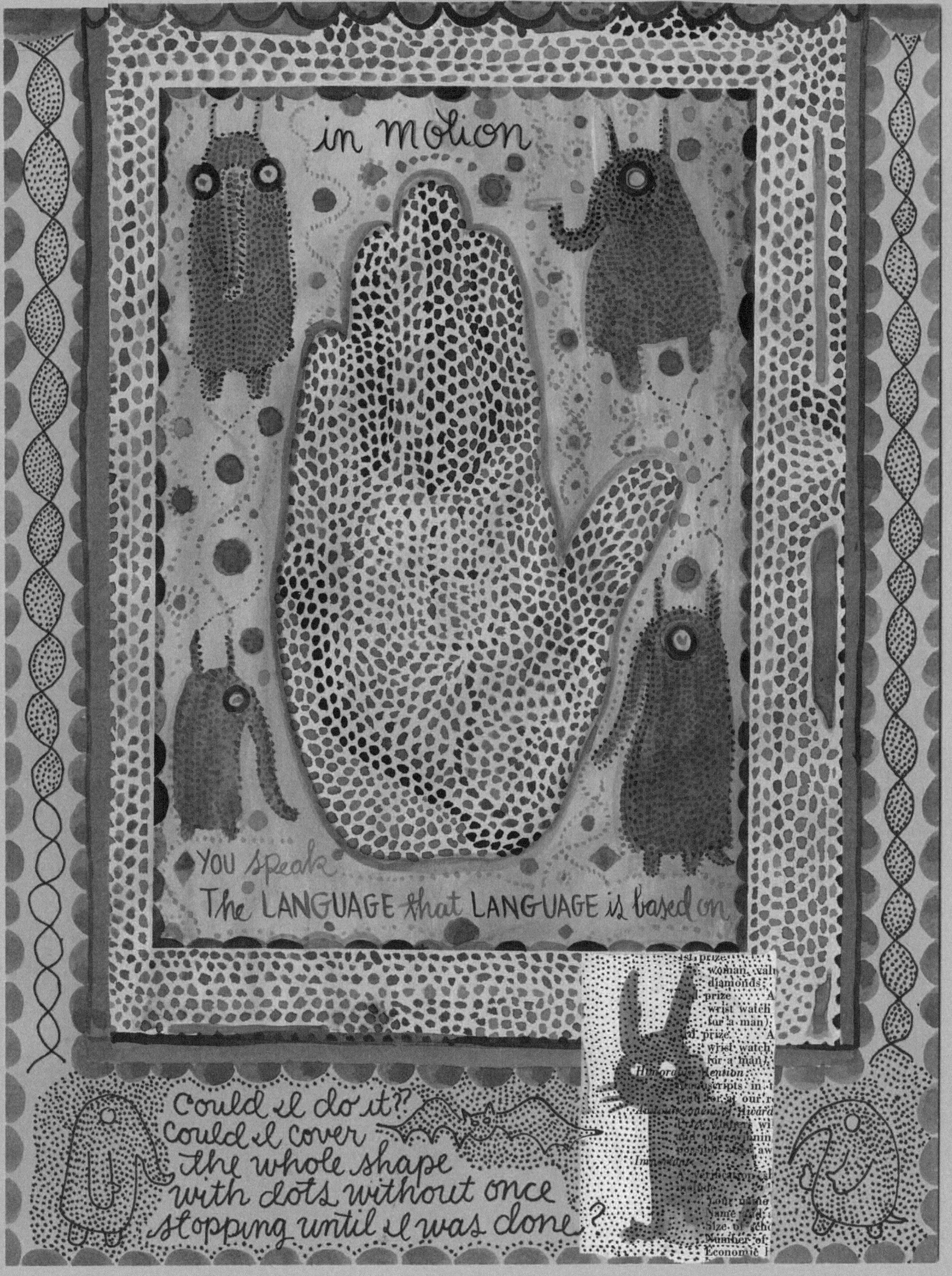
in motion
YOU speak
The LANGUAGE that LANGUAGE is based on
Could I do it?
Could I cover
the whole shape
with dots without once
stopping until I was done?

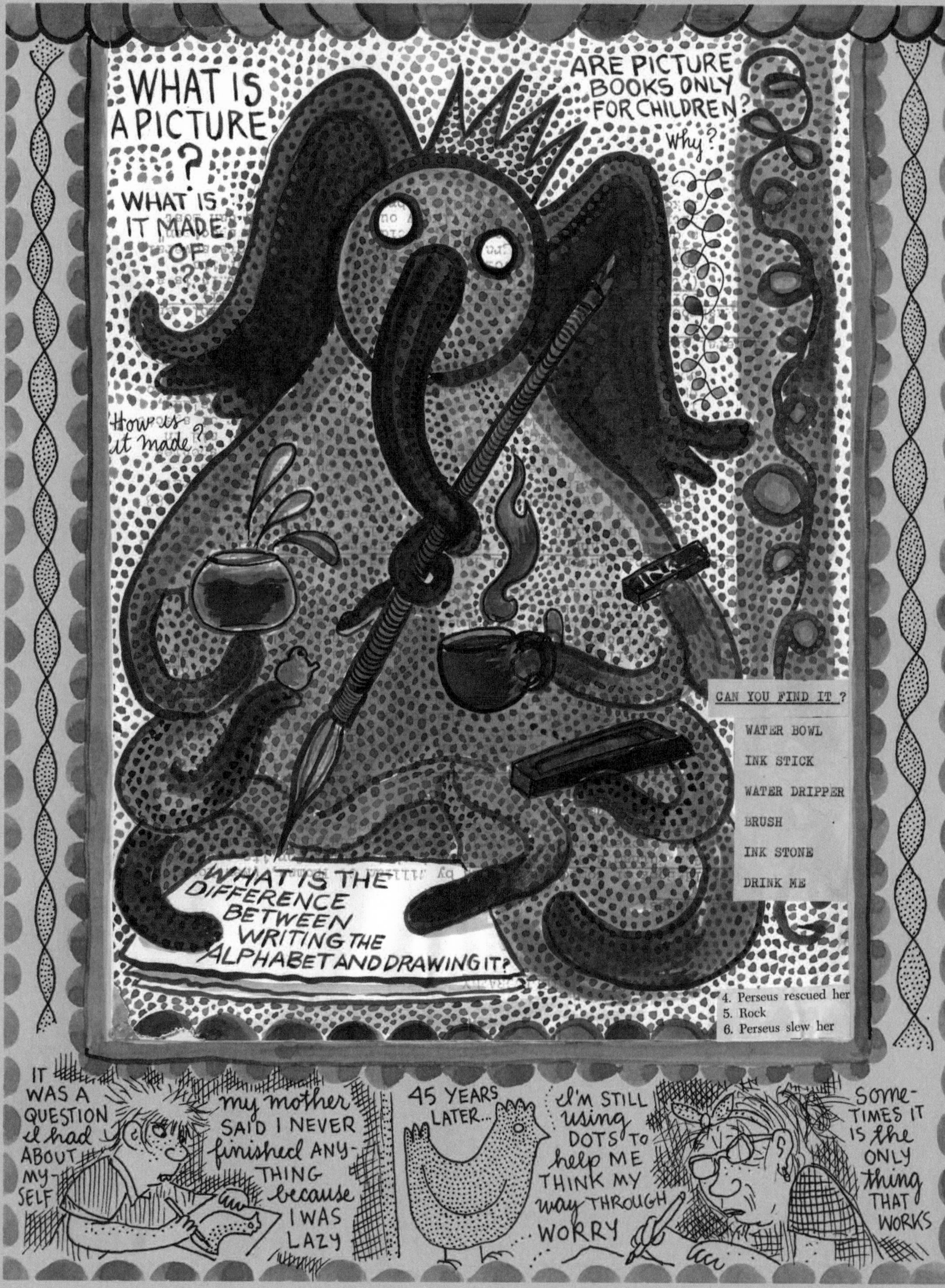

WHAT IS A PICTURE ?
WHAT IS IT MADE OF ?
ARE PICTURE BOOKS ONLY FOR CHILDREN ?
Why ?
How is it made ?
INK
CAN YOU FIND IT ?
WATER BOWL
INK STICK
WATER DRIPPER
BRUSH
INK STONE
DRINK ME
WHAT IS THE DIFFERENCE BETWEEN WRITING THE ALPHABET AND DRAWING IT?
4. Perseus rescued her
5. Rock
6. Perseus slew her
IT WAS A QUESTION I HAD ABOUT MYSELF
MY MOTHER SAID I NEVER FINISHED ANYTHING BECAUSE I WAS LAZY
45 YEARS LATER...
I'M STILL USING DOTS TO HELP ME THINK MY WAY THROUGH WORRY
SOMETIMES IT IS THE ONLY THING THAT WORKS

Here are some shapes you can cover with dots. It is OK to have the TV on. Let your mind drift. Let your fingers do the walking. Let the dots connect themselves

37

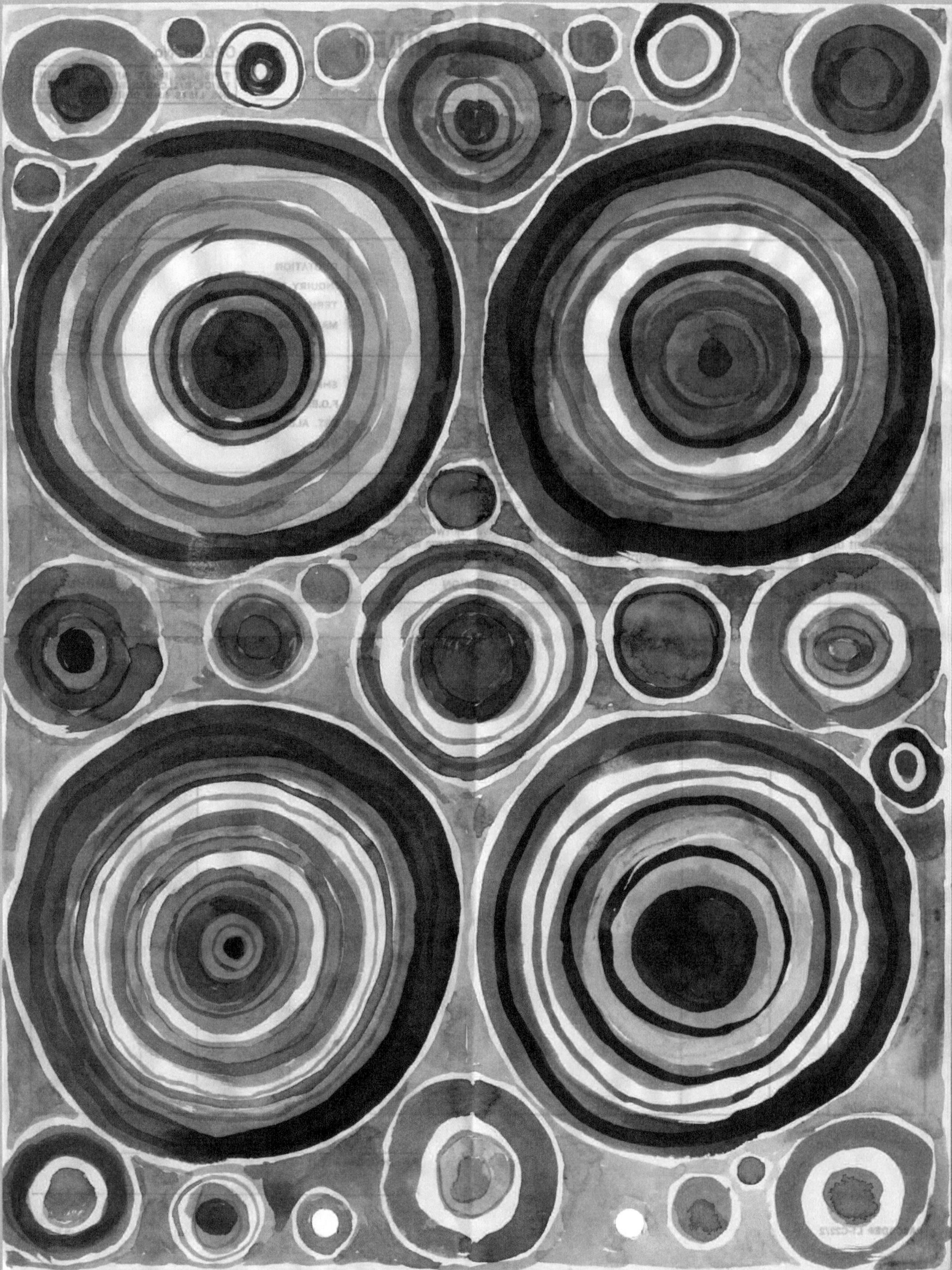

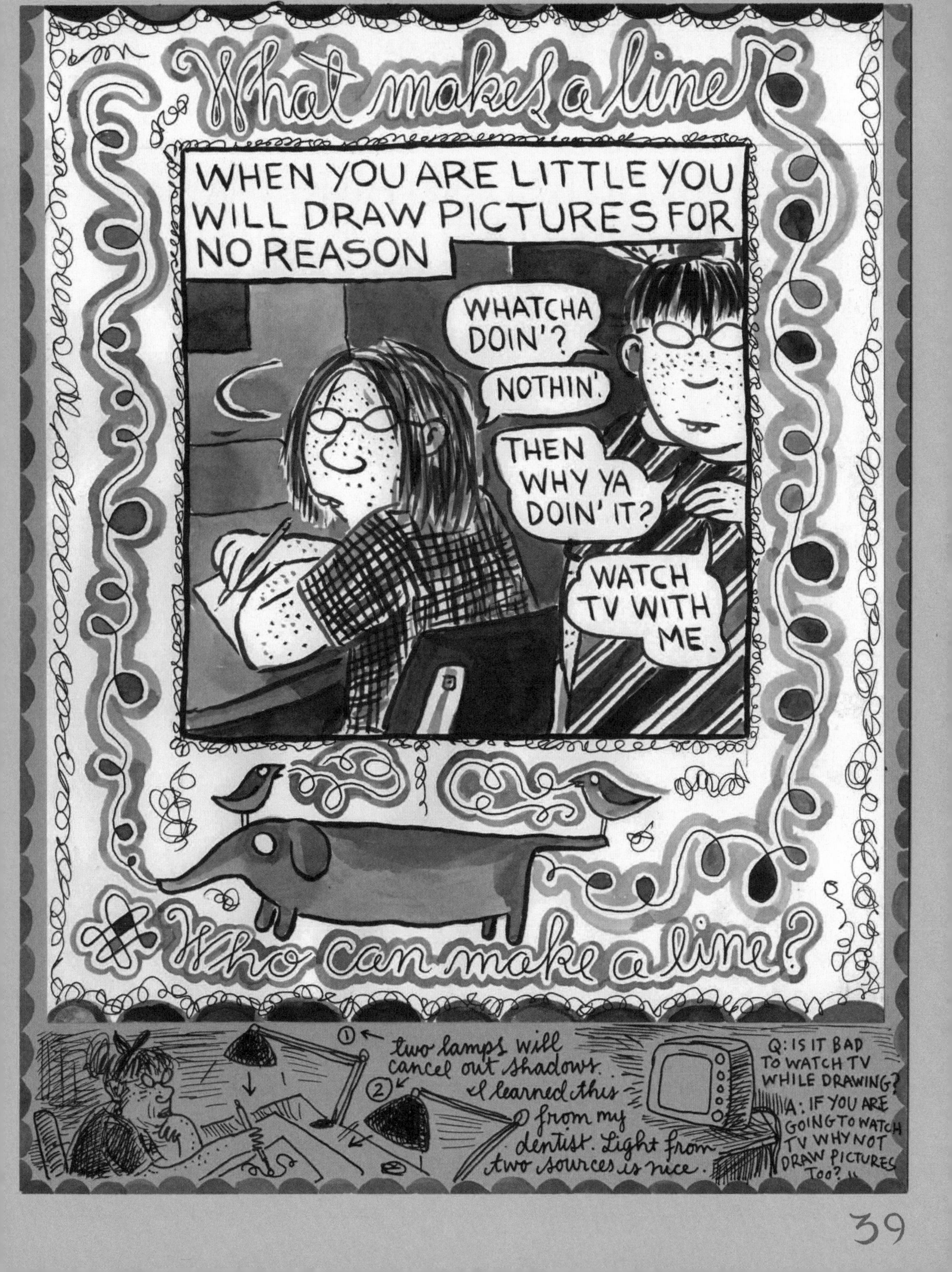

What makes a line?
WHEN YOU ARE LITTLE YOU WILL DRAW PICTURES FOR NO REASON
WHATCHA DOIN'?
NOTHIN'.
THEN WHY YA DOIN' IT?
WATCH TV WITH ME.
Who can make a line?
① ← two lamps will cancel out shadows. ② I learned this from my dentist. Light from two sources is nice.
Q: IS IT BAD TO WATCH TV WHILE DRAWING?
A: IF YOU ARE GOING TO WATCH TV WHY NOT DRAW PICTURES TOO?

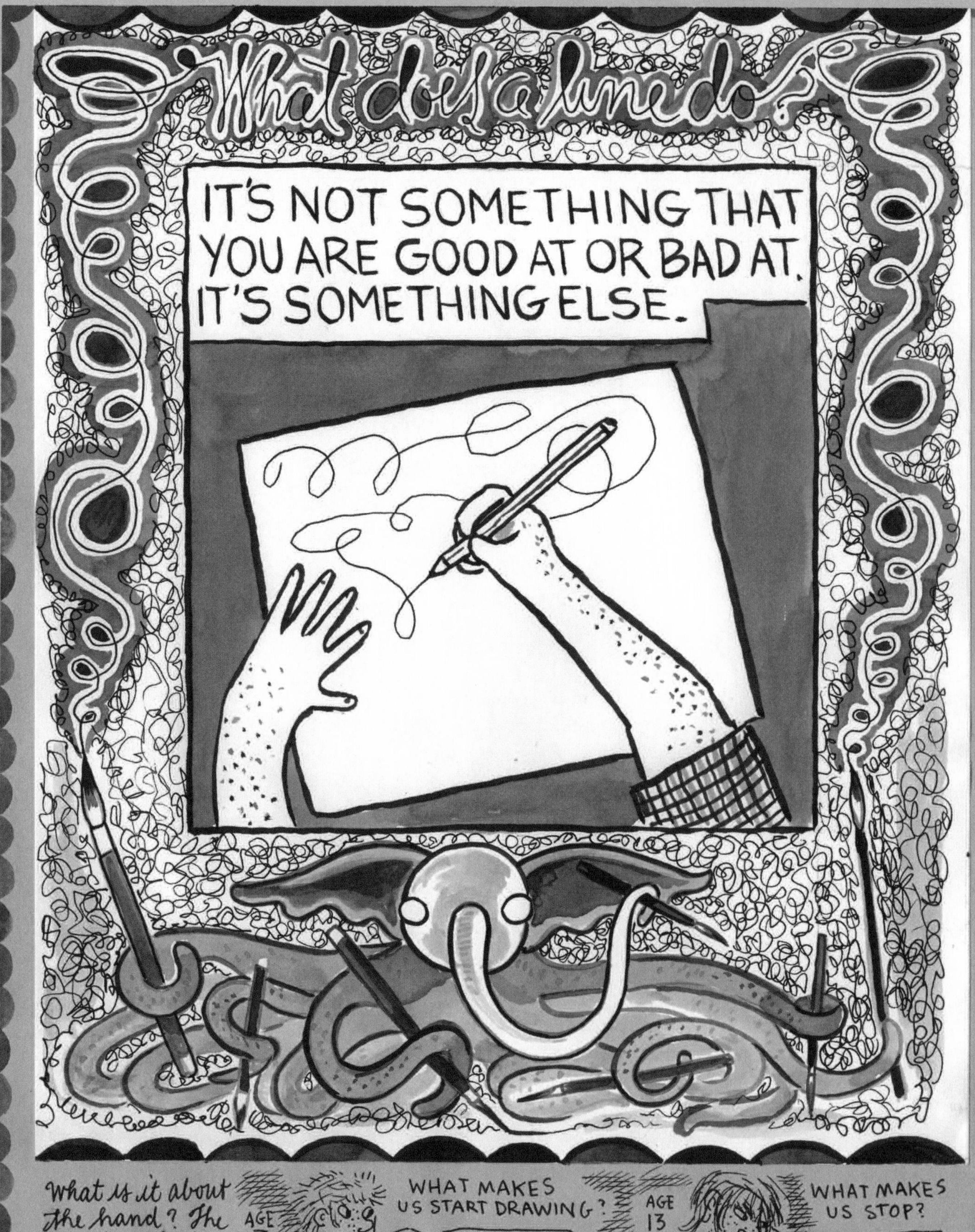
What does a line do?
IT'S NOT SOMETHING THAT YOU ARE GOOD AT OR BAD AT. IT'S SOMETHING ELSE.
What is it about the hand? The hand and the motion we call handwriting?
AGE 3
WHAT MAKES US START DRAWING?
AGE 13
WHAT MAKES US STOP?

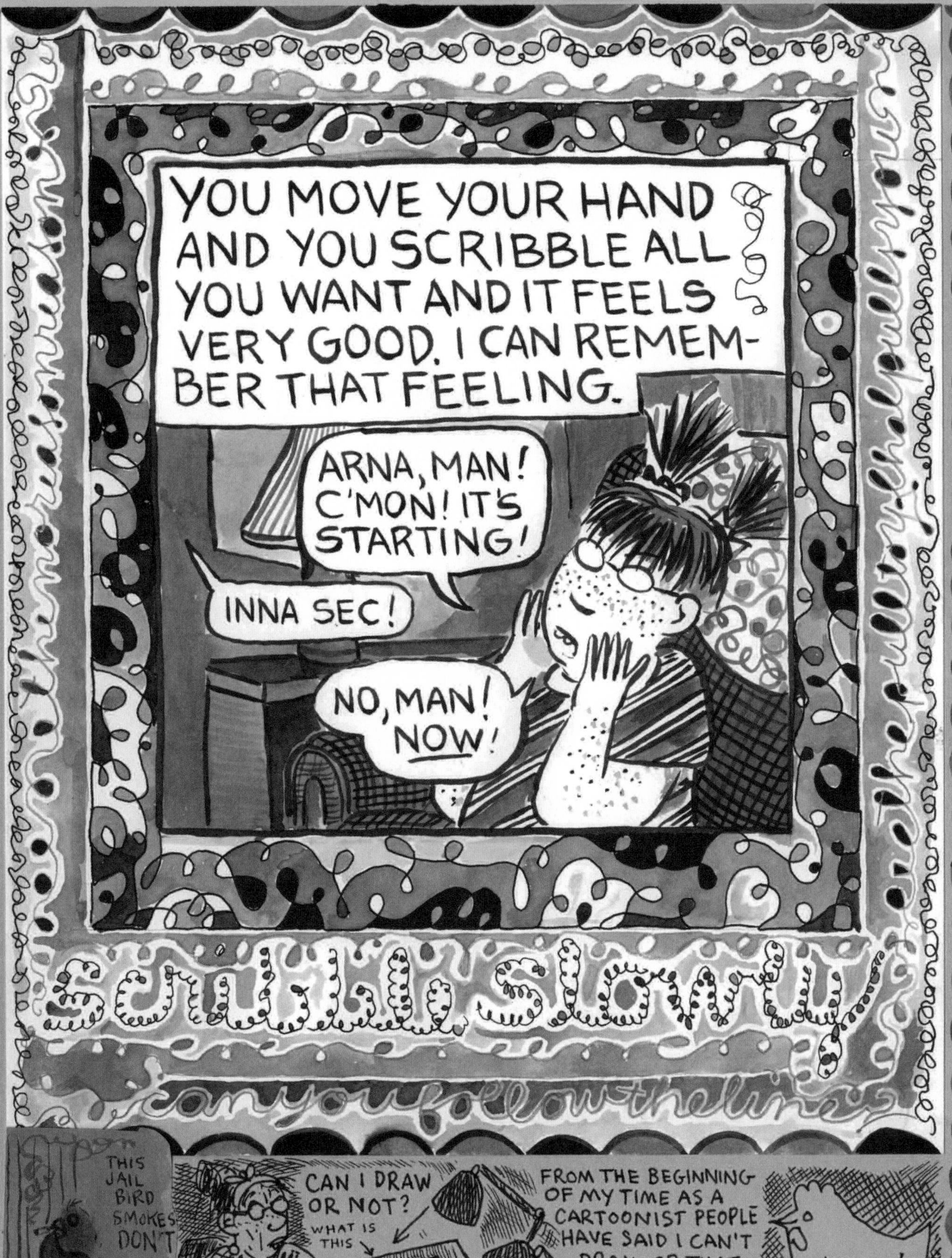
YOU MOVE YOUR HAND AND YOU SCRIBBLE ALL YOU WANT AND IT FEELS VERY GOOD. I CAN REMEMBER THAT FEELING.
ARNA, MAN! C'MON! IT'S STARTING!
INNA SEC!
NO, MAN! NOW!
scribble slowly
can you follow the line
THIS JAIL BIRD SMOKES DON'T
CAN I DRAW OR NOT?
WHAT IS THIS
FROM THE BEGINNING OF MY TIME AS A CARTOONIST PEOPLE HAVE SAID I CAN'T DRAW OR THAT MY DRAWING IS BAD.

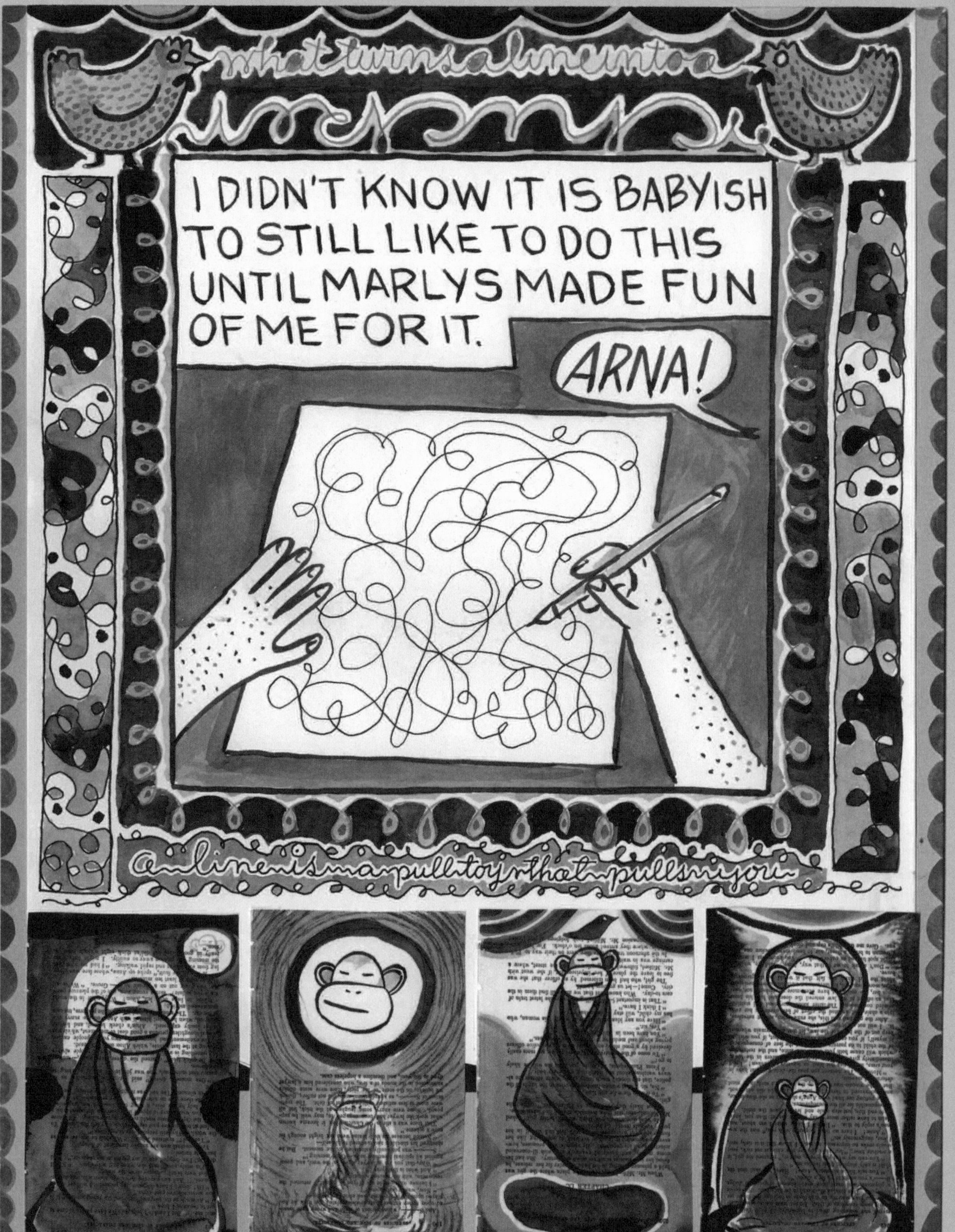
what turns a line into a
I DIDN'T KNOW IT IS BABYISH TO STILL LIKE TO DO THIS UNTIL MARLYS MADE FUN OF ME FOR IT.
ARNA!
a line is a pull toy that pulls you

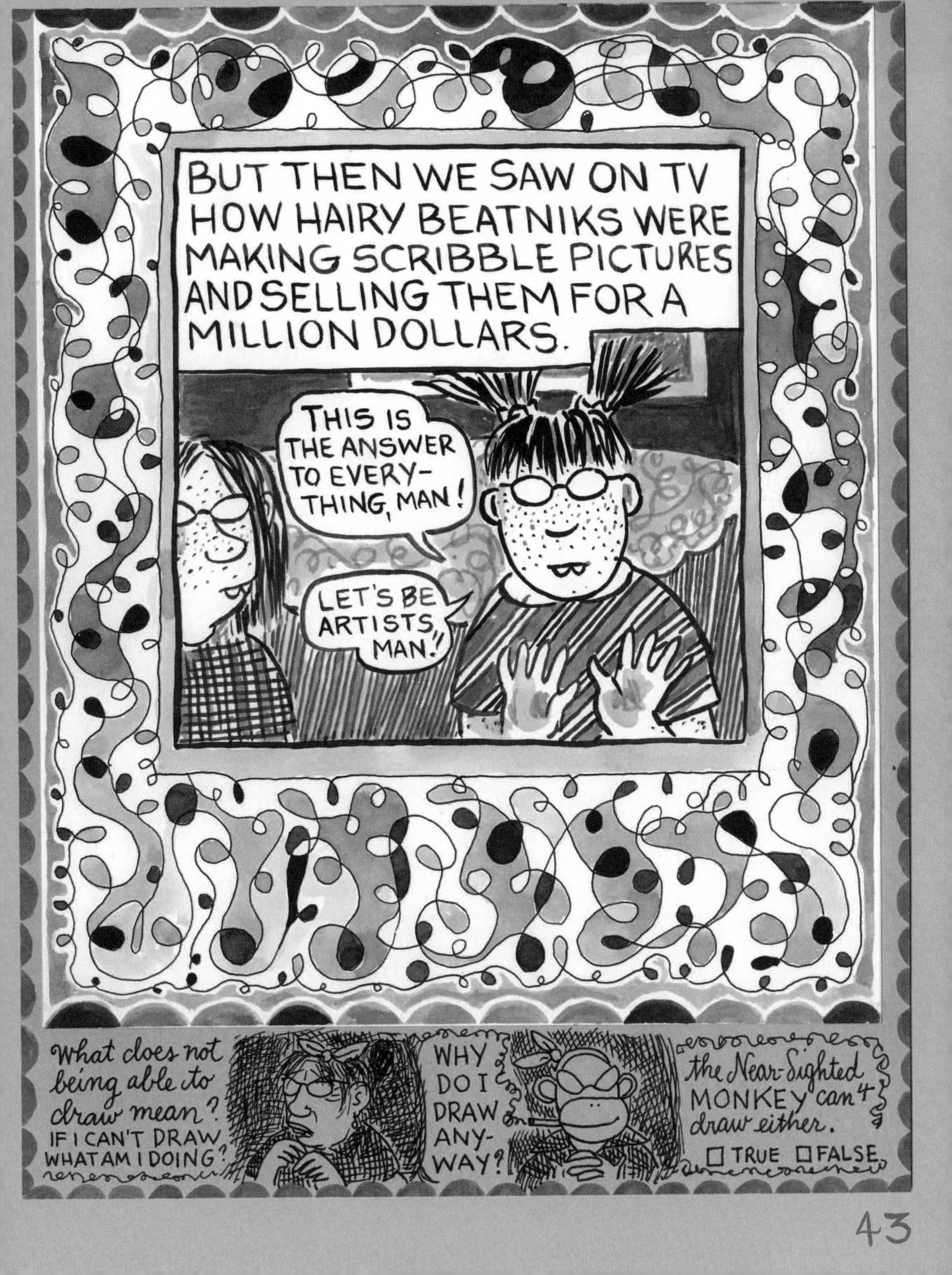

BUT THEN WE SAW ON TV HOW HAIRY BEATNIKS WERE MAKING SCRIBBLE PICTURES AND SELLING THEM FOR A MILLION DOLLARS.
THIS IS THE ANSWER TO EVERY-THING, MAN!
LET'S BE ARTISTS, MAN!!
What does not being able to draw mean?
IF I CAN'T DRAW WHAT AM I DOING?
WHY DO I DRAW ANY-WAY?
the Near-Sighted MONKEY can't draw either.
☐ TRUE ☐ FALSE

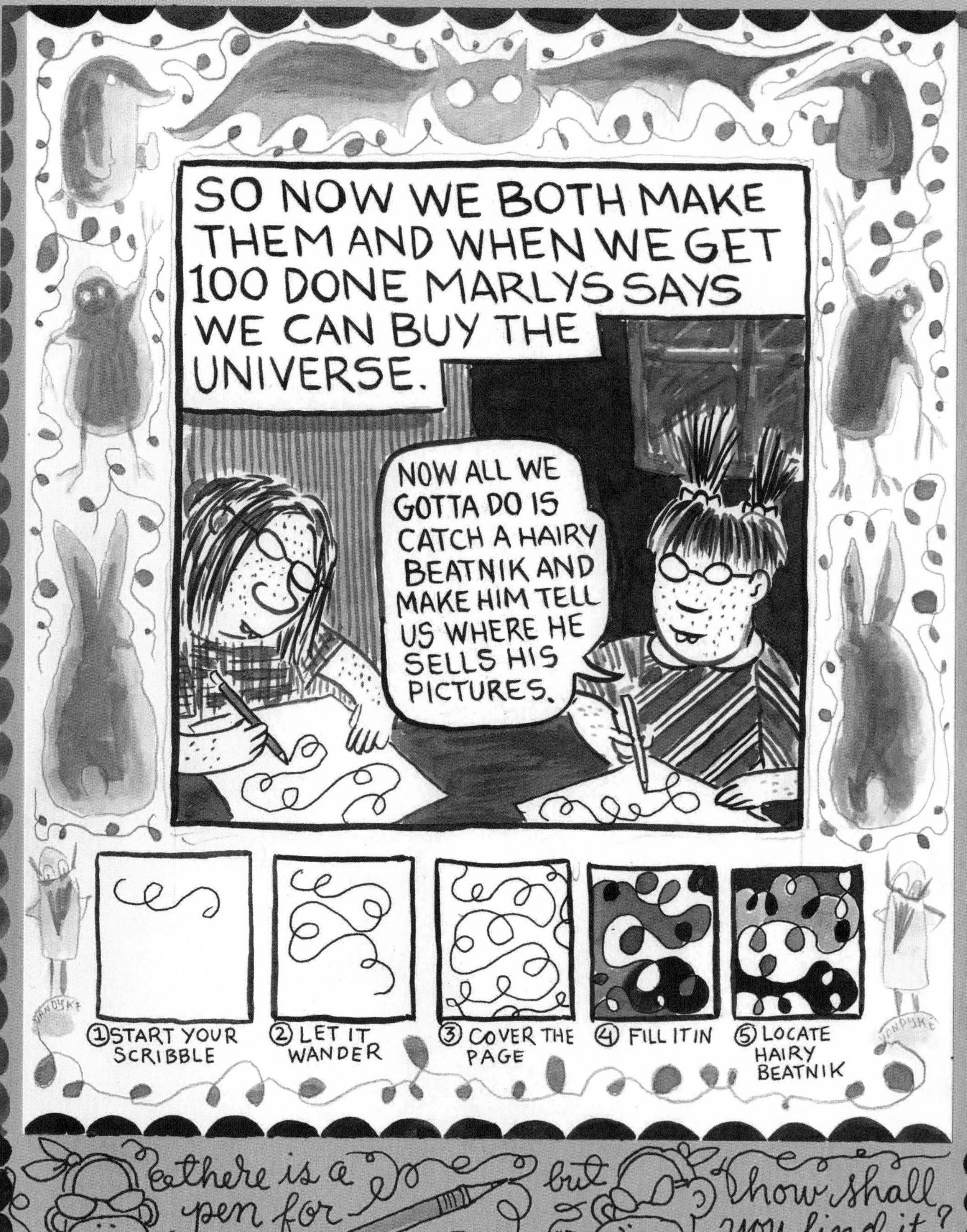
SO NOW WE BOTH MAKE THEM AND WHEN WE GET 100 DONE MARLYS SAYS WE CAN BUY THE UNIVERSE.
NOW ALL WE GOTTA DO IS CATCH A HAIRY BEATNIK AND MAKE HIM TELL US WHERE HE SELLS HIS PICTURES.
① START YOUR SCRIBBLE
② LET IT WANDER
③ COVER THE PAGE
④ FILL IT IN
⑤ LOCATE HAIRY BEATNIK
there is a pen for you
but how shall you find it?

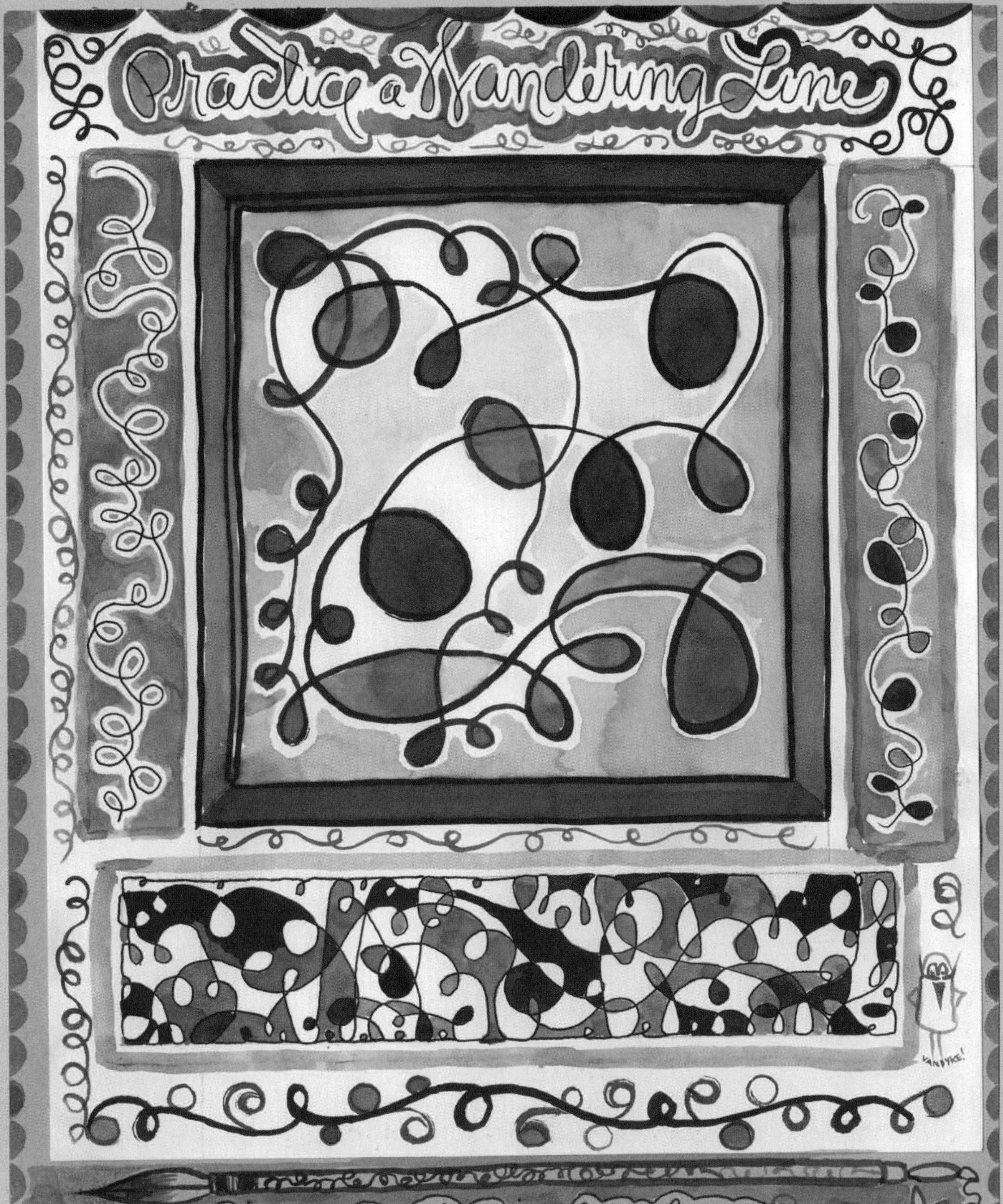
Practice a Wandering Line
VANDYKE!
understanding your paintbrush
and pretending it's alive and
has a living sense of direction is recommended by The Monkey

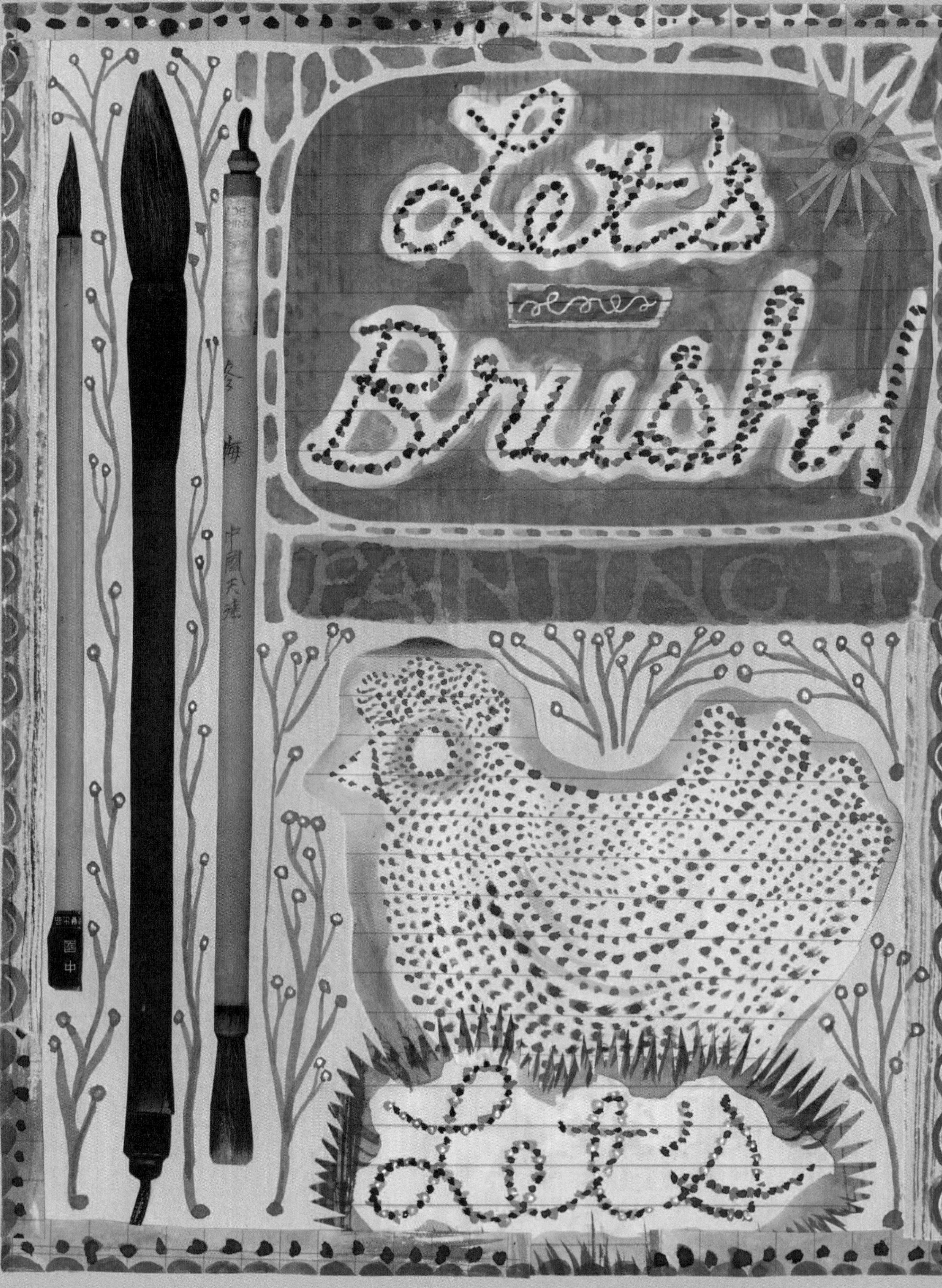
Let's
Brush!
PAINTING
Let's

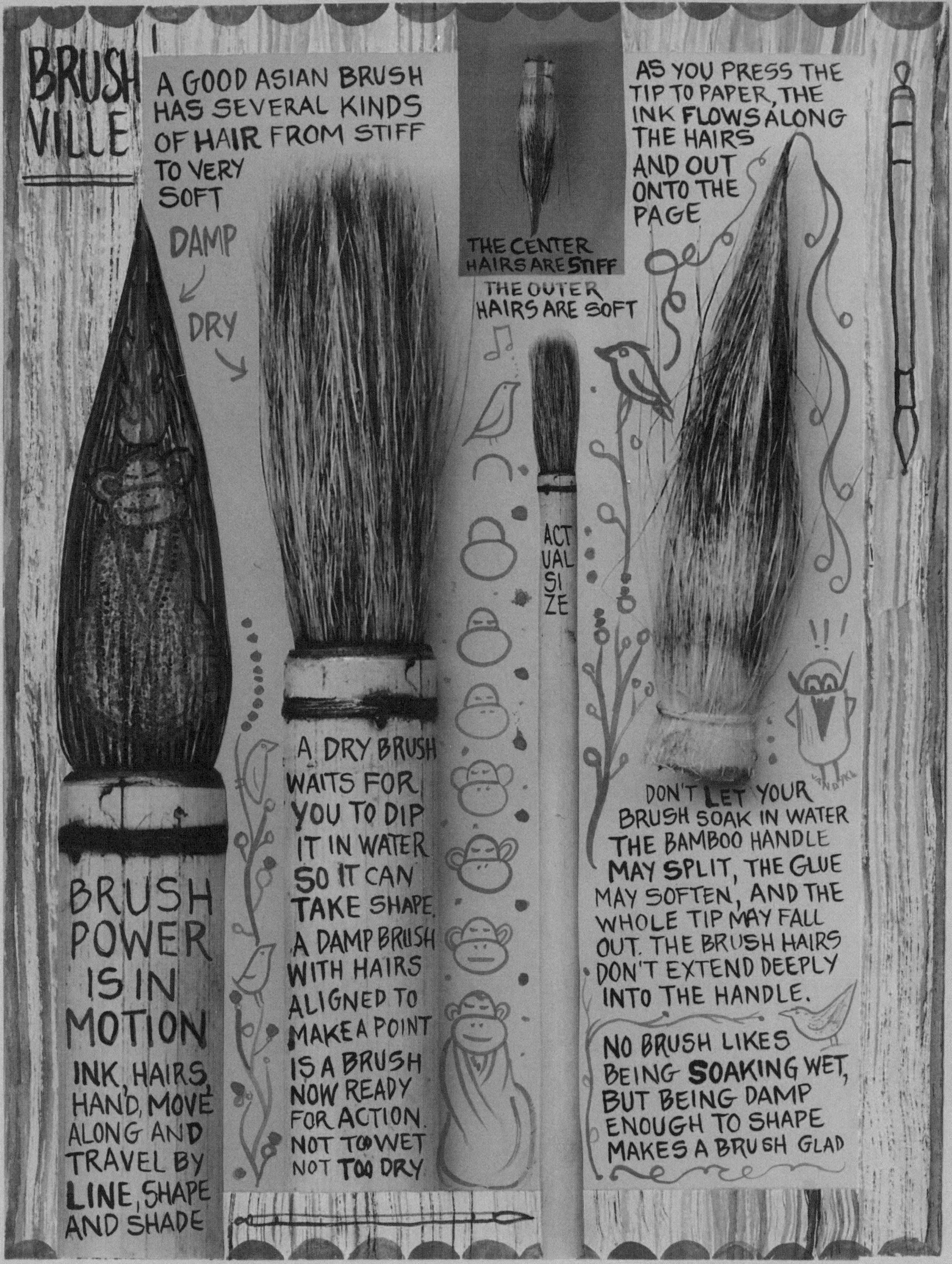
BRUSH VILLE
A GOOD ASIAN BRUSH HAS SEVERAL KINDS OF HAIR FROM STIFF TO VERY SOFT
DAMP
DRY
THE CENTER HAIRS ARE STIFF
THE OUTER HAIRS ARE SOFT
AS YOU PRESS THE TIP TO PAPER, THE INK FLOWS ALONG THE HAIRS AND OUT ONTO THE PAGE
ACTUAL SIZE
BRUSH POWER IS IN MOTION
INK, HAIRS, HAND, MOVE ALONG AND TRAVEL BY LINE, SHAPE AND SHADE
A DRY BRUSH WAITS FOR YOU TO DIP IT IN WATER SO IT CAN TAKE SHAPE.
A DAMP BRUSH WITH HAIRS ALIGNED TO MAKE A POINT IS A BRUSH NOW READY FOR ACTION.
NOT TOO WET NOT TOO DRY
!!
DON'T LET YOUR BRUSH SOAK IN WATER THE BAMBOO HANDLE MAY SPLIT, THE GLUE MAY SOFTEN, AND THE WHOLE TIP MAY FALL OUT. THE BRUSH HAIRS DON'T EXTEND DEEPLY INTO THE HANDLE.
NO BRUSH LIKES BEING SOAKING WET, BUT BEING DAMP ENOUGH TO SHAPE MAKES A BRUSH GLAD

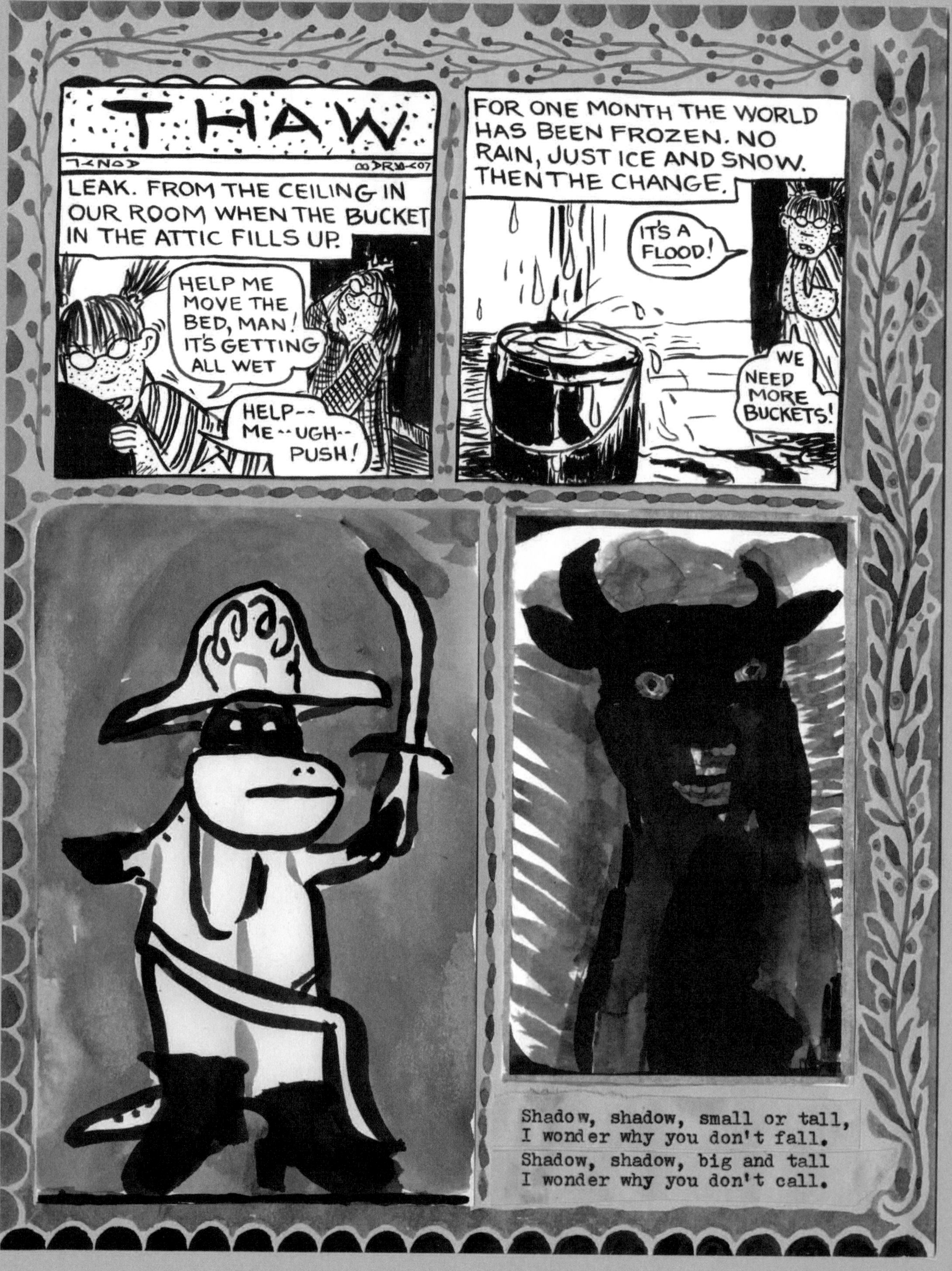
THAW
LEAK. FROM THE CEILING IN OUR ROOM WHEN THE BUCKET IN THE ATTIC FILLS UP.
HELP ME MOVE THE BED, MAN! IT'S GETTING ALL WET
HELP-- ME--UGH-- PUSH!
FOR ONE MONTH THE WORLD HAS BEEN FROZEN. NO RAIN, JUST ICE AND SNOW. THEN THE CHANGE.
IT'S A FLOOD!
WE NEED MORE BUCKETS!
Shadow, shadow, small or tall,
I wonder why you don't fall.
Shadow, shadow, big and tall
I wonder why you don't call.

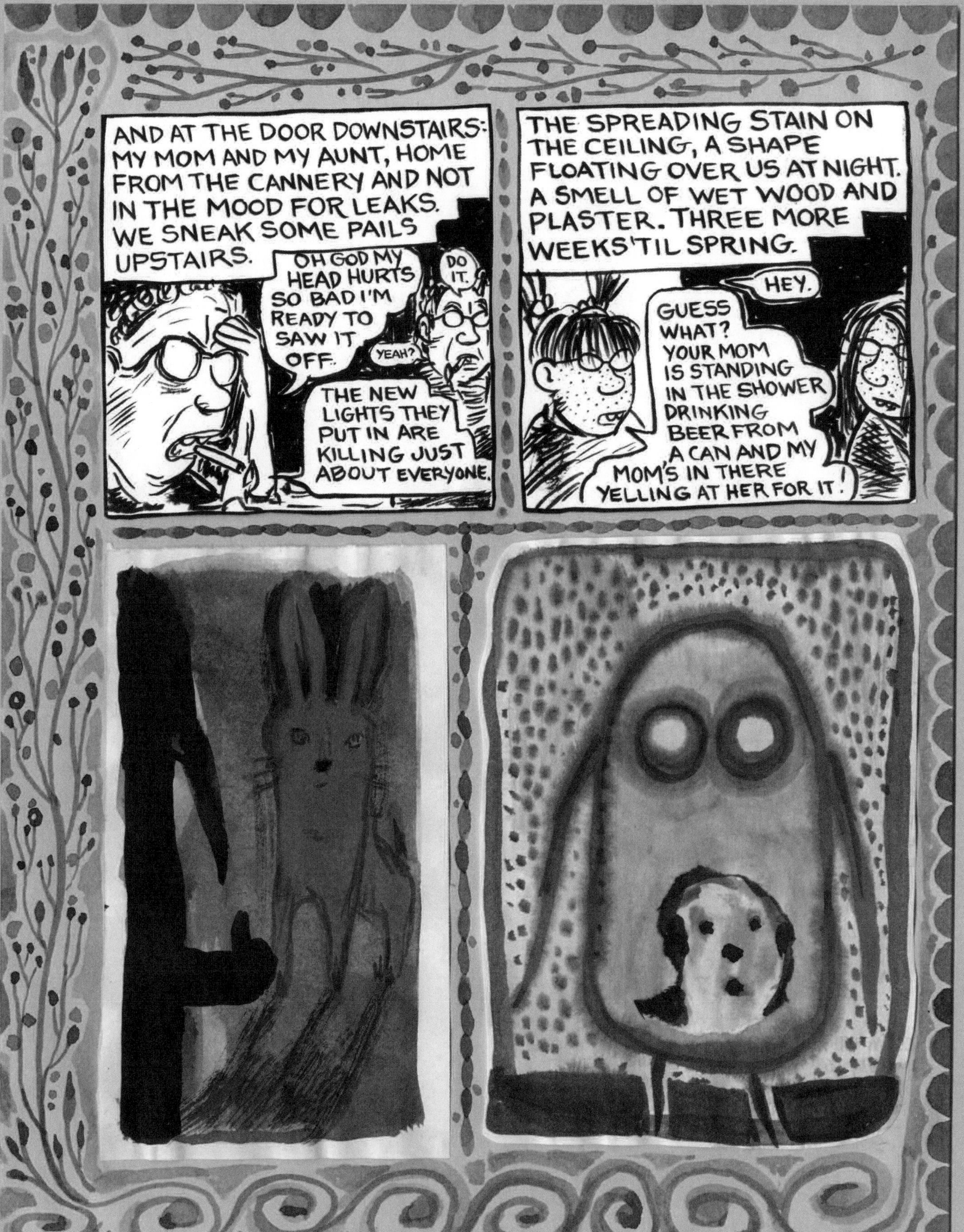
AND AT THE DOOR DOWNSTAIRS: MY MOM AND MY AUNT, HOME FROM THE CANNERY AND NOT IN THE MOOD FOR LEAKS. WE SNEAK SOME PAILS UPSTAIRS.
OH GOD MY HEAD HURTS SO BAD I'M READY TO SAW IT OFF.
DO IT.
YEAH?
THE NEW LIGHTS THEY PUT IN ARE KILLING JUST ABOUT EVERYONE.
THE SPREADING STAIN ON THE CEILING, A SHAPE FLOATING OVER US AT NIGHT. A SMELL OF WET WOOD AND PLASTER. THREE MORE WEEKS 'TIL SPRING.
HEY.
GUESS WHAT? YOUR MOM IS STANDING IN THE SHOWER DRINKING BEER FROM A CAN AND MY MOM'S IN THERE YELLING AT HER FOR IT!

TAKING SHAPE

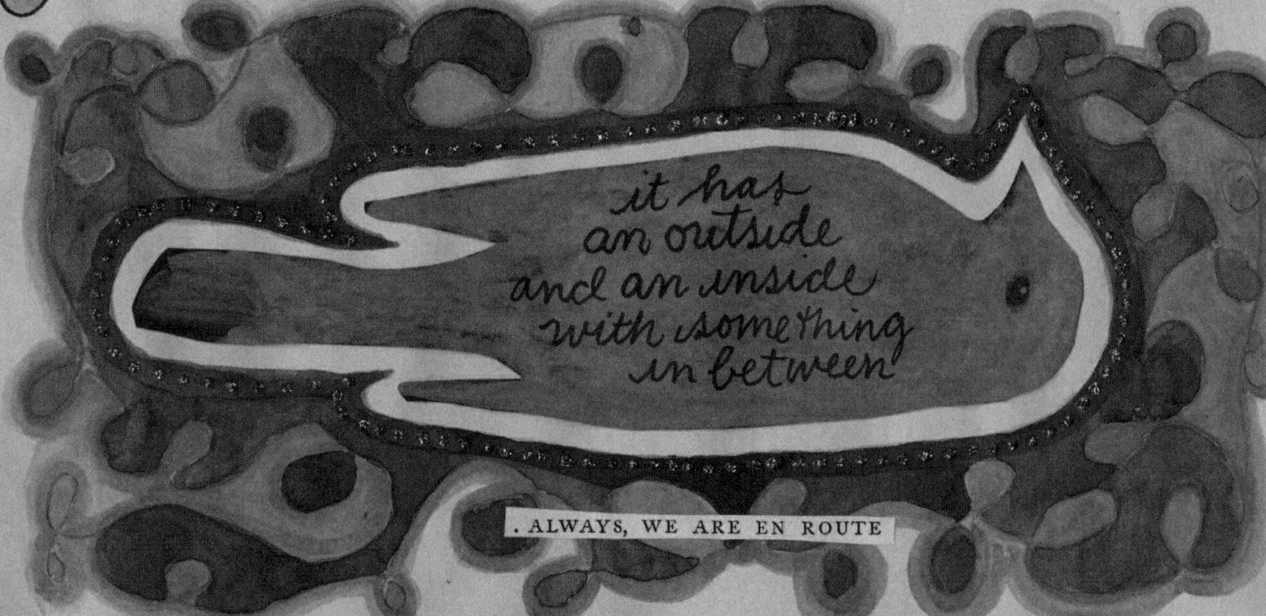
it has
an outside
and an inside
with something
in between
. ALWAYS, WE ARE EN ROUTE

1. COVER THE BACKGROUND OF A PHOTO OF A BIRD WITH BLACK INK.

2. COVER THE BIRD IN THE PICTURE WITH BLUE PAINT.

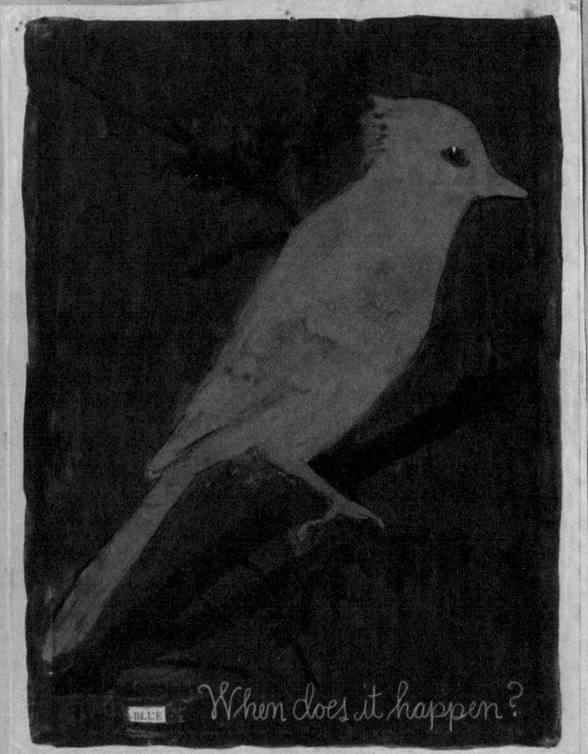
BLUE
When does it happen?

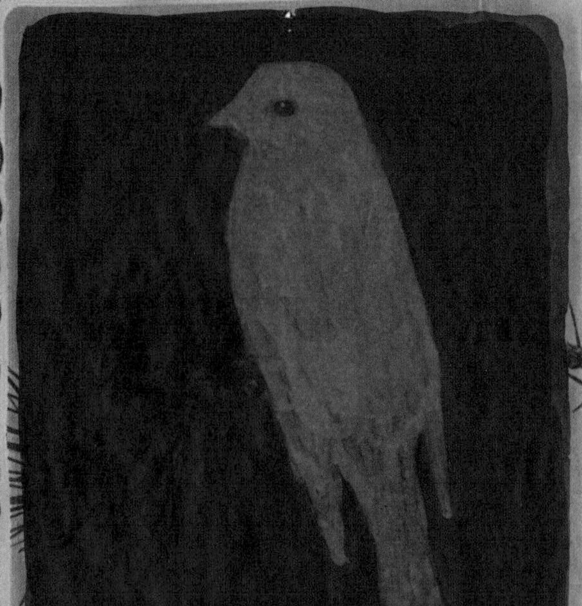
When does something take shape?

"At last!" he cried, when he saw us; "I thought you were never coming. What in the world has kept you?"

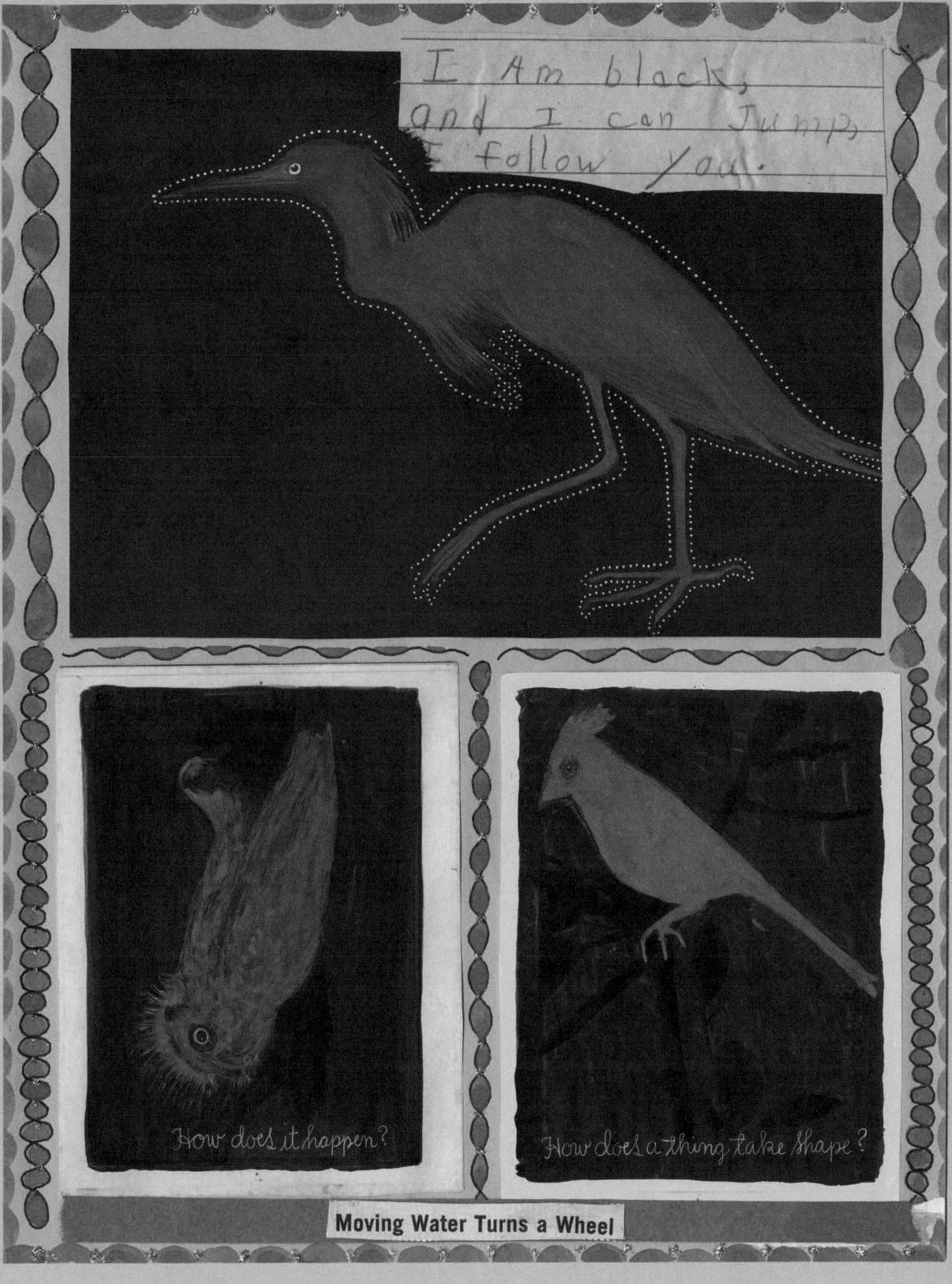
I Am black,
and I can Jump,
I follow you.
How does it happen?
How does a thing take Shape?
Moving Water Turns a Wheel

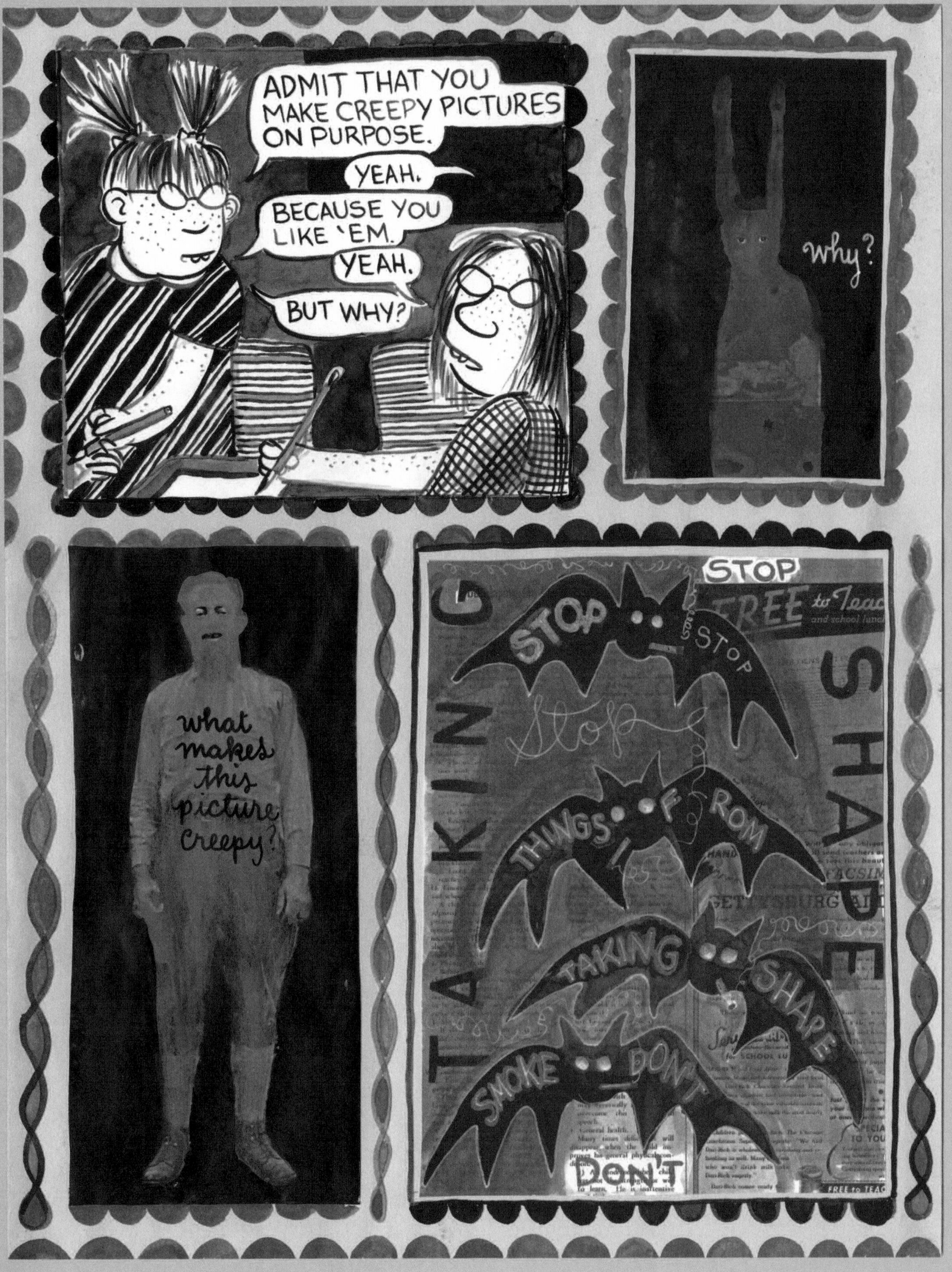
ADMIT THAT YOU MAKE CREEPY PICTURES ON PURPOSE.
YEAH.
BECAUSE YOU LIKE 'EM.
YEAH.
BUT WHY?
why?
what makes this picture creepy?
TAKING
SHAPE
STOP
STOP
STOP
Stop
THINGS FROM
TAKING SHAPE
SMOKE DON'T
DON'T

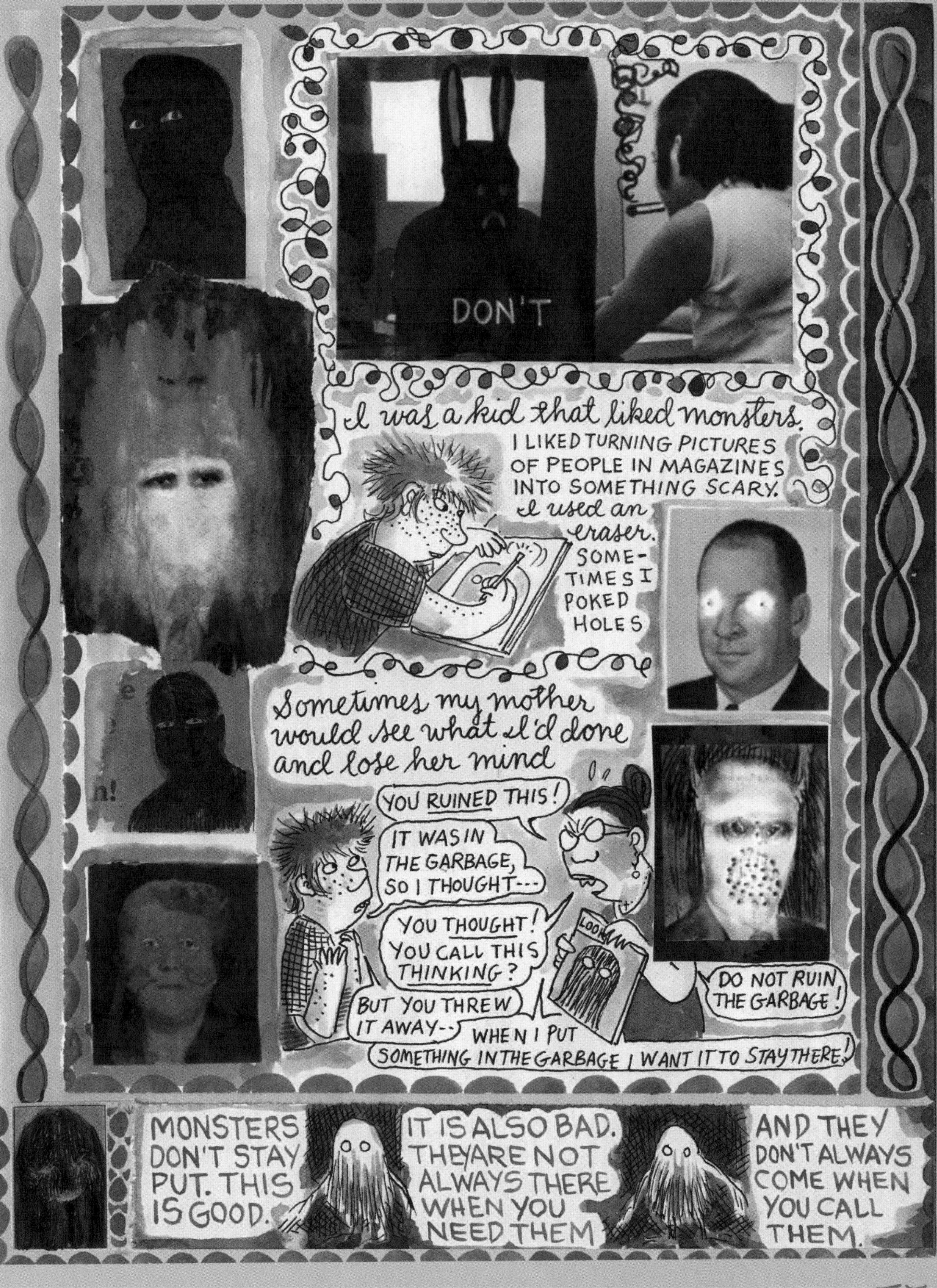
DON'T
I was a kid that liked monsters.
I LIKED TURNING PICTURES OF PEOPLE IN MAGAZINES INTO SOMETHING SCARY.
I used an eraser.
SOMETIMES I POKED HOLES
Sometimes my mother would see what I'd done and lose her mind
YOU RUINED THIS!
IT WAS IN THE GARBAGE, SO I THOUGHT---
YOU THOUGHT! YOU CALL THIS THINKING?
BUT YOU THREW IT AWAY--
DO NOT RUIN THE GARBAGE!
WHEN I PUT SOMETHING IN THE GARBAGE I WANT IT TO STAY THERE!
MONSTERS DON'T STAY PUT. THIS IS GOOD.
IT IS ALSO BAD. THEY ARE NOT ALWAYS THERE WHEN YOU NEED THEM
AND THEY DON'T ALWAYS COME WHEN YOU CALL THEM.

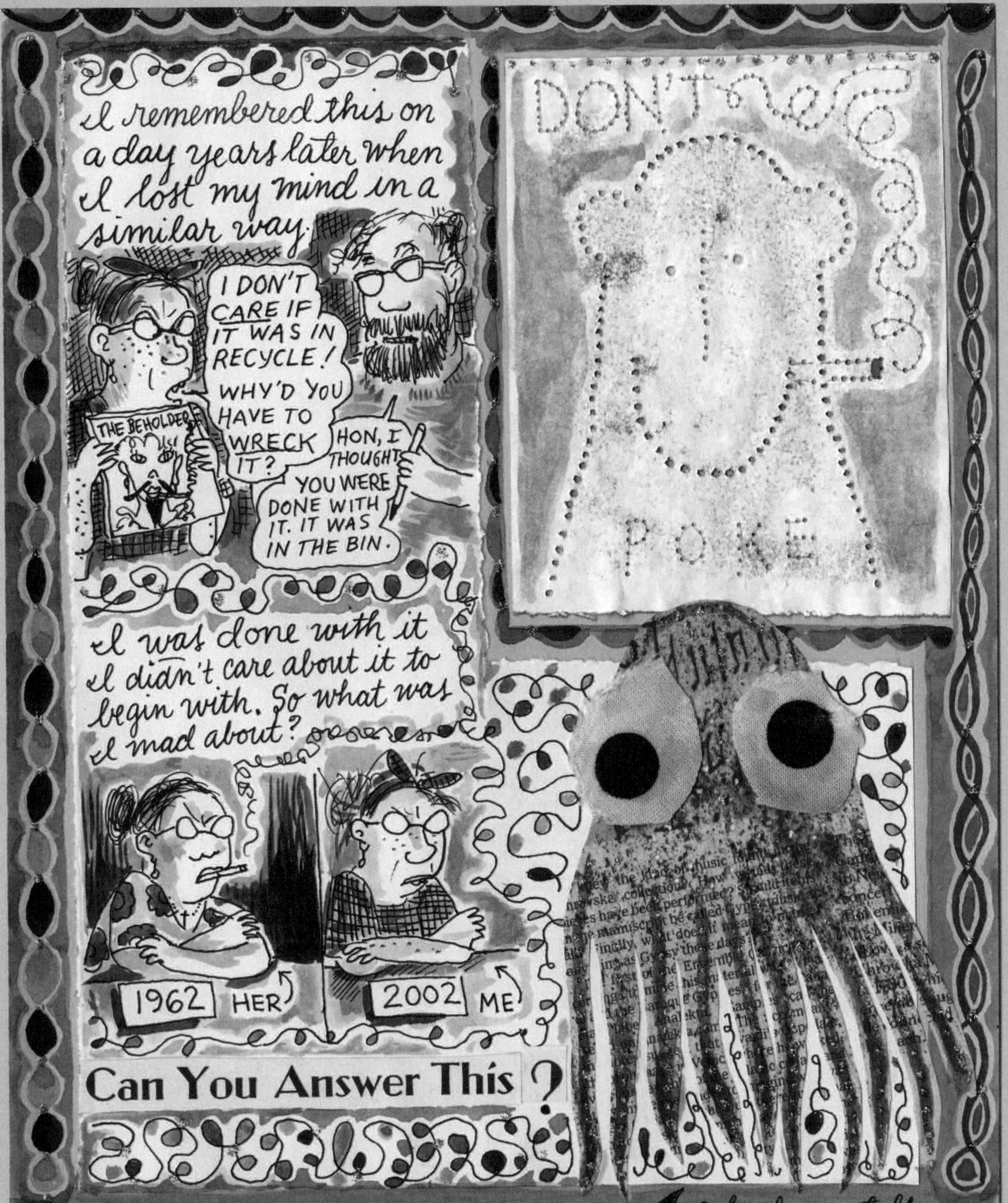

I remembered this on a day years later when I lost my mind in a similar way.
I DON'T CARE IF IT WAS IN RECYCLE! WHY'D YOU HAVE TO WRECK IT?
THE BEHOLDER
HON, I THOUGHT YOU WERE DONE WITH IT. IT WAS IN THE BIN.
DON'T
POKE
I was done with it I didn't care about it to begin with. So what was I mad about?
1962 HER
2002 ME
Can You Answer This ?
DOES EXPERIENCE HAVE A SHAPE? Can this shape be passed from one person to another?
Why do we talk about things that shape character? OR SHAPE THE COURSE OF OUR LIVES?
what IS IT THAT 'TAKES SHAPE'?

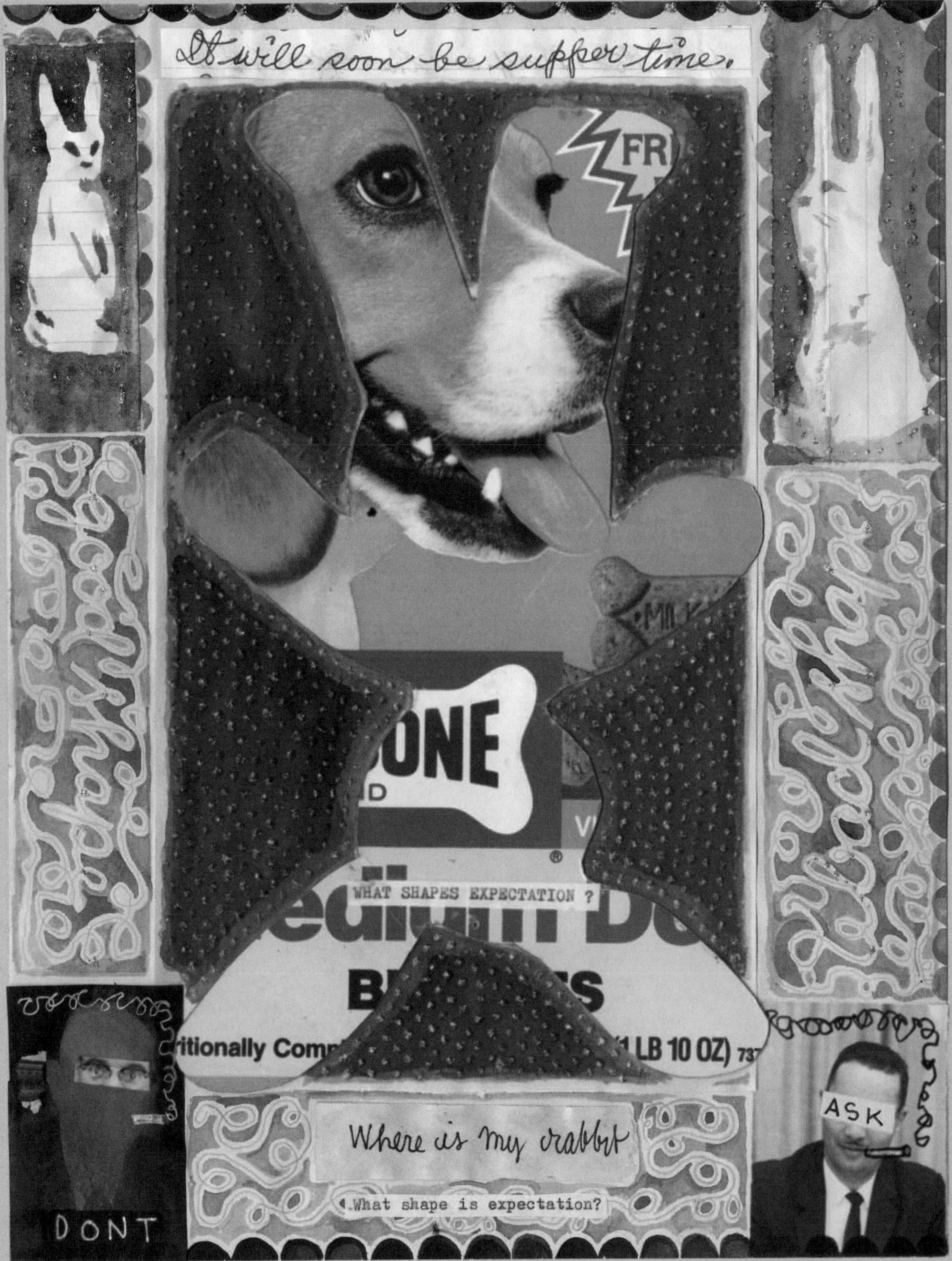

It will soon be supper time.
WHAT SHAPES EXPECTATION ?
Where is my rabbit
What shape is expectation?
DONT
ASK

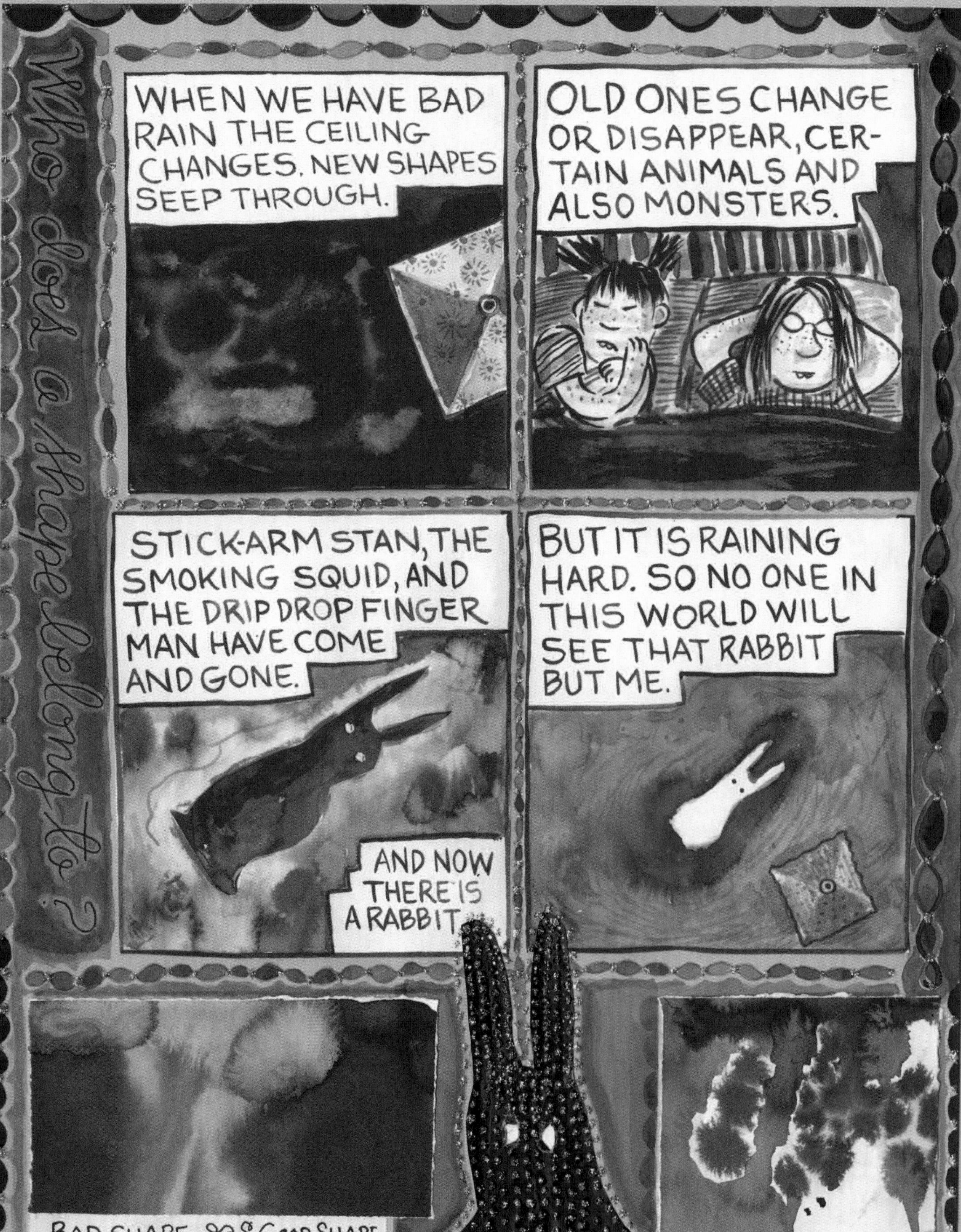
Who does a shape belong to?
WHEN WE HAVE BAD RAIN THE CEILING CHANGES. NEW SHAPES SEEP THROUGH.
OLD ONES CHANGE OR DISAPPEAR, CERTAIN ANIMALS AND ALSO MONSTERS.
STICK-ARM STAN, THE SMOKING SQUID, AND THE DRIP DROP FINGER MAN HAVE COME AND GONE.
AND NOW THERE IS A RABBIT.
BUT IT IS RAINING HARD. SO NO ONE IN THIS WORLD WILL SEE THAT RABBIT BUT ME.
BAD SHAPE
GOOD SHAPE

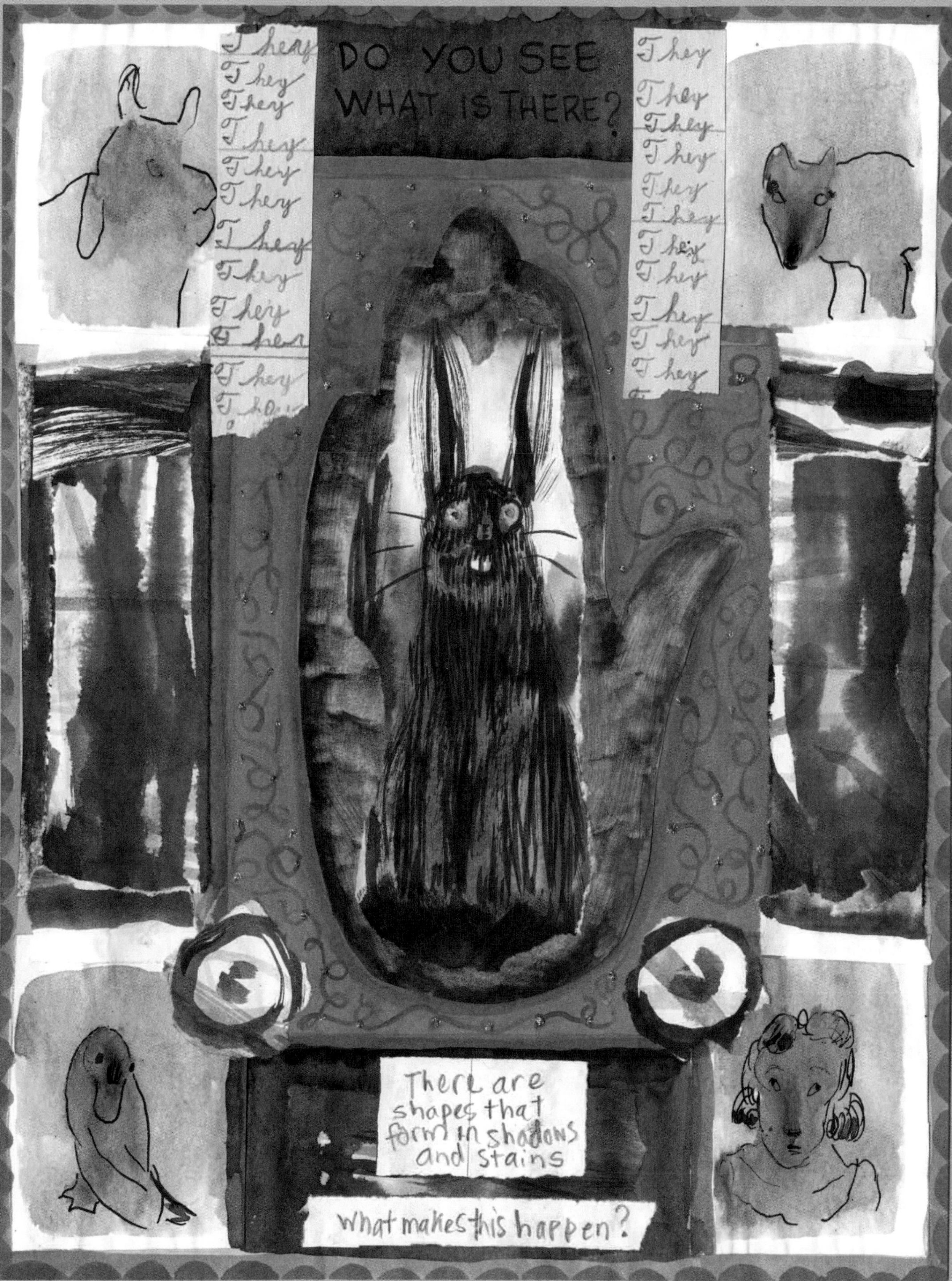

DO YOU SEE WHAT IS THERE?
They
They
They
They
They
They
They
They
They
They
They
They
They
They
They
They
They
They
They
They
They
They
They
They
There are shapes that form in shadows and stains
what makes this happen?

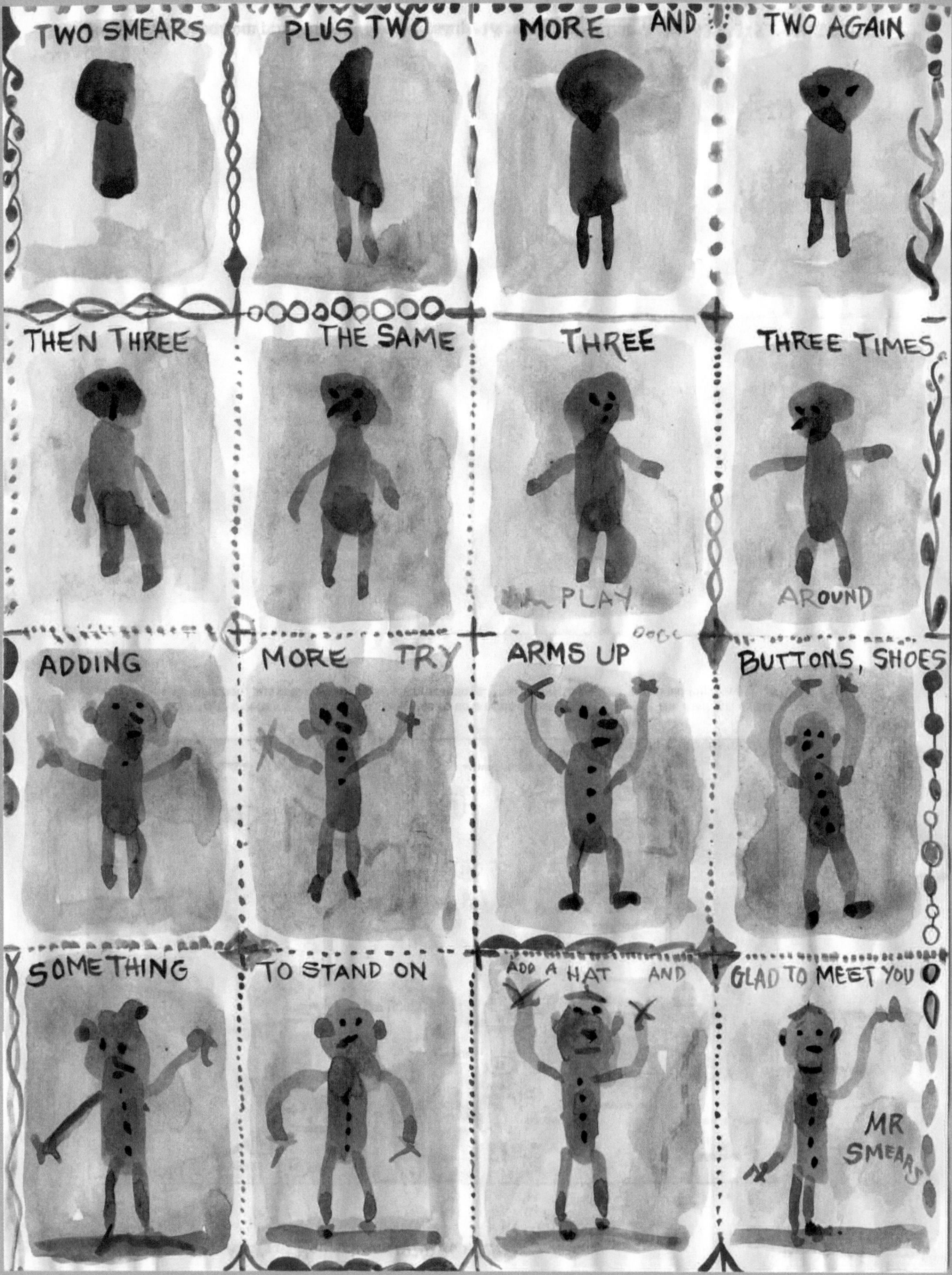
TWO SMEARS
PLUS TWO
MORE AND
TWO AGAIN
THEN THREE
THE SAME
THREE
THREE TIMES
PLAY
AROUND
ADDING
MORE TRY
ARMS UP
BUTTONS, SHOES
SOMETHING
TO STAND ON
ADD A HAT AND
GLAD TO MEET YOU
MR SMEARS

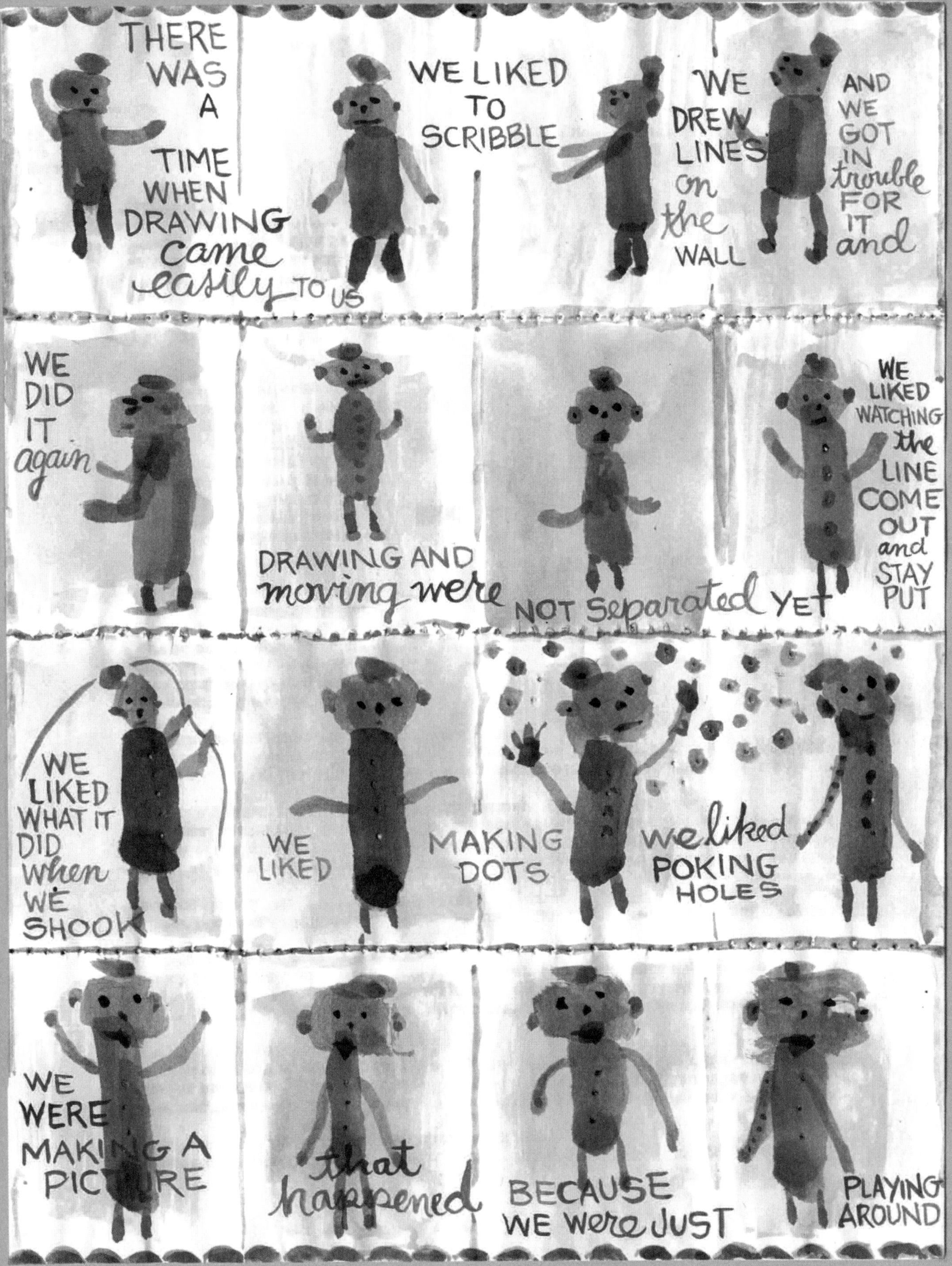
THERE WAS A TIME WHEN DRAWING came easily TO US
WE LIKED TO SCRIBBLE
WE DREW LINES on the WALL
AND WE GOT IN trouble FOR IT and
WE DID IT again
DRAWING AND moving were NOT Separated YET
WE LIKED WATCHING the LINE COME OUT and STAY PUT
WE LIKED WHAT IT DID when WE SHOOK
WE LIKED MAKING DOTS
we liked POKING HOLES
WE WERE MAKING A PICTURE
that happened BECAUSE WE were JUST PLAYING AROUND

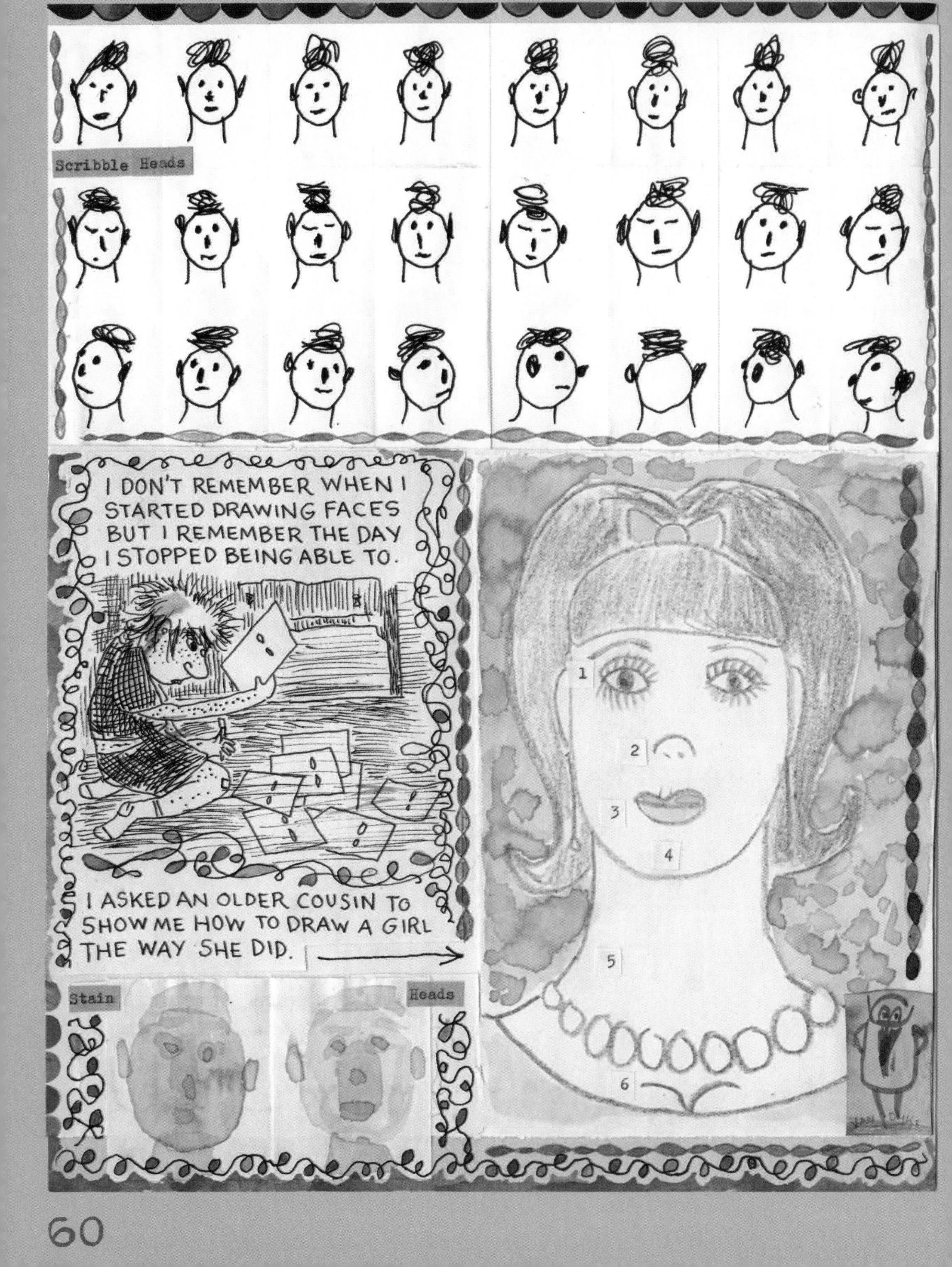
Scribble Heads
I DON'T REMEMBER WHEN I STARTED DRAWING FACES BUT I REMEMBER THE DAY I STOPPED BEING ABLE TO.
I ASKED AN OLDER COUSIN TO SHOW ME HOW TO DRAW A GIRL THE WAY SHE DID.
1
2
3
4
5
6
Stain
Heads

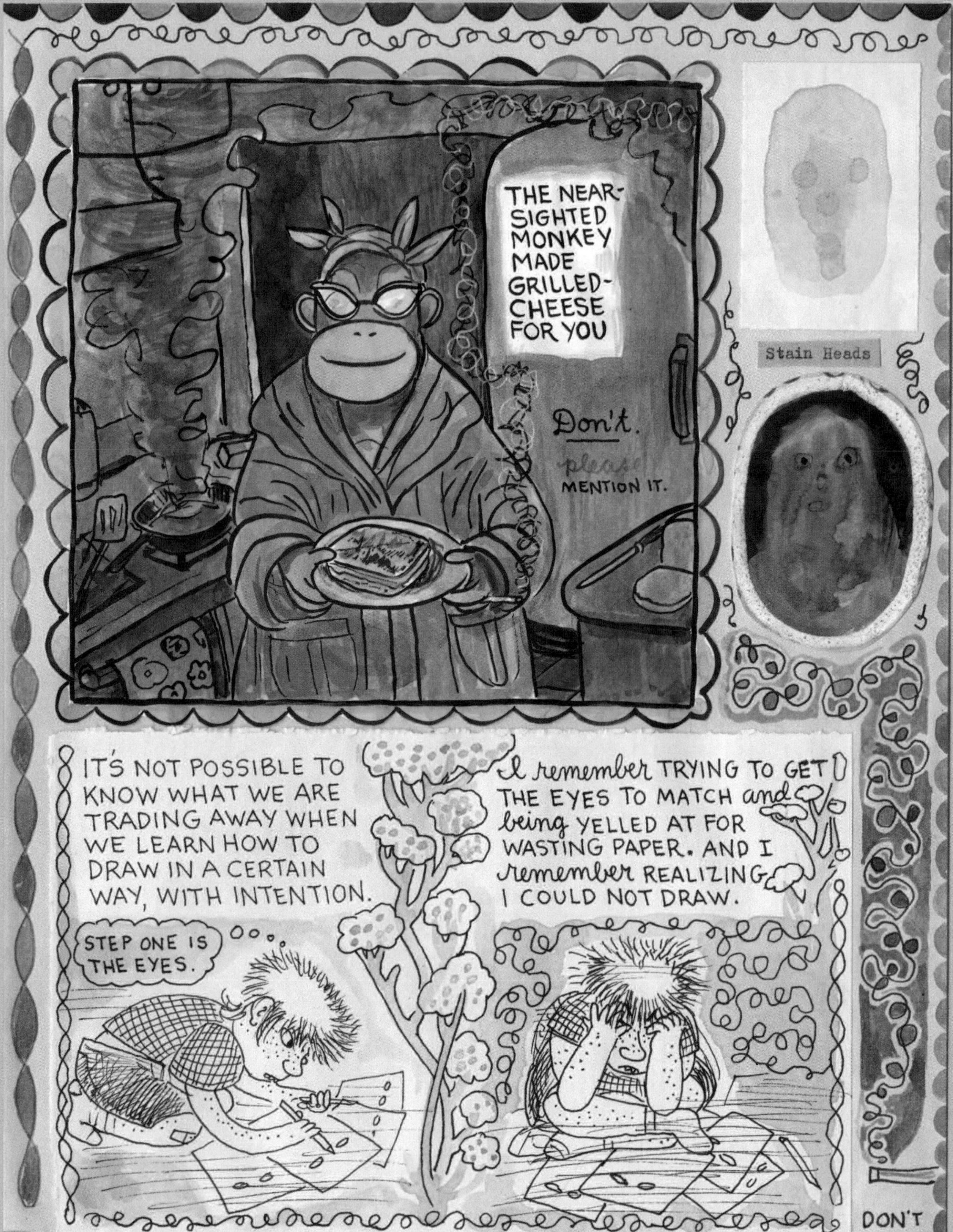
THE NEAR-SIGHTED MONKEY MADE GRILLED-CHEESE FOR YOU
Don't. please MENTION IT.
Stain Heads
IT'S NOT POSSIBLE TO KNOW WHAT WE ARE TRADING AWAY WHEN WE LEARN HOW TO DRAW IN A CERTAIN WAY, WITH INTENTION.
I remember TRYING TO GET THE EYES TO MATCH and being YELLED AT FOR WASTING PAPER. AND I remember REALIZING I COULD NOT DRAW.
STEP ONE IS THE EYES.
DON'T

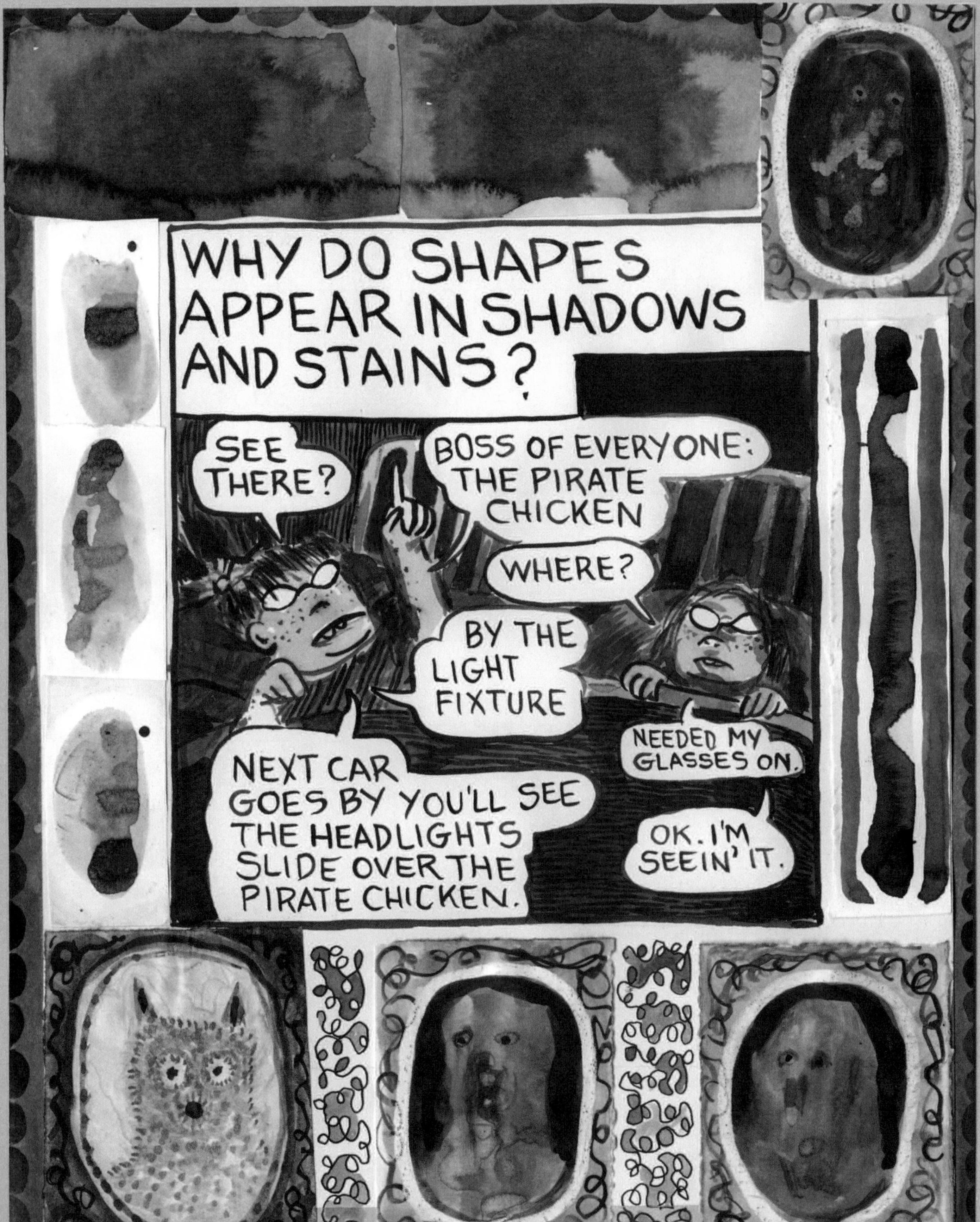
WHY DO SHAPES APPEAR IN SHADOWS AND STAINS?
SEE THERE?
BOSS OF EVERYONE: THE PIRATE CHICKEN
WHERE?
BY THE LIGHT FIXTURE
NEEDED MY GLASSES ON.
NEXT CAR GOES BY YOU'LL SEE THE HEADLIGHTS SLIDE OVER THE PIRATE CHICKEN.
OK. I'M SEEIN' IT.

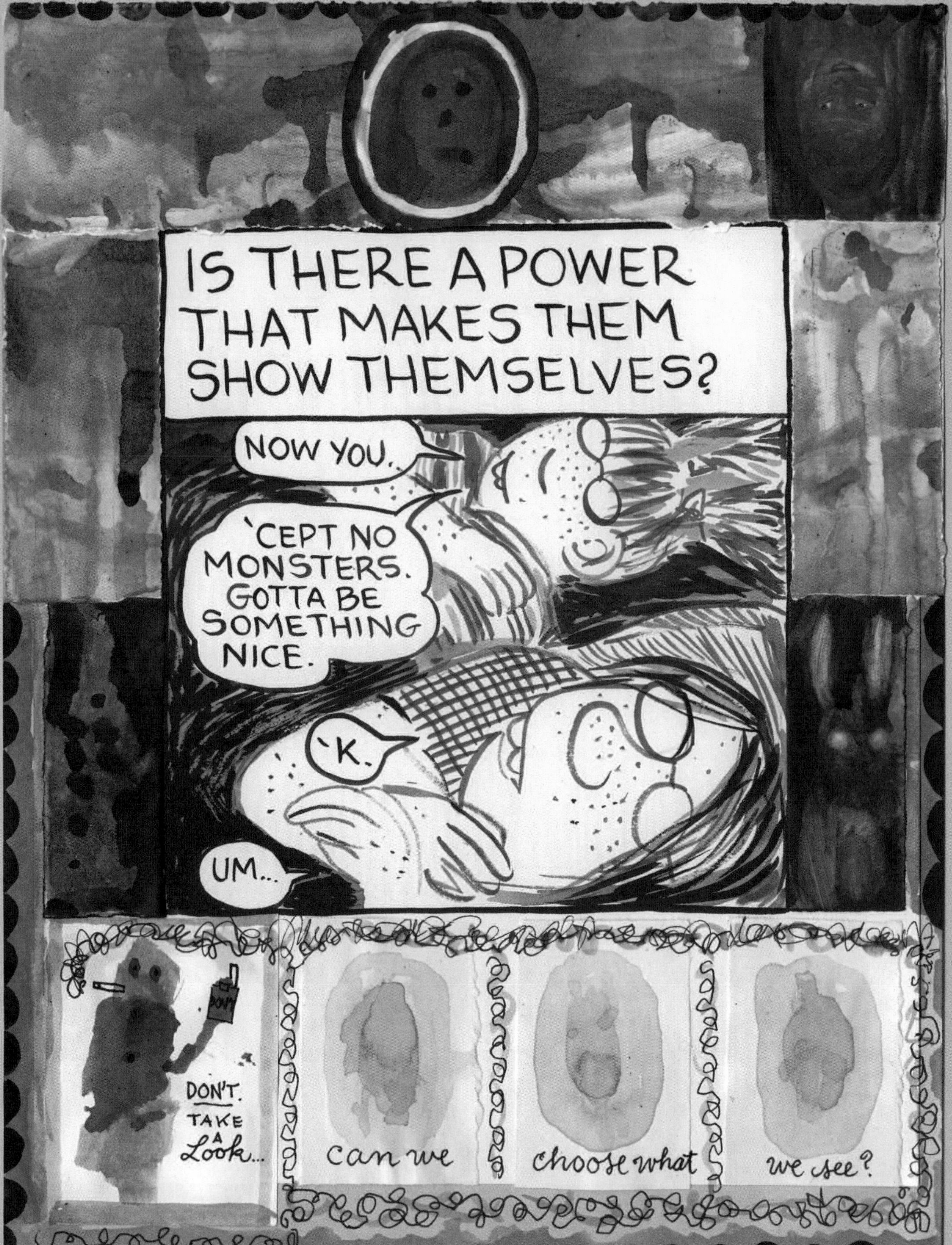

IS THERE A POWER THAT MAKES THEM SHOW THEMSELVES?
NOW YOU.
`CEPT NO MONSTERS. GOTTA BE SOMETHING NICE.
`K.
UM...
DON'T.
DON'T. TAKE A Look...
can we
choose what
we see?

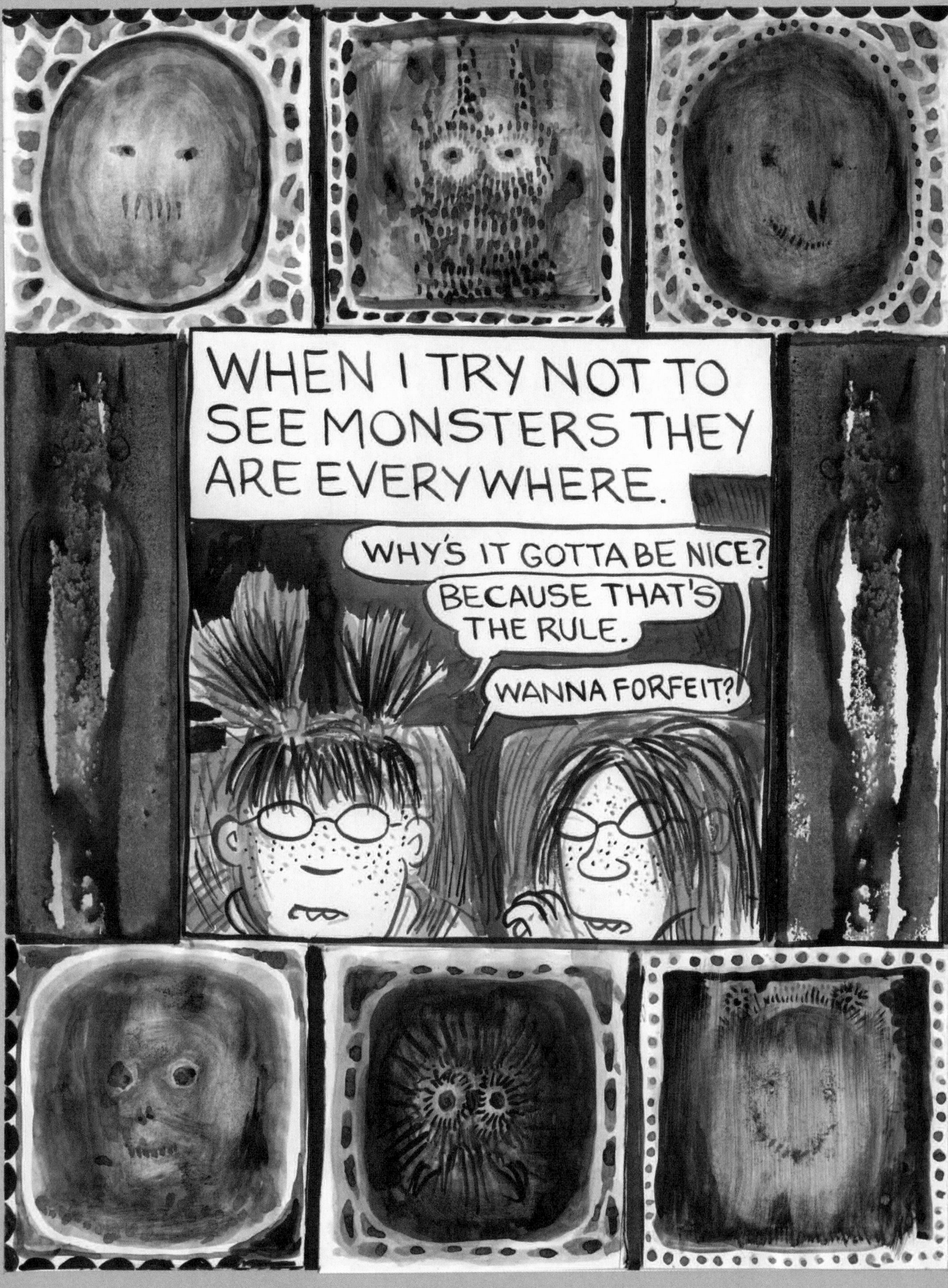
WHEN I TRY NOT TO SEE MONSTERS THEY ARE EVERYWHERE.
WHY'S IT GOTTA BE NICE?
BECAUSE THAT'S THE RULE.
WANNA FORFEIT?

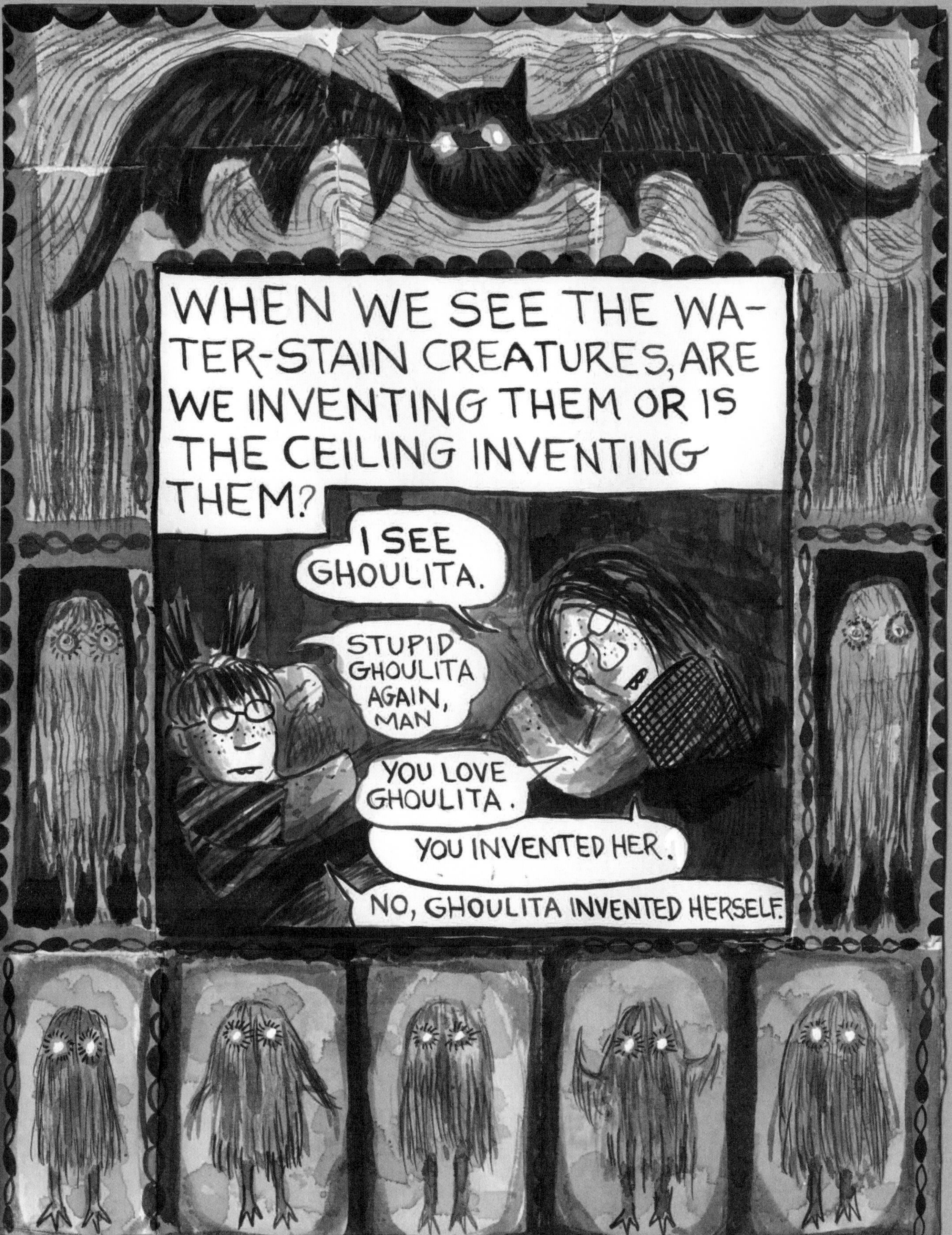
WHEN WE SEE THE WATER-STAIN CREATURES, ARE WE INVENTING THEM OR IS THE CEILING INVENTING THEM?
I SEE GHOULITA.
STUPID GHOULITA AGAIN, MAN
YOU LOVE GHOULITA.
YOU INVENTED HER.
NO, GHOULITA INVENTED HERSELF.

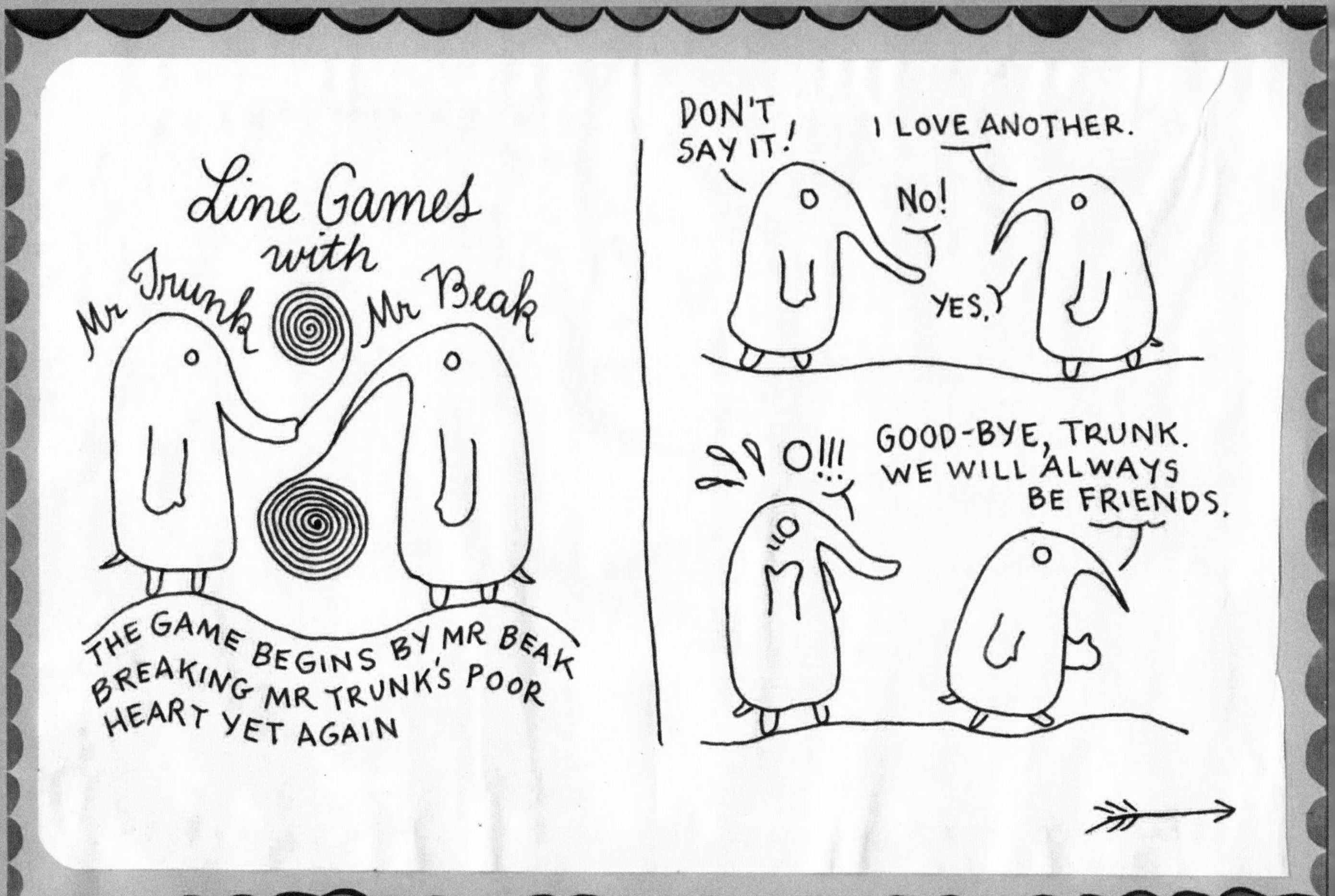
Line Games with
Mr Trunk
Mr Beak
THE GAME BEGINS BY MR BEAK BREAKING MR TRUNK'S POOR HEART YET AGAIN
DON'T SAY IT!
I LOVE ANOTHER.
NO!
YES.
O!!!
GOOD-BYE, TRUNK. WE WILL ALWAYS BE FRIENDS.

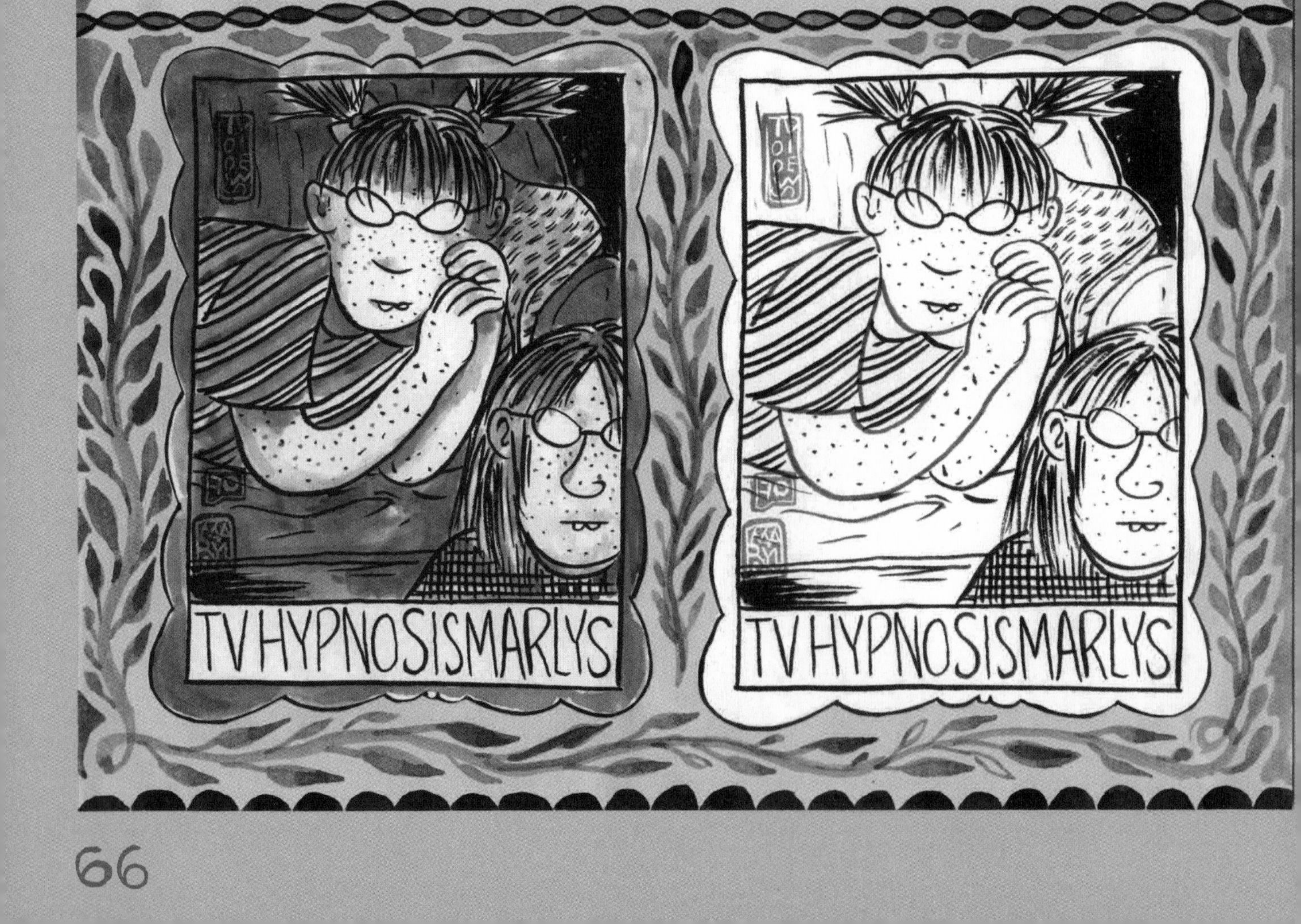
TV HYPNOSIS MARLYS
TV HYPNOSIS MARLYS

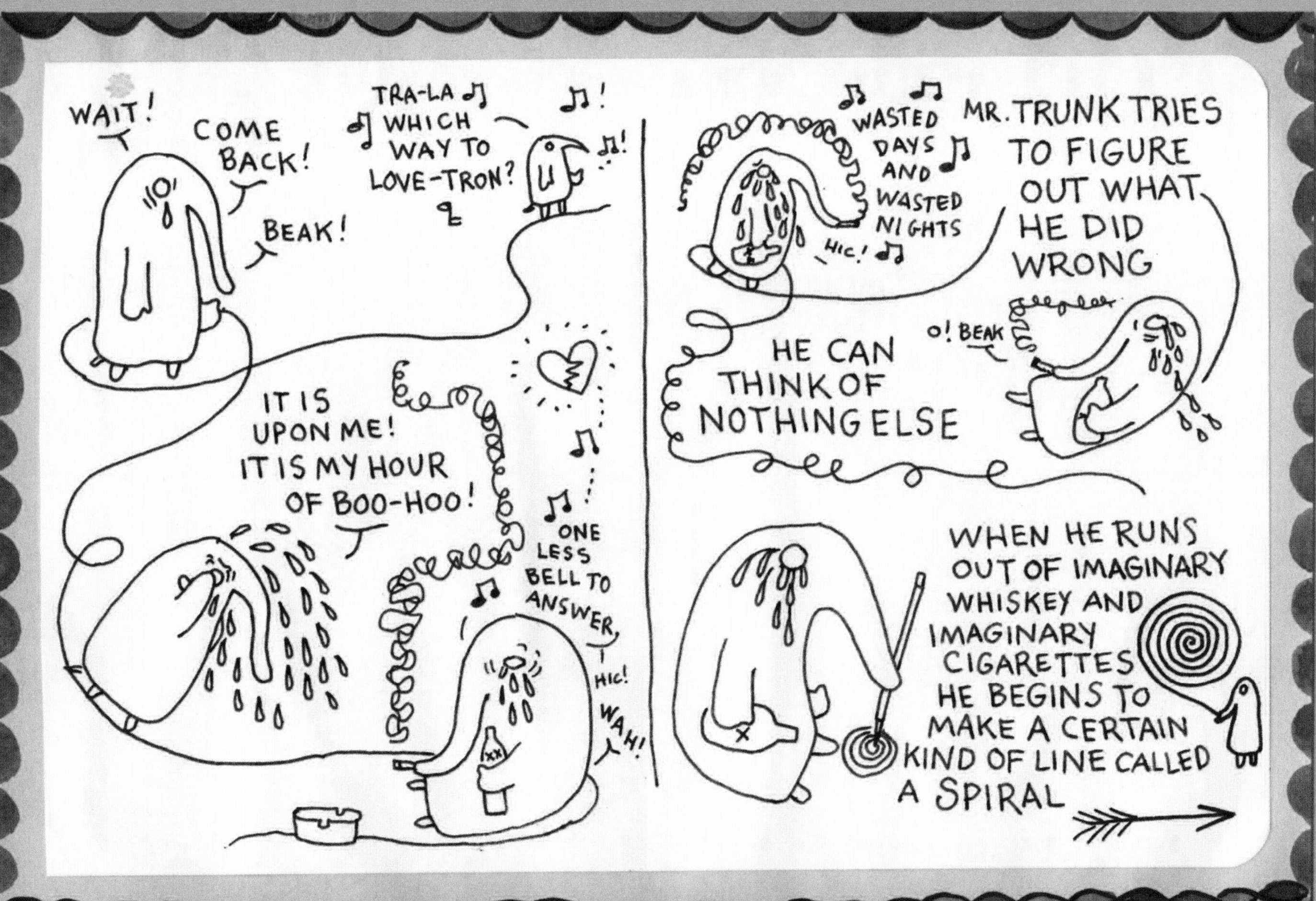
WAIT!
COME BACK!
BEAK!
TRA-LA WHICH WAY TO LOVE-TRON?
IT IS UPON ME! IT IS MY HOUR OF BOO-HOO!
ONE LESS BELL TO ANSWER
HIC!
WAH!
WASTED DAYS AND WASTED NIGHTS
HIC!
MR. TRUNK TRIES TO FIGURE OUT WHAT HE DID WRONG
HE CAN THINK OF NOTHING ELSE
O! BEAK
WHEN HE RUNS OUT OF IMAGINARY WHISKEY AND IMAGINARY CIGARETTES HE BEGINS TO MAKE A CERTAIN KIND OF LINE CALLED A SPIRAL

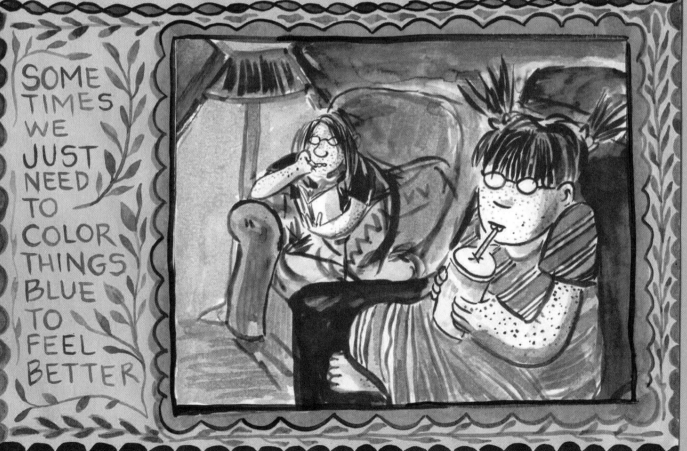

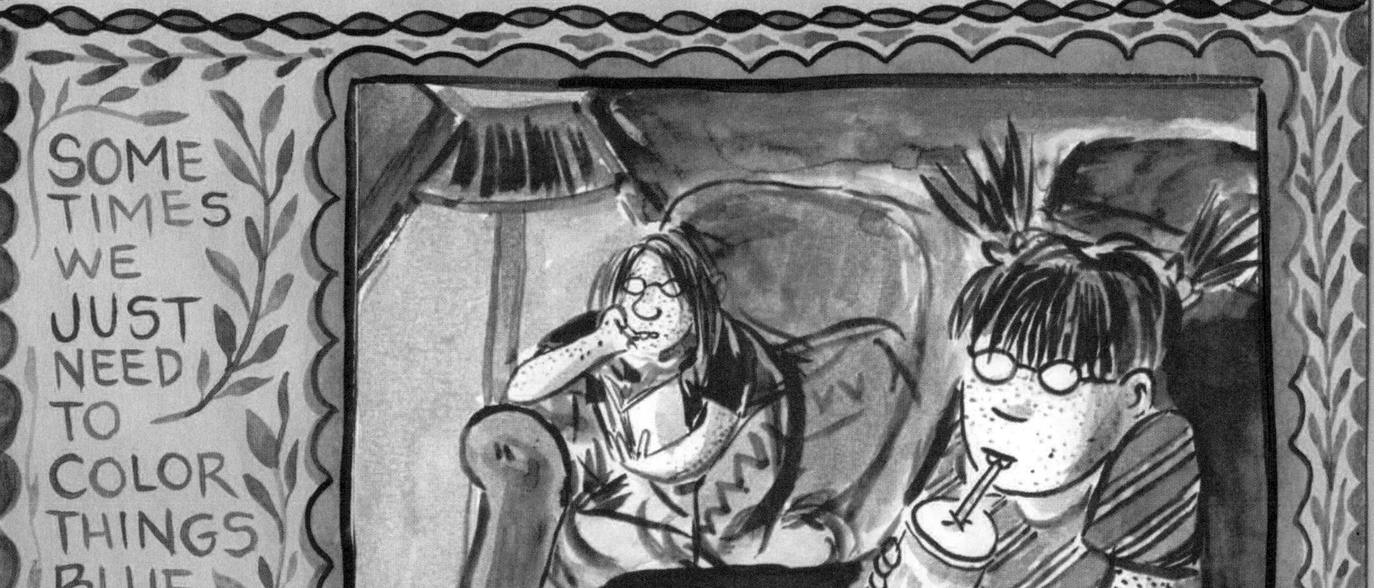
SOME TIMES WE JUST NEED TO COLOR THINGS BLUE TO FEEL BETTER

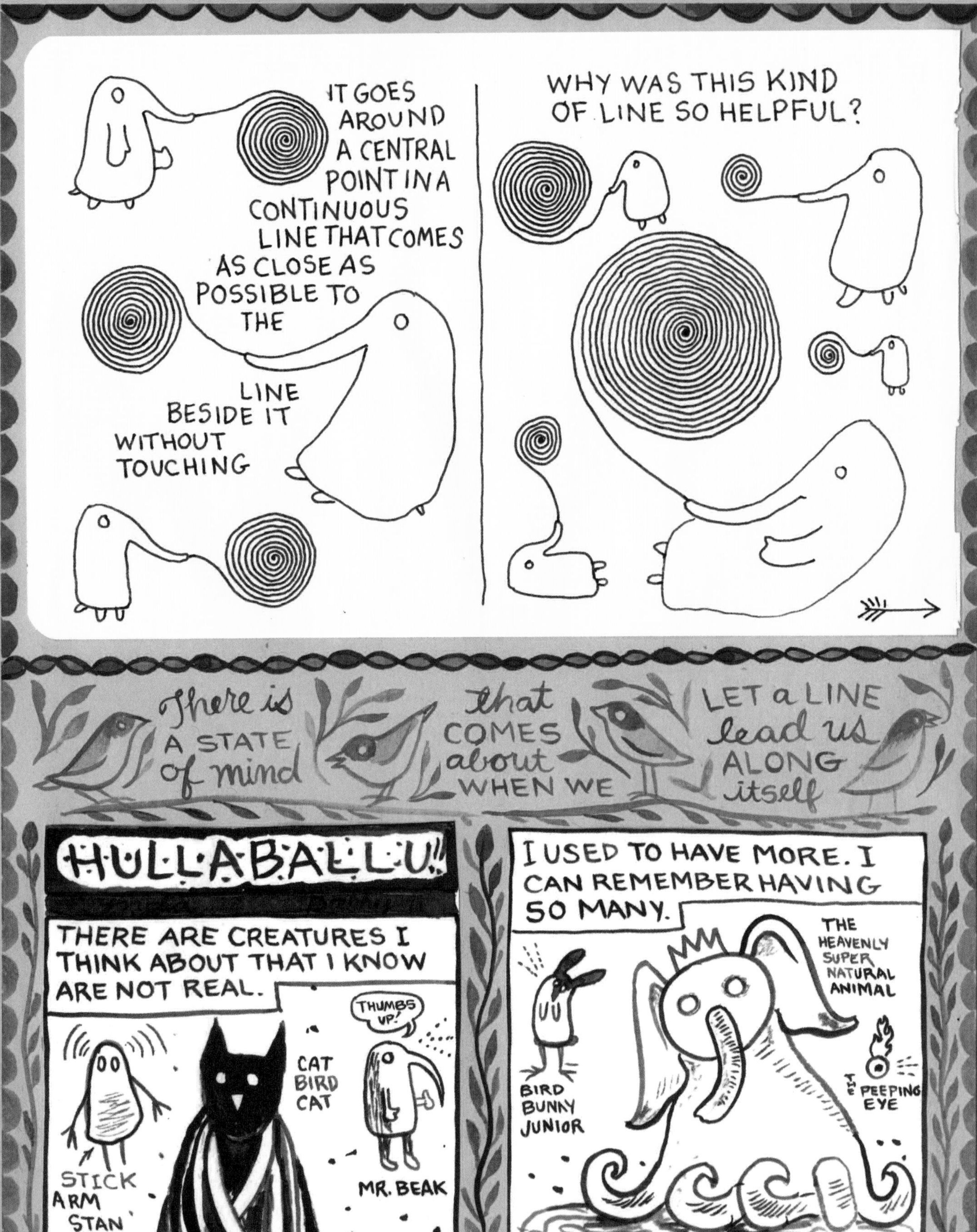
IT GOES AROUND A CENTRAL POINT IN A CONTINUOUS LINE THAT COMES AS CLOSE AS POSSIBLE TO THE LINE BESIDE IT WITHOUT TOUCHING
WHY WAS THIS KIND OF LINE SO HELPFUL?
There is a STATE of mind that COMES about WHEN WE LET a LINE lead us ALONG itself
HULLABALLU!
THERE ARE CREATURES I THINK ABOUT THAT I KNOW ARE NOT REAL.
THUMBS UP!
STICK ARM STAN
CAT BIRD CAT
MR. BEAK
I USED TO HAVE MORE. I CAN REMEMBER HAVING SO MANY.
THE HEAVENLY SUPER NATURAL ANIMAL
BIRD BUNNY JUNIOR
THE PEEPING EYE

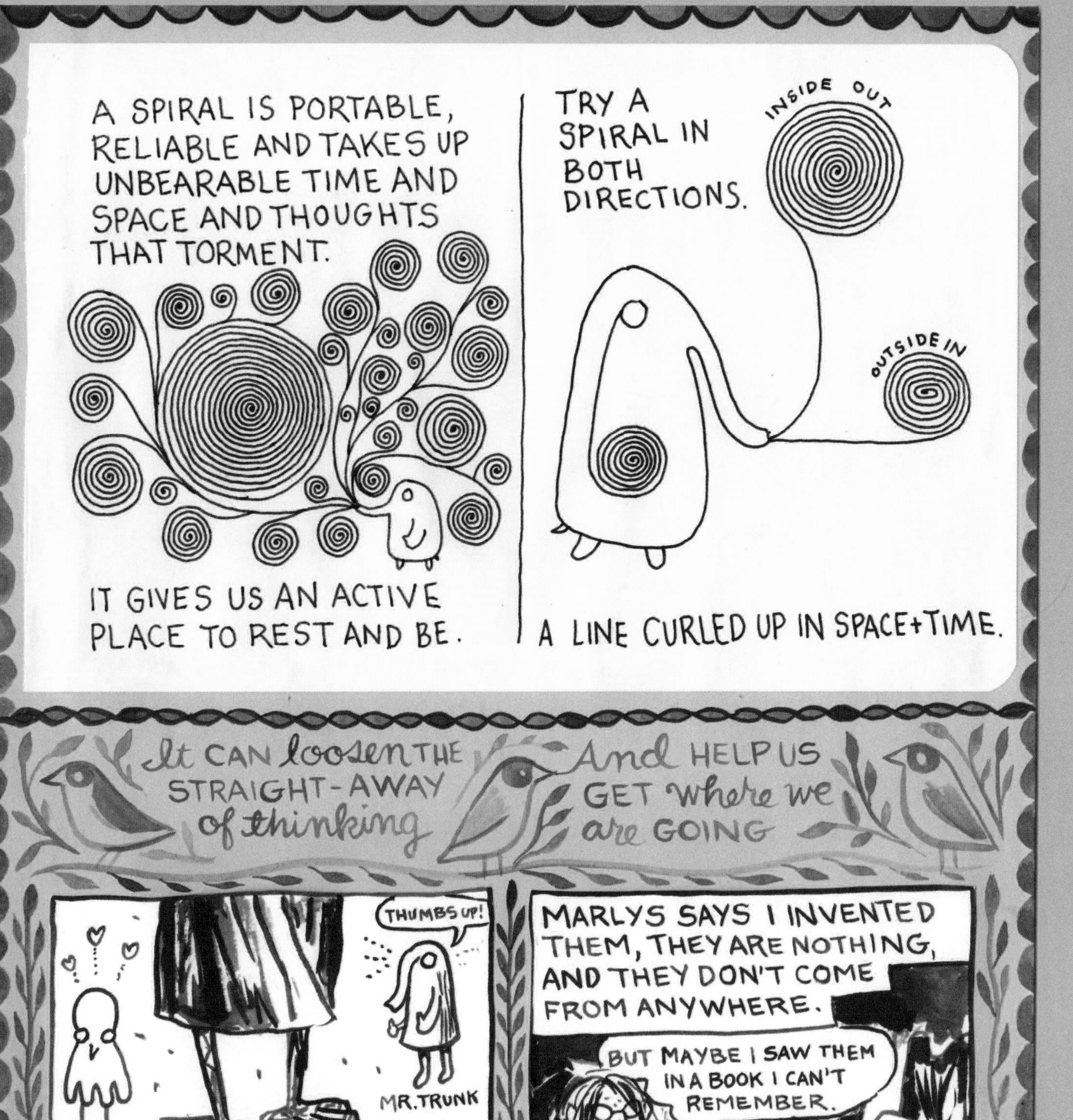
A SPIRAL IS PORTABLE, RELIABLE AND TAKES UP UNBEARABLE TIME AND SPACE AND THOUGHTS THAT TORMENT.
IT GIVES US AN ACTIVE PLACE TO REST AND BE.
TRY A SPIRAL IN BOTH DIRECTIONS.
INSIDE OUT
OUTSIDE IN
A LINE CURLED UP IN SPACE+TIME.
It CAN loosen THE STRAIGHT-AWAY of thinking
And HELP US GET where we are GOING
BIRD SQUID ROMANTIC VERSION
THUMBS UP!
MR. TRUNK
DR. 13
I DIDN'T KNOW WHERE THEY CAME FROM.
I THOUGHT THEY WERE IN EVERYONES MIND. BUT NO.
MARLYS SAYS I INVENTED THEM, THEY ARE NOTHING, AND THEY DON'T COME FROM ANYWHERE.
BUT MAYBE I SAW THEM IN A BOOK I CAN'T REMEMBER.
THAT WOULD HAVE TO BE A BOOK TOO MESSED UP TO EXIST.
HEY WE SHOULD WRITE IT!
CALL IT HULLABALLU!

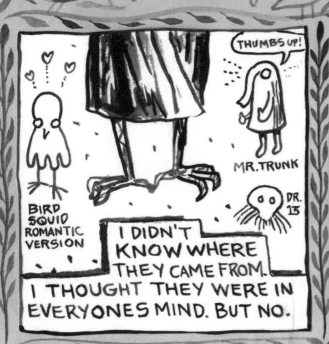

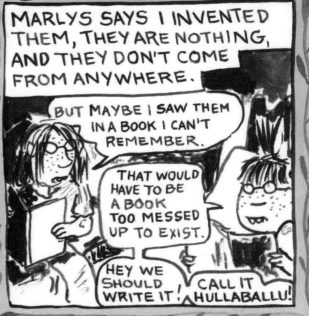

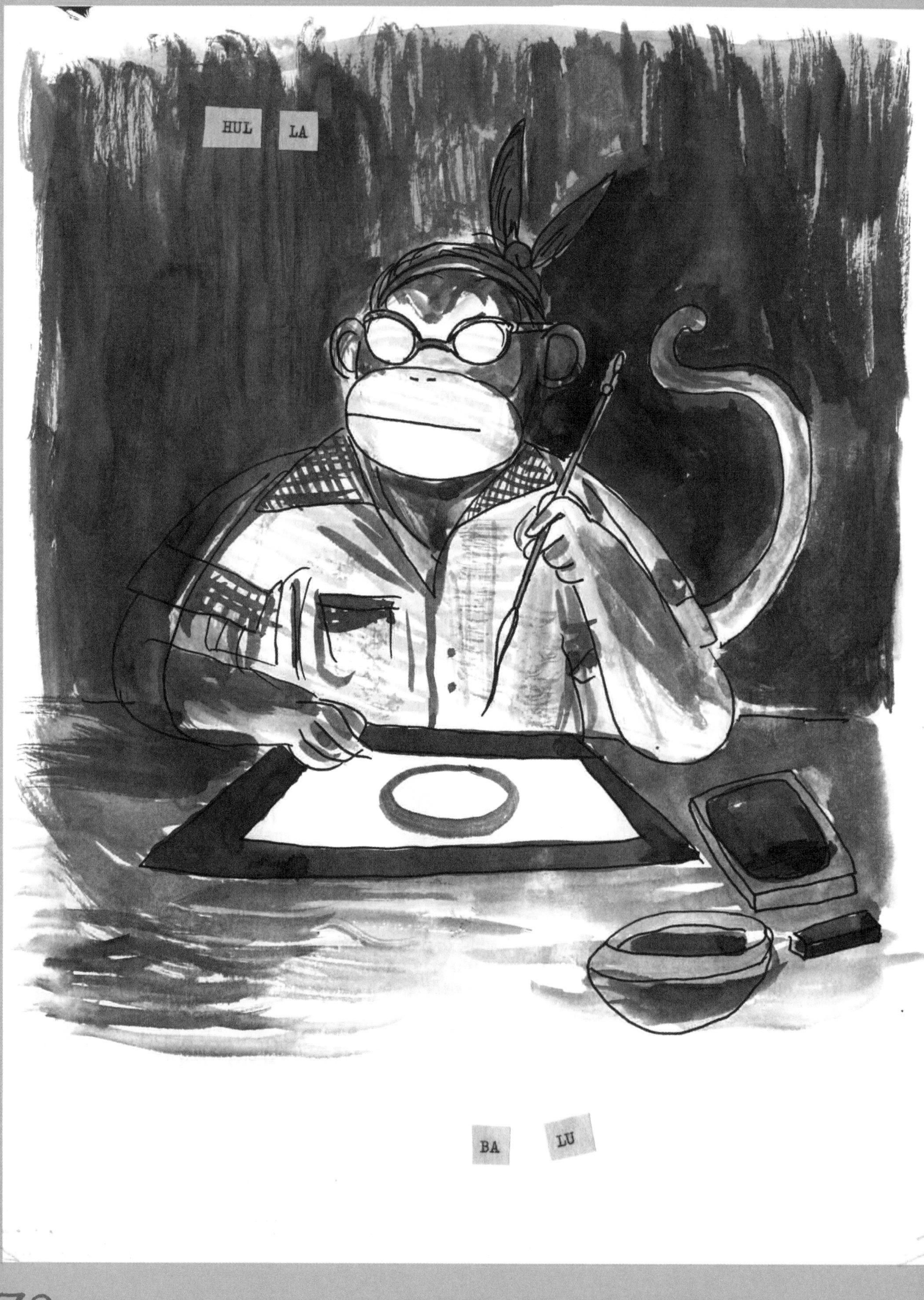
HUL LA
BA LU

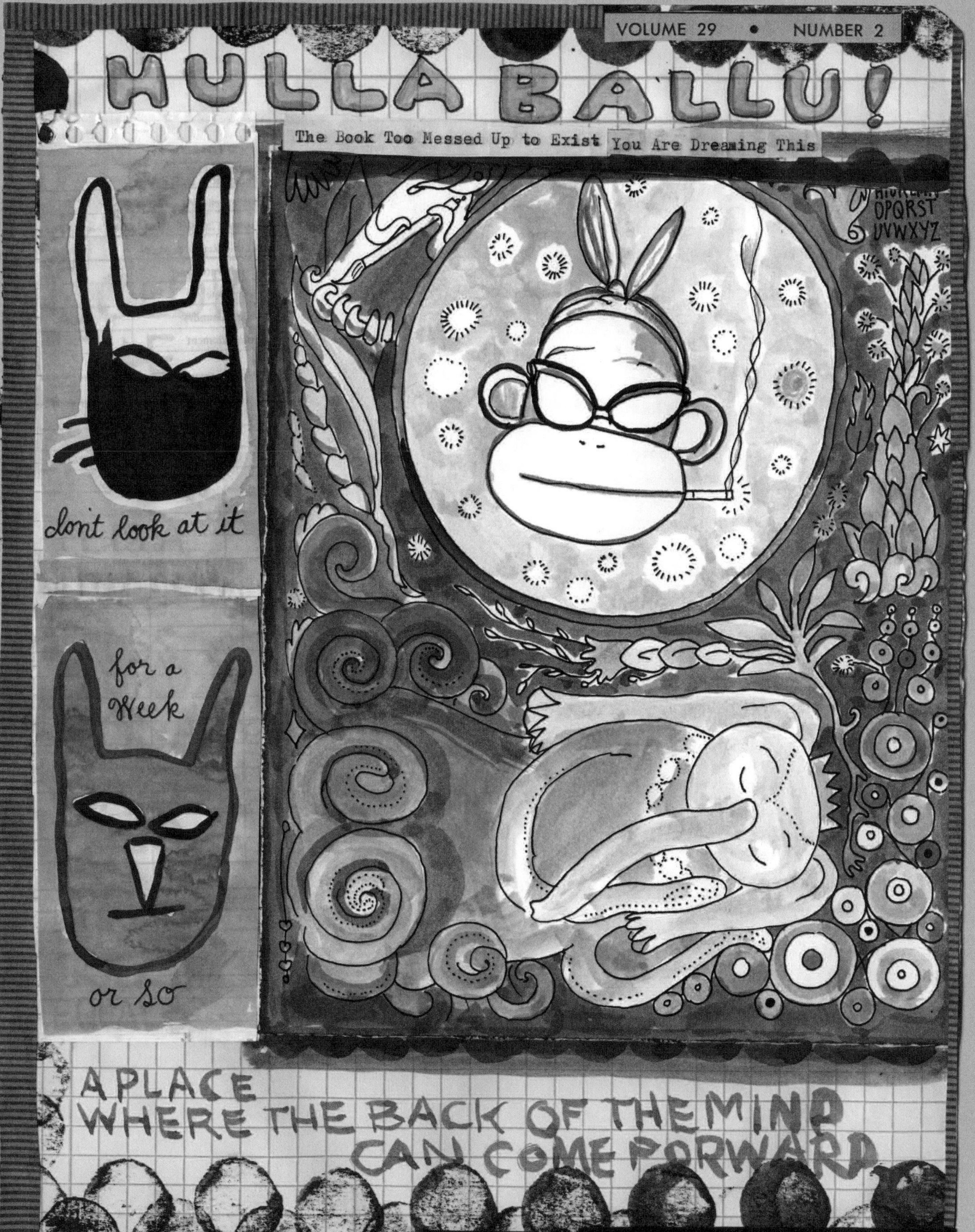
VOLUME 29 • NUMBER 2
HULLA BALLU!
The Book Too Messed Up to Exist
You Are Dreaming This
OPQRST
UVWXYZ
dont look at it
for a week
or so
A PLACE WHERE THE BACK OF THE MIND CAN COME FORWARD
A TIMELY ACTIVITY SUGGESTION

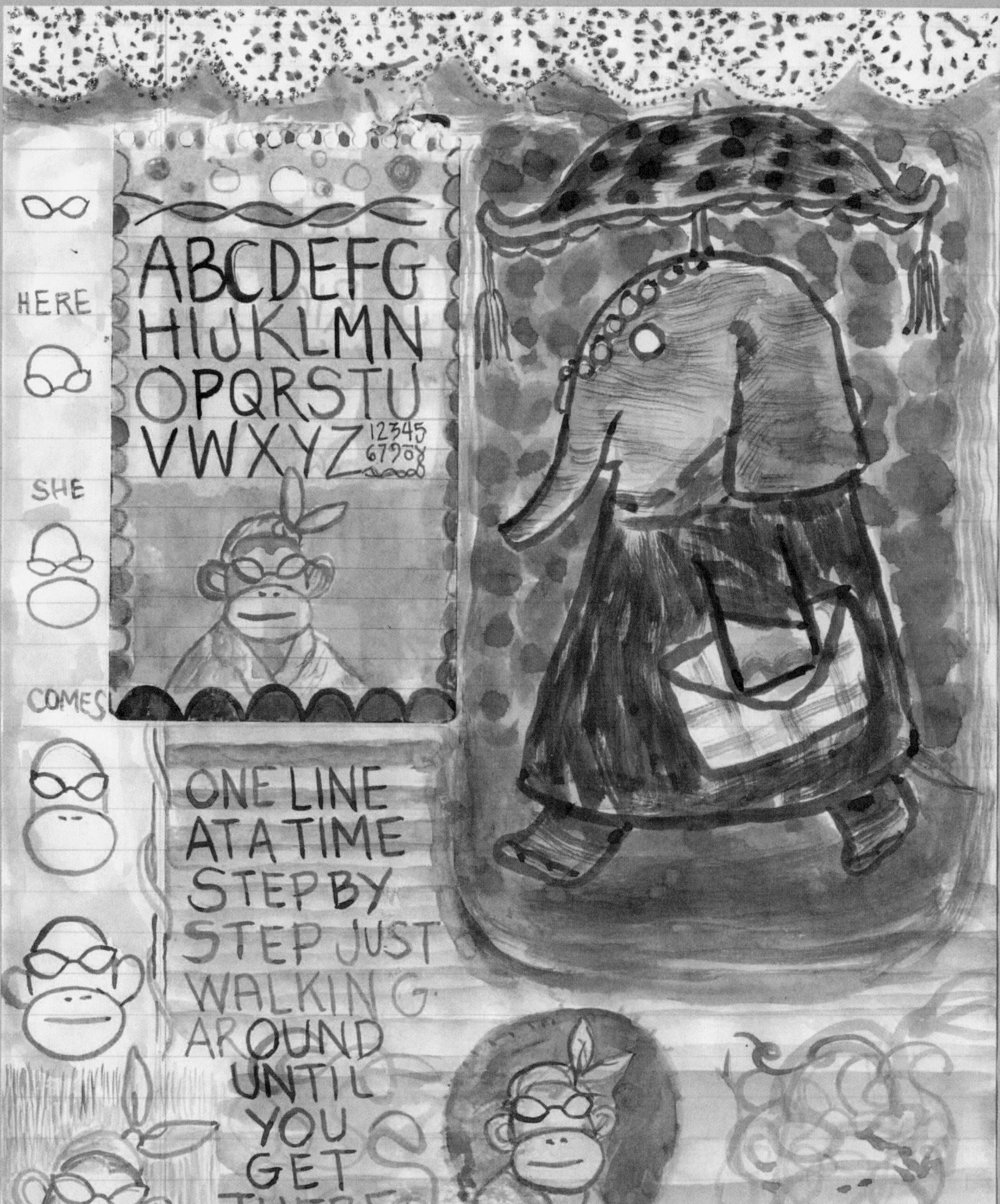
HERE
SHE
COMES
ABCDEFG
HIJKLMN
OPQRSTU
VWXYZ
12345
67890
ONE LINE
AT A TIME
STEP BY
STEP JUST
WALKING
AROUND
UNTIL
YOU
GET
THERE

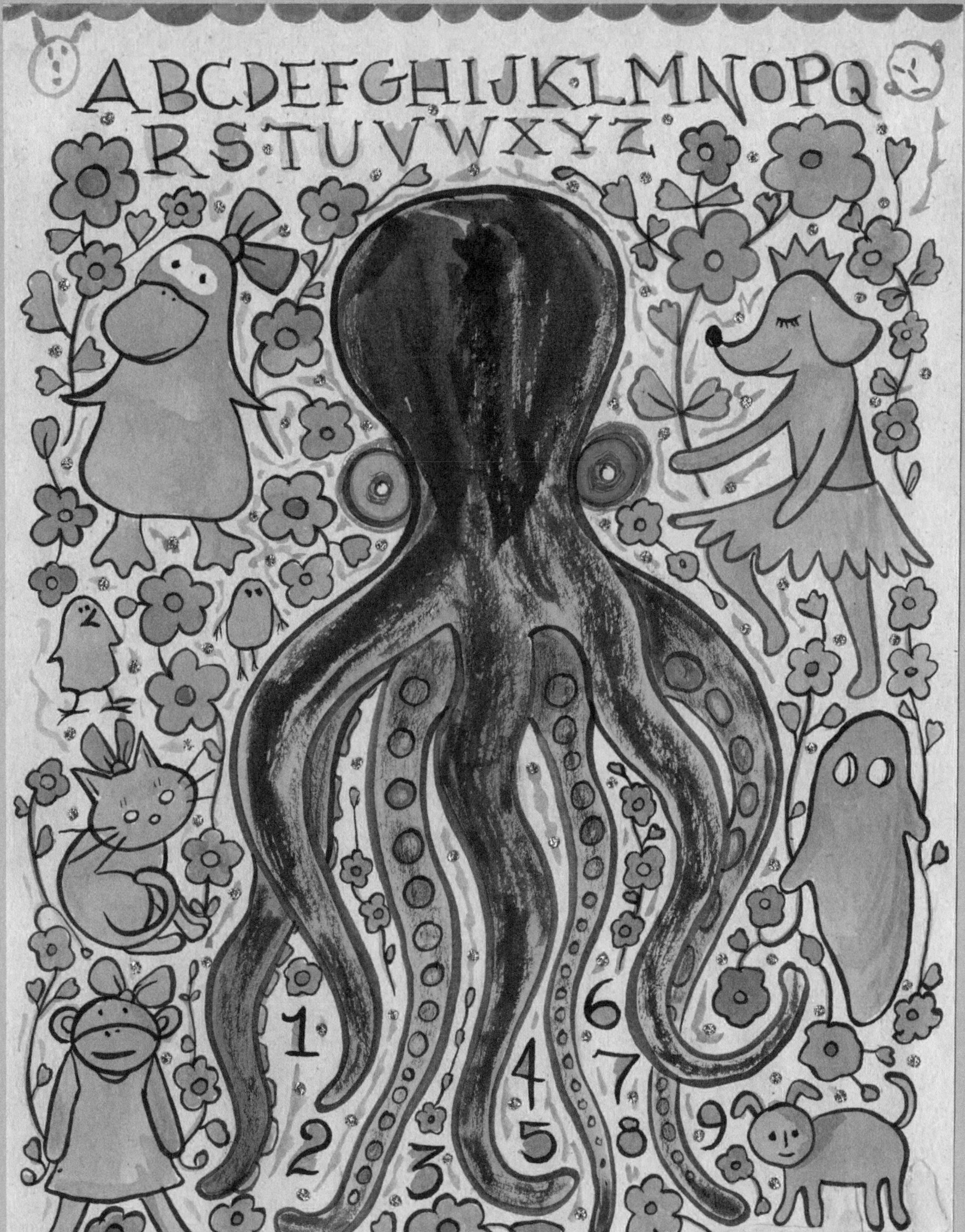
ABCDEFGHIJKLMNOPQ
RSTUVWXYZ
1
2
3
4
5
6
7
8
9

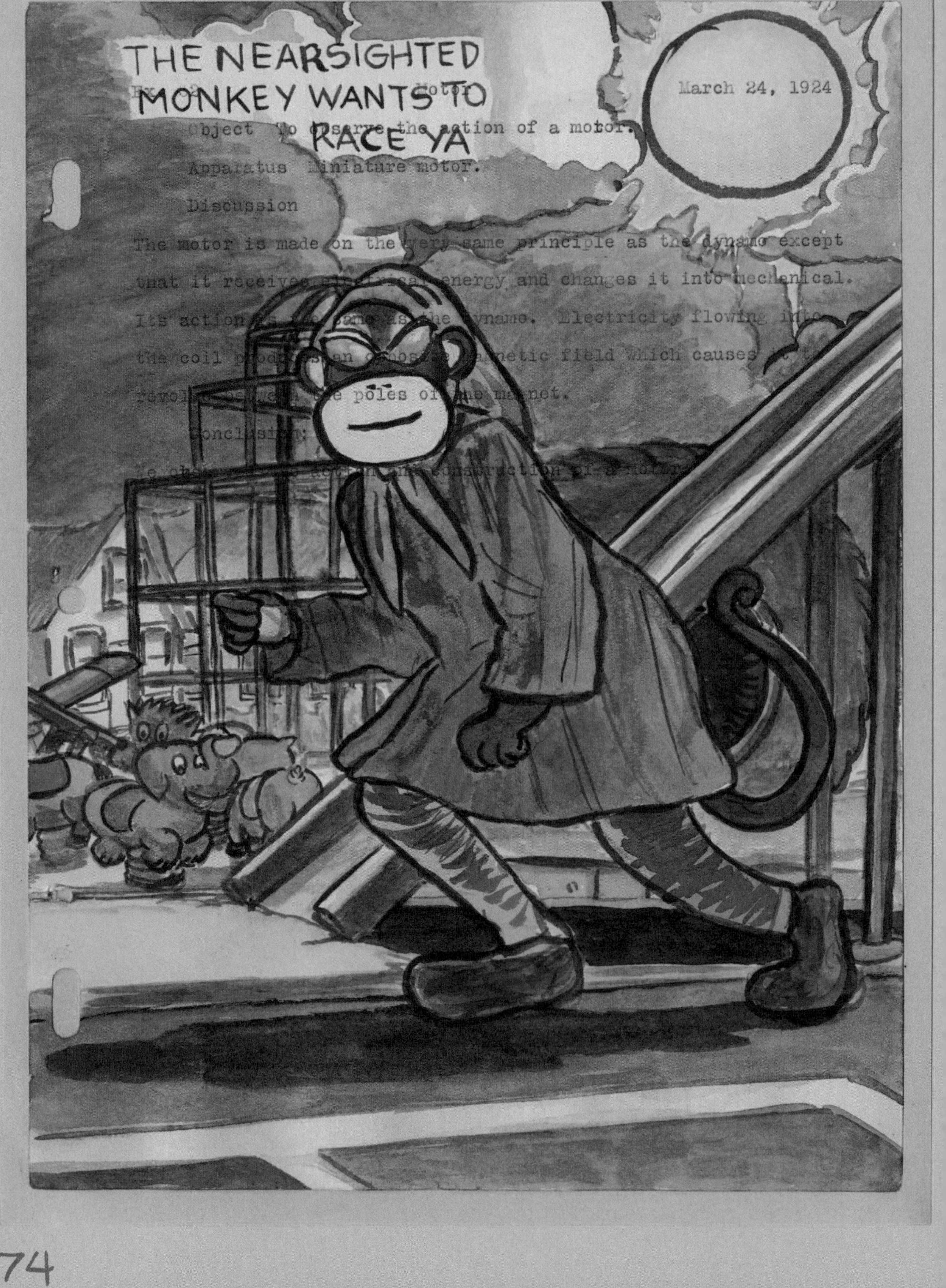
THE NEARSIGHTED MONKEY WANTS TO RACE YA
March 24, 1924
Object
Apparatus
Discussion
The motor is made on the very same principle as the dynamo except
that it receives
energy and changes it into mechanical.
Its action
Electricity flowing
the coil
netic field which causes
the poles of
net.
construction of a motor

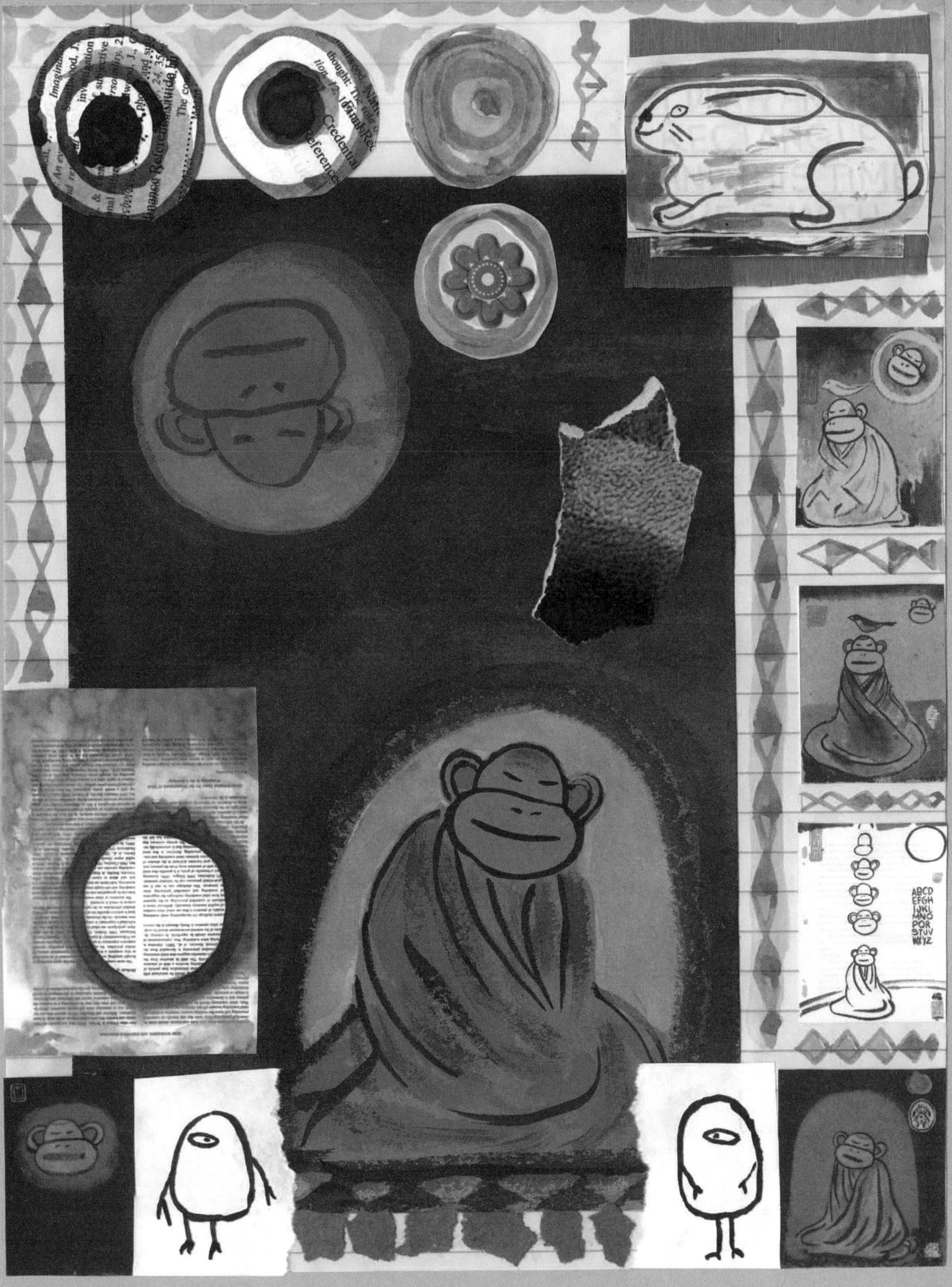

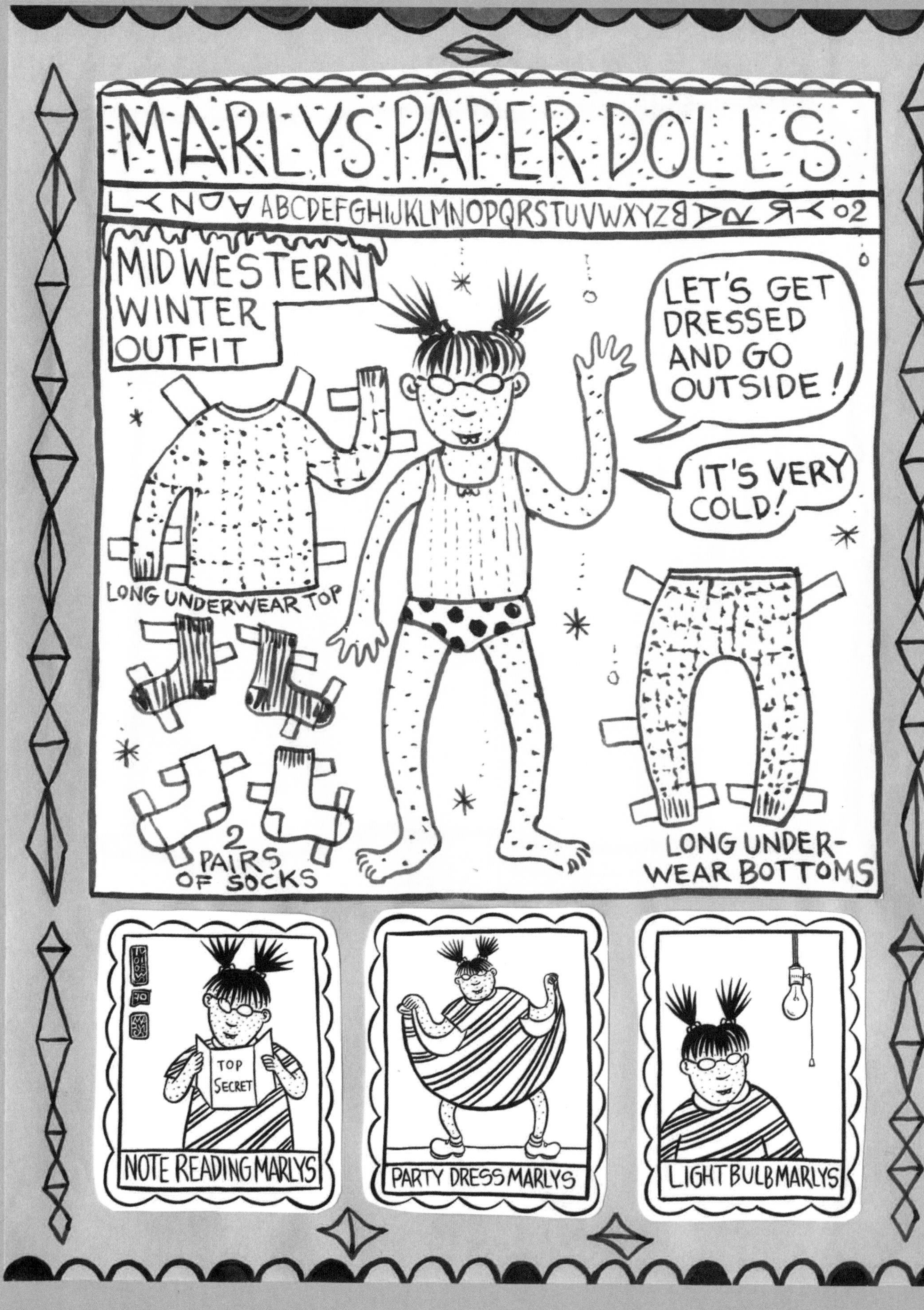

MARLYS PAPER DOLLS
ABCDEFGHIJKLMNOPQRSTUVWXYZ
MIDWESTERN WINTER OUTFIT
LET'S GET DRESSED AND GO OUTSIDE!
IT'S VERY COLD!
LONG UNDERWEAR TOP
2 PAIRS OF SOCKS
LONG UNDER-WEAR BOTTOMS
TOP SECRET
NOTE READING MARLYS
PARTY DRESS MARLYS
LIGHT BULB MARLYS

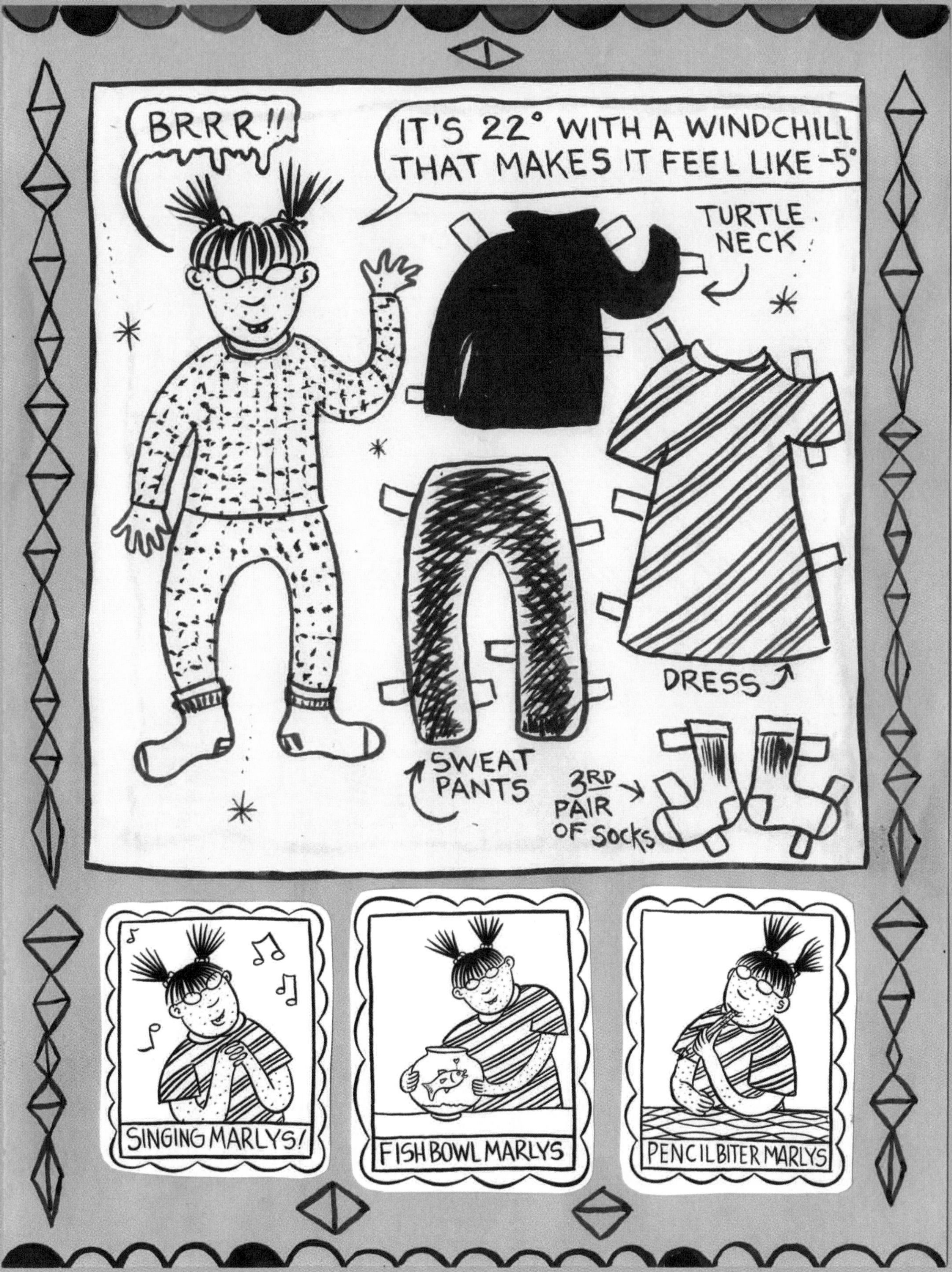
BRRR!!
IT'S 22° WITH A WINDCHILL THAT MAKES IT FEEL LIKE -5°
TURTLE NECK
DRESS
SWEAT PANTS
3RD PAIR OF SOCKS
SINGING MARLYS!
FISHBOWL MARLYS
PENCILBITER MARLYS

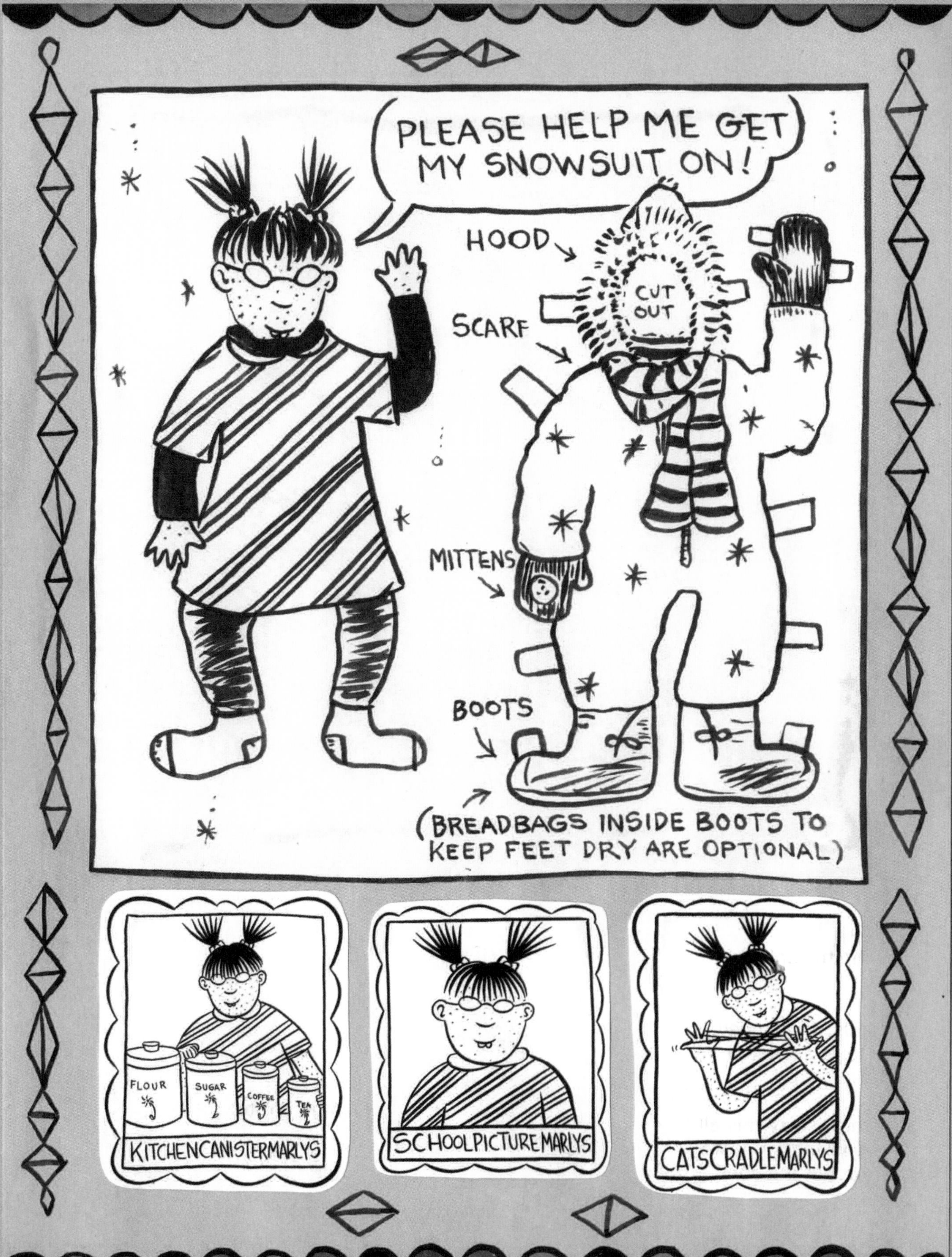
PLEASE HELP ME GET MY SNOWSUIT ON!
HOOD
CUT OUT
SCARF
MITTENS
BOOTS
(BREADBAGS INSIDE BOOTS TO KEEP FEET DRY ARE OPTIONAL)
FLOUR
SUGAR
COFFEE
TEA
KITCHENCANISTERMARLYS
SCHOOLPICTUREMARLYS
CATSCRADLEMARLYS

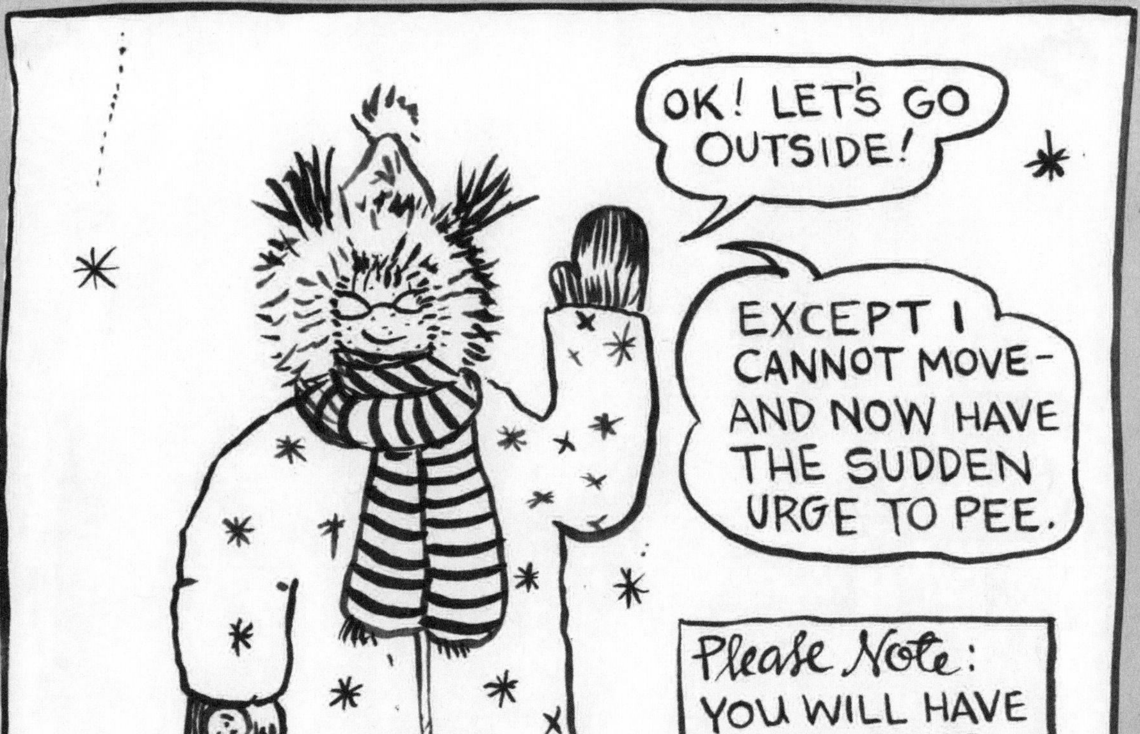
OK! LET'S GO OUTSIDE!
EXCEPT I CANNOT MOVE- AND NOW HAVE THE SUDDEN URGE TO PEE.
Please Note: YOU WILL HAVE TO TIE YOUR MARLYS PAPER DOLL TO SOMETHING STURDY TO KEEP HER FROM FALLING ON HER FACE WHEN WEARING THE MIDWESTERN OUTFIT.

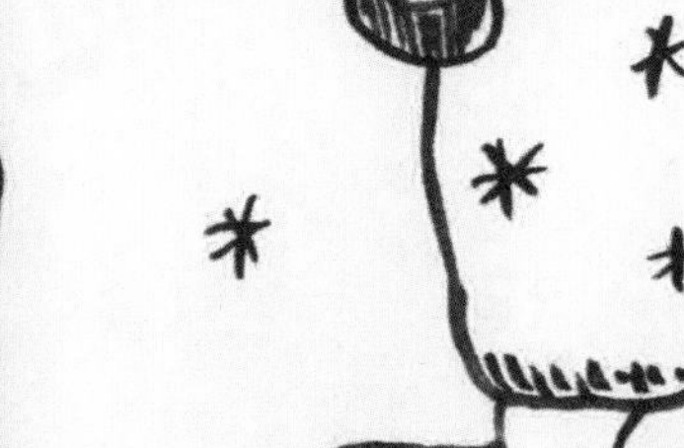
TRANSISTOR MARLYS

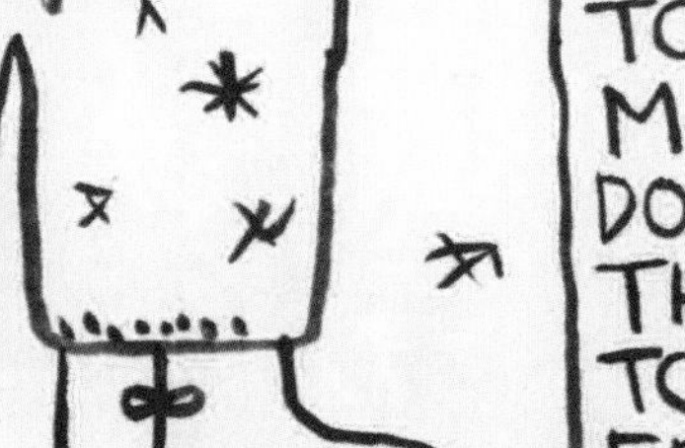
MICROSCOPE MARLYS!

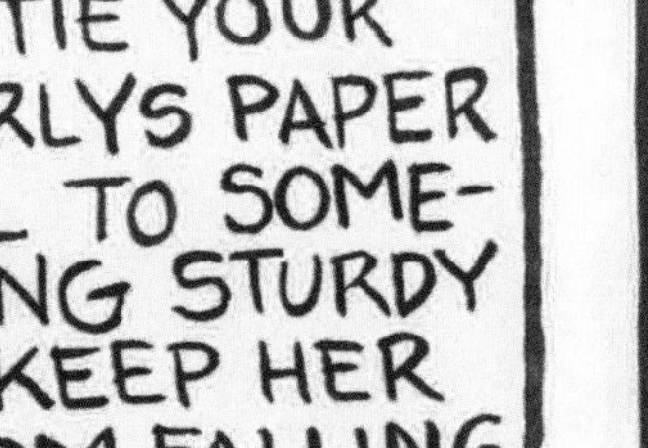
BAT PAL MARLYS

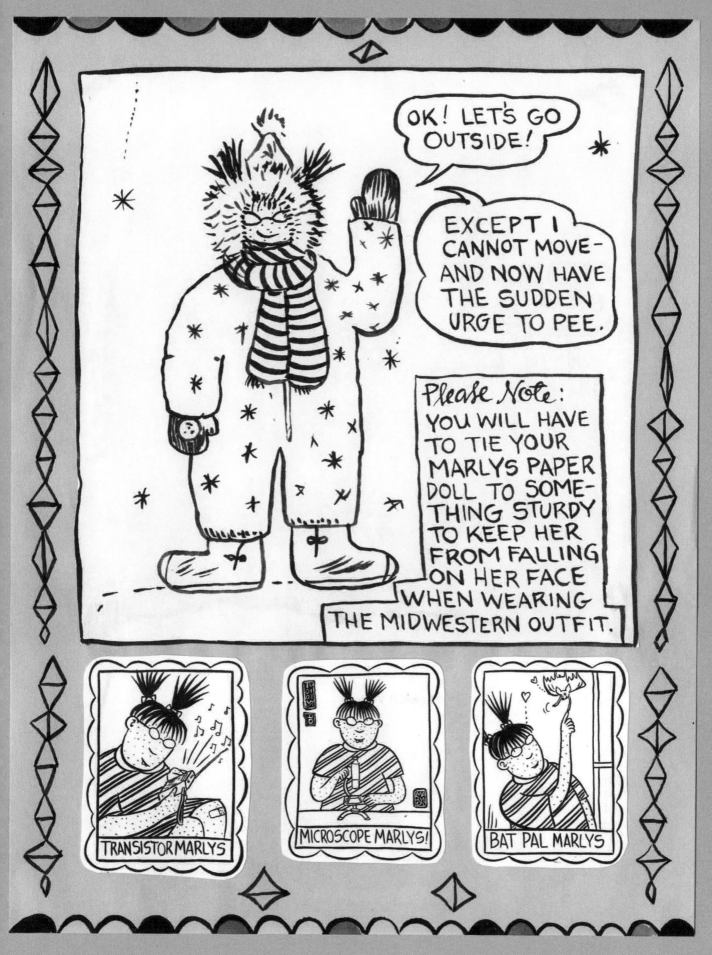

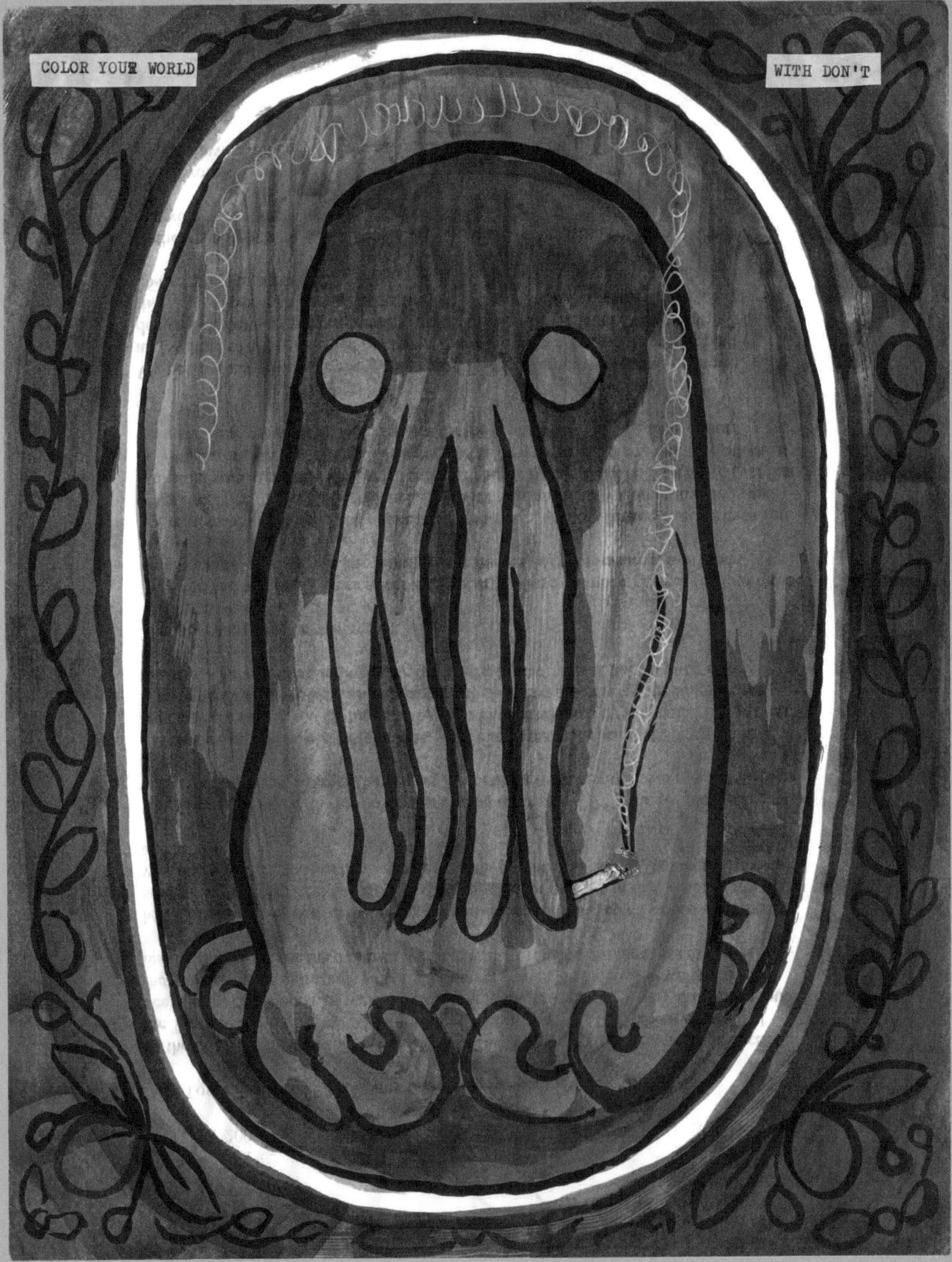
COLOR YOUR WORLD
WITH DON'T

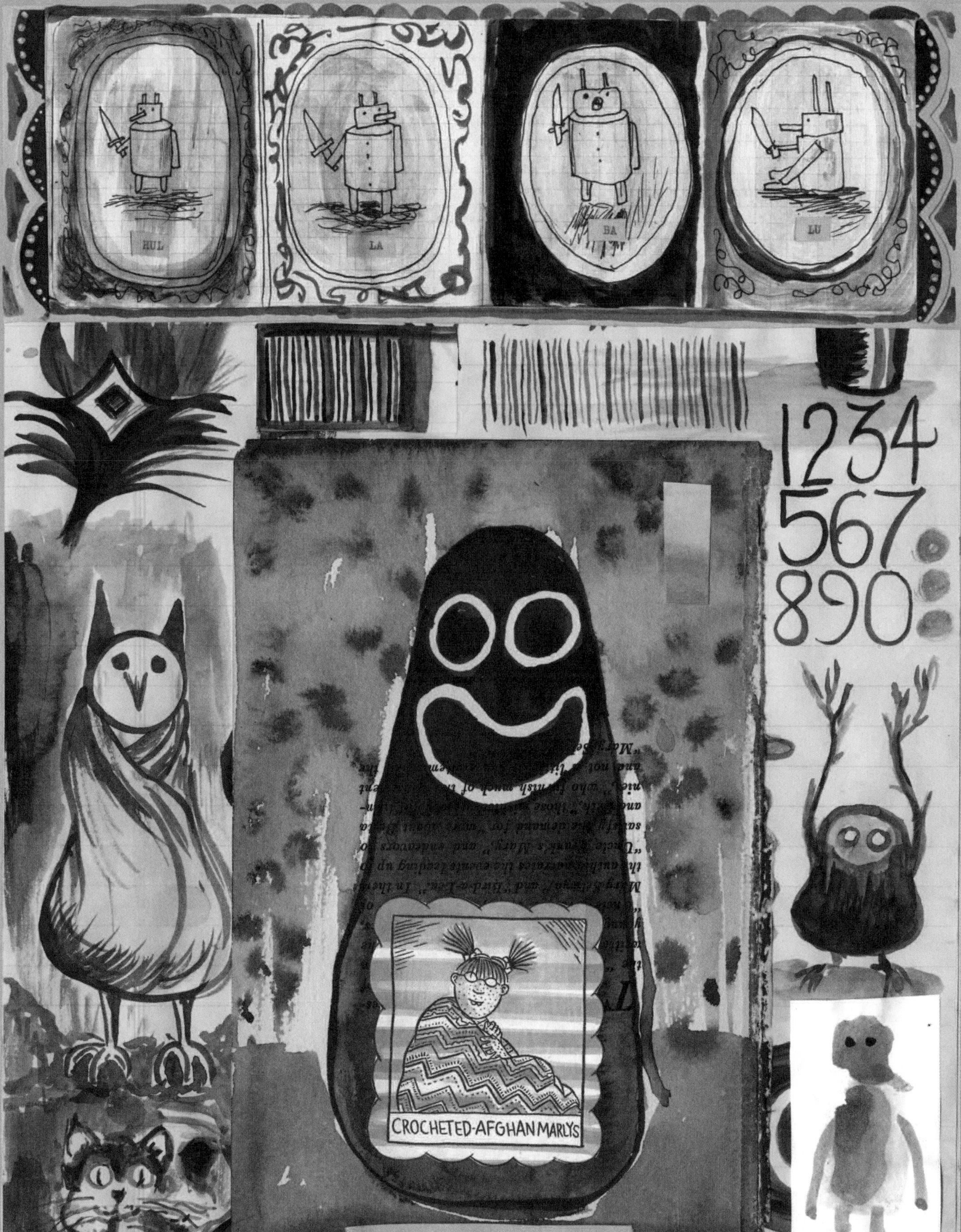
HUL
LA
BA
LU
1234
567
890
CROCHETED-AFGHAN MARLYS

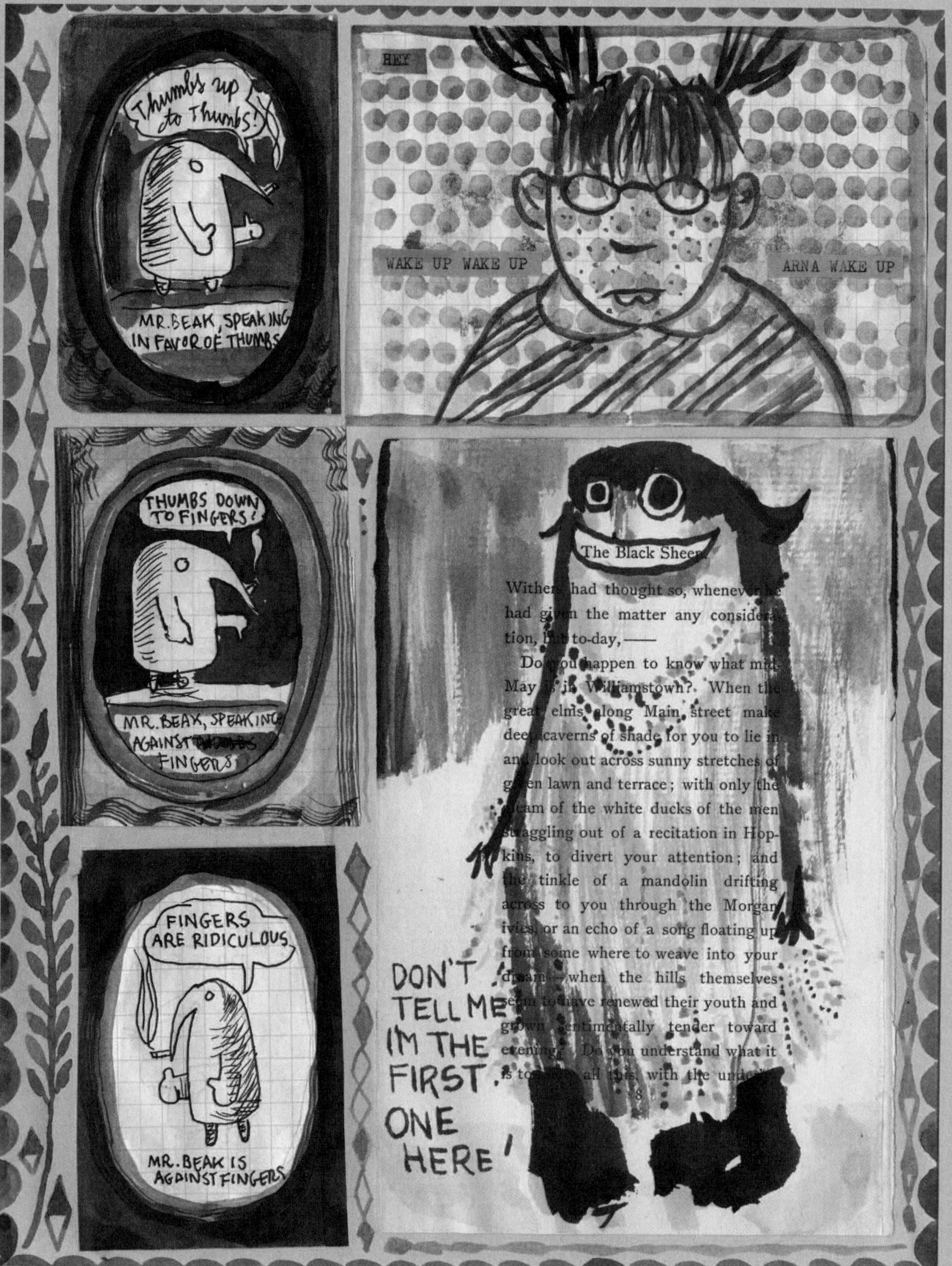
Thumbs up to Thumbs!
MR. BEAK, SPEAKING IN FAVOR OF THUMBS
HEY
WAKE UP WAKE UP
ARNA WAKE UP
THUMBS DOWN TO FINGERS!
MR. BEAK, SPEAKING AGAINST FINGERS
The Black Shee
had given the matter any considera-
tion, but to-day, ——
Do you happen to know what mid-
May is in Williamstown? When the
great elms along Main street make
deep caverns of shade for you to lie in
and look out across sunny stretches of
green lawn and terrace; with only the
gleam of the white ducks of the men
straggling out of a recitation in Hop-
kins, to divert your attention; and
the tinkle of a mandolin drifting
across to you through the Morgan
ivies, or an echo of a song floating up
from some where to weave into your
dream — when the hills themselves
seem to have renewed their youth and
grown sentimentally tender toward
evening? Do you understand what it
DON'T TELL ME I'M THE FIRST ONE HERE'
FINGERS ARE RIDICULOUS
MR. BEAK IS AGAINST FINGERS

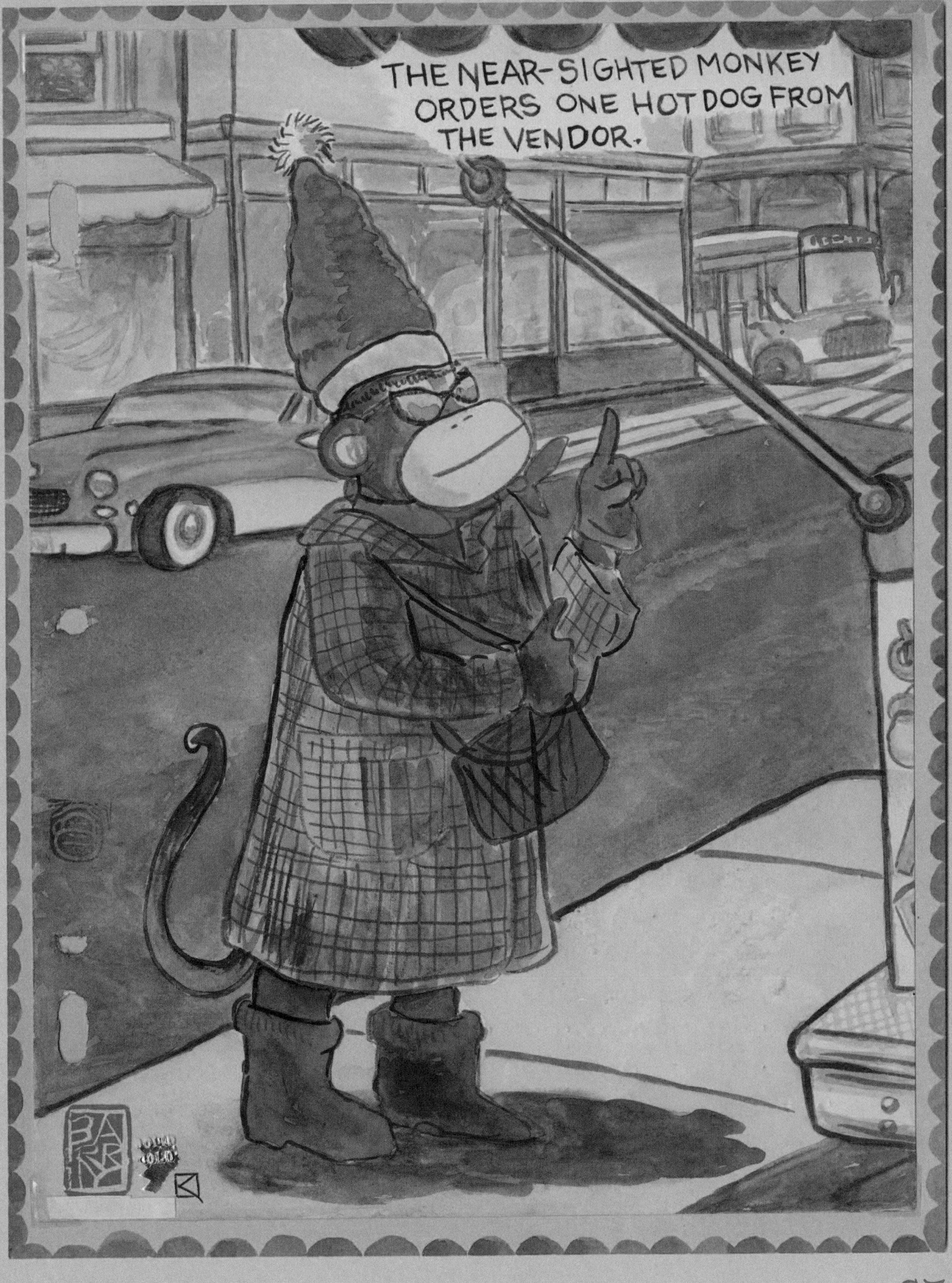
THE NEAR-SIGHTED MONKEY ORDERS ONE HOT DOG FROM THE VENDOR.

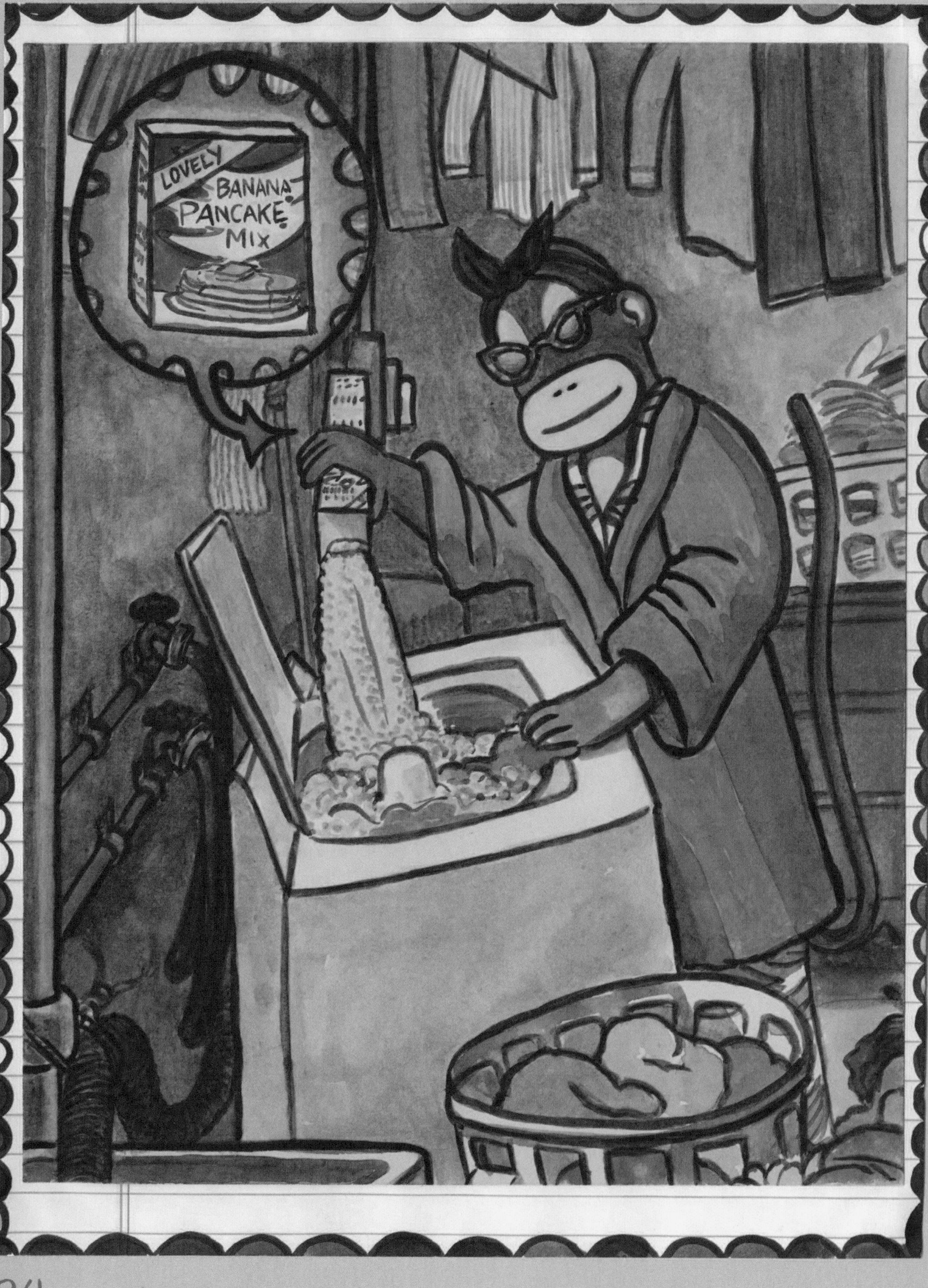
LOVELY
BANANA
PANCAKE
MIX

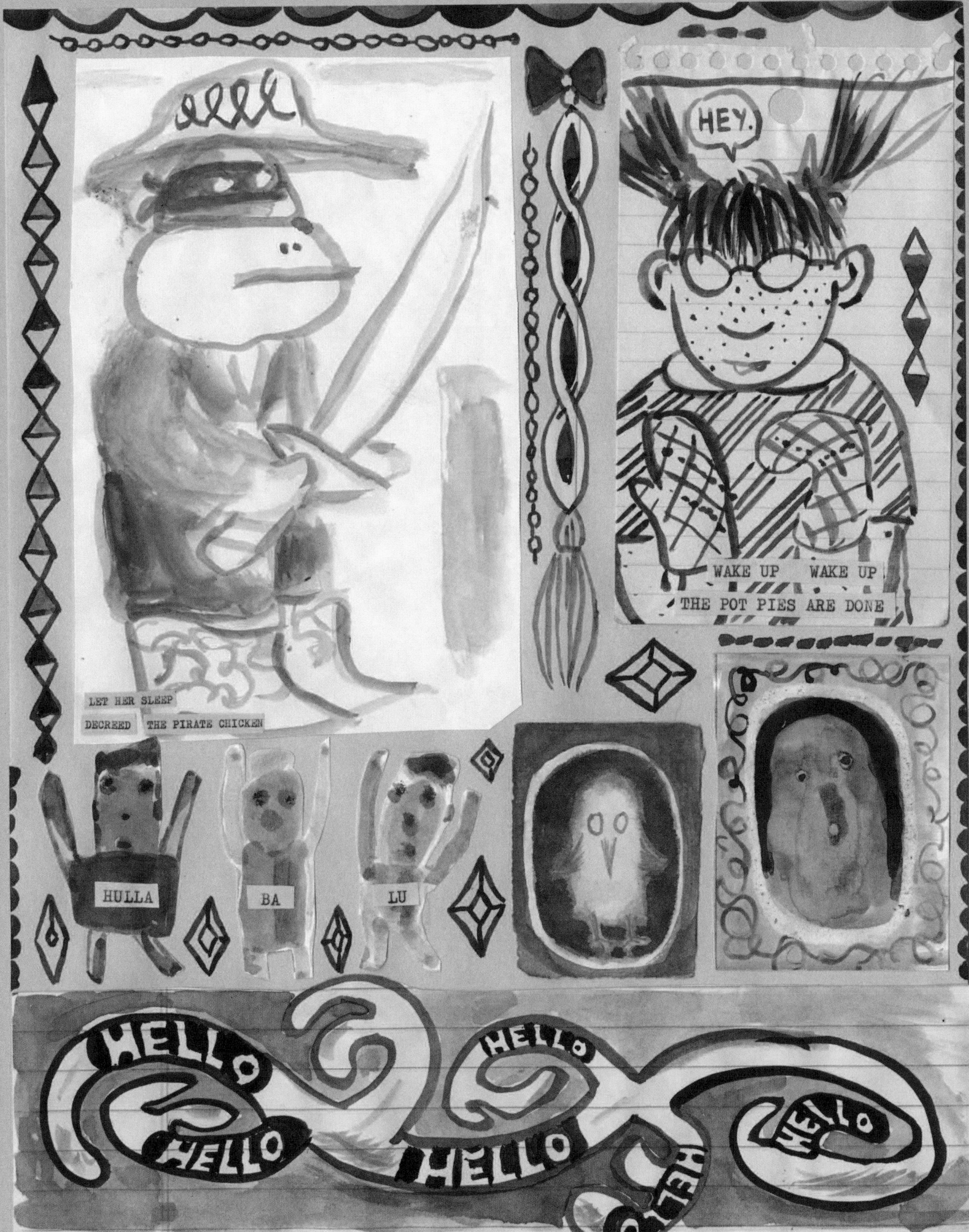
LET HER SLEEP
DECREED THE PIRATE CHICKEN
HEY.
WAKE UP WAKE UP
THE POT PIES ARE DONE
HULLA
BA
LU
HELLO
HELLO
HELLO
HELLO
HELLO
HELLO

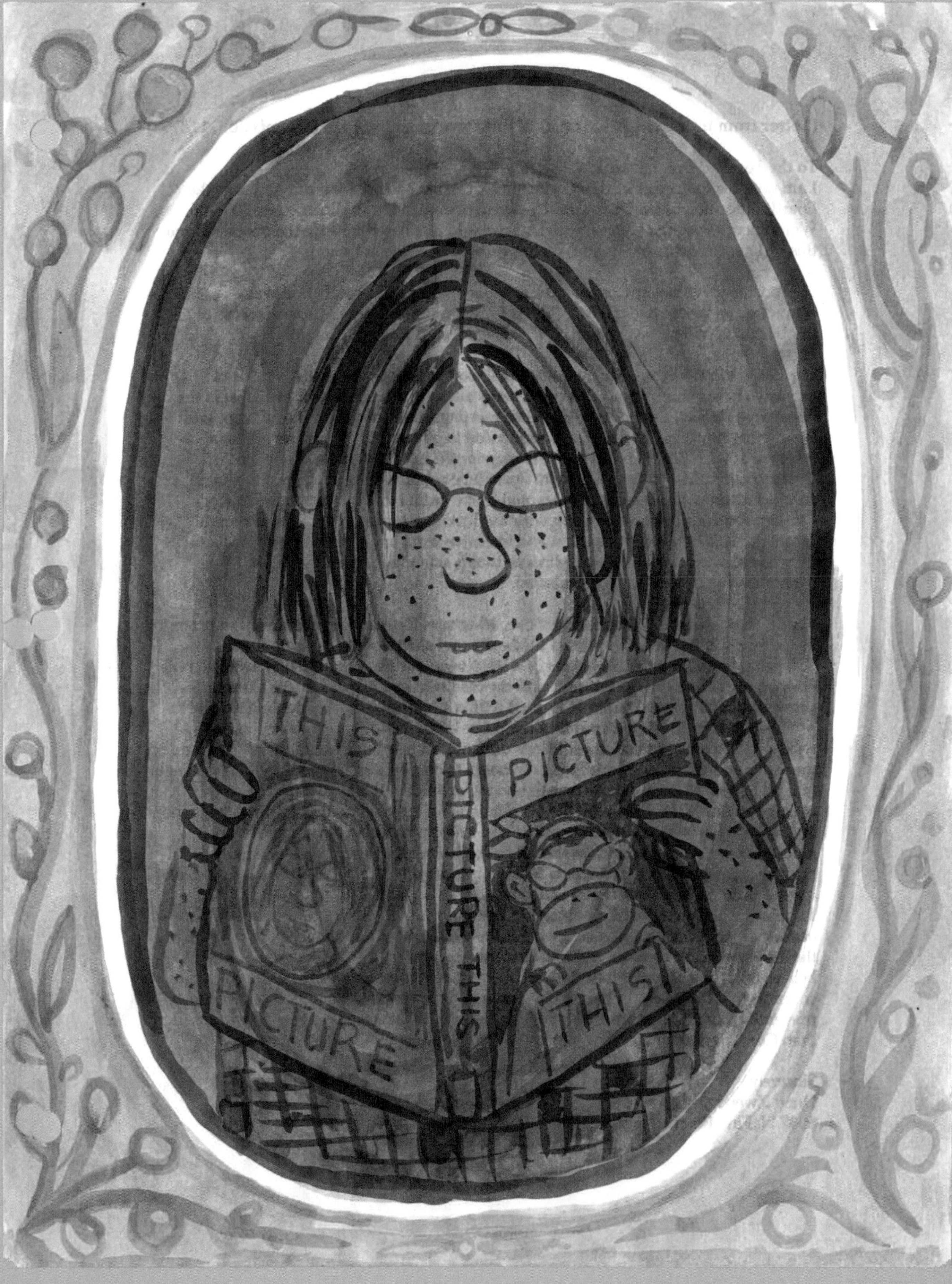
THIS PICTURE
PICTURE THIS
PICTURE
THIS

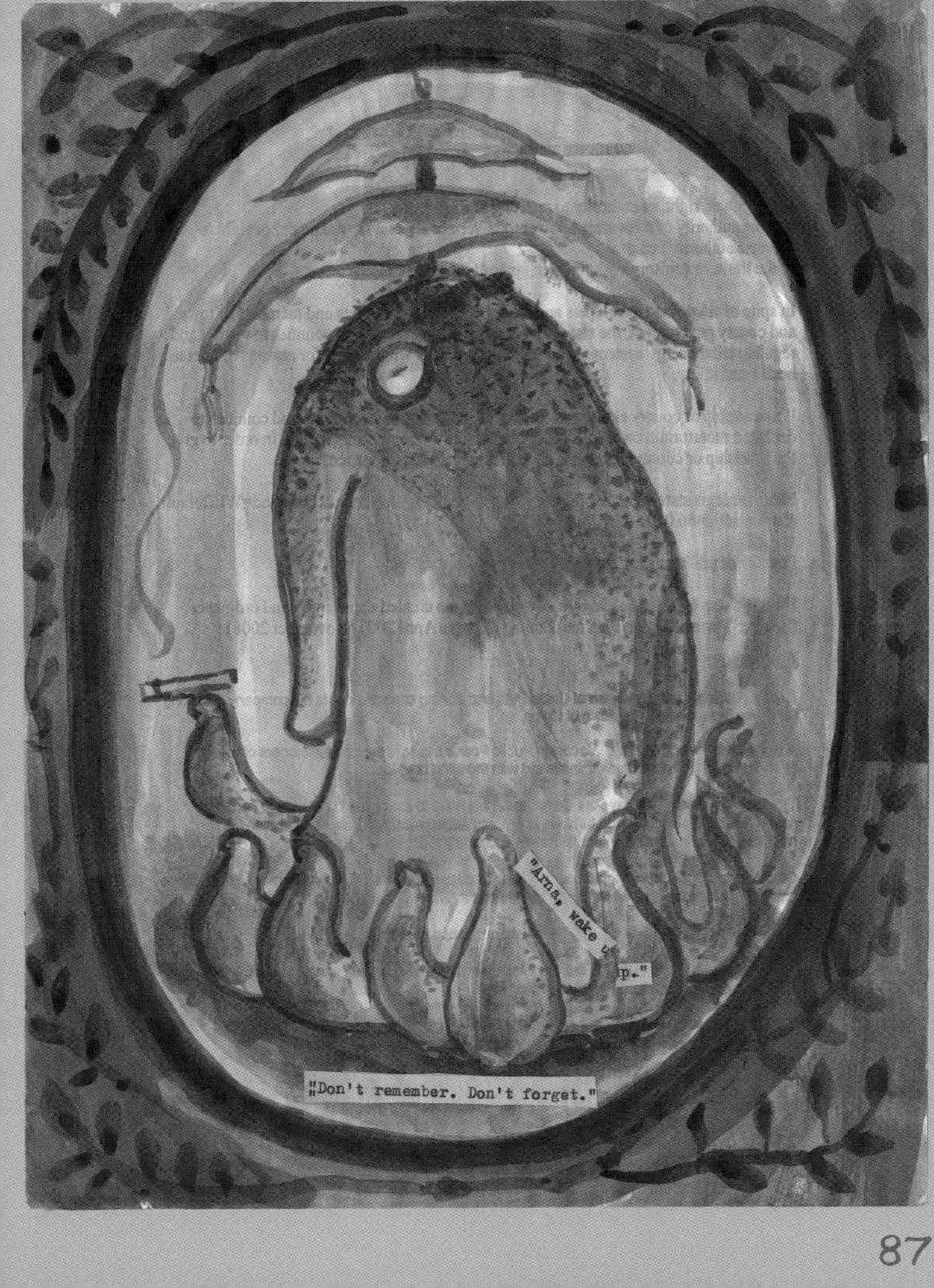
"Arna, wake up."
"Don't remember. Don't forget."

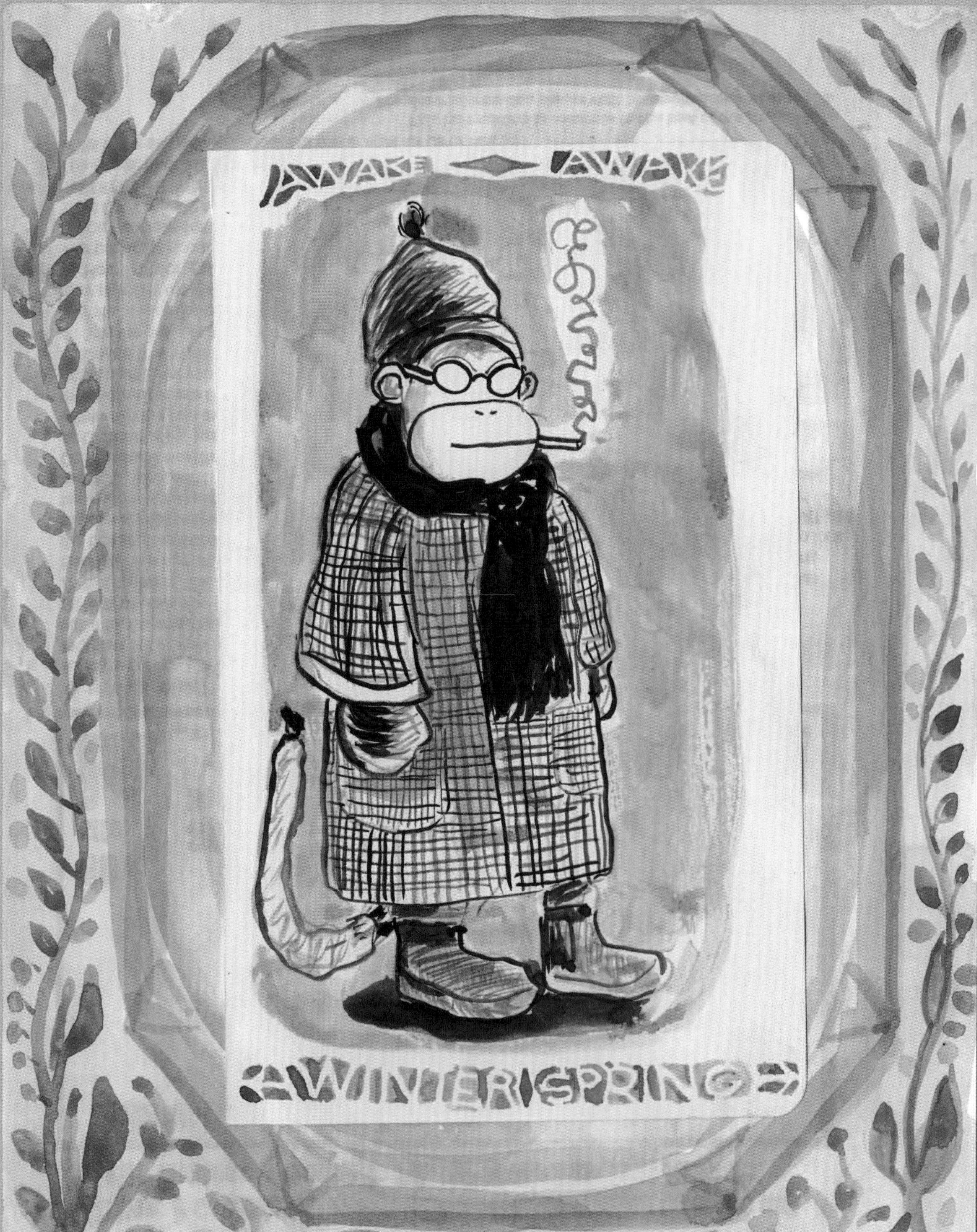
AWAKE AWAKE
WINTER SPRING

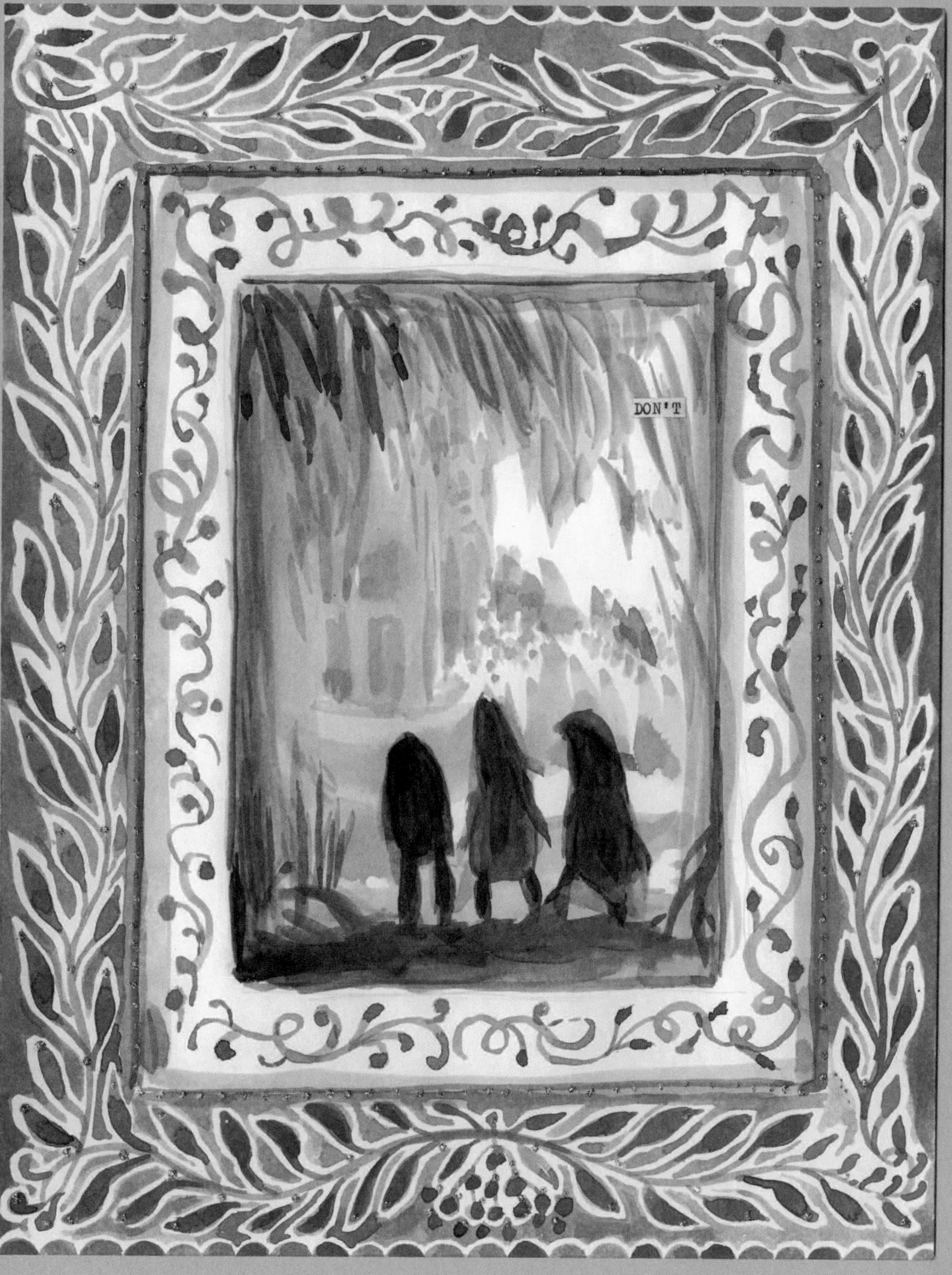
DON'T

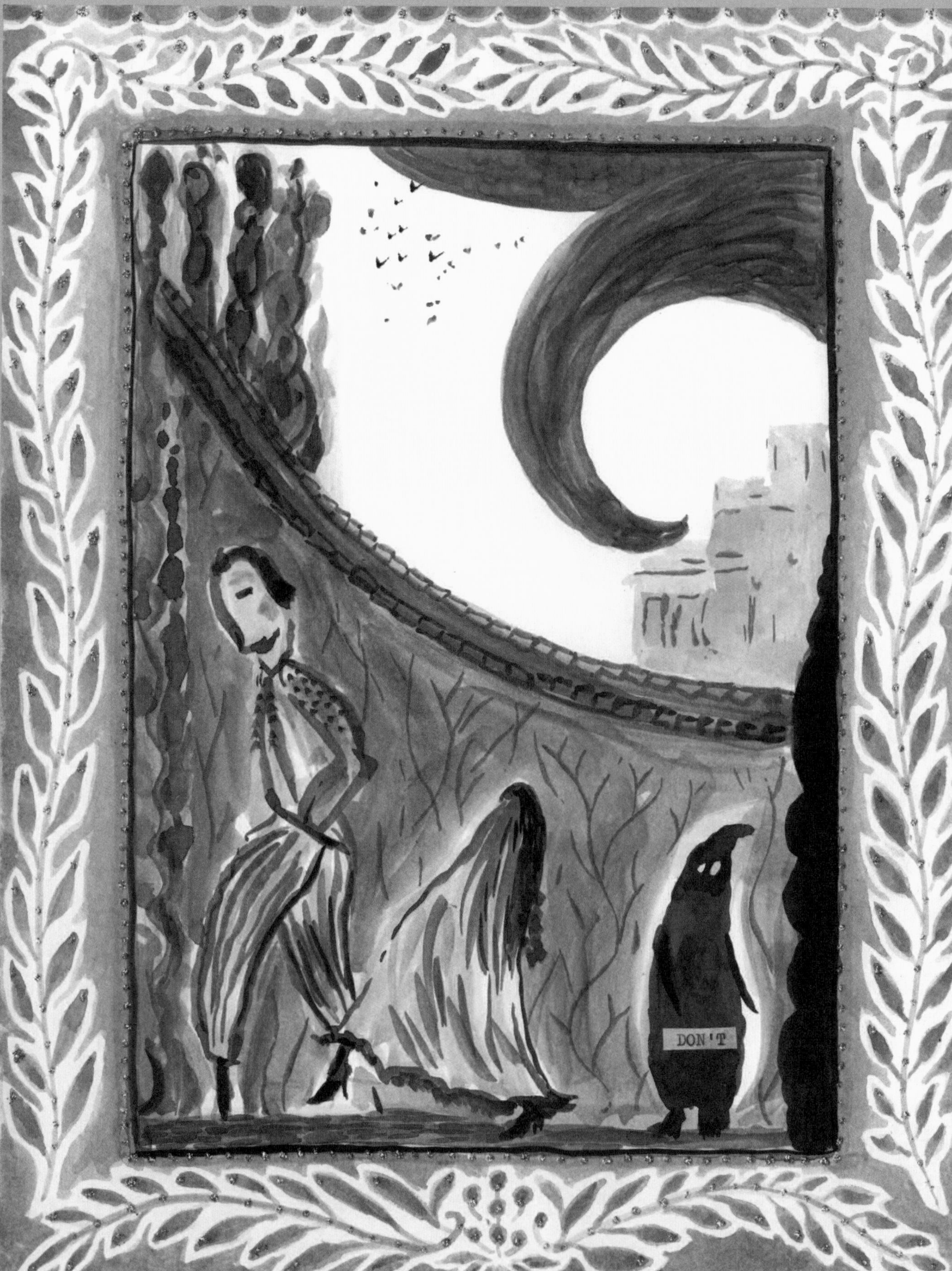
DON'T

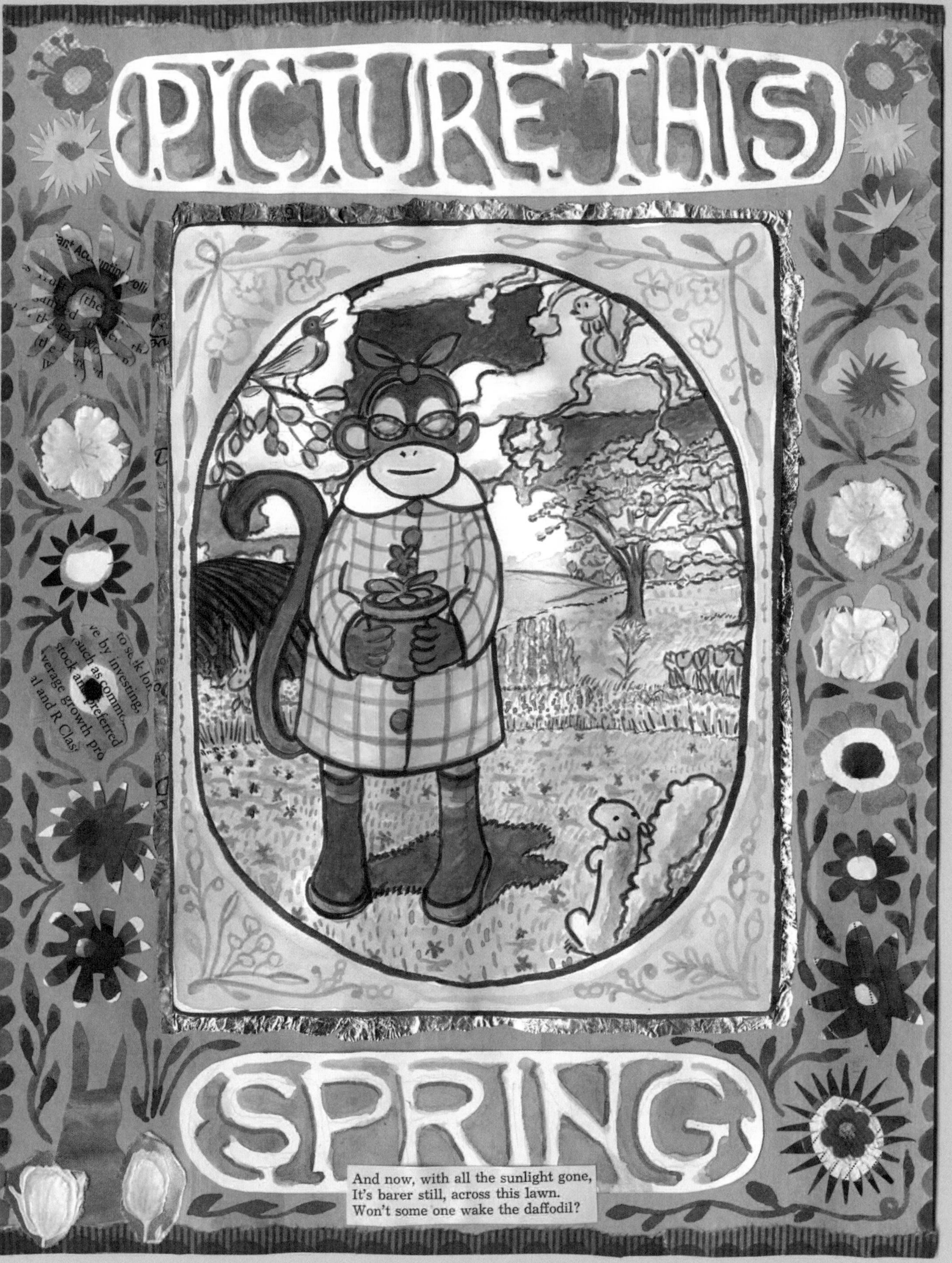
PICTURE THIS
SPRING
And now, with all the sunlight gone,
It's barer still, across this lawn.
Won't some one wake the daffodil?

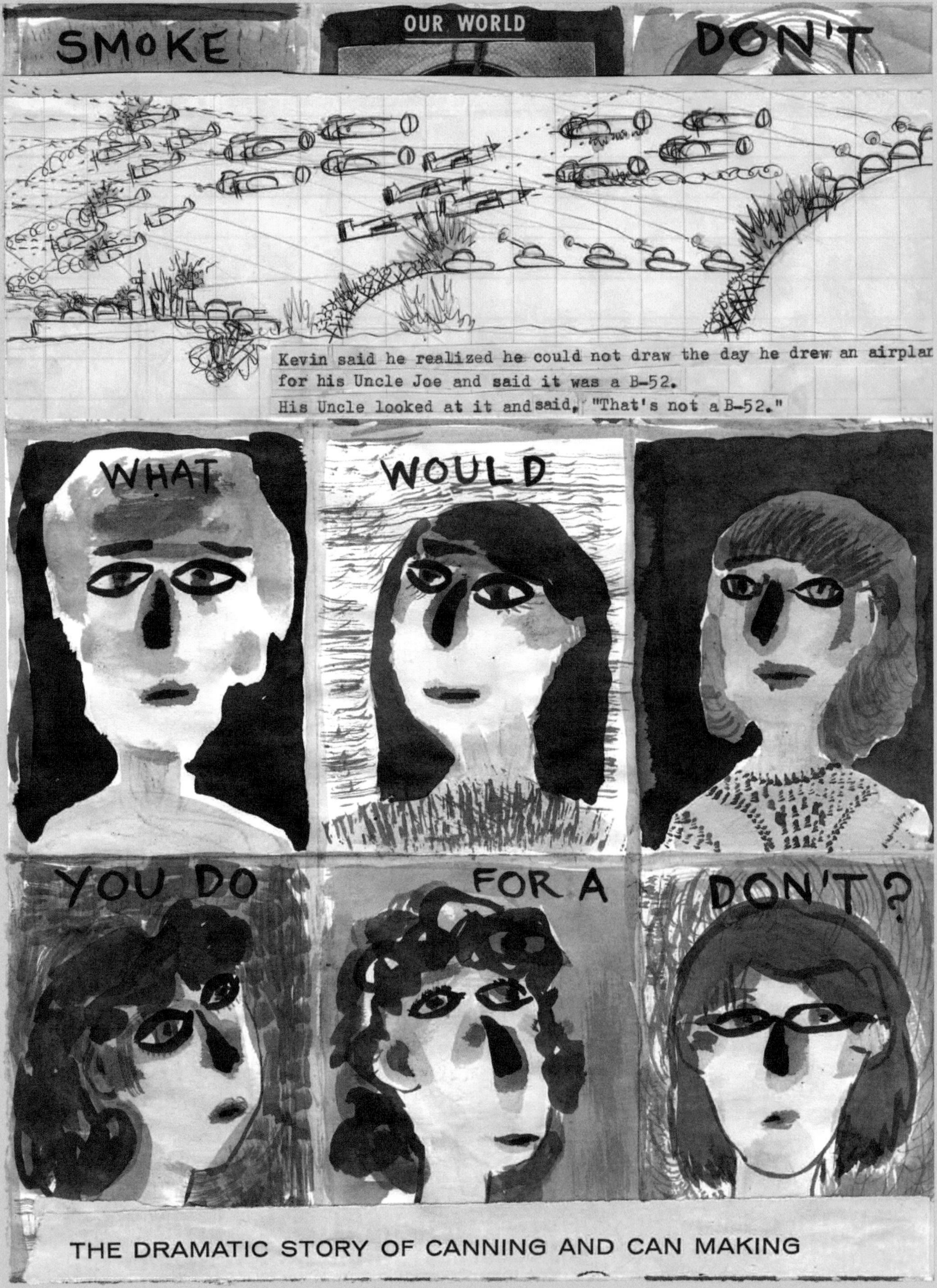
SMOKE
OUR WORLD
DON'T
Kevin said he realized he could not draw the day he drew an airplan
for his Uncle Joe and said it was a B-52.
His Uncle looked at it and said, "That's not a B-52."
WHAT
WOULD
YOU DO
FOR A
DON'T?
THE DRAMATIC STORY OF CANNING AND CAN MAKING

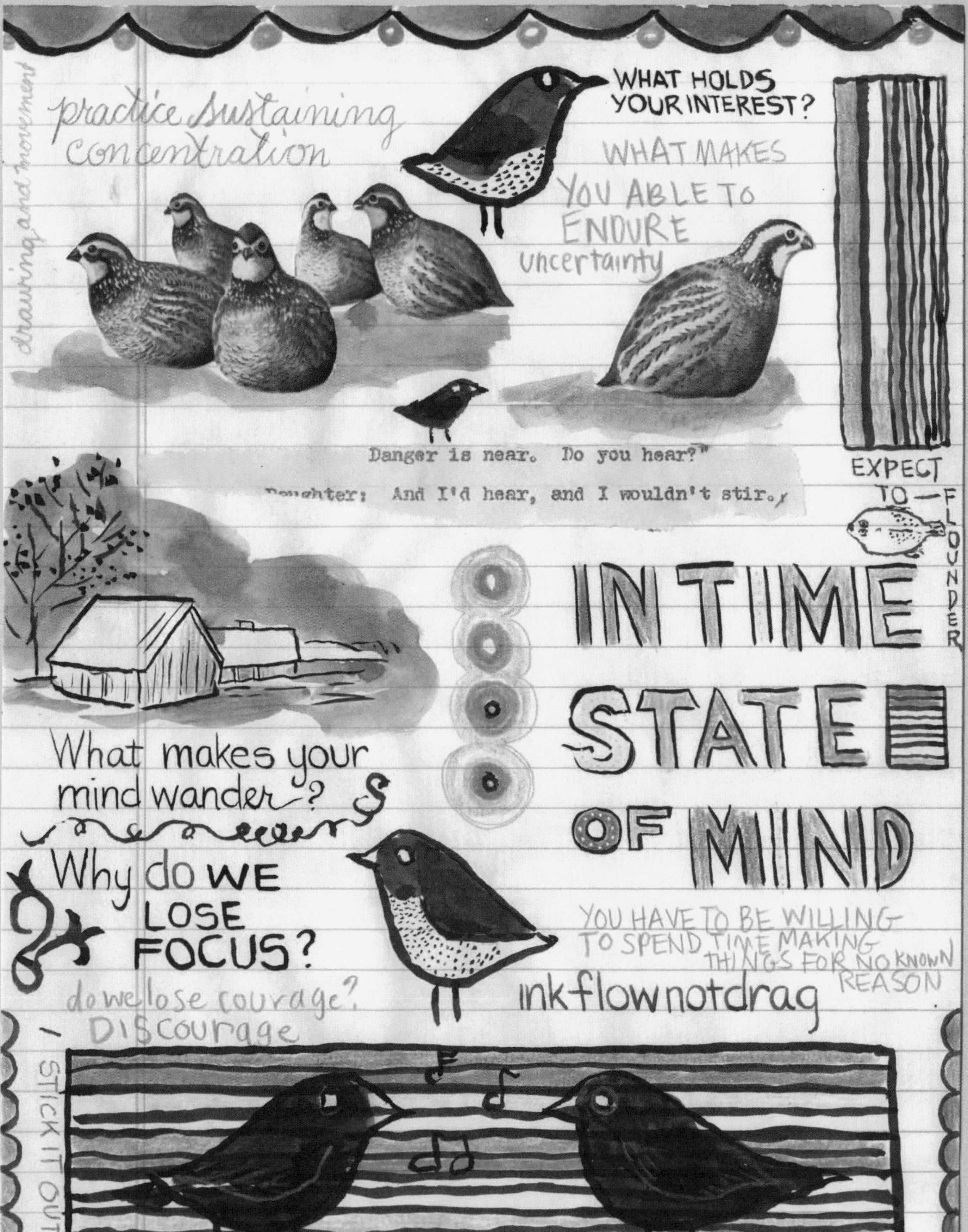
drawing and movement
practice sustaining concentration
WHAT HOLDS YOUR INTEREST?
WHAT MAKES YOU ABLE TO ENDURE uncertainty
Danger is near. Do you hear?"
And I'd hear, and I wouldn't stir.
EXPECT TO—FLOUNDER
IN TIME STATE OF MIND
What makes your mind wander?
Why do WE LOSE FOCUS?
do we lose courage?
DISCOURAGE
YOU HAVE TO BE WILLING TO SPEND TIME MAKING THINGS FOR NO KNOWN REASON
inkflownotdrag
STICK IT OUT

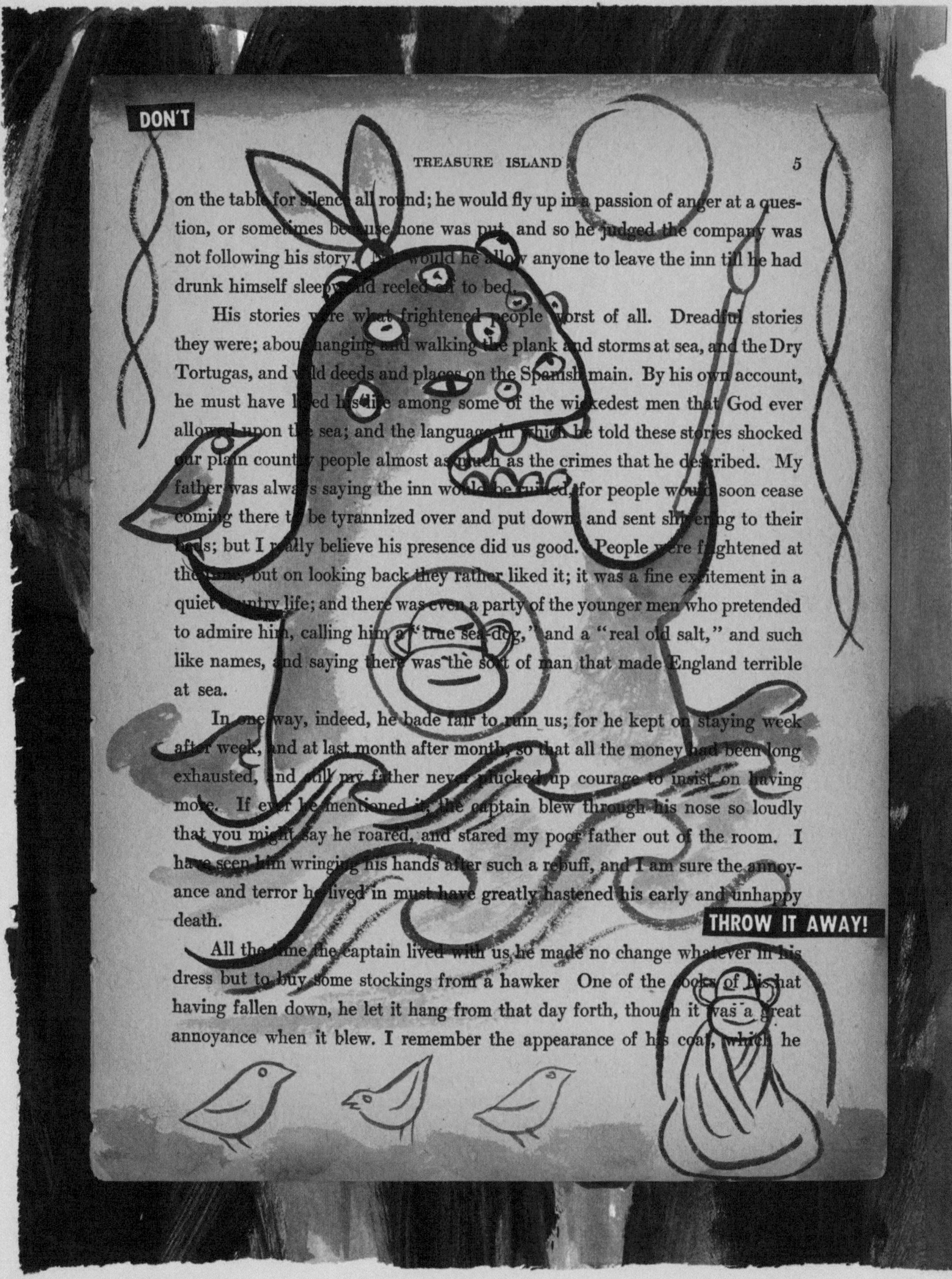

DON'T
THROW IT AWAY!

on the table for silence all round; he would fly up in a passion of anger at a question, or sometimes because none was put, and so he judged the company was not following his story. Nor would he allow anyone to leave the inn till he had drunk himself sleepy and reeled off to bed.

His stories were what frightened people worst of all. Dreadful stories they were; about hanging and walking the plank and storms at sea, and the Dry Tortugas, and wild deeds and places on the Spanish main. By his own account, he must have lived his life among some of the wickedest men that God ever allowed upon the sea; and the language in which he told these stories shocked our plain country people almost as much as the crimes that he described. My father was always saying the inn would be ruined, for people would soon cease coming there to be tyrannized over and put down, and sent shivering to their beds; but I really believe his presence did us good. People were frightened at the time, but on looking back they rather liked it; it was a fine excitement in a quiet country life; and there was even a party of the younger men who pretended to admire him, calling him a "true sea-dog," and a "real old salt," and such like names, and saying there was the sort of man that made England terrible at sea.

In one way, indeed, he bade fair to ruin us; for he kept on staying week after week, and at last month after month, so that all the money had been long exhausted, and still my father never plucked up courage to insist on having more. If ever he mentioned it, the captain blew through his nose so loudly that you might say he roared, and stared my poor father out of the room. I have seen him wringing his hands after such a rebuff, and I am sure the annoyance and terror he lived in must have greatly hastened his early and unhappy death.

All the time the captain lived with us he made no change whatever in his dress but to buy some stockings from a hawker One of the cocks of his hat having fallen down, he let it hang from that day forth, though it was a great annoyance when it blew. I remember the appearance of his coat, which he

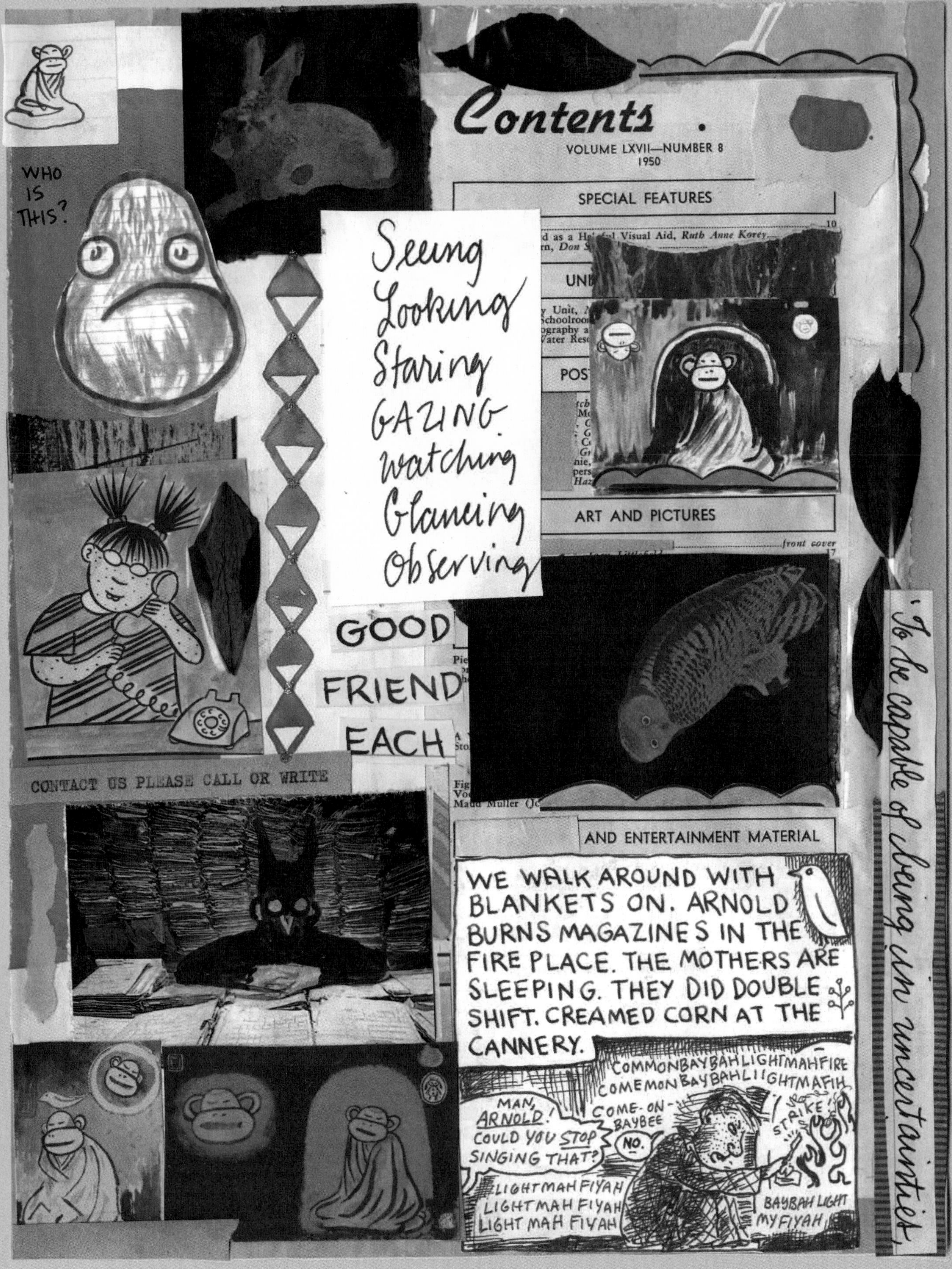

WHO IS THIS?
Contents
VOLUME LXVII—NUMBER 8
1950
SPECIAL FEATURES
Seeing
Looking
Staring
GAZING
watching
Glancing
Observing
ART AND PICTURES
front cover
GOOD
FRIEND
EACH
CONTACT US PLEASE CALL OR WRITE
AND ENTERTAINMENT MATERIAL
WE WALK AROUND WITH BLANKETS ON. ARNOLD BURNS MAGAZINES IN THE FIRE PLACE. THE MOTHERS ARE SLEEPING. THEY DID DOUBLE SHIFT. CREAMED CORN AT THE CANNERY.
COMMONBAYBAHLIGHTMAHFIRE
COMEMONBAYBAHLIIGHTMAFIH
MAN, ARNOLD! COULD YOU STOP SINGING THAT?
COME-ON-BAYBEE
NO.
STRIKE!
LIGHTMAHFIYAH
LIGHTMAHFIYAH
LIGHT MAH FIYAH
BAYBAH LIGHT MYFIYAH
'To be capable of being in uncertainties,

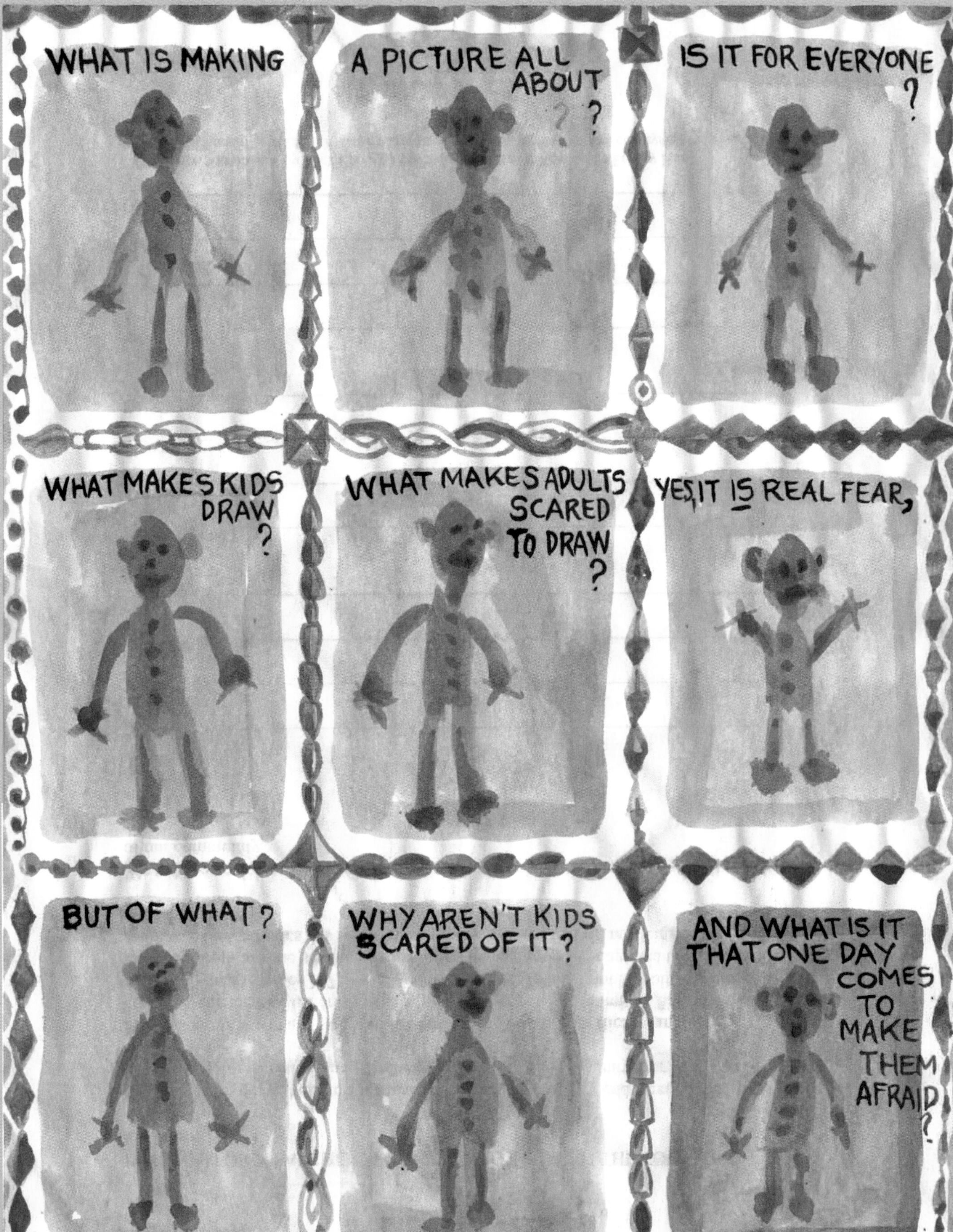
WHAT IS MAKING
A PICTURE ALL ABOUT ? ?
IS IT FOR EVERYONE ?
WHAT MAKES KIDS DRAW ?
WHAT MAKES ADULTS SCARED TO DRAW ?
YES, IT IS REAL FEAR,
BUT OF WHAT ?
WHY AREN'T KIDS SCARED OF IT ?
AND WHAT IS IT THAT ONE DAY COMES TO MAKE THEM AFRAID ?

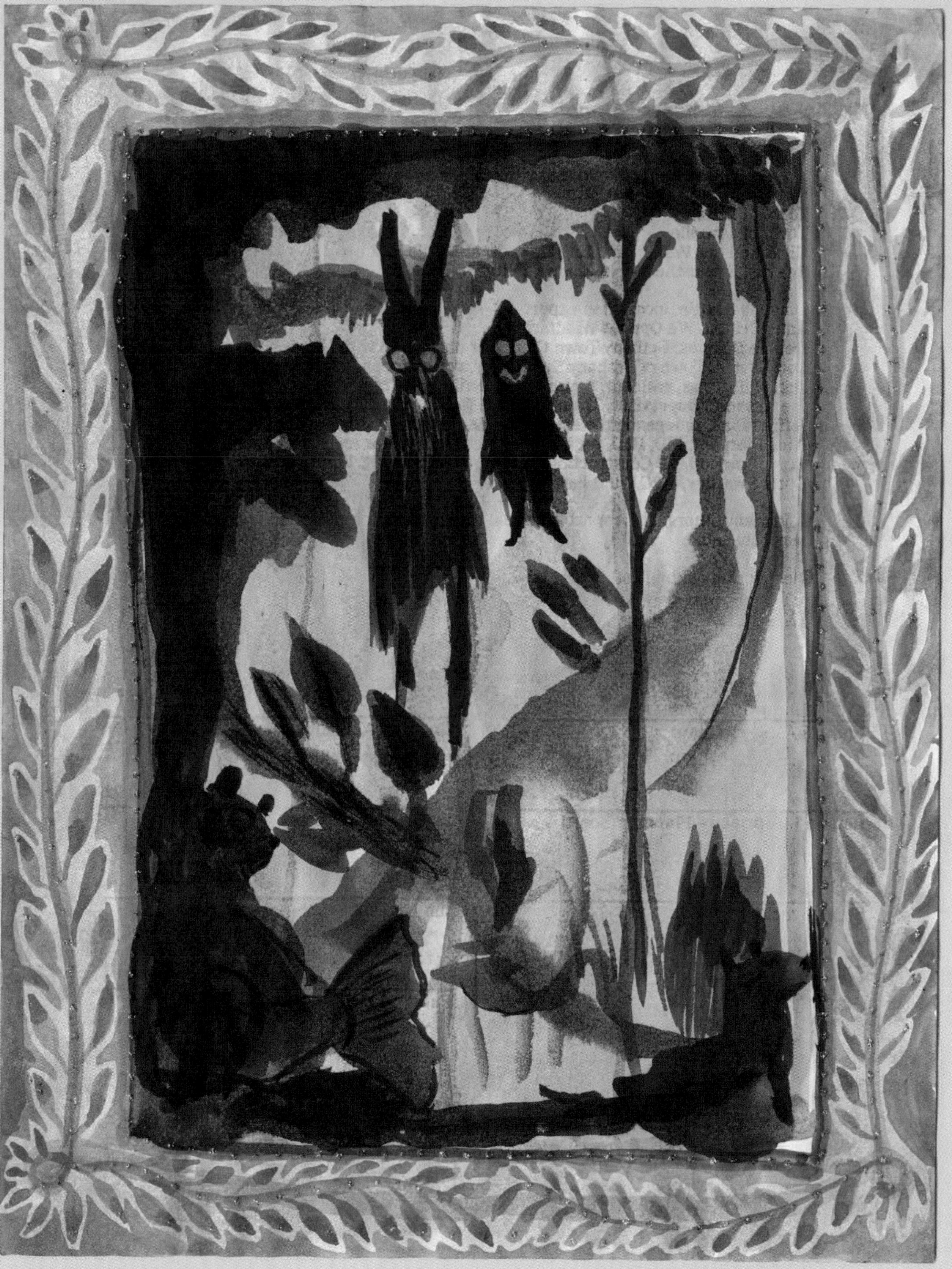

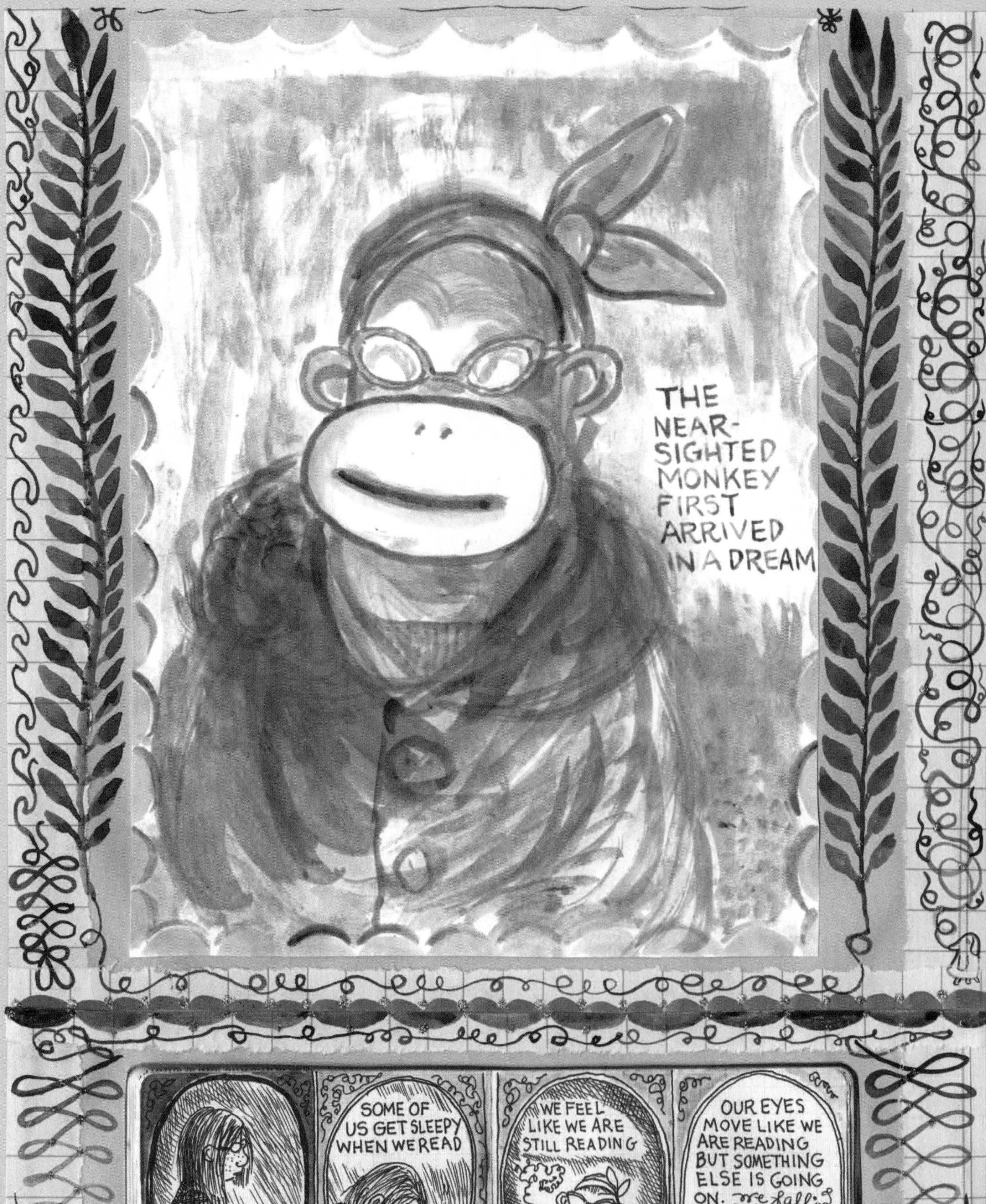
THE NEAR-SIGHTED MONKEY FIRST ARRIVED IN A DREAM
SOME OF US GET SLEEPY WHEN WE READ
WE FEEL LIKE WE ARE STILL READING
DON'T CIGS
OUR EYES MOVE LIKE WE ARE READING BUT SOMETHING ELSE IS GOING ON. we fall into Sleep

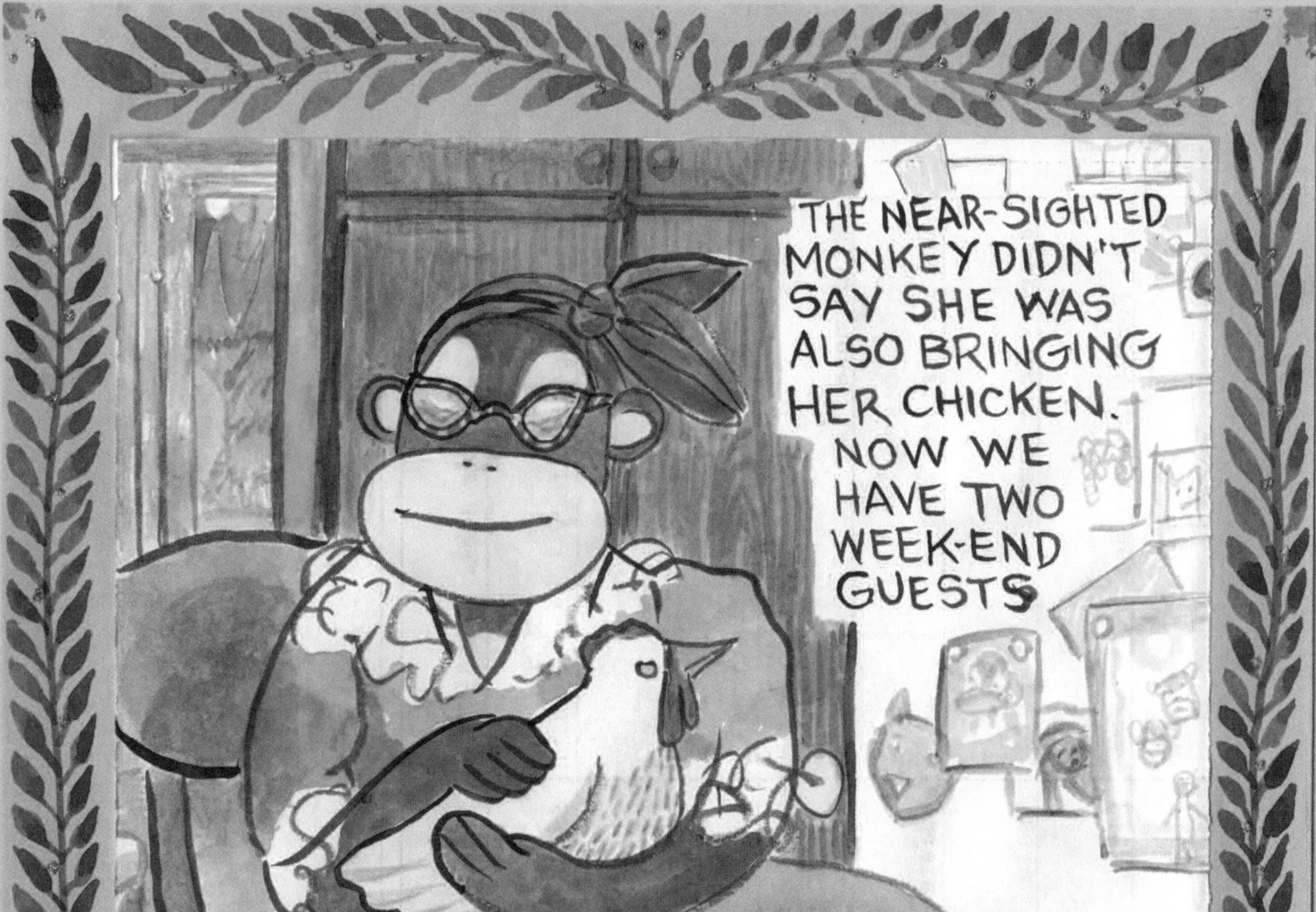
THE NEAR-SIGHTED MONKEY DIDN'T SAY SHE WAS ALSO BRINGING HER CHICKEN. NOW WE HAVE TWO WEEK-END GUESTS

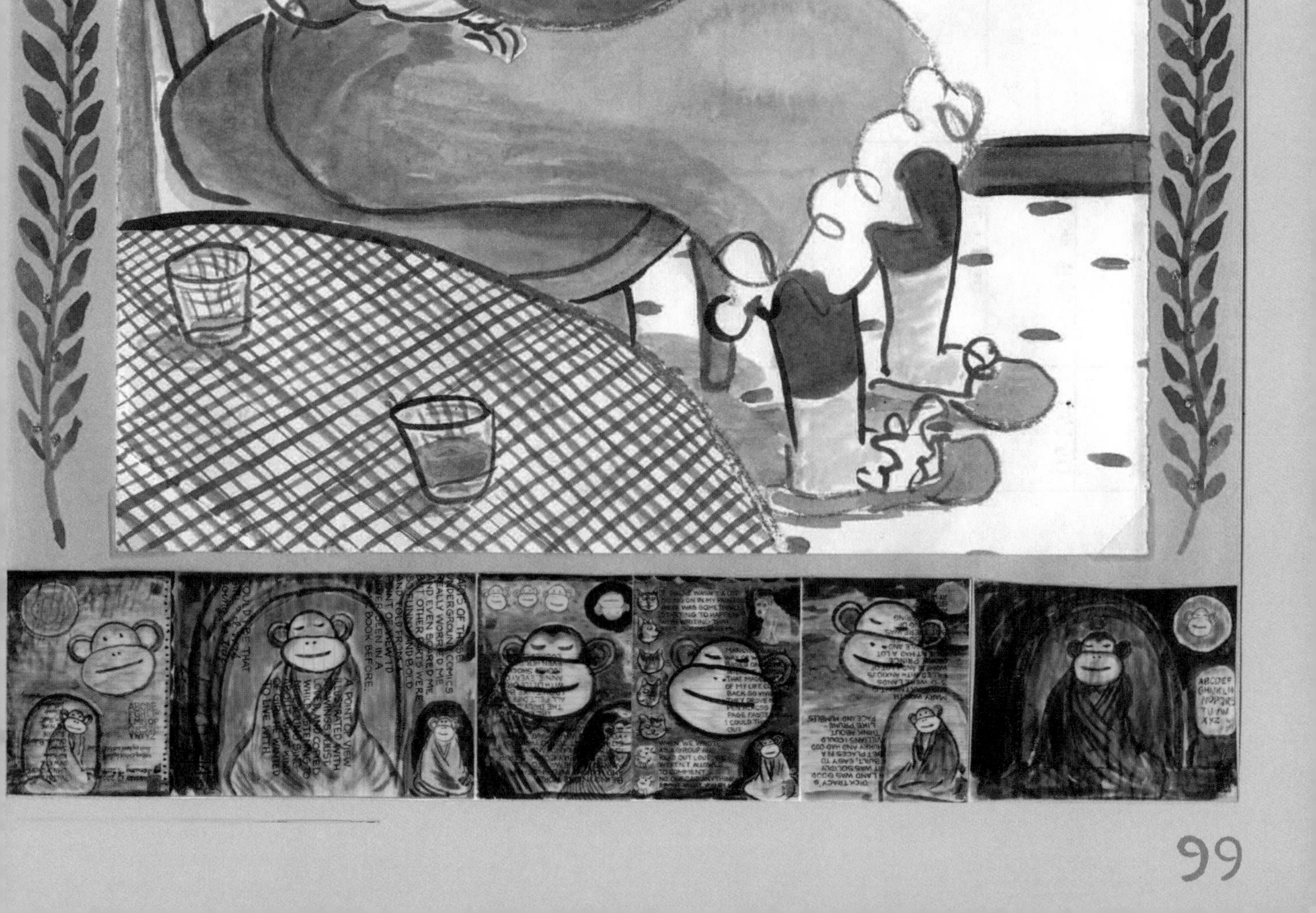

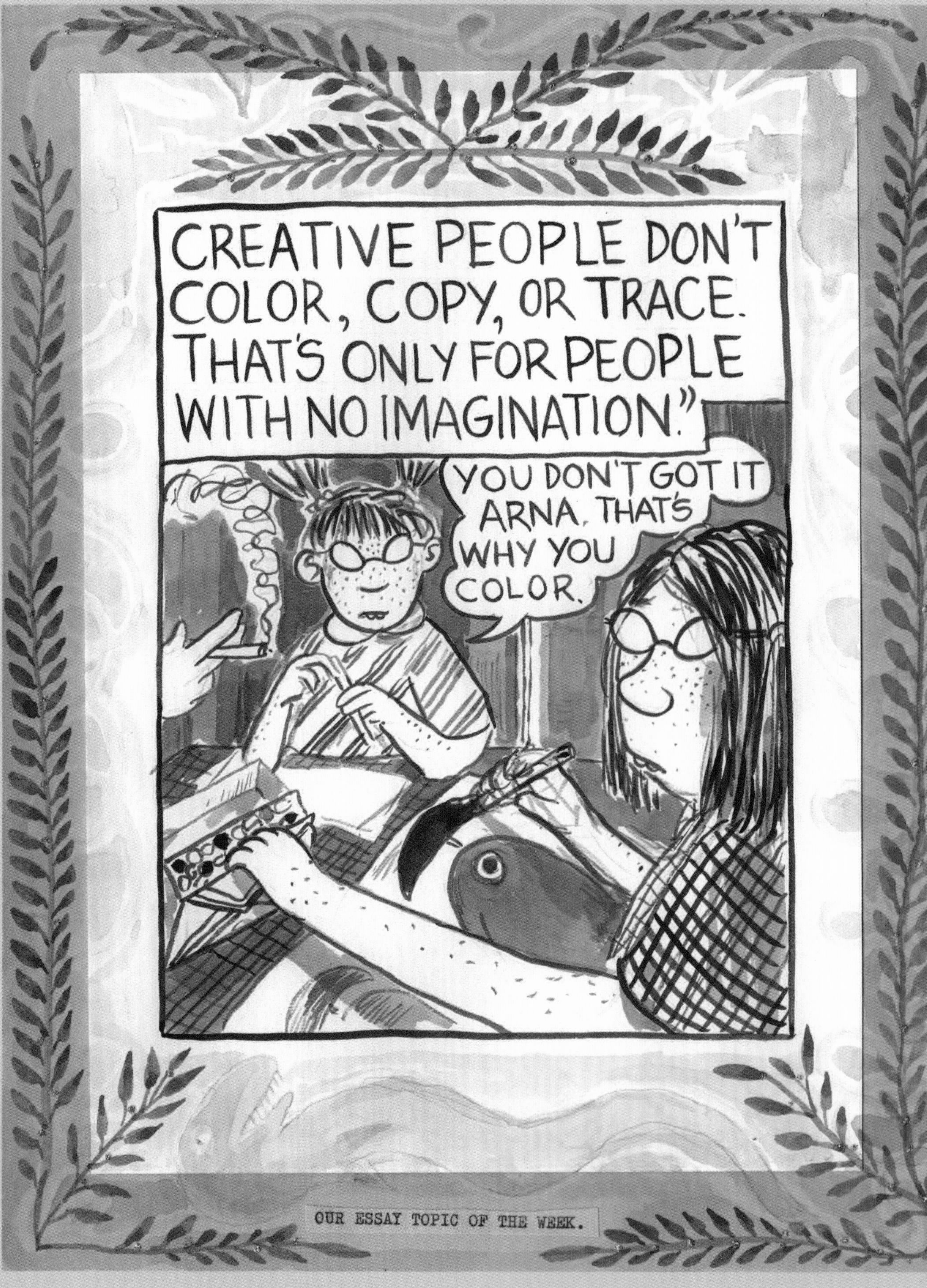
CREATIVE PEOPLE DON'T COLOR, COPY, OR TRACE. THAT'S ONLY FOR PEOPLE WITH NO IMAGINATION."
YOU DON'T GOT IT ARNA. THAT'S WHY YOU COLOR.
OUR ESSAY TOPIC OF THE WEEK.

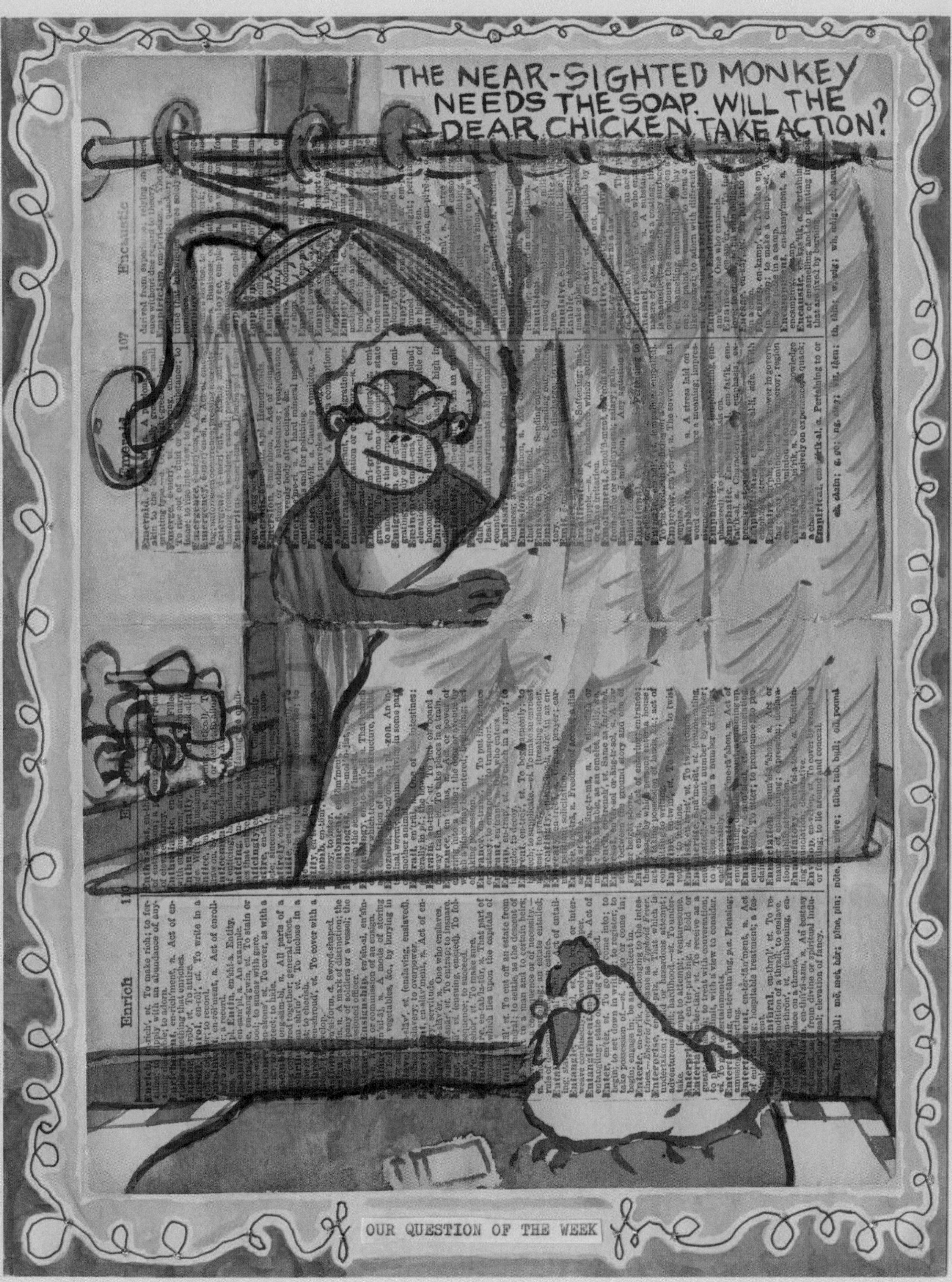
THE NEAR-SIGHTED MONKEY NEEDS THE SOAP. WILL THE DEAR CHICKEN TAKE ACTION?
OUR QUESTION OF THE WEEK

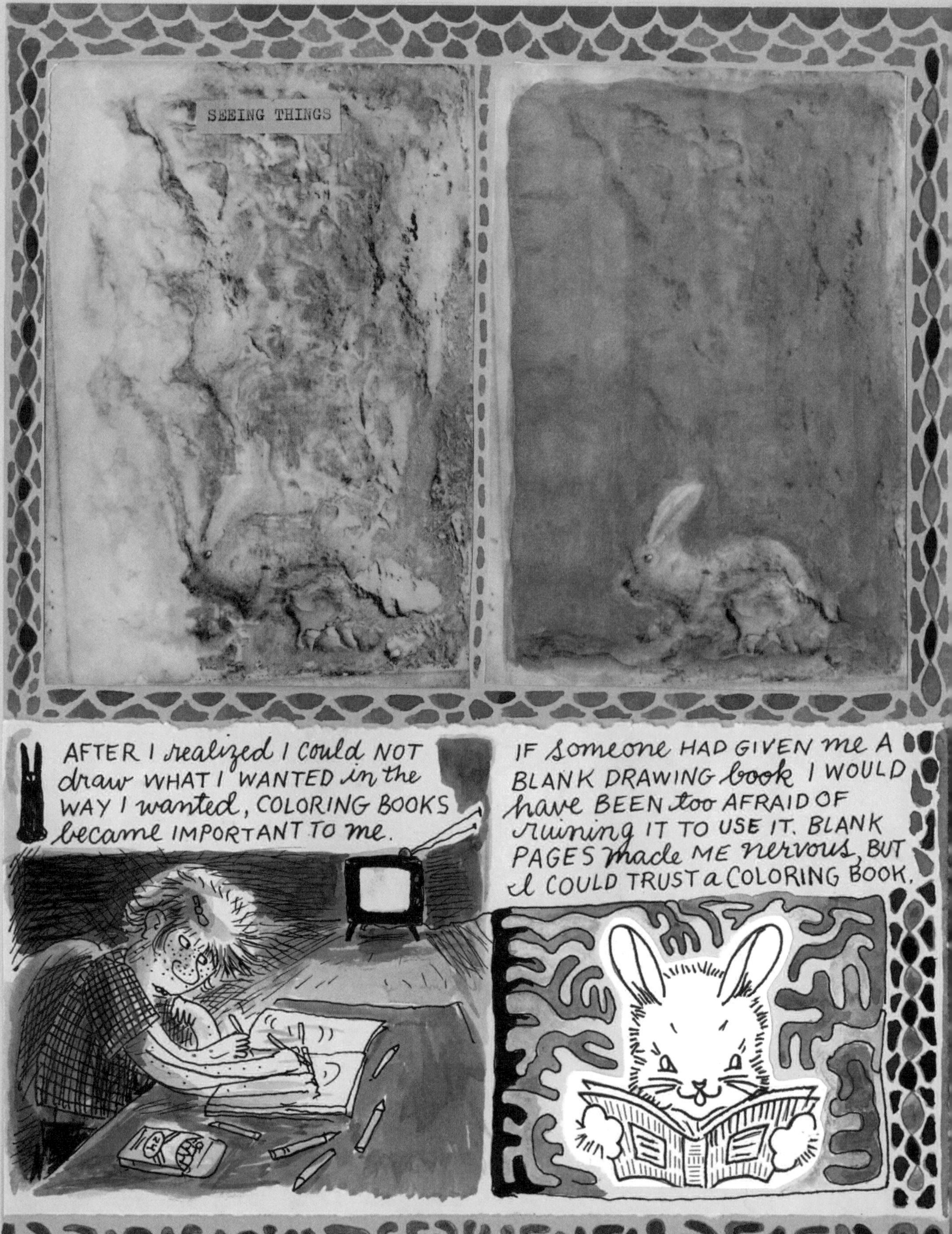
SEEING THINGS
AFTER I realized I could NOT draw WHAT I WANTED in the WAY I wanted, COLORING BOOKS became IMPORTANT TO me.
IF someone HAD GIVEN me A BLANK DRAWING book I WOULD have BEEN too AFRAID OF ruining IT TO USE IT. BLANK PAGES made ME nervous, BUT I COULD TRUST a COLORING BOOK.

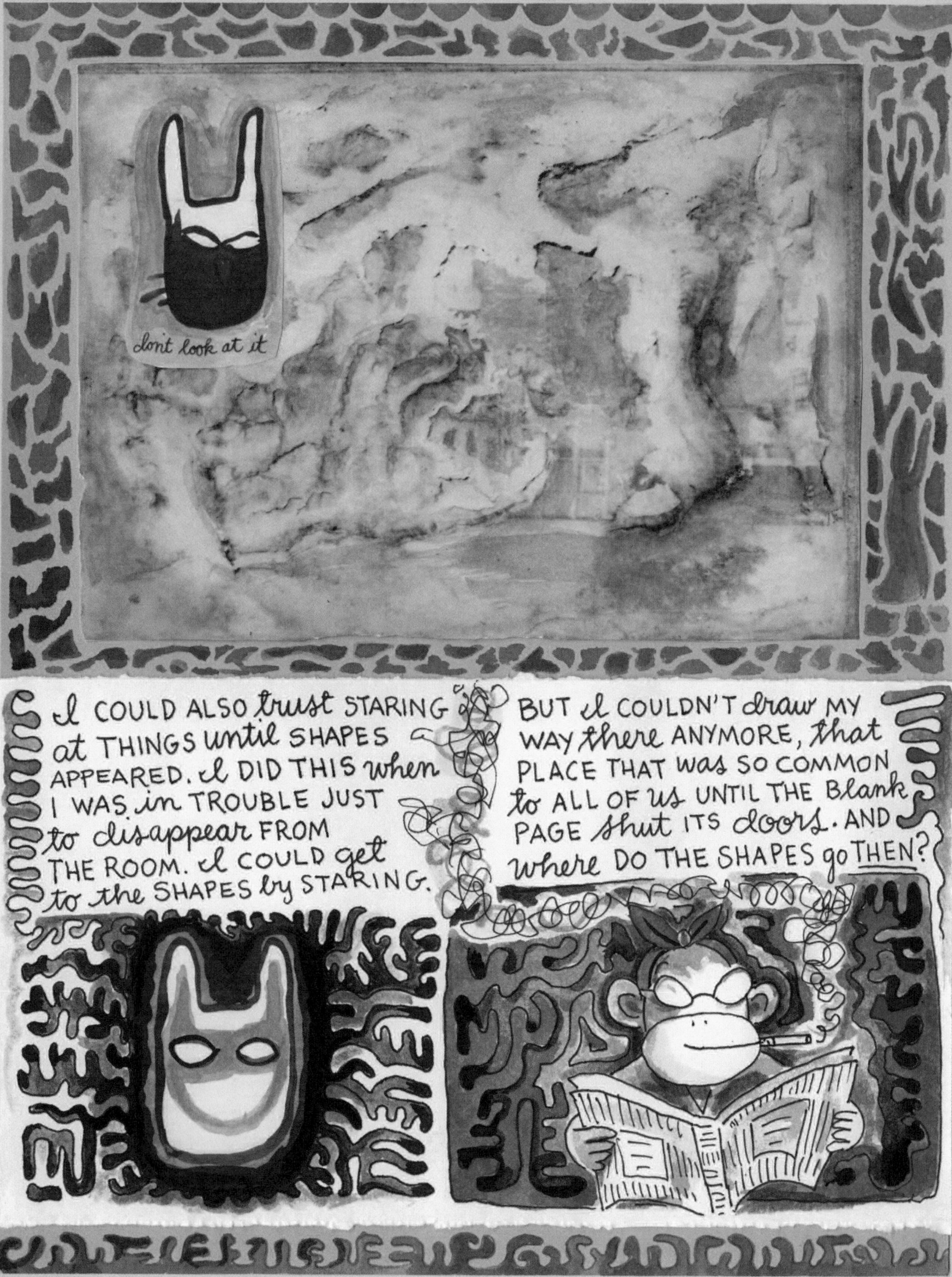

don't look at it
I COULD ALSO trust STARING at THINGS until SHAPES APPEARED. I DID THIS when I WAS in TROUBLE JUST to disappear FROM THE ROOM. I COULD get to the SHAPES by STARING.
BUT I COULDN'T draw MY WAY there ANYMORE, that PLACE THAT was SO COMMON to ALL OF us UNTIL THE Blank PAGE shut ITS doors. AND where DO THE SHAPES go THEN?

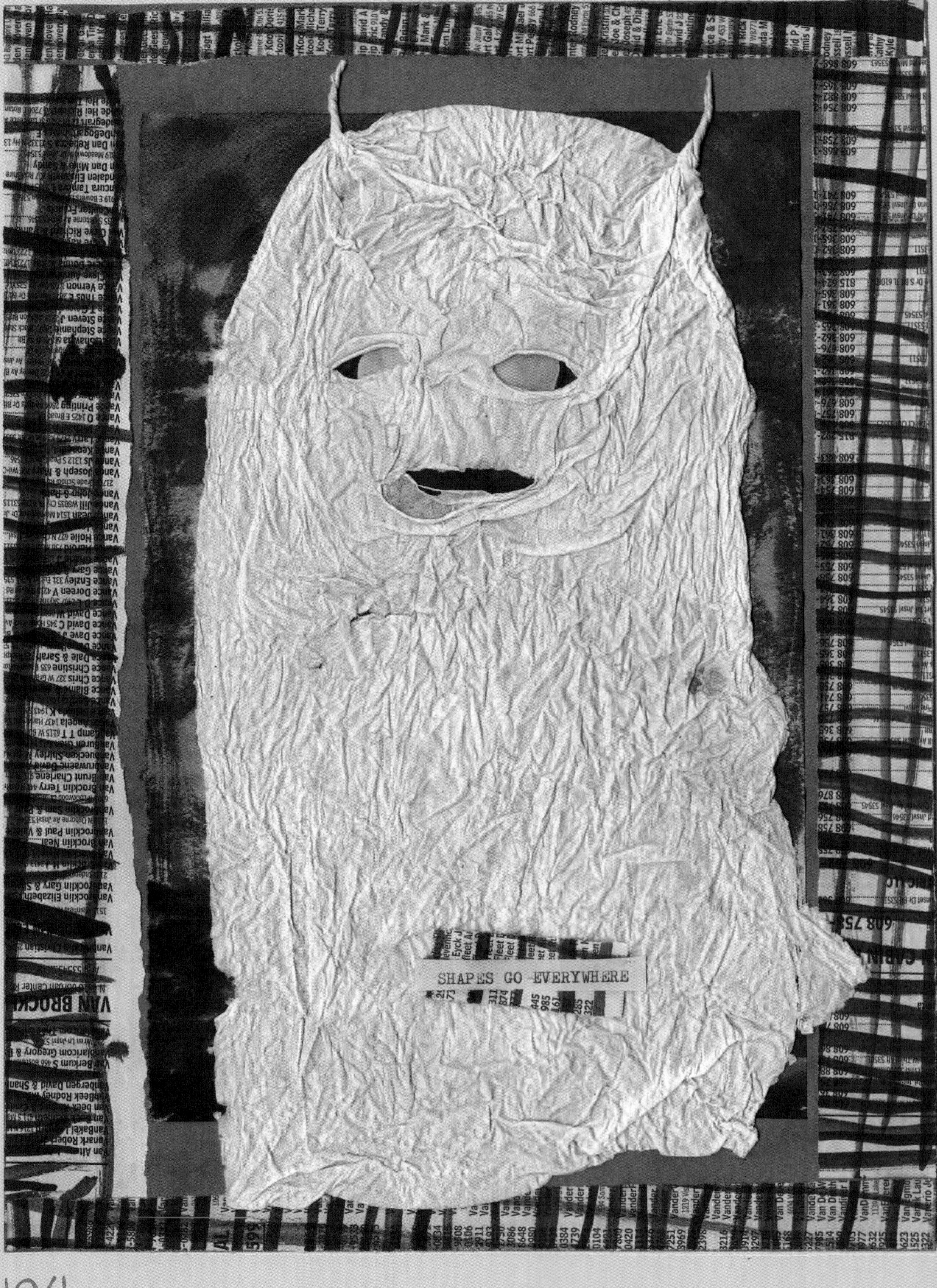
SHAPES GO EVERYWHERE

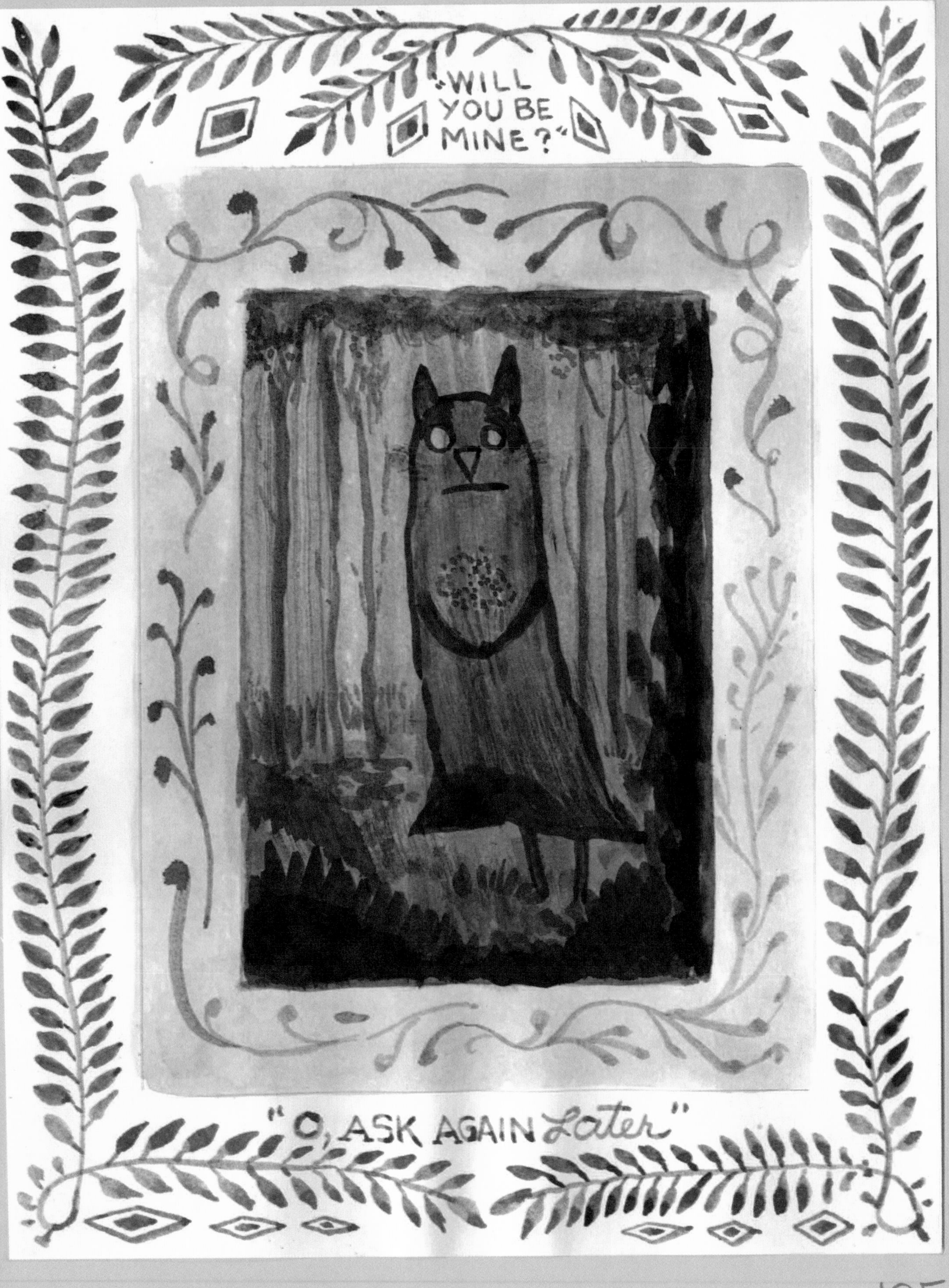
"WILL YOU BE MINE?"
"O, ASK AGAIN Later"

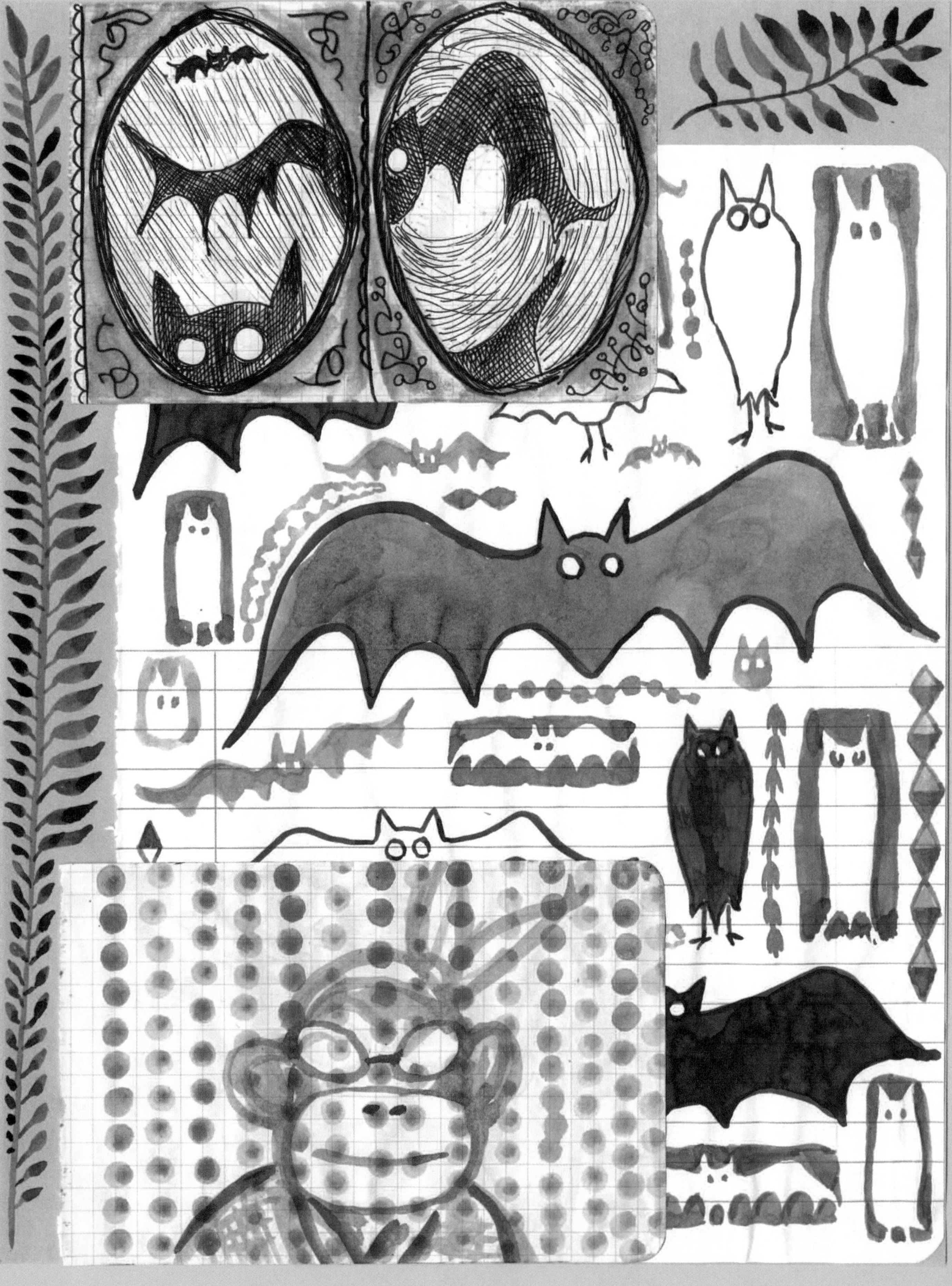

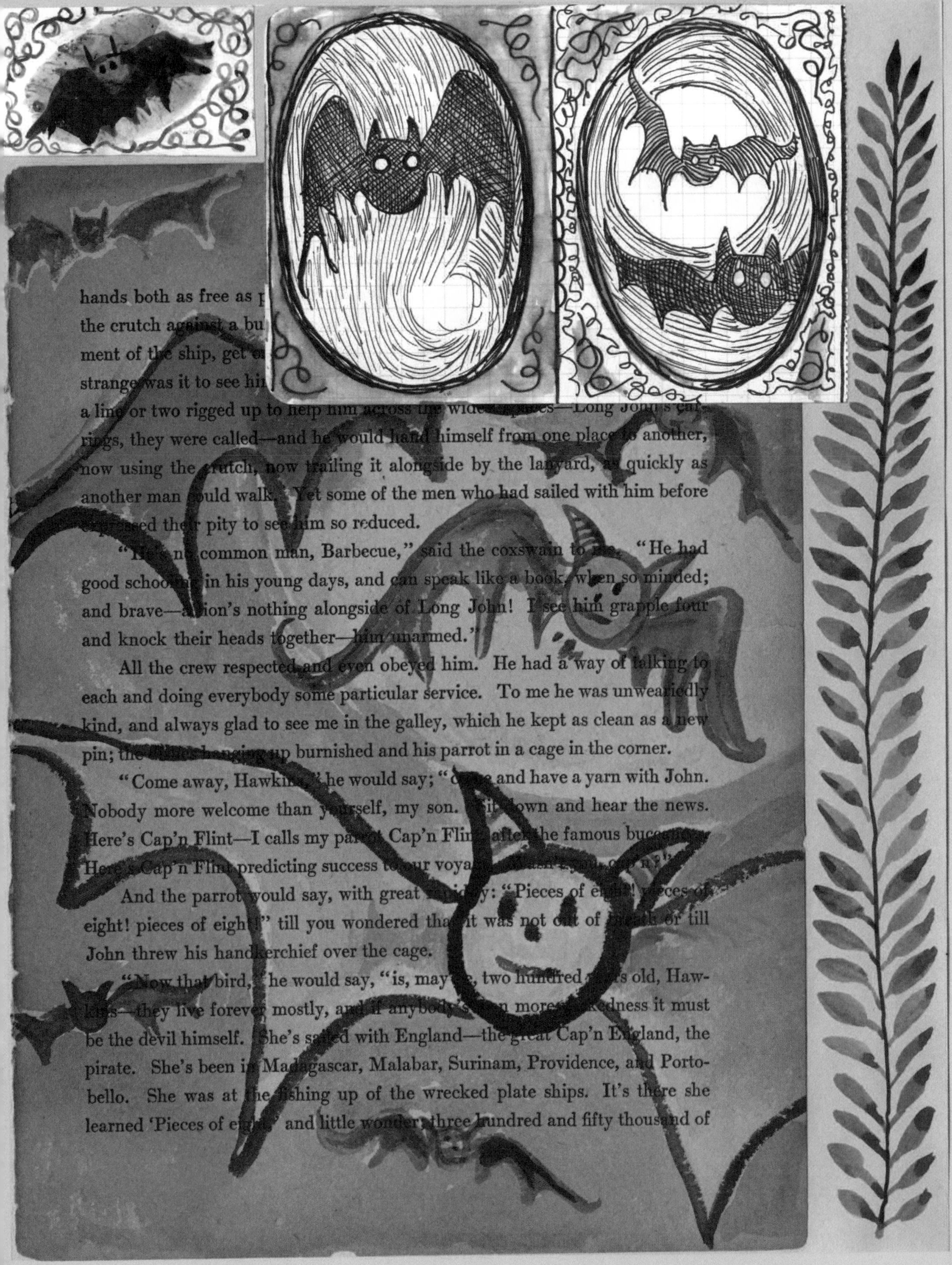
hands both as free as p
the crutch against a bu
ment of the ship, get o
strange was it to see hi
a line or two rigged up to help him across the widest spaces—Long John's ear-rings, they were called—and he would hand himself from one place to another, now using the crutch, now trailing it alongside by the lanyard, as quickly as another man could walk. Yet some of the men who had sailed with him before expressed their pity to see him so reduced.

"He's no common man, Barbecue," said the coxswain to me. "He had good schooling in his young days, and can speak like a book when so minded; and brave—a lion's nothing alongside of Long John! I see him grapple four and knock their heads together—him unarmed."

All the crew respected and even obeyed him. He had a way of talking to each and doing everybody some particular service. To me he was unweariedly kind, and always glad to see me in the galley, which he kept as clean as a new pin; the dishes hanging up burnished and his parrot in a cage in the corner.

"Come away, Hawkins," he would say; "come and have a yarn with John. Nobody more welcome than yourself, my son. Sit you down and hear the news. Here's Cap'n Flint—I calls my parrot Cap'n Flint, after the famous buccaneer—Here's Cap'n Flint predicting success to our voyage. Wasn't you, cap'n?"

And the parrot would say, with great rapidity: "Pieces of eight! pieces of eight! pieces of eight!" till you wondered that it was not out of breath, or till John threw his handkerchief over the cage.

"Now that bird," he would say, "is, may be, two hundred years old, Hawkins—they live forever mostly, and if anybody's seen more wickedness it must be the devil himself. She's sailed with England—the great Cap'n England, the pirate. She's been in Madagascar, Malabar, Surinam, Providence, and Portobello. She was at the fishing up of the wrecked plate ships. It's there she learned 'Pieces of eight,' and little wonder: three hundred and fifty thousand of

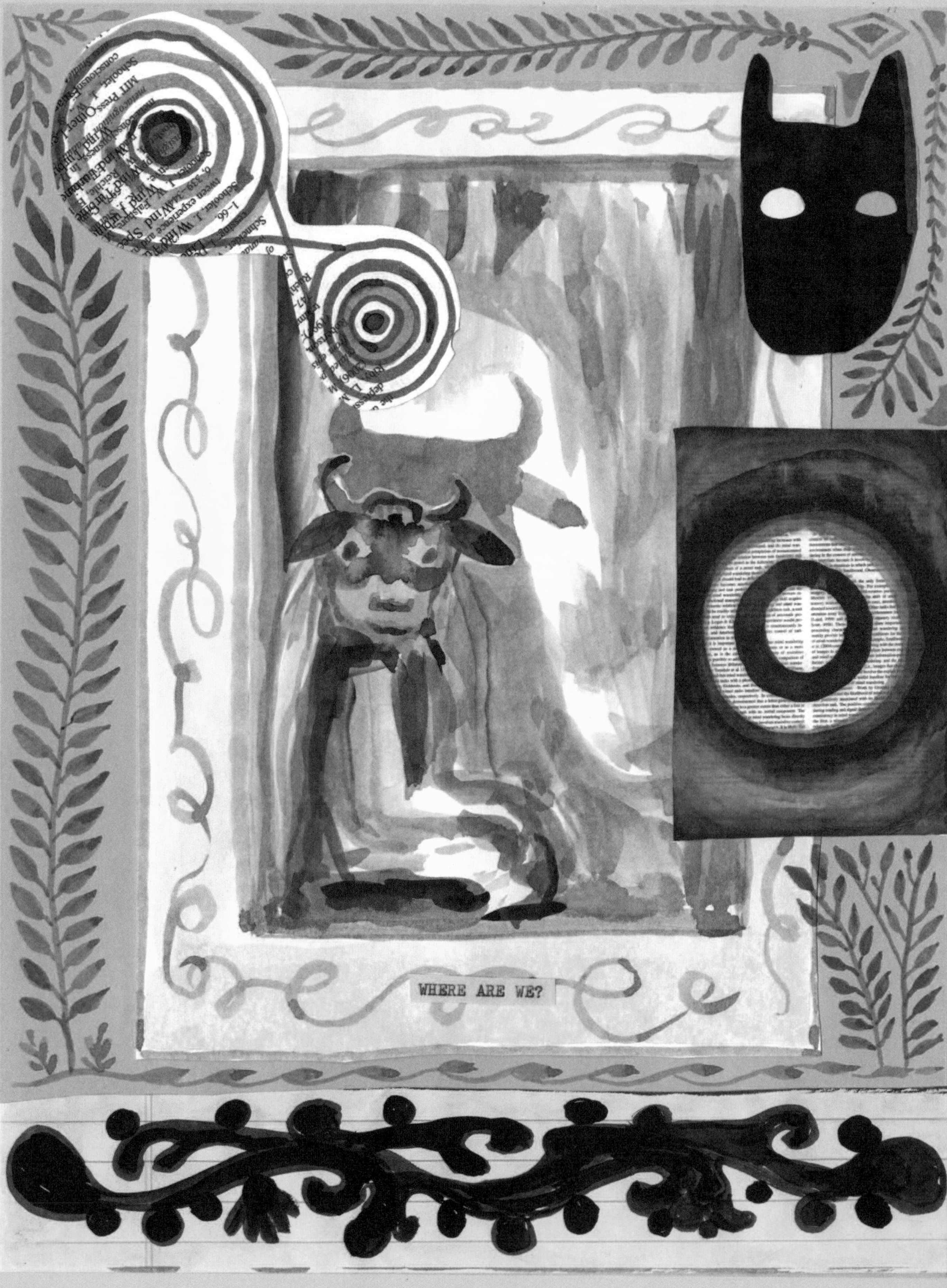
WHERE ARE WE?

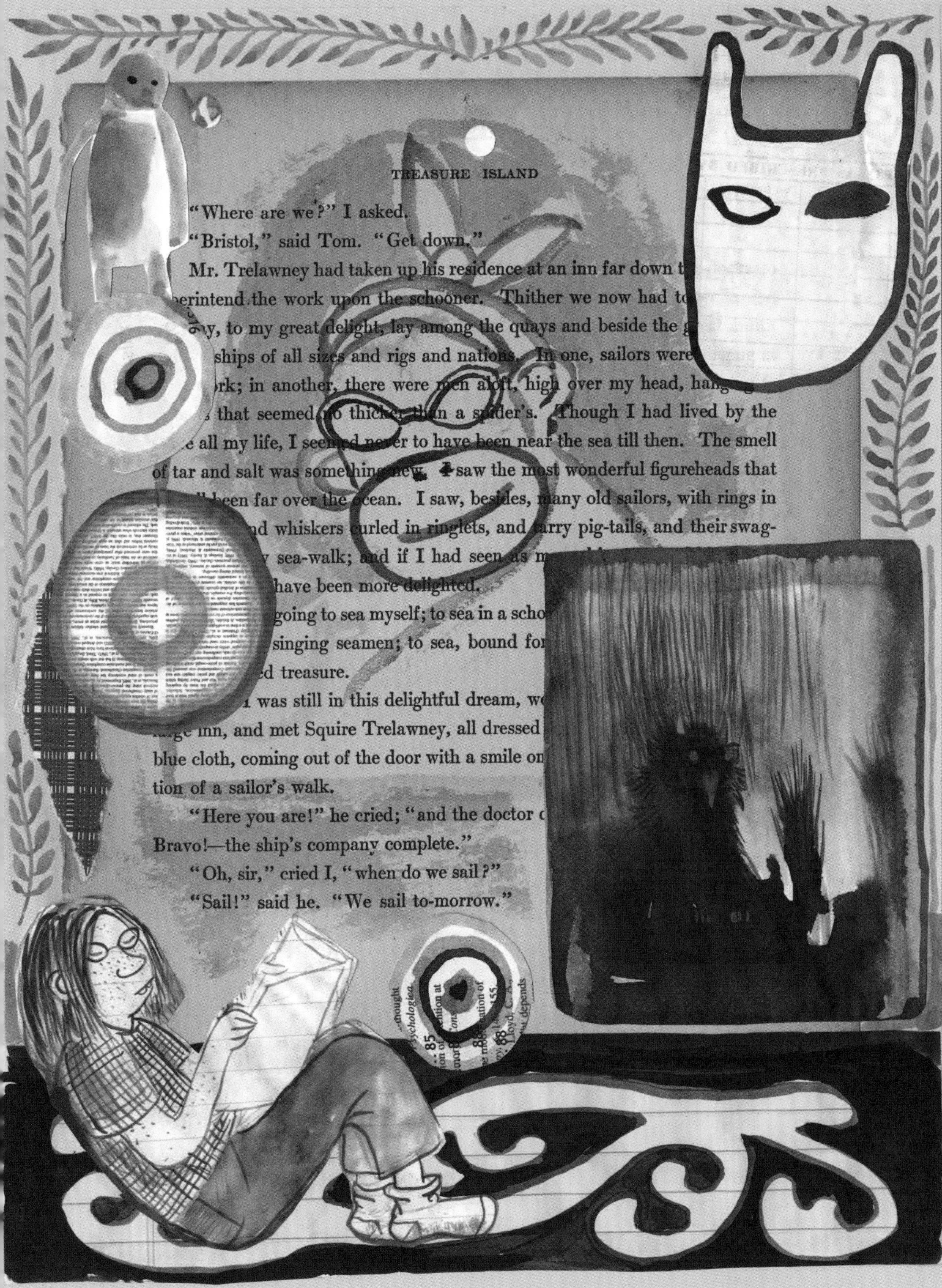
TREASURE ISLAND
"Where are we?" I asked.
"Bristol," said Tom. "Get down."
Mr. Trelawney had taken up his residence at an inn far down t
perintend the work upon the schooner. Thither we now had to
y, to my great delight, lay among the quays and beside the g
ships of all sizes and rigs and nations. In one, sailors were
rk; in another, there were men aloft, high over my head, hang
s that seemed no thicker than a spider's. Though I had lived by the
e all my life, I seemed never to have been near the sea till then. The smell
of tar and salt was something new. I saw the most wonderful figureheads that
been far over the ocean. I saw, besides, many old sailors, with rings in
d whiskers curled in ringlets, and tarry pig-tails, and their swag-
sea-walk; and if I had seen
have been more delighted.
going to sea myself; to sea in a scho
singing seamen; to sea, bound fo
d treasure.
was still in this delightful dream, w
inn, and met Squire Trelawney, all dressed
blue cloth, coming out of the door with a smile on
tion of a sailor's walk.
"Here you are!" he cried; "and the doctor c
Bravo!—the ship's company complete."
"Oh, sir," cried I, "when do we sail?"
"Sail!" said he. "We sail to-morrow."

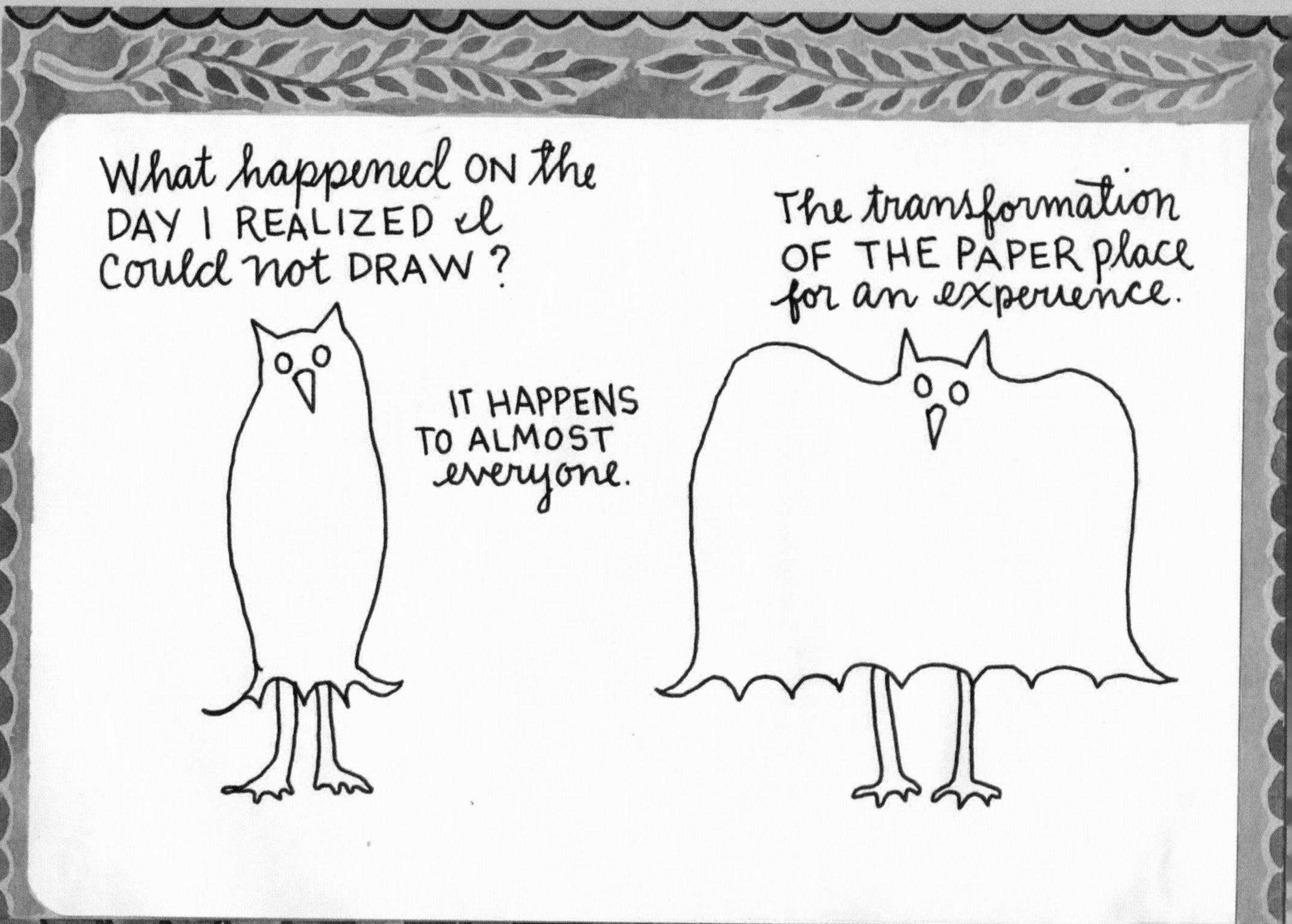
What happened ON the DAY I REALIZED I Could not DRAW?
IT HAPPENS TO ALMOST everyone.
The transformation OF THE PAPER place for an experience.

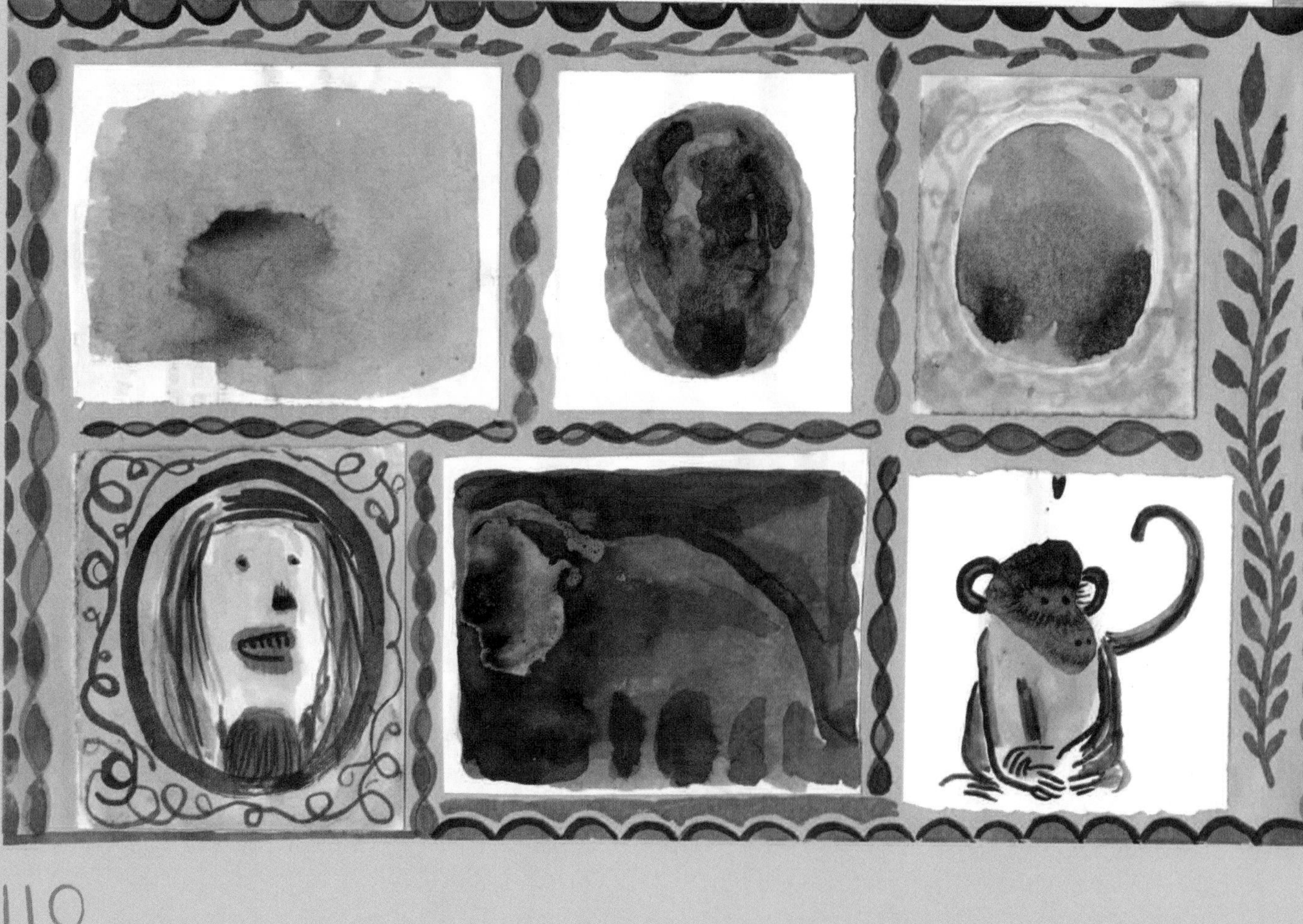

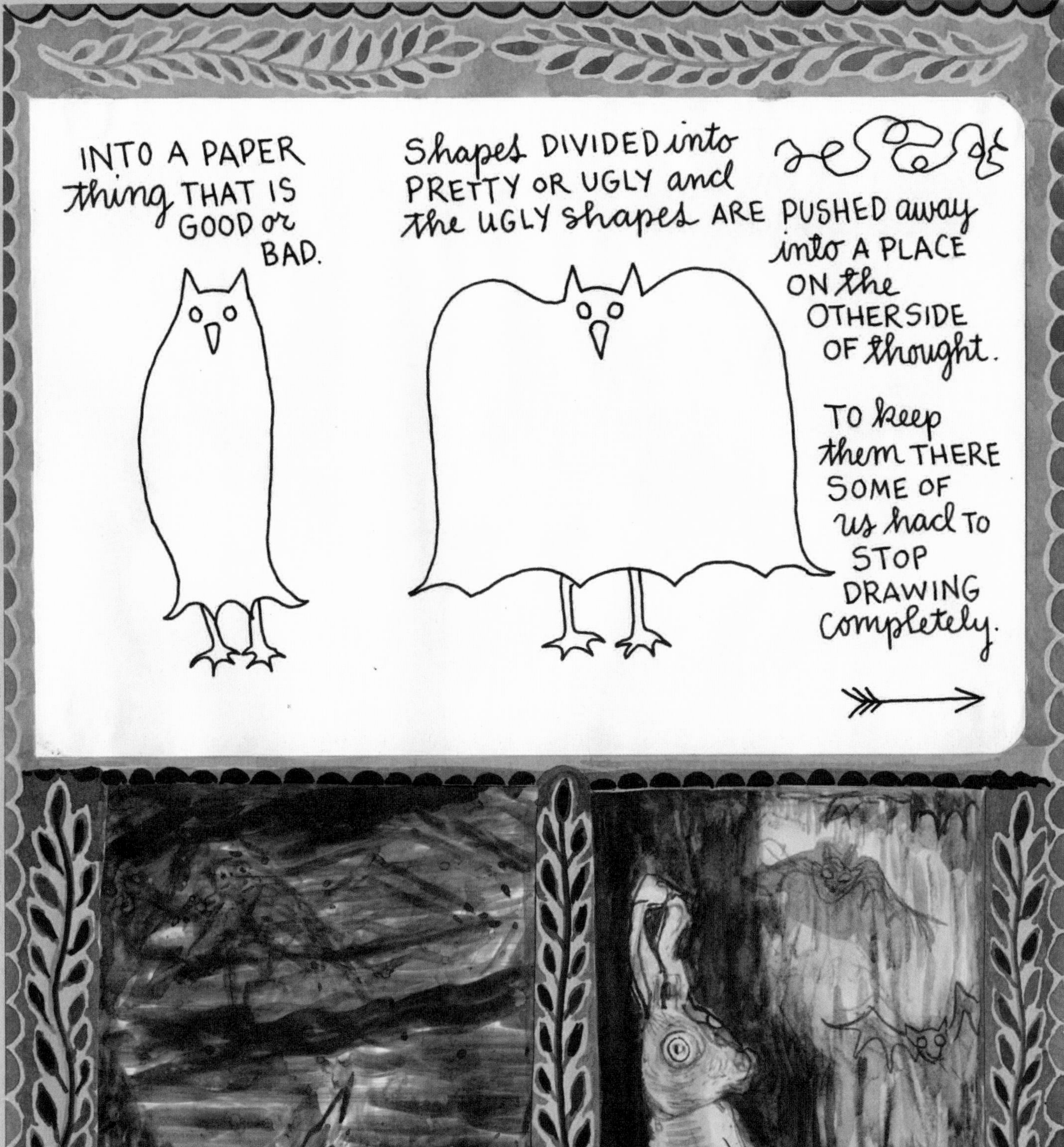
INTO A PAPER thing THAT IS GOOD or BAD.
Shapes DIVIDED into PRETTY OR UGLY and the UGLY shapes ARE PUSHED away into A PLACE ON the OTHERSIDE OF thought.
TO keep them THERE SOME OF us had TO STOP DRAWING completely.

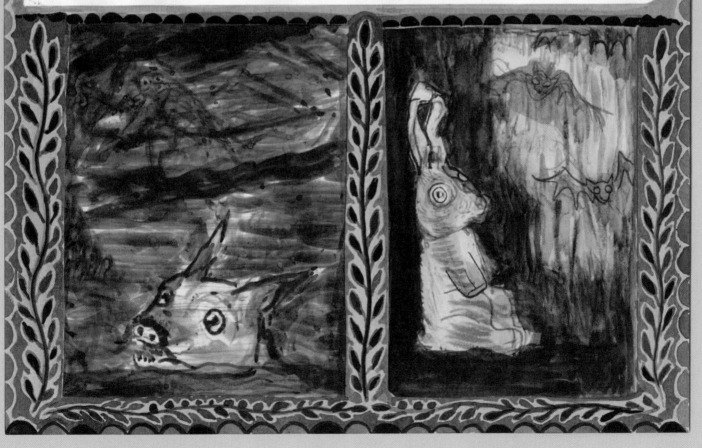

OR WE *had* TO LEARN *how* TO DRAW *in* AN *Organized* WAY *that* OTHERS *could* RECOGNIZE AND *Say* YES TO.

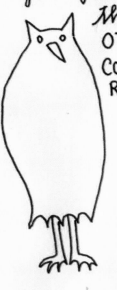

YES THAT IS *A nice* DRAWING.

SO YOU *have* *not* WASTED TIME *or* PAPER.

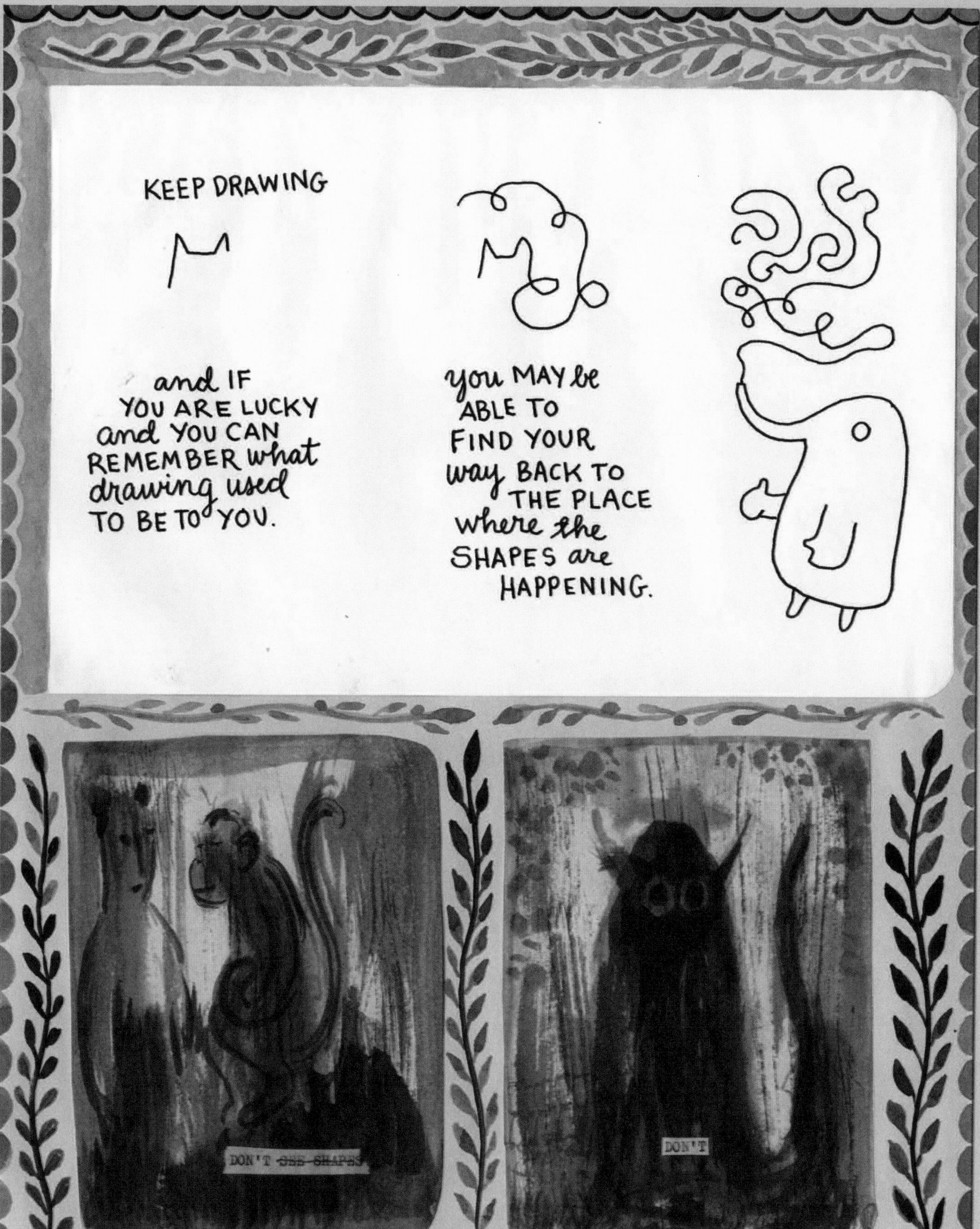
KEEP DRAWING
and IF YOU ARE LUCKY and YOU CAN REMEMBER what drawing used TO BE TO YOU.
you MAY be ABLE TO FIND YOUR way BACK TO THE PLACE where the SHAPES are HAPPENING.
DON'T ~~SEE SHAPES~~
DON'T

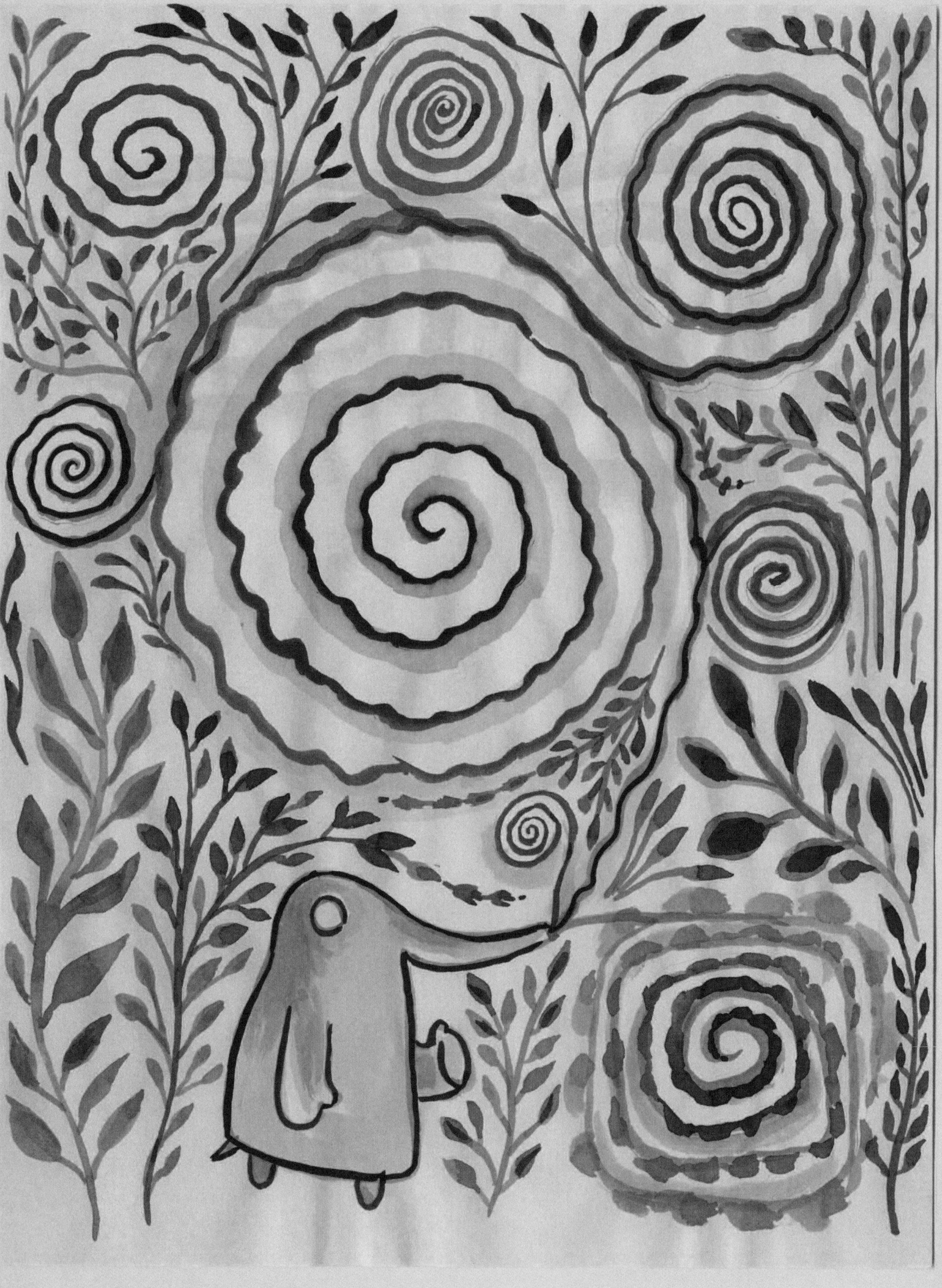

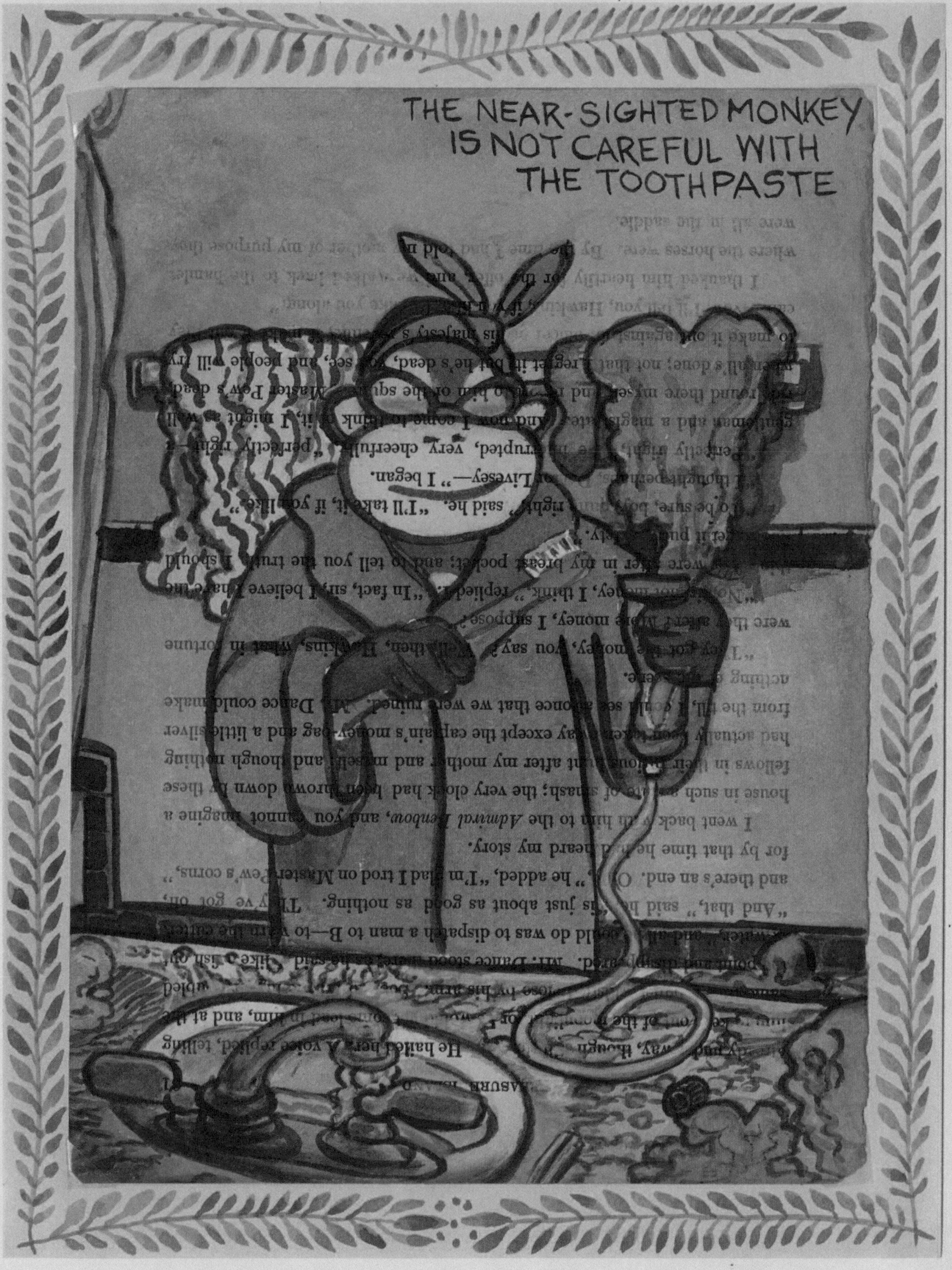
THE NEAR-SIGHTED MONKEY IS NOT CAREFUL WITH THE TOOTHPASTE

IT IS FUNNY TO THINK OF THE CHARACTERS IN MY COMICS AS BEING MINE. I DIDN'T PLAN THEIR ARRIVAL. I DIDN'T KNOW THEY WERE COMING. AND WHEN THEY FIRST SHOWED UP THEY DIDN'T STAND OUT.

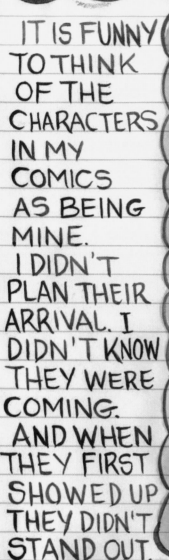

I DON'T KNOW WHY I DREW THEM AGAIN AT FIRST, BUT THEY QUICKLY TOOK OVER MY COMIC STRIP. WHEN I MOVED MY BRUSH ACROSS THE PAPER WALL, THEY WERE THERE. WHEN I STOPPED MY BRUSH, I'D LOSE THE SIGNAL. AND I COULDN'T GET IT BACK BY THINKING.

THAT IS MARLYS

THIS IS ARNA

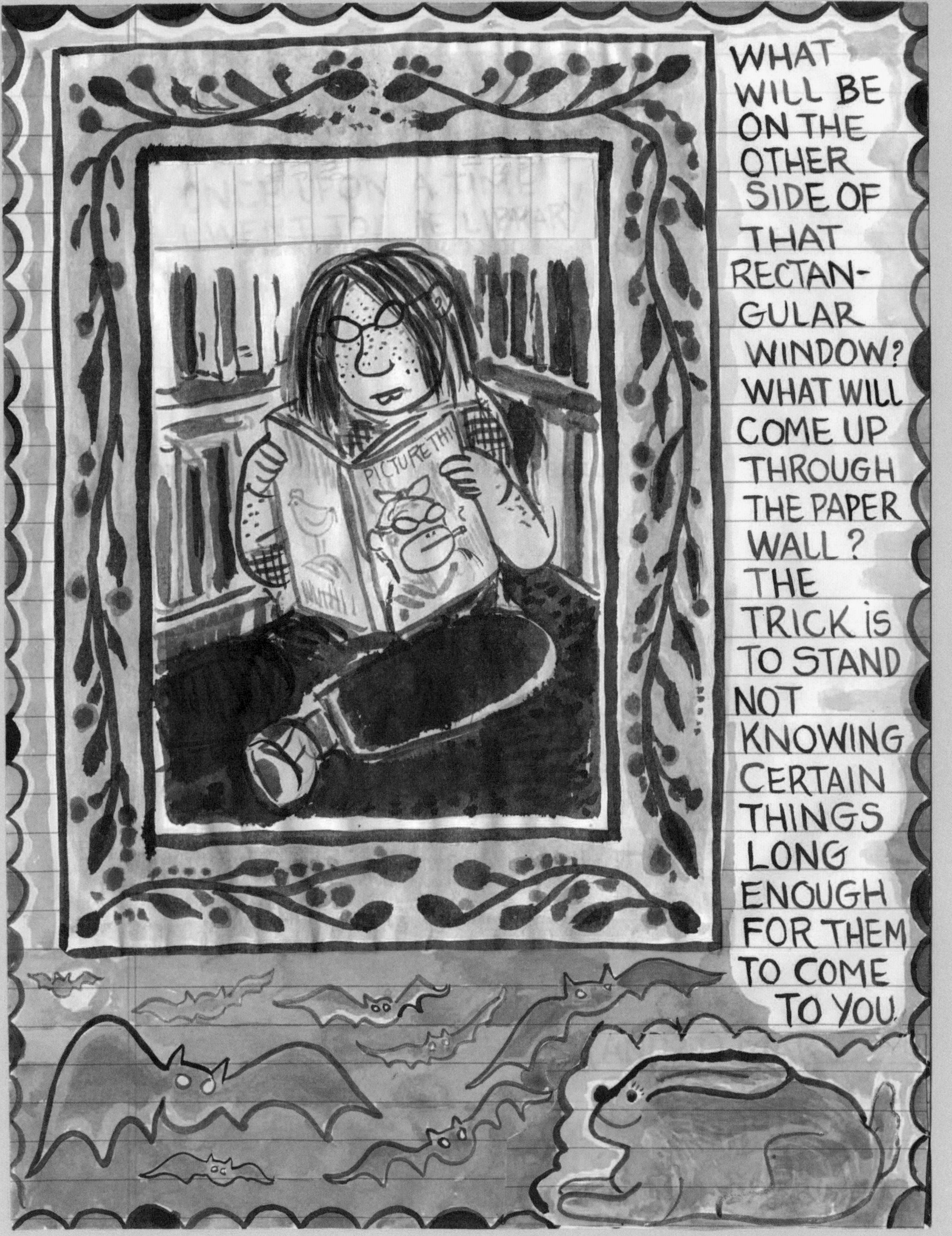
WHAT WILL BE ON THE OTHER SIDE OF THAT RECTAN-GULAR WINDOW? WHAT WILL COME UP THROUGH THE PAPER WALL? THE TRICK IS TO STAND NOT KNOWING CERTAIN THINGS LONG ENOUGH FOR THEM TO COME TO YOU.
PICTURE THIS

CHARACTERS
A
FIGURES
4

"Mysterious symbols curving and twisting across the page, black ink on white paper, can have a fascination nonetheless powerful for their not being understood." Ryokushu Kuiseko 1988

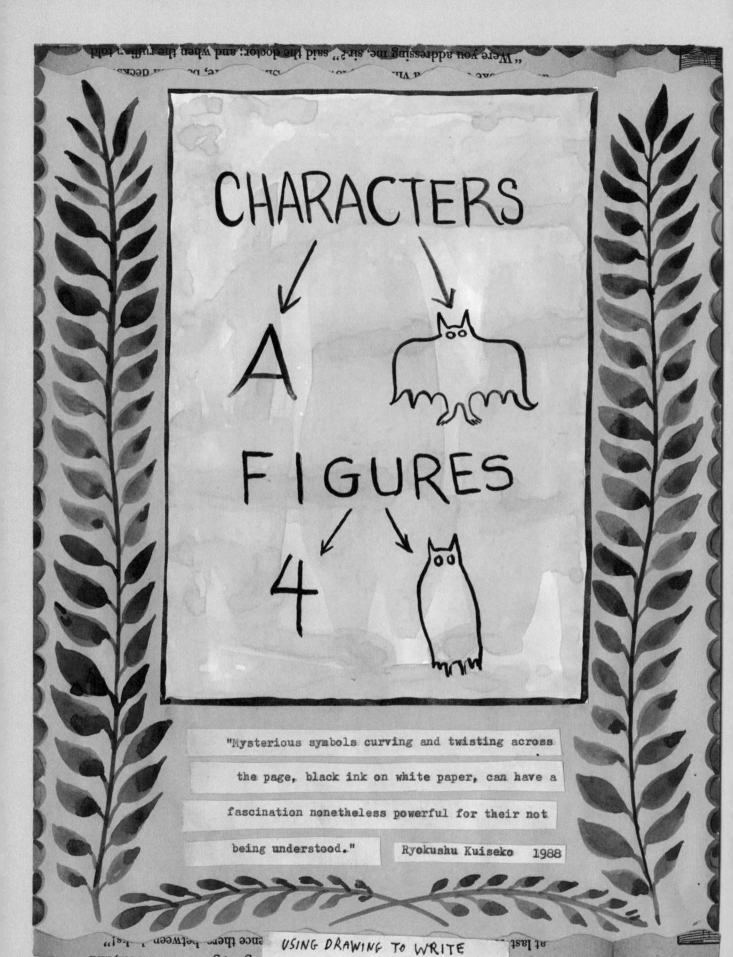

USING DRAWING TO WRITE

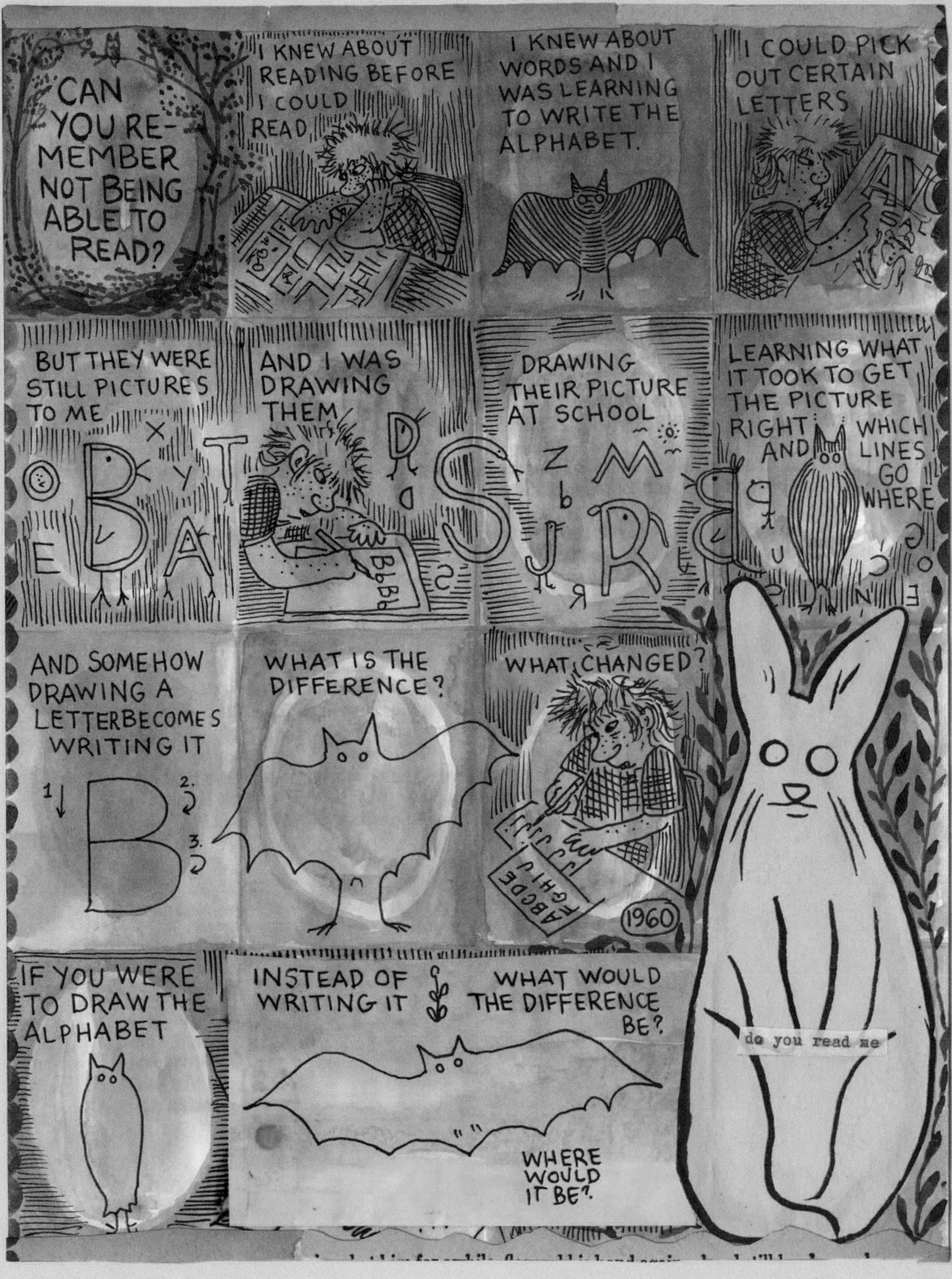

CAN YOU RE-MEMBER NOT BEING ABLE TO READ?
I KNEW ABOUT READING BEFORE I COULD READ.
I KNEW ABOUT WORDS AND I WAS LEARNING TO WRITE THE ALPHABET.
I COULD PICK OUT CERTAIN LETTERS
BUT THEY WERE STILL PICTURES TO ME
AND I WAS DRAWING THEM
DRAWING THEIR PICTURE AT SCHOOL
LEARNING WHAT IT TOOK TO GET THE PICTURE RIGHT: AND WHICH LINES GO WHERE
AND SOMEHOW DRAWING A LETTER BECOMES WRITING IT
WHAT IS THE DIFFERENCE?
WHAT CHANGED?
1960
IF YOU WERE TO DRAW THE ALPHABET
INSTEAD OF WRITING IT
WHAT WOULD THE DIFFERENCE BE?
WHERE WOULD IT BE?
do you read me

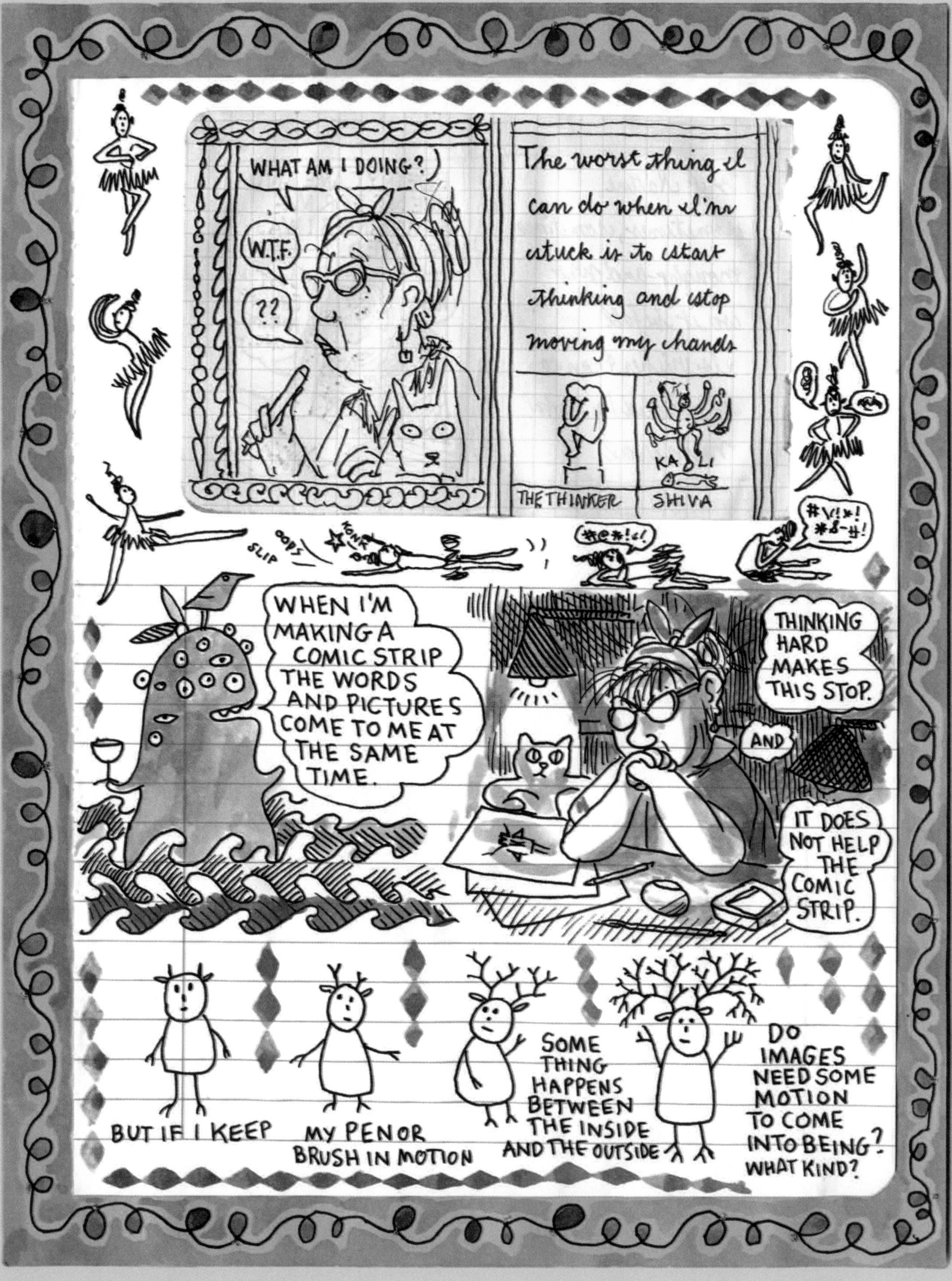
WHAT AM I DOING?
W.T.F.
??
The worst thing I can do when I'm stuck is to start thinking and stop moving my hands
THE THINKER
KA LI
SHIVA
SLIP
OOPS
KONK
#@*!&!
#V!*! *&-#!
WHEN I'M MAKING A COMIC STRIP THE WORDS AND PICTURES COME TO ME AT THE SAME TIME.
THINKING HARD MAKES THIS STOP.
AND
IT DOES NOT HELP THE COMIC STRIP.
BUT IF I KEEP
MY PEN OR BRUSH IN MOTION
SOME THING HAPPENS BETWEEN THE INSIDE AND THE OUTSIDE
DO IMAGES NEED SOME MOTION TO COME INTO BEING? WHAT KIND?

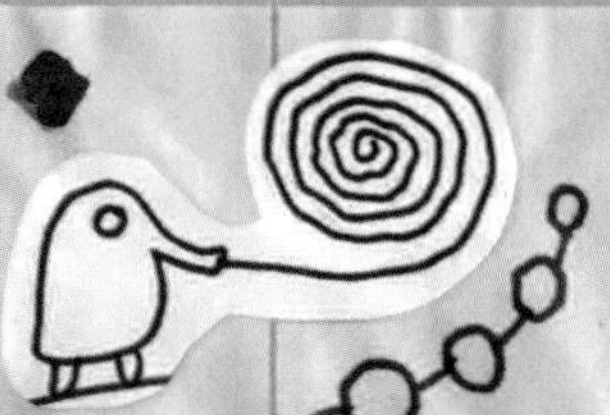

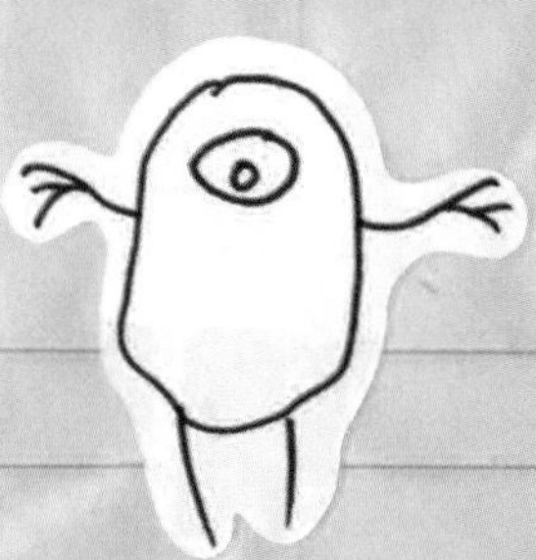

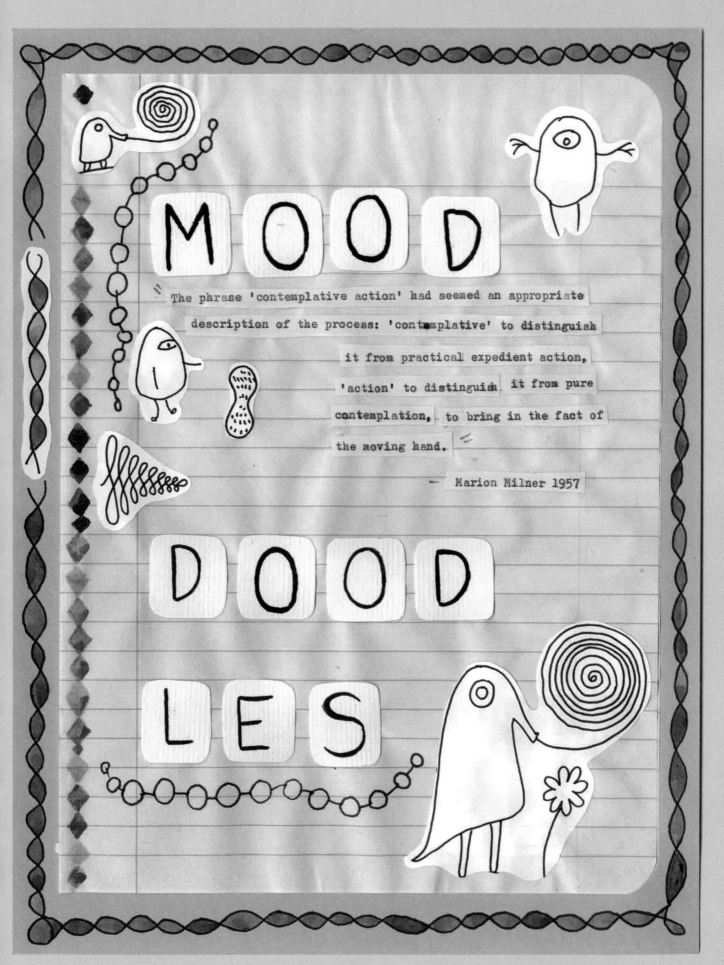

MOOD DOODLES

"The phrase 'contemplative action' had seemed an appropriate description of the process: 'contemplative' to distinguish it from practical expedient action, 'action' to distinguish it from pure contemplation, to bring in the fact of the moving hand."

— Marion Milner 1957

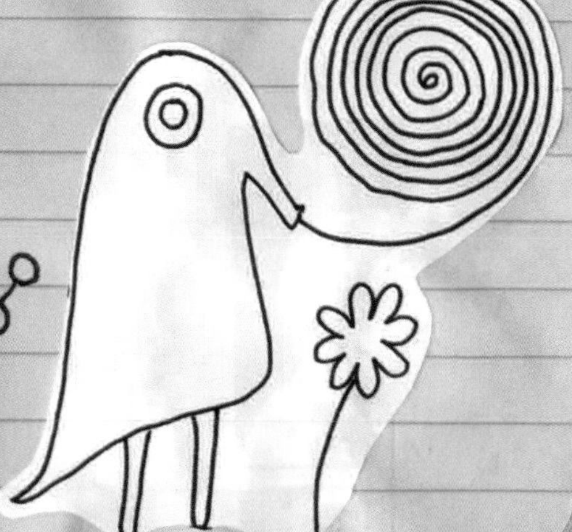

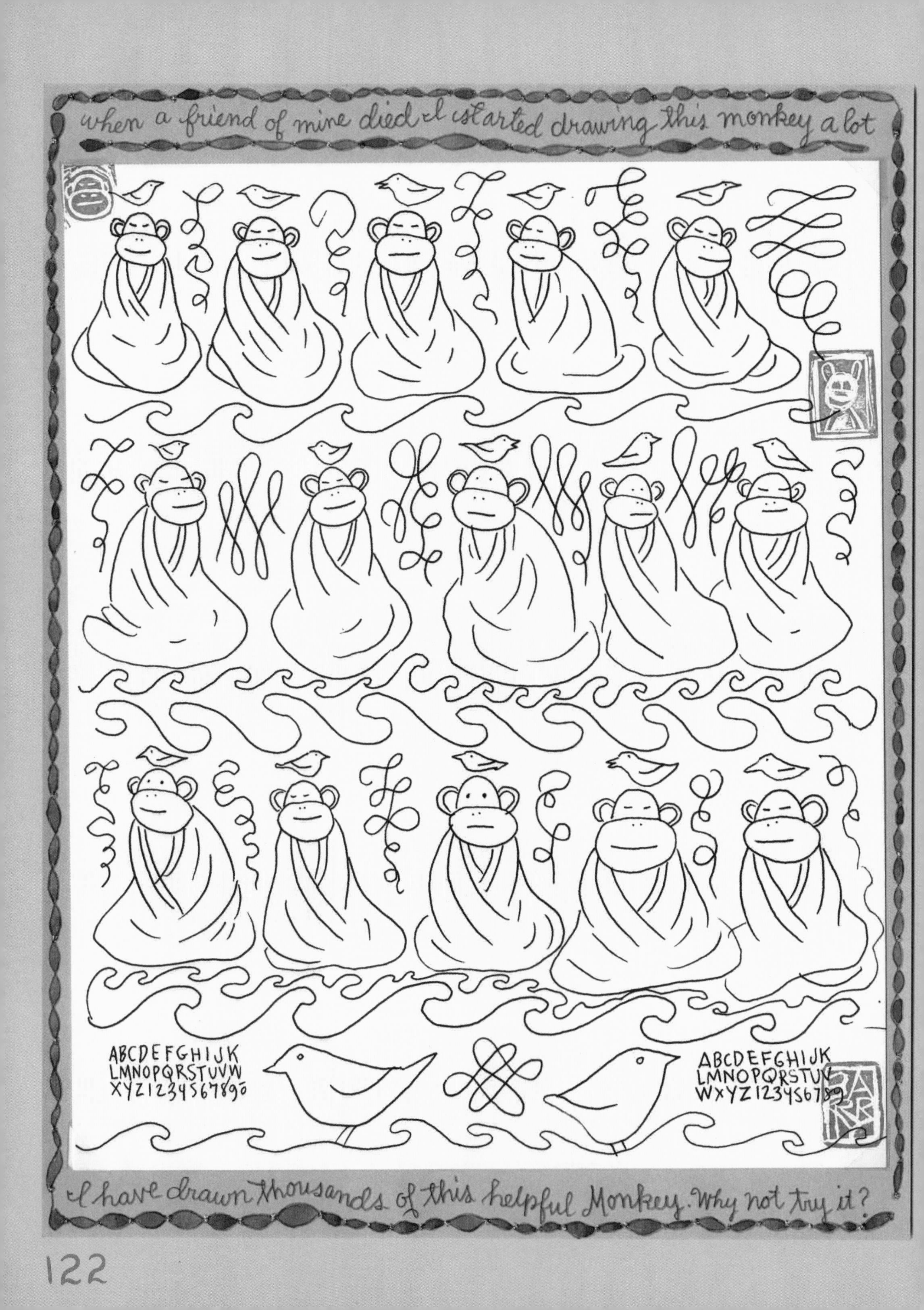
when a friend of mine died I started drawing this monkey a lot
ABCDEFGHIJK
LMNOPQRSTUVW
XYZ1234567890
ABCDEFGHIJK
LMNOPQRSTUV
WXYZ123456789
I have drawn thousands of this helpful Monkey. Why not try it?

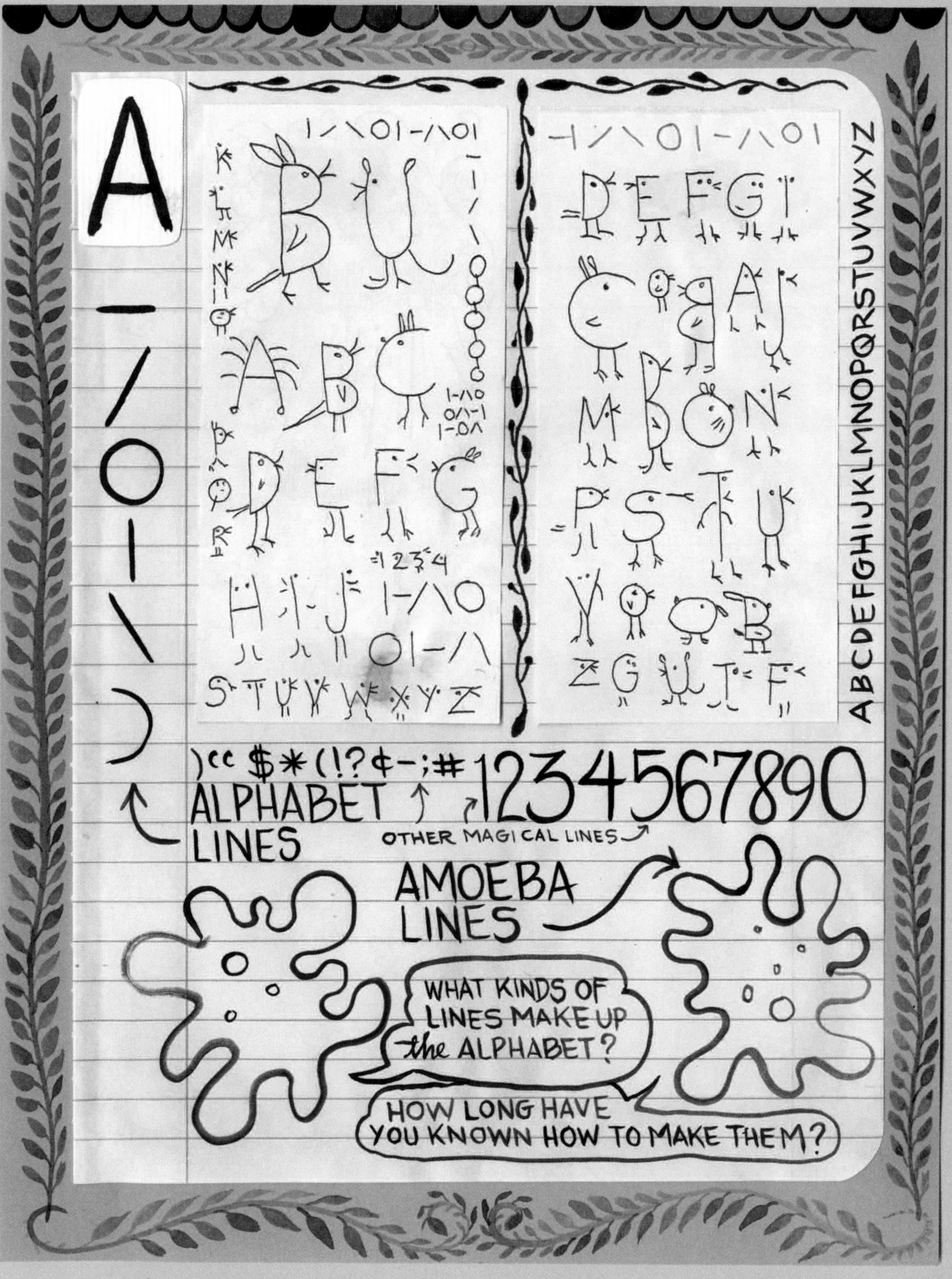
A
ABCDEFGHIJKLMNOPQRSTUVWXYZ
)cc $*(!?¢–;#
ALPHABET
LINES
1234567890
OTHER MAGICAL LINES
AMOEBA
LINES
WHAT KINDS OF LINES MAKE UP the ALPHABET?
HOW LONG HAVE YOU KNOWN HOW TO MAKE THEM?

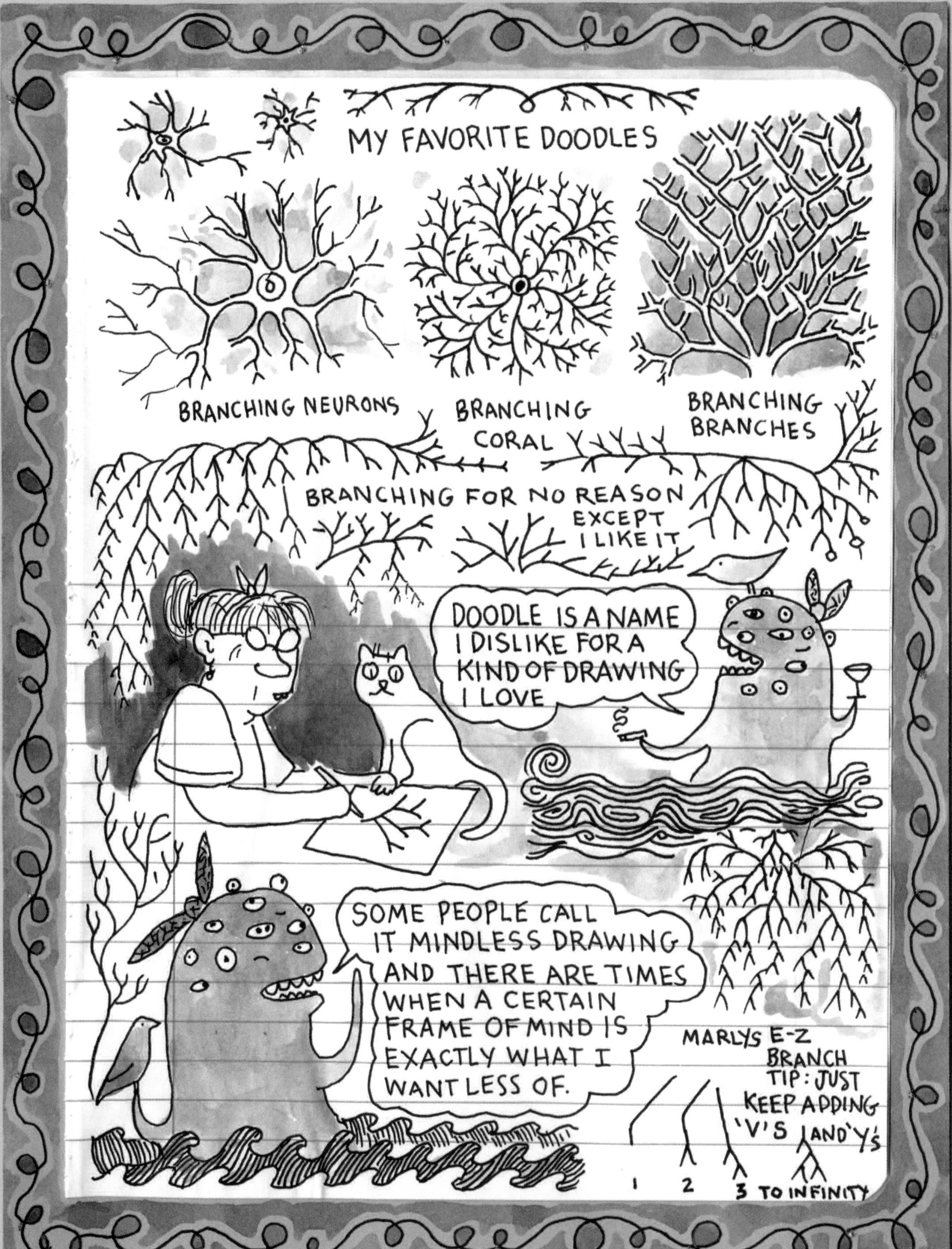
MY FAVORITE DOODLES
BRANCHING NEURONS
BRANCHING CORAL
BRANCHING BRANCHES
BRANCHING FOR NO REASON EXCEPT I LIKE IT
DOODLE IS A NAME I DISLIKE FOR A KIND OF DRAWING I LOVE
SOME PEOPLE CALL IT MINDLESS DRAWING AND THERE ARE TIMES WHEN A CERTAIN FRAME OF MIND IS EXACTLY WHAT I WANT LESS OF.
MARLYS E-Z BRANCH TIP: JUST KEEP ADDING 'V'S AND 'Y'S
1
2
3 TO INFINITY

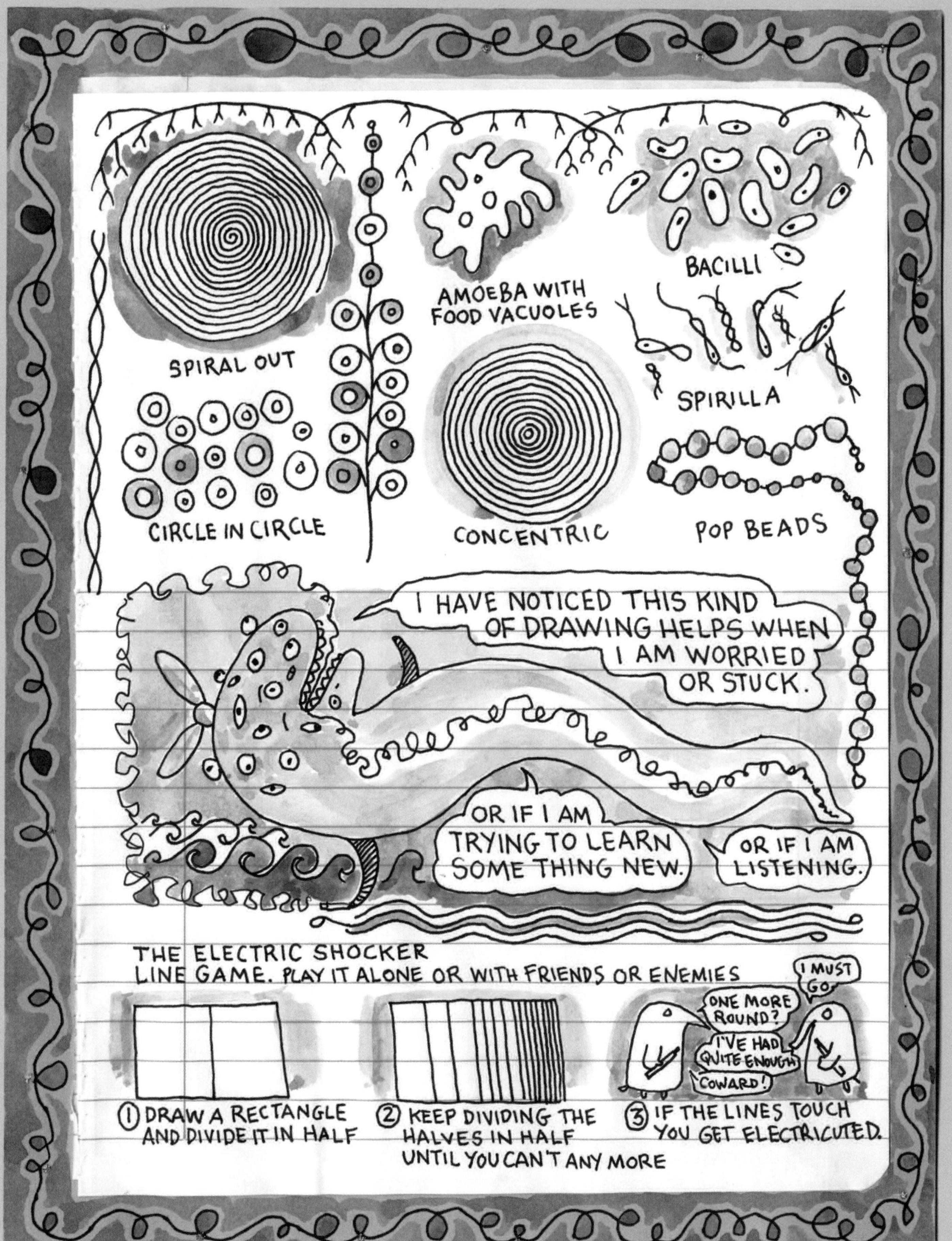

SPIRAL OUT
AMOEBA WITH FOOD VACUOLES
BACILLI
SPIRILLA
CIRCLE IN CIRCLE
CONCENTRIC
POP BEADS
I HAVE NOTICED THIS KIND OF DRAWING HELPS WHEN I AM WORRIED OR STUCK.
OR IF I AM TRYING TO LEARN SOME THING NEW.
OR IF I AM LISTENING.
THE ELECTRIC SHOCKER LINE GAME. PLAY IT ALONE OR WITH FRIENDS OR ENEMIES
① DRAW A RECTANGLE AND DIVIDE IT IN HALF
② KEEP DIVIDING THE HALVES IN HALF UNTIL YOU CAN'T ANY MORE
③ IF THE LINES TOUCH YOU GET ELECTRICUTED.
I MUST GO.
ONE MORE ROUND?
I'VE HAD QUITE ENOUGH
COWARD!

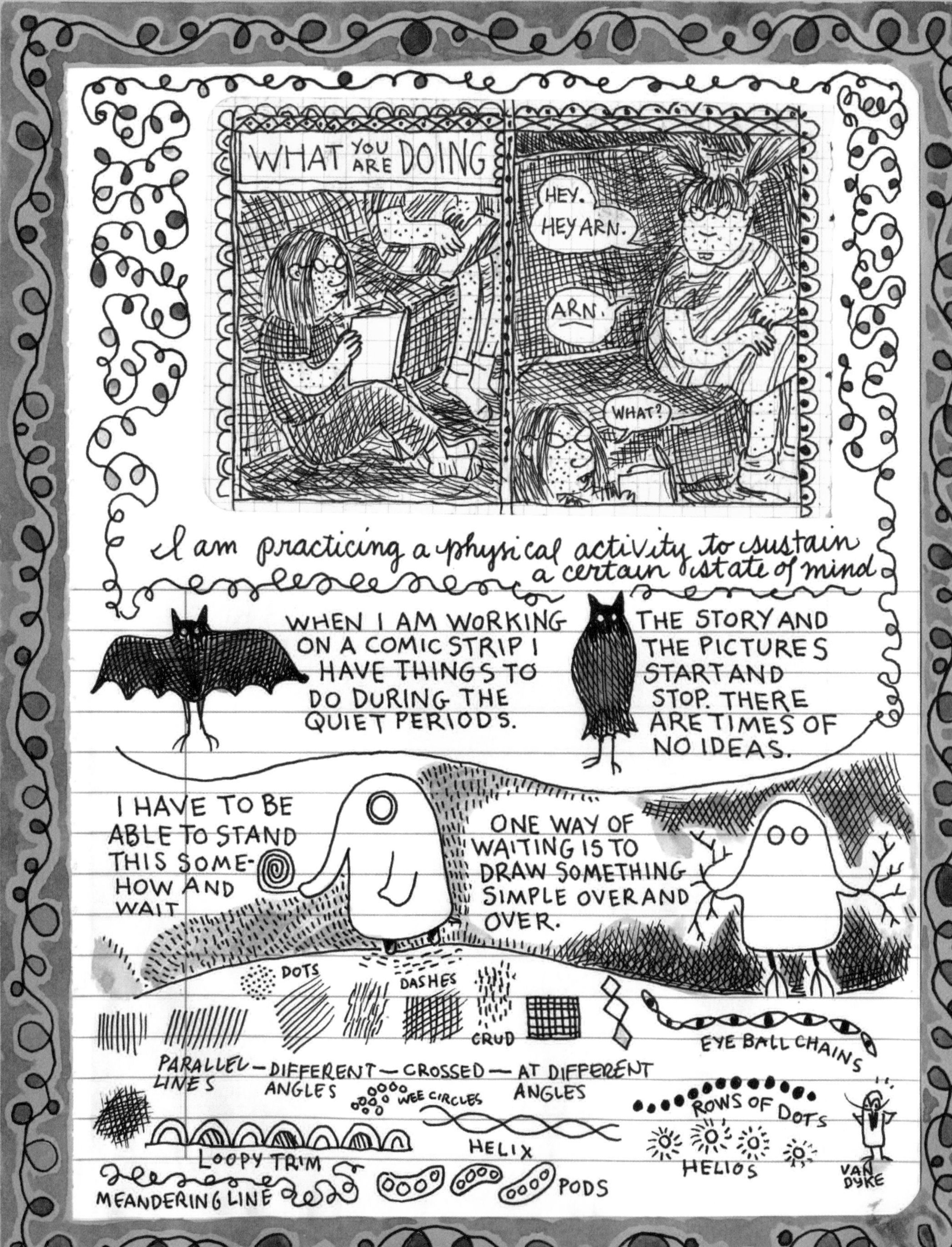
WHAT YOU ARE DOING
HEY.
HEY ARN.
ARN.
WHAT?
I am practicing a physical activity to sustain a certain state of mind
WHEN I AM WORKING ON A COMIC STRIP I HAVE THINGS TO DO DURING THE QUIET PERIODS.
THE STORY AND THE PICTURES START AND STOP. THERE ARE TIMES OF NO IDEAS.
I HAVE TO BE ABLE TO STAND THIS SOMEHOW AND WAIT
ONE WAY OF WAITING IS TO DRAW SOMETHING SIMPLE OVER AND OVER.
DOTS
DASHES
CRUD
EYE BALL CHAINS
PARALLEL LINES — DIFFERENT ANGLES — CROSSED — AT DIFFERENT ANGLES
WEE CIRCLES
ROWS OF DOTS
LOOPY TRIM
HELIX
HELIOS
VAN DYKE
MEANDERING LINE
PODS

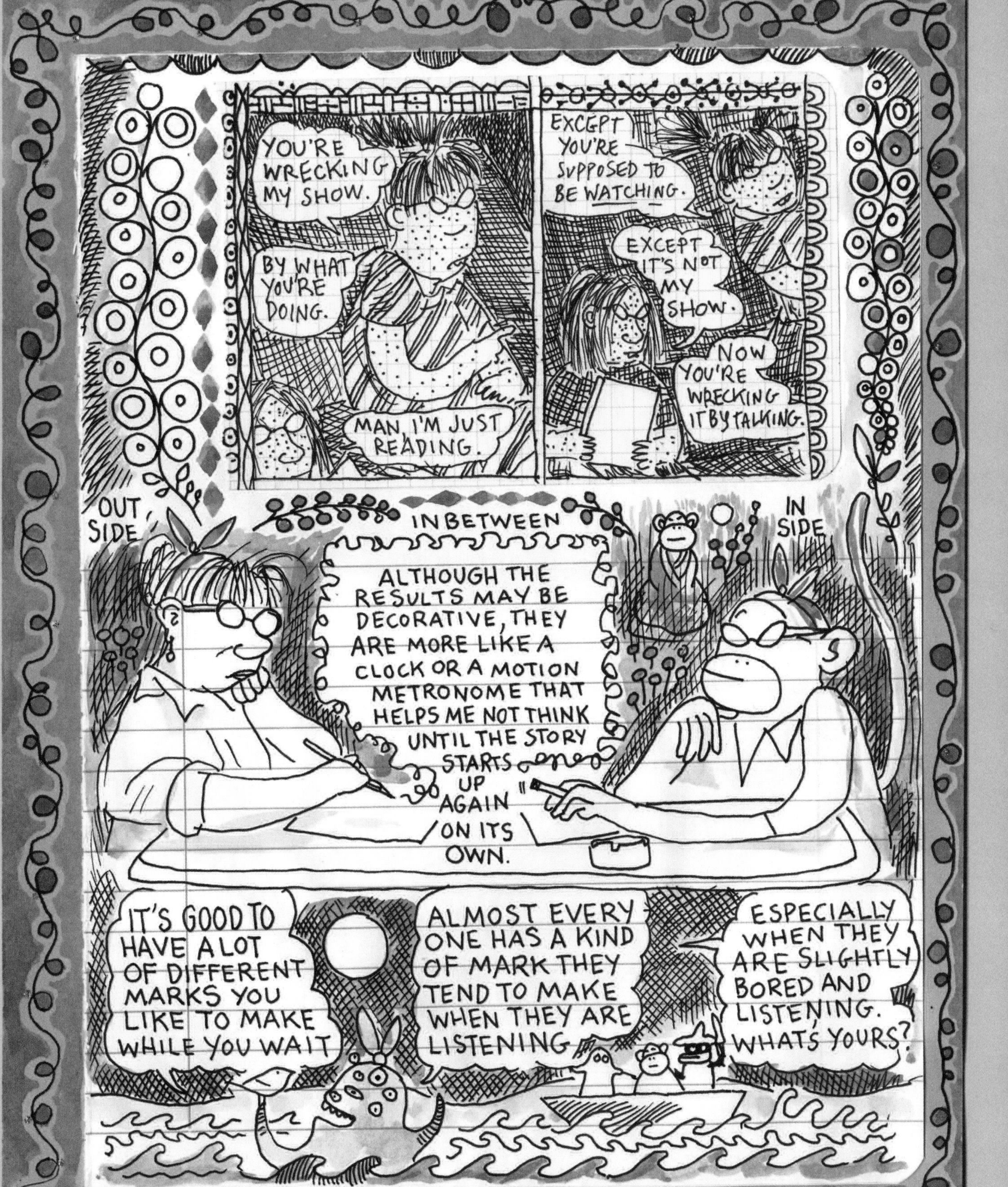
YOU'RE WRECKING MY SHOW.
BY WHAT YOU'RE DOING.
MAN I'M JUST READING.
EXCEPT YOU'RE SUPPOSED TO BE WATCHING.
EXCEPT IT'S NOT MY SHOW.
NOW YOU'RE WRECKING IT BY TALKING.
OUT SIDE
IN BETWEEN
IN SIDE
ALTHOUGH THE RESULTS MAY BE DECORATIVE, THEY ARE MORE LIKE A CLOCK OR A MOTION METRONOME THAT HELPS ME NOT THINK UNTIL THE STORY STARTS UP AGAIN ON ITS OWN.
IT'S GOOD TO HAVE A LOT OF DIFFERENT MARKS YOU LIKE TO MAKE WHILE YOU WAIT
ALMOST EVERY ONE HAS A KIND OF MARK THEY TEND TO MAKE WHEN THEY ARE LISTENING
ESPECIALLY WHEN THEY ARE SLIGHTLY BORED AND LISTENING. WHAT'S YOURS?

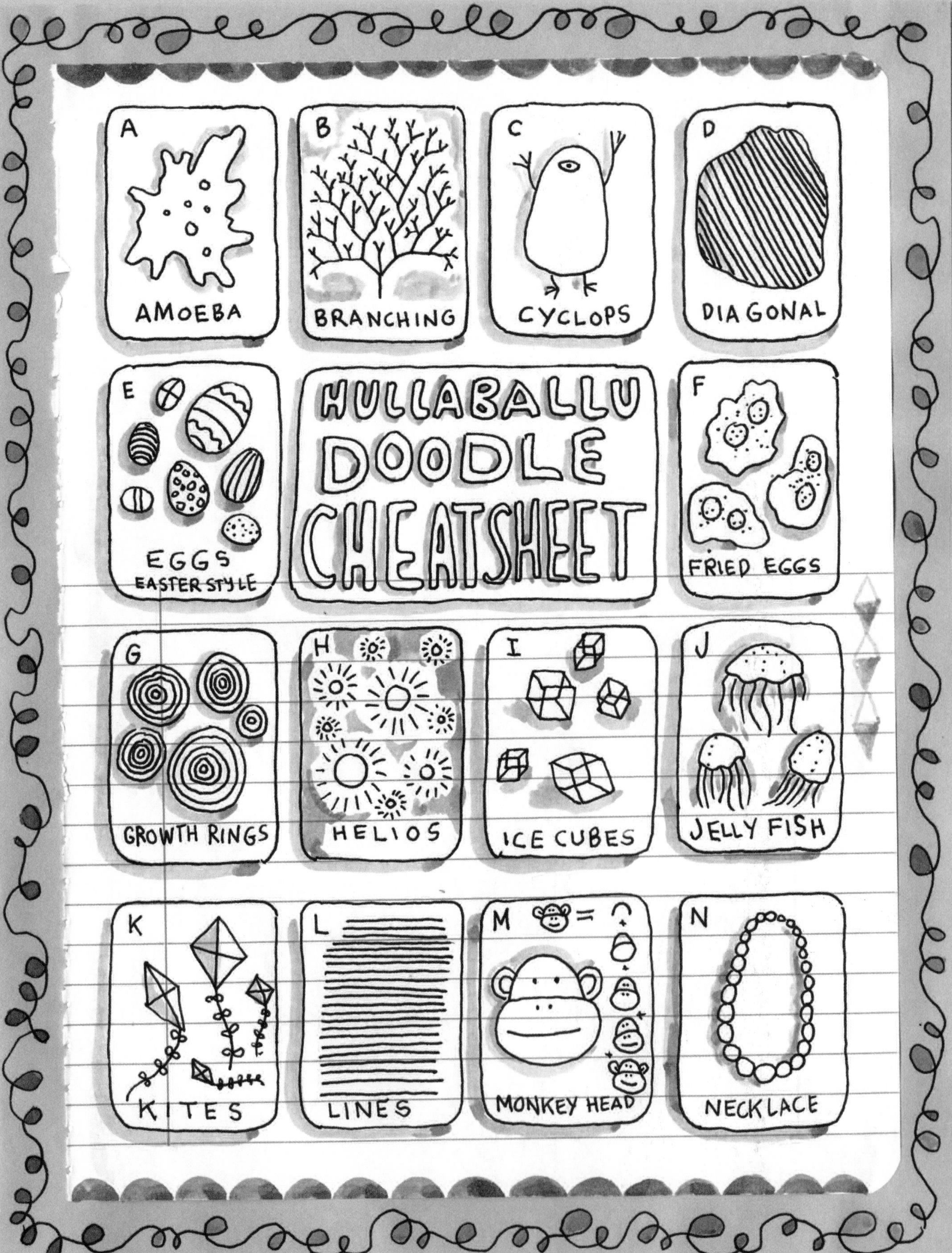
HULLABALLU DOODLE CHEATSHEET
A
AMOEBA
B
BRANCHING
C
CYCLOPS
D
DIAGONAL
E
EGGS
EASTER STYLE
F
FRIED EGGS
G
GROWTH RINGS
H
HELIOS
I
ICE CUBES
J
JELLY FISH
K
KITES
L
LINES
M
MONKEY HEAD
N
NECKLACE

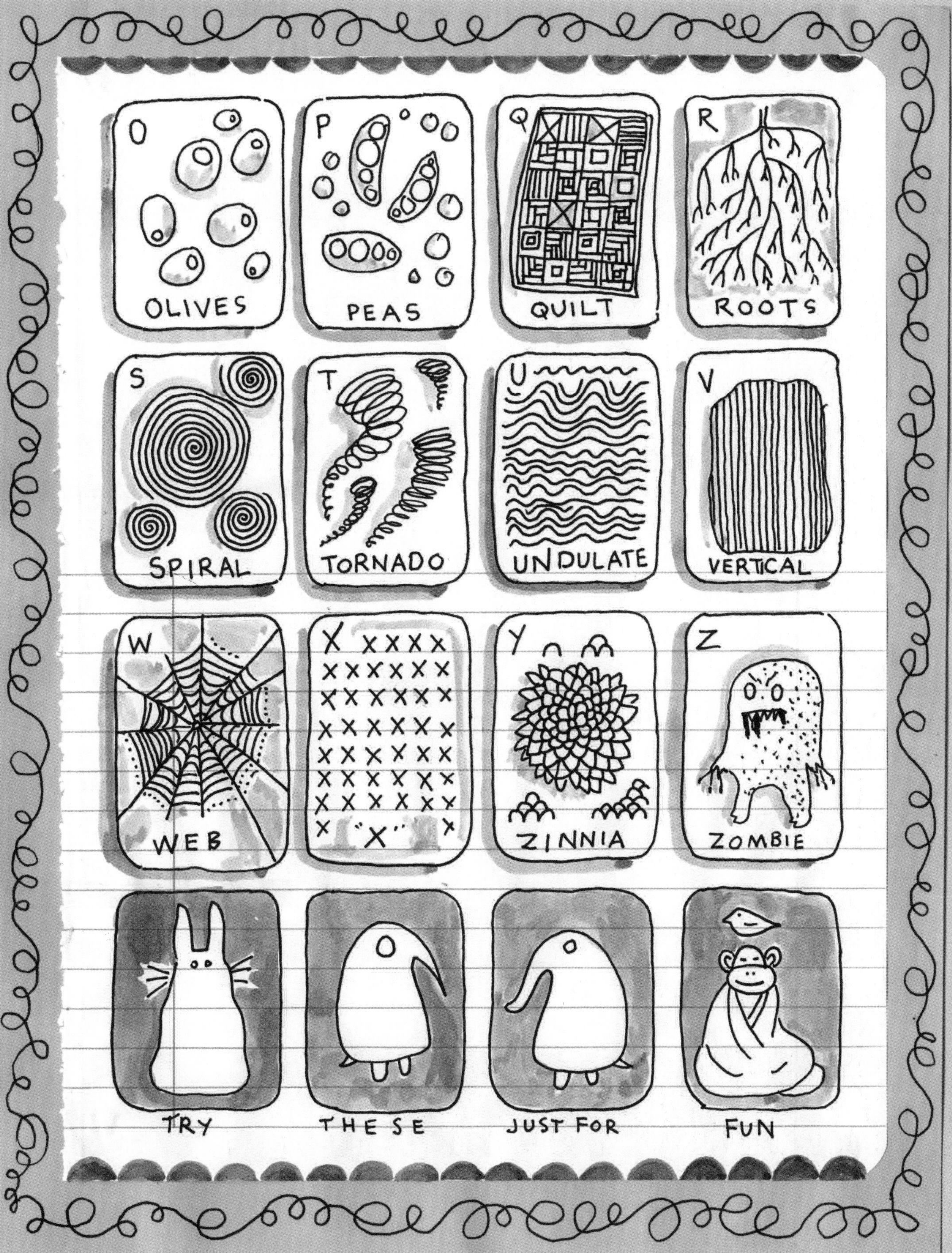
O
OLIVES
P
PEAS
Q
QUILT
R
ROOTS
S
SPIRAL
T
TORNADO
U
UNDULATE
V
VERTICAL
W
WEB
X
"X"
Y
ZINNIA
Z
ZOMBIE
TRY
THESE
JUST FOR
FUN

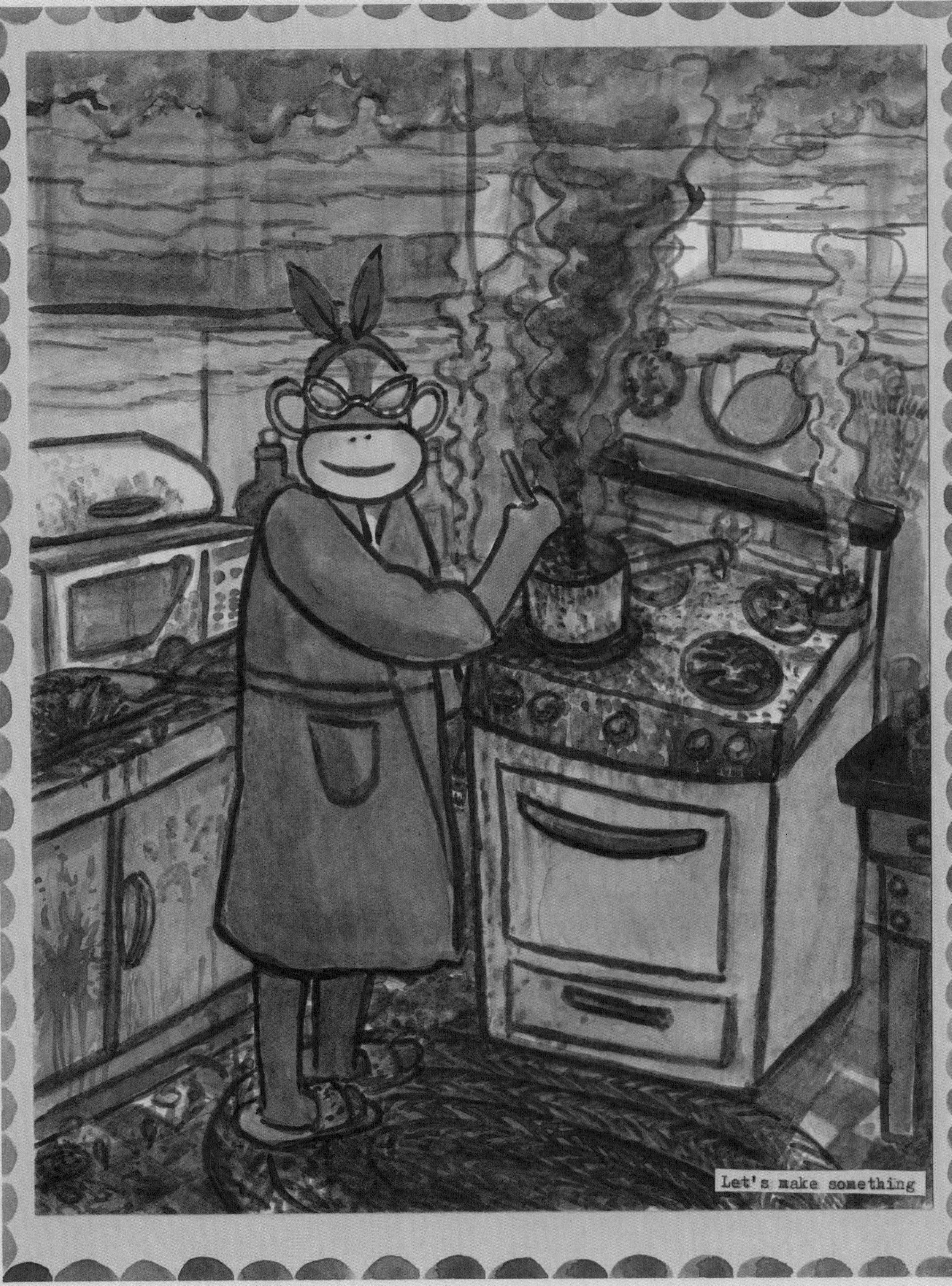
Let's make something

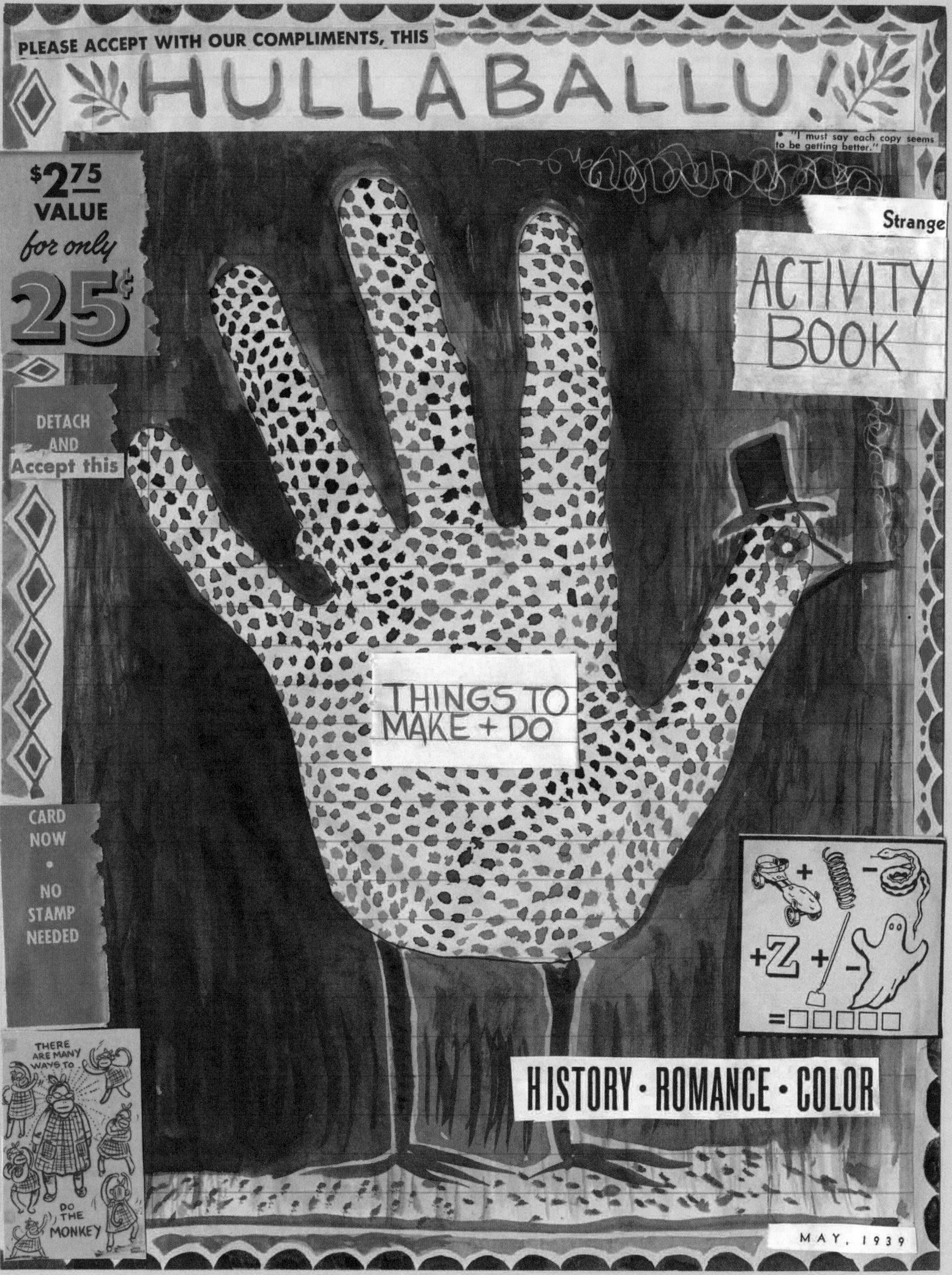

PLEASE ACCEPT WITH OUR COMPLIMENTS, THIS
HULLABALLU!
• "I must say each copy seems to be getting better."
$2.75 VALUE for only 25¢
Strange
ACTIVITY BOOK
DETACH AND Accept this
THINGS TO MAKE + DO
CARD NOW • NO STAMP NEEDED
+ Z + − =
THERE ARE MANY WAYS TO DO THE MONKEY
HISTORY · ROMANCE · COLOR
MAY, 1939

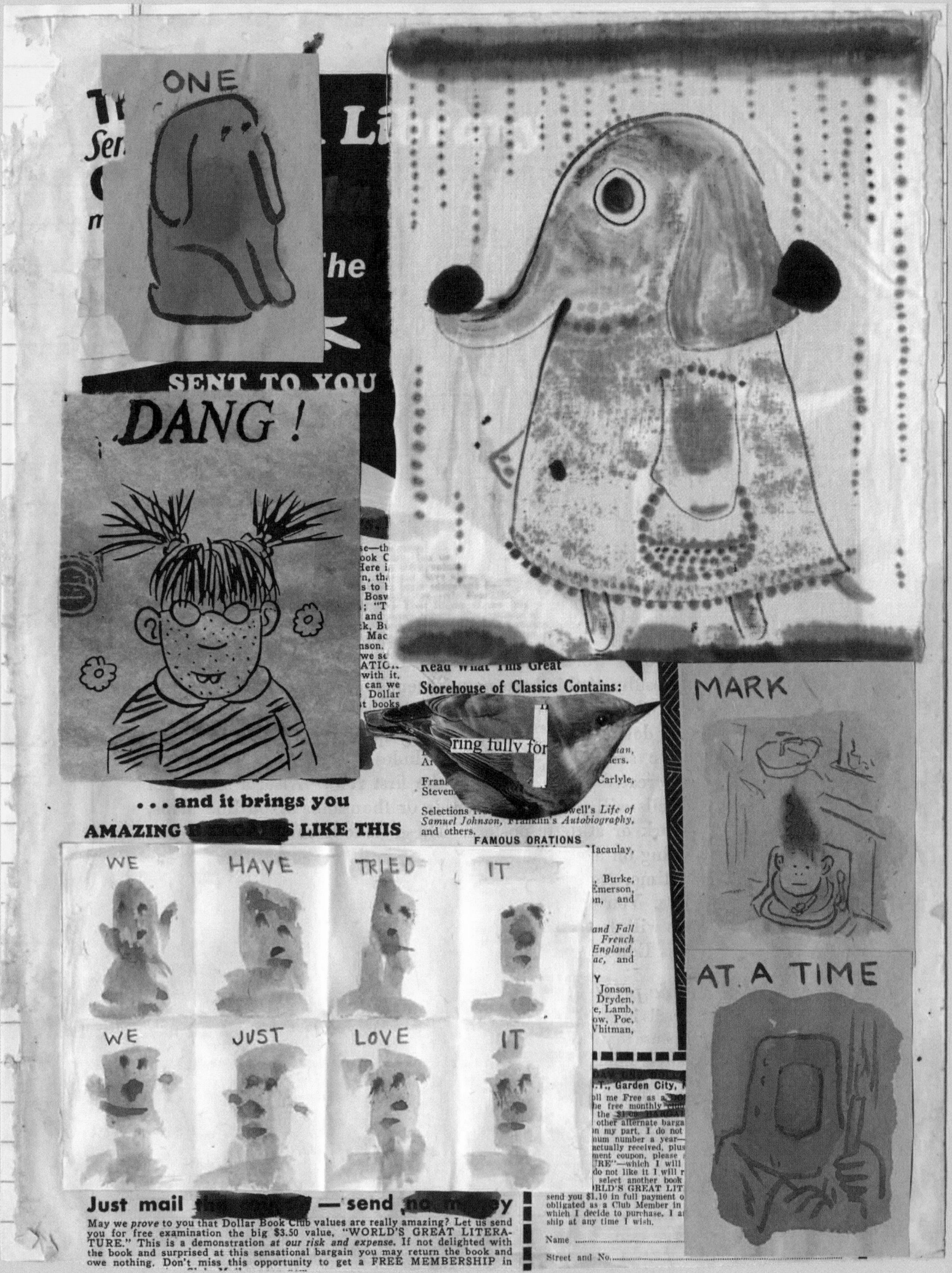
ONE
SENT TO YOU
DANG !
... and it brings you
AMAZING [redacted] LIKE THIS
WE HAVE TRIED IT
WE JUST LOVE IT
Storehouse of Classics Contains:
FAMOUS ORATIONS
MARK
AT A TIME
Just mail [redacted] — send [redacted]
May we prove to you that Dollar Book Club values are really amazing? Let us send you for free examination the big $3.50 value, "WORLD'S GREAT LITERATURE." This is a demonstration at our risk and expense. If not delighted with the book and surprised at this sensational bargain you may return the book and owe nothing. Don't miss this opportunity to get a FREE MEMBERSHIP in

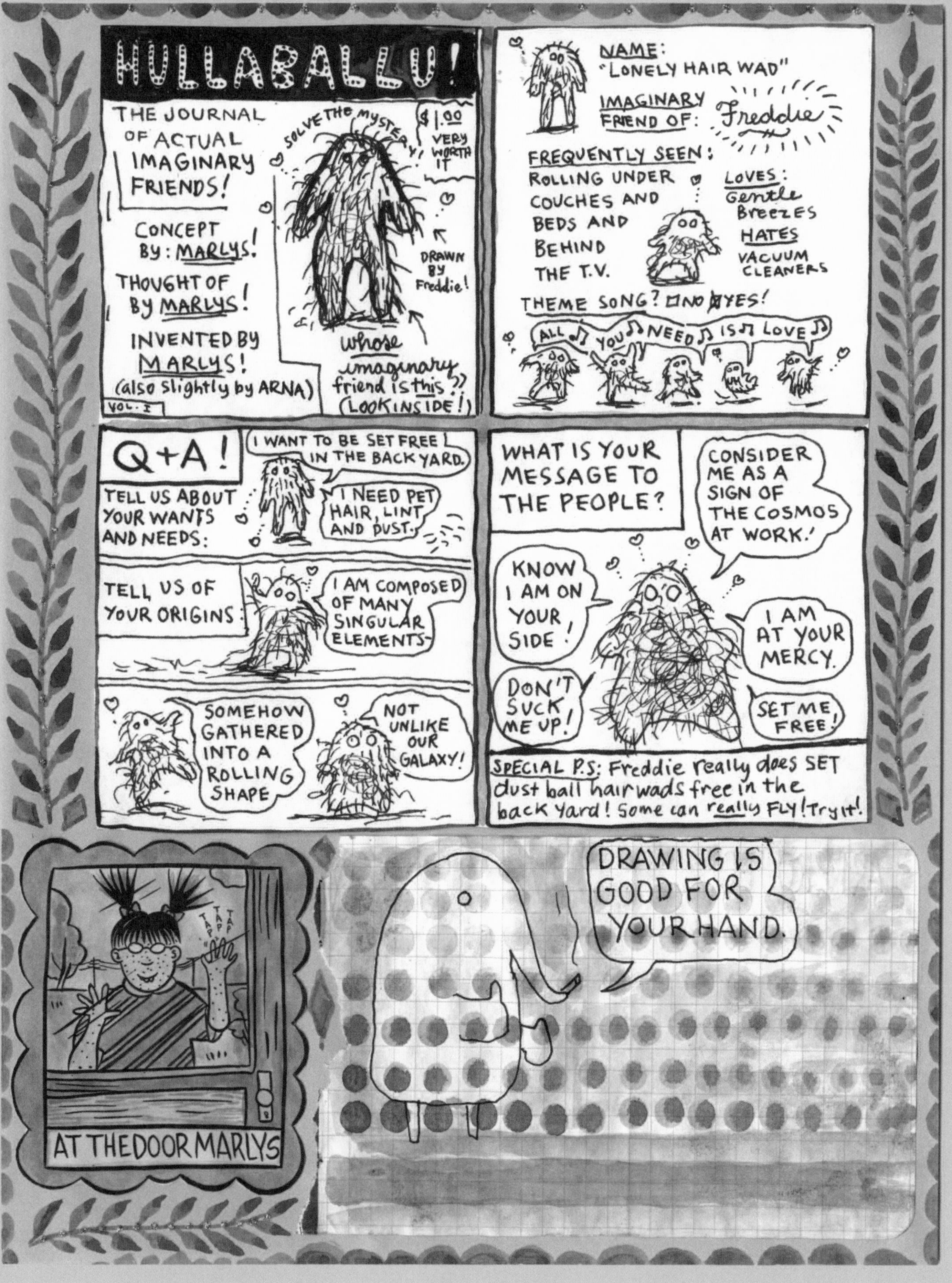
HULLABALLU!
THE JOURNAL OF ACTUAL IMAGINARY FRIENDS!
CONCEPT BY: MARLYS!
THOUGHT OF BY MARLYS!
INVENTED BY MARLYS!
(also slightly by ARNA)
VOL. I
SOLVE THE MYSTERY!
$1.00 VERY WORTH IT
DRAWN BY Freddie!
whose imaginary friend is this?? (LOOK INSIDE!)
NAME: "LONELY HAIR WAD"
IMAGINARY FRIEND OF: Freddie
FREQUENTLY SEEN: ROLLING UNDER COUCHES AND BEDS AND BEHIND THE T.V.
LOVES: Gentle Breezes
HATES VACUUM CLEANERS
THEME SONG? ☐NO ☒YES!
ALL YOU NEED IS LOVE
Q+A!
TELL US ABOUT YOUR WANTS AND NEEDS:
I WANT TO BE SET FREE IN THE BACK YARD.
I NEED PET HAIR, LINT AND DUST.
TELL US OF YOUR ORIGINS:
I AM COMPOSED OF MANY SINGULAR ELEMENTS-
SOMEHOW GATHERED INTO A ROLLING SHAPE
NOT UNLIKE OUR GALAXY!
WHAT IS YOUR MESSAGE TO THE PEOPLE?
CONSIDER ME AS A SIGN OF THE COSMOS AT WORK!
KNOW I AM ON YOUR SIDE!
I AM AT YOUR MERCY.
DON'T SUCK ME UP!
SET ME FREE!
SPECIAL P.S: Freddie really does SET dust ball hairwads free in the back yard! Some can really FLY! Try it!
TAP TAP TAP
AT THE DOOR MARLYS
DRAWING IS GOOD FOR YOUR HAND.

Pictures to copy, trace, color and paste

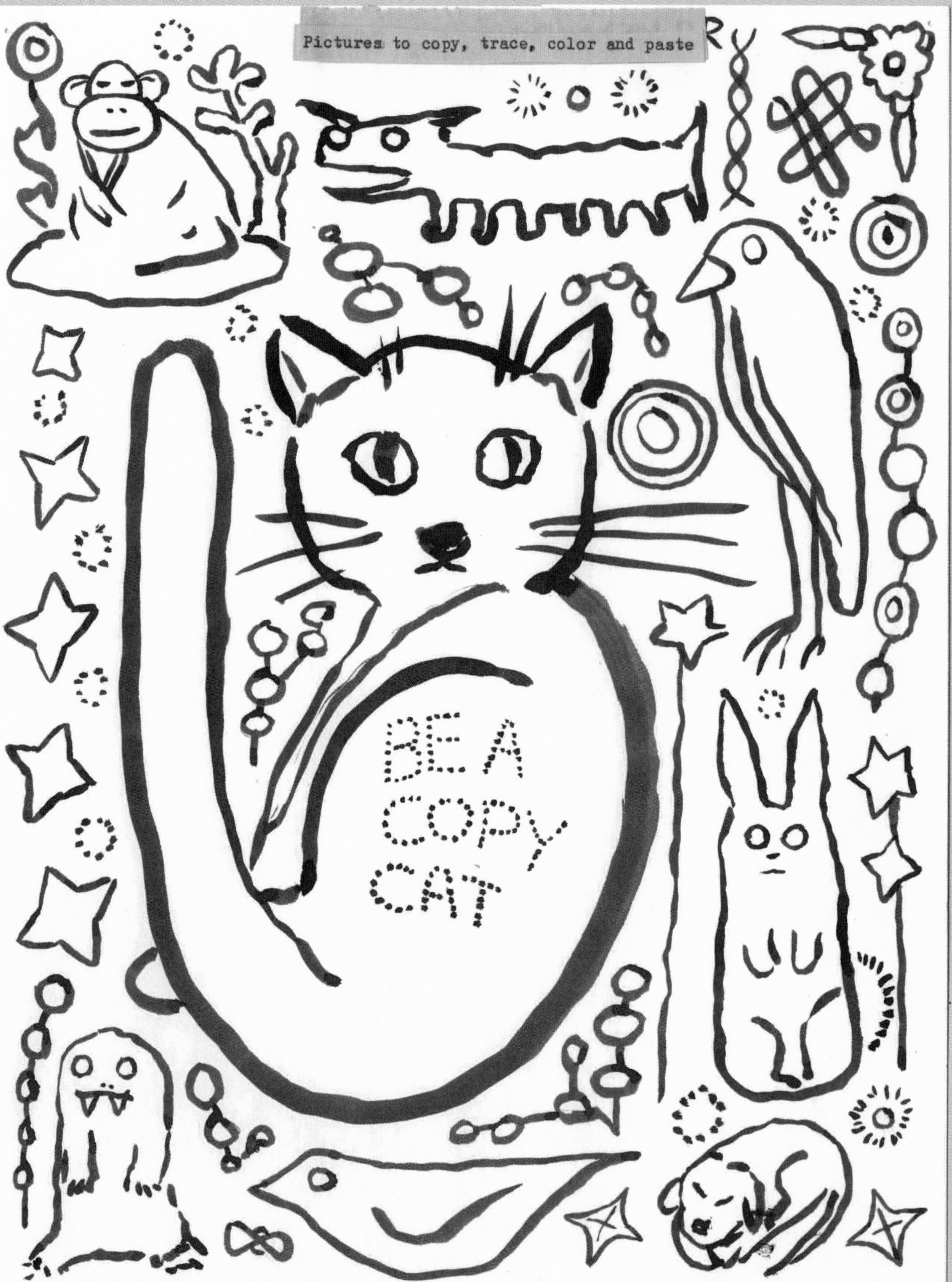
BE A
COPY
CAT

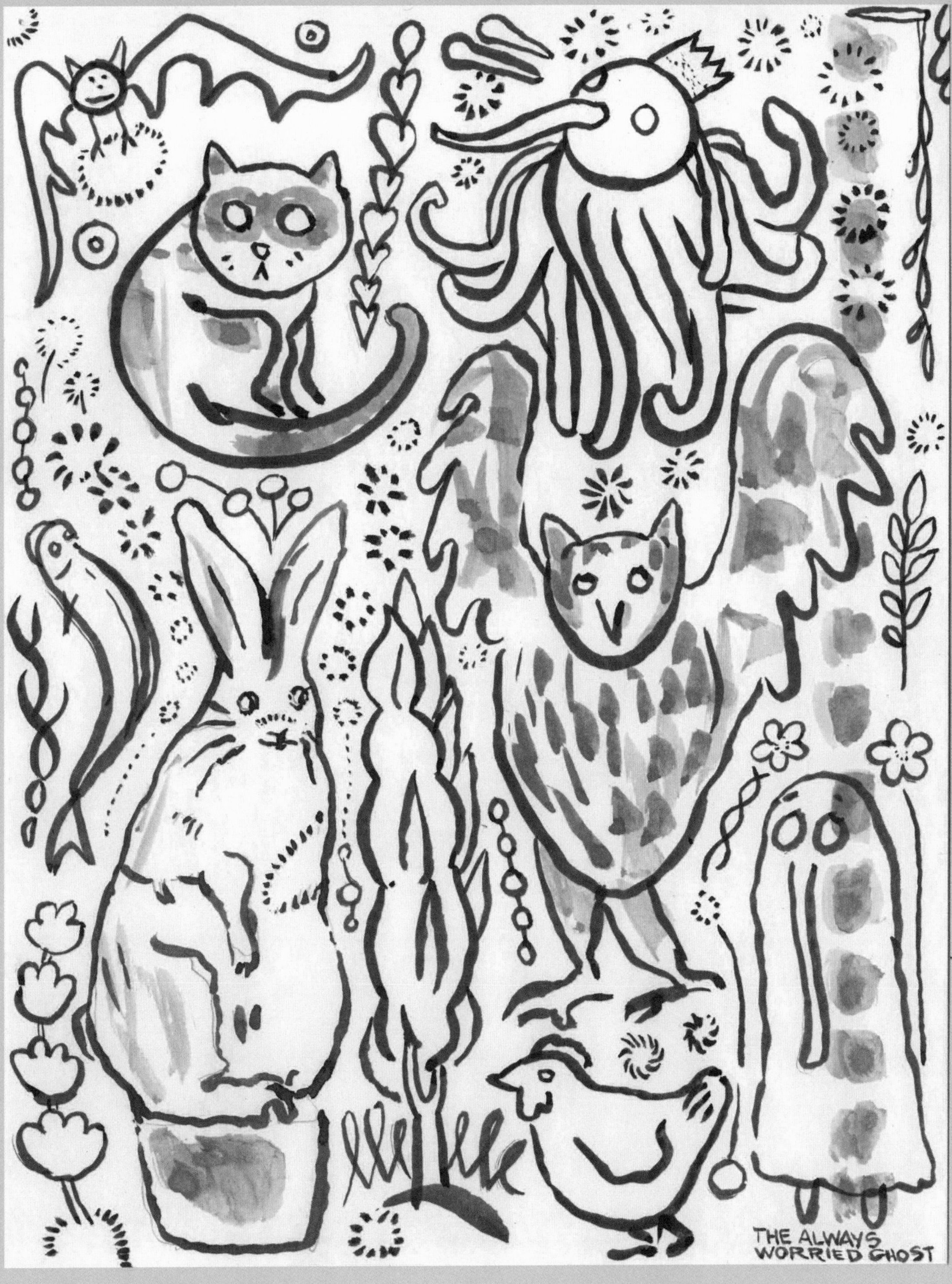
THE ALWAYS
WORRIED GHOST

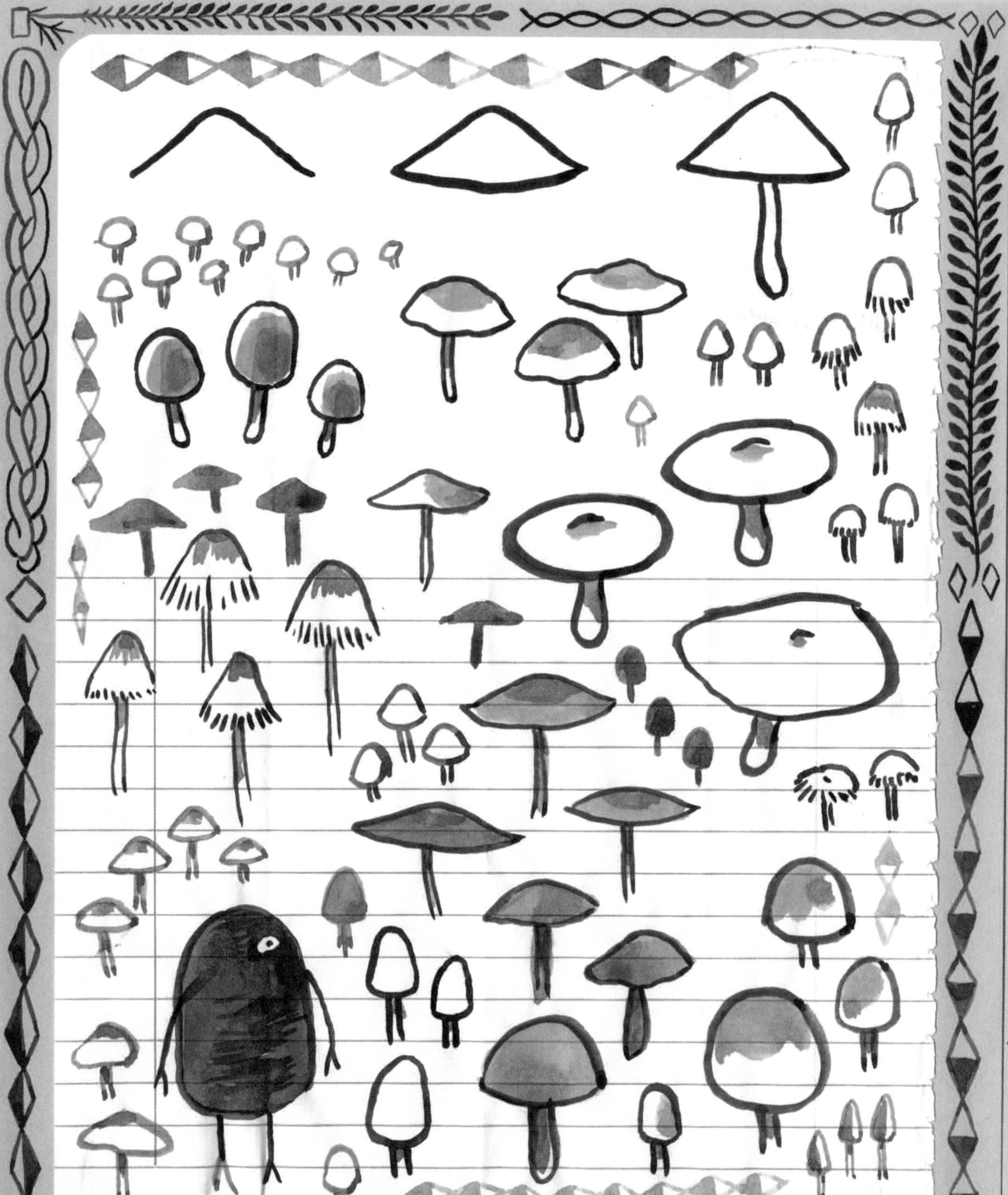
PLEASE NOTE: THERE IS NOTHIHG LAME ABOUT DRAWING FUNGUS.

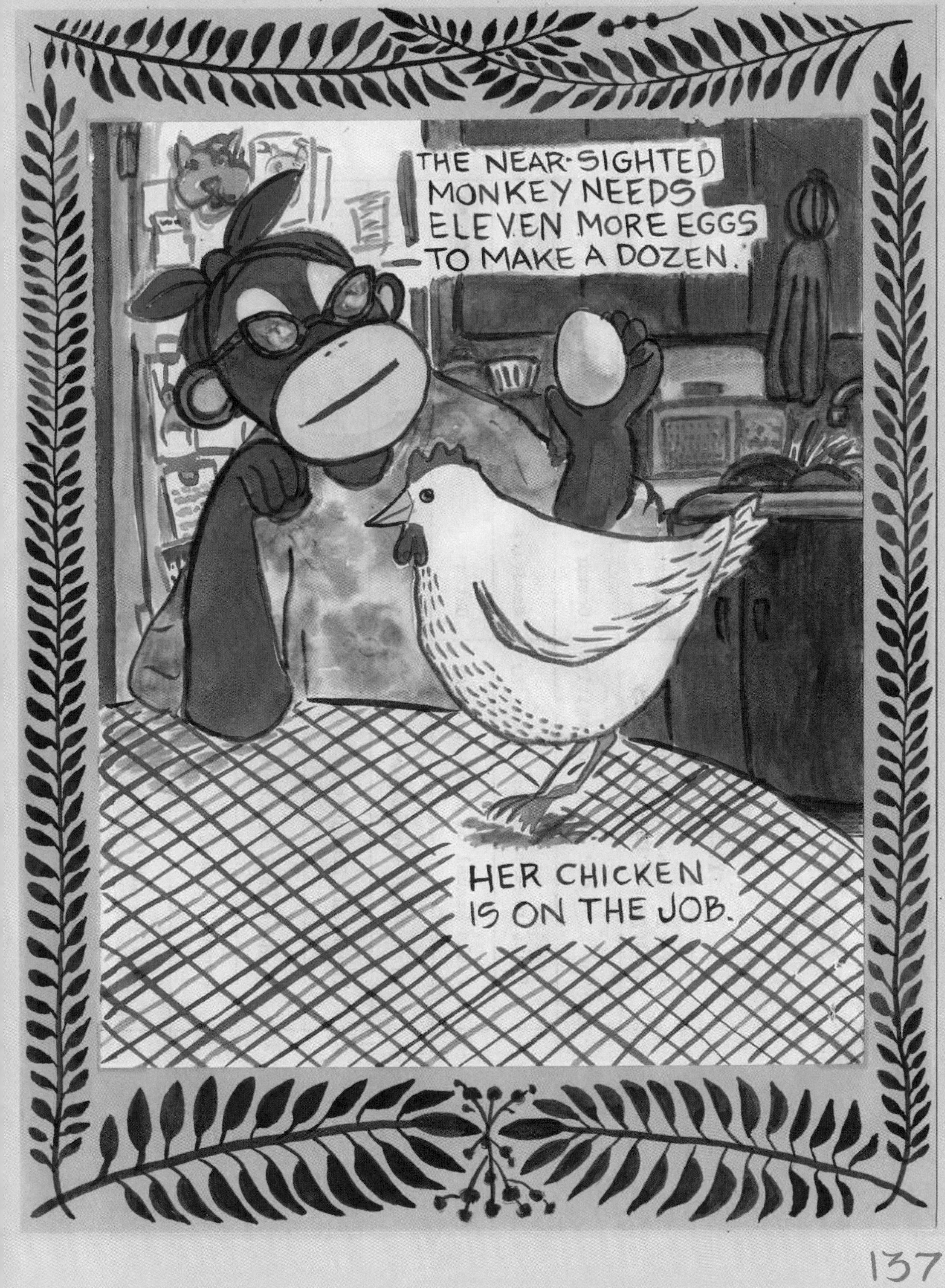
THE NEAR-SIGHTED MONKEY NEEDS ELEVEN MORE EGGS TO MAKE A DOZEN.
HER CHICKEN IS ON THE JOB.

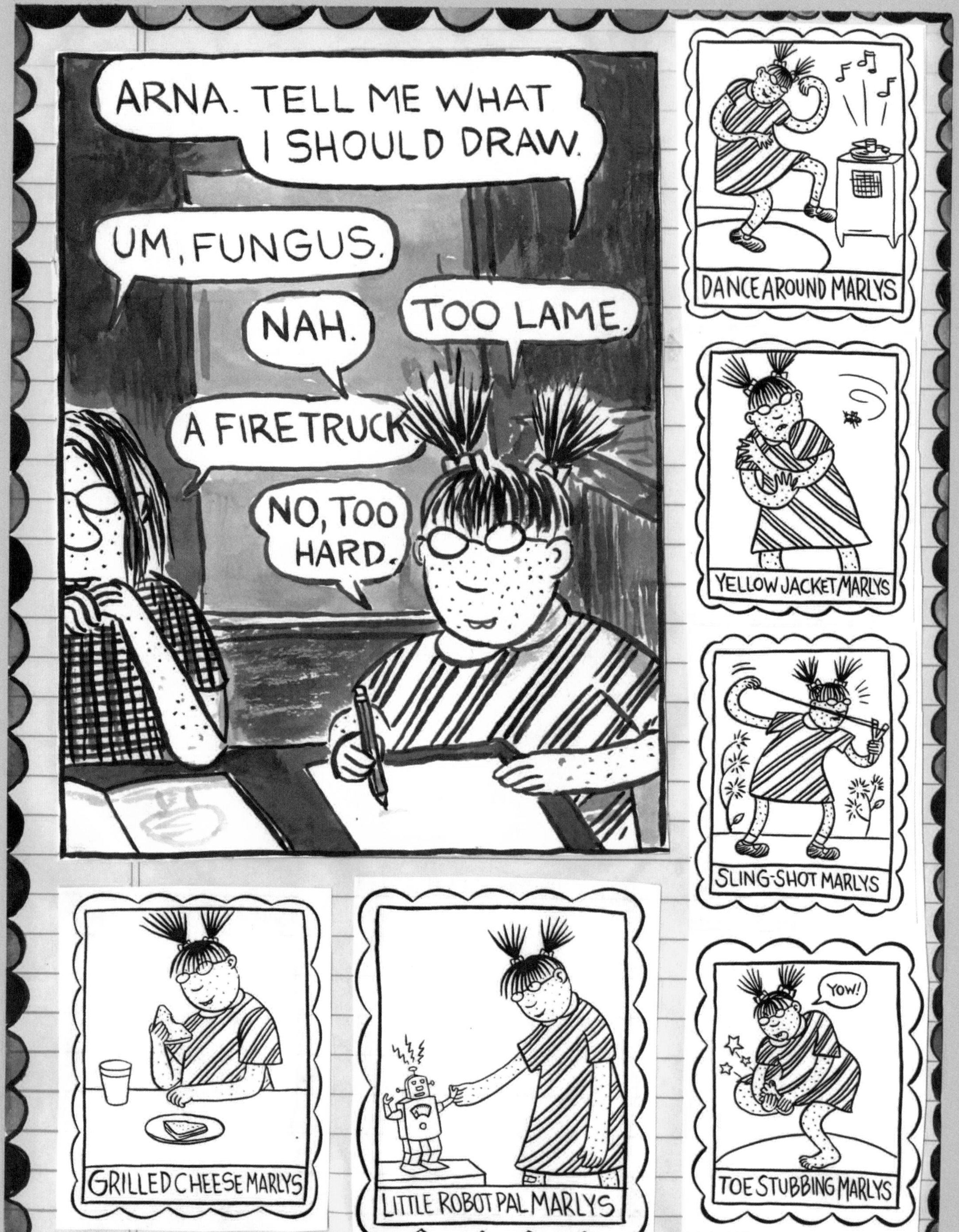
ARNA. TELL ME WHAT I SHOULD DRAW.
UM, FUNGUS.
NAH.
TOO LAME.
A FIRETRUCK.
NO, TOO HARD.
DANCE AROUND MARLYS
YELLOW JACKET MARLYS
SLING-SHOT MARLYS
GRILLED CHEESE MARLYS
LITTLE ROBOT PAL MARLYS
YOW!
TOE STUBBING MARLYS

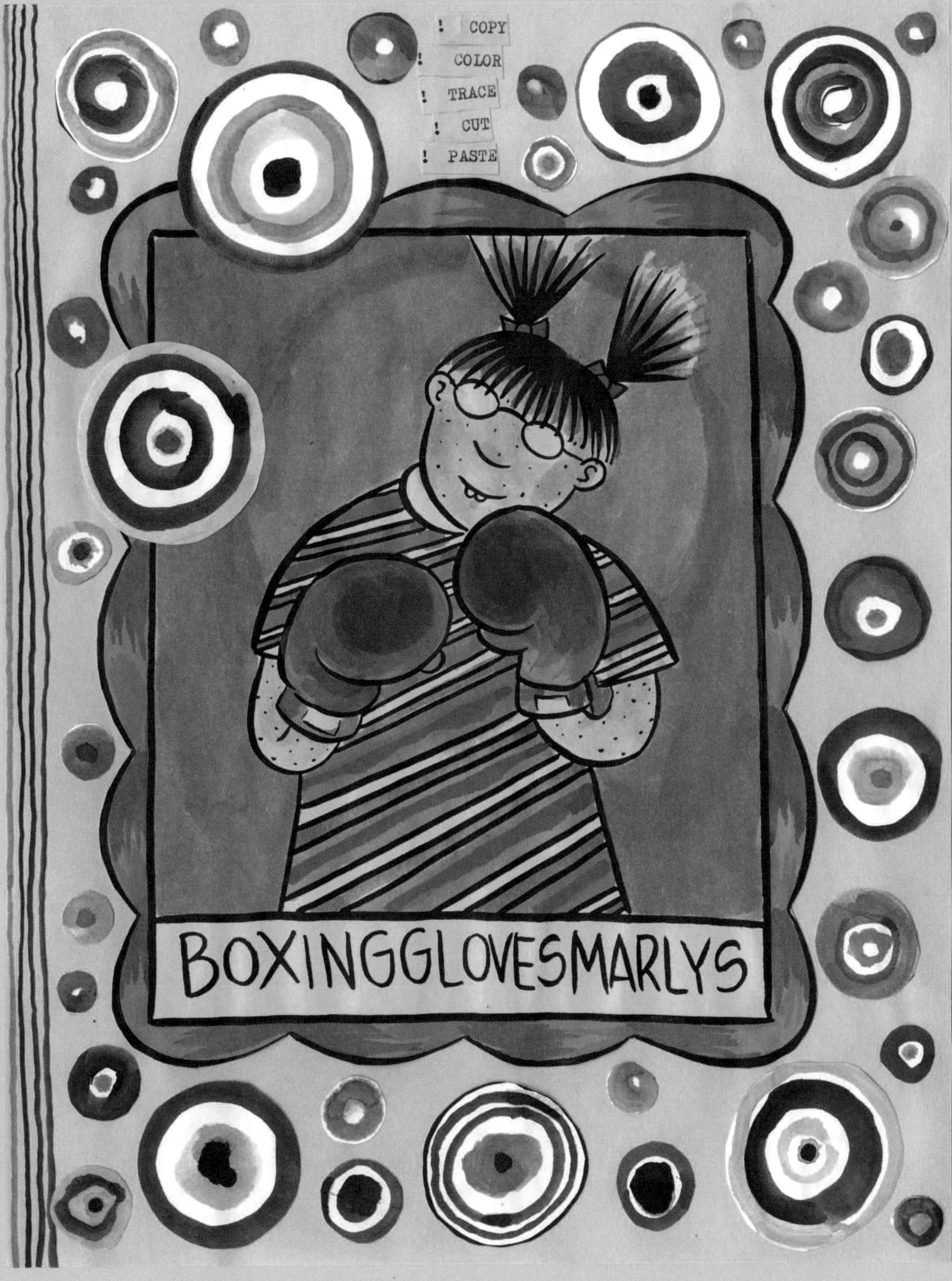
! COPY
! COLOR
! TRACE
! CUT
! PASTE
BOXINGGLOVESMARLYS

COPY

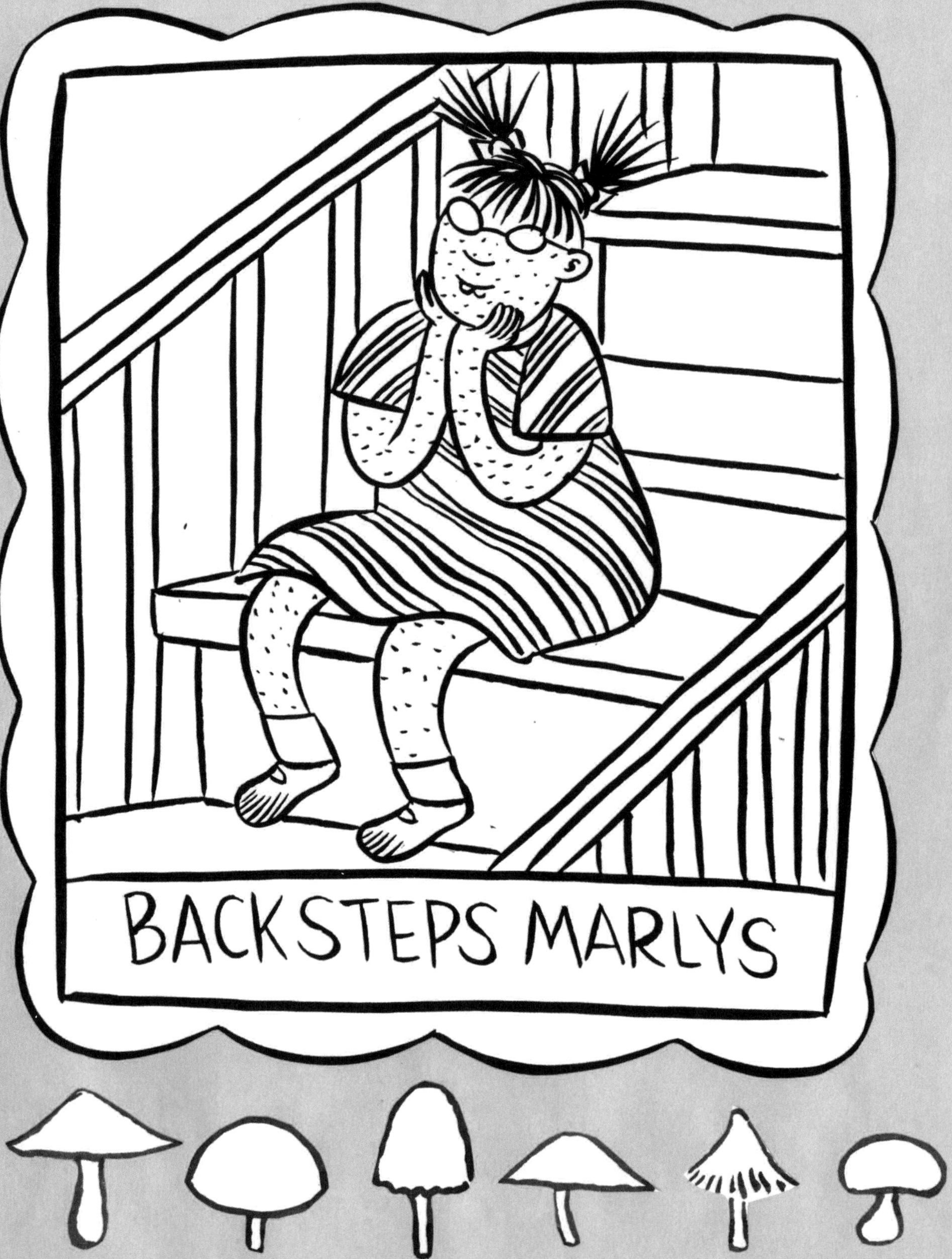
BACKSTEPS MARLYS

COLOR

HULA MARLYS!

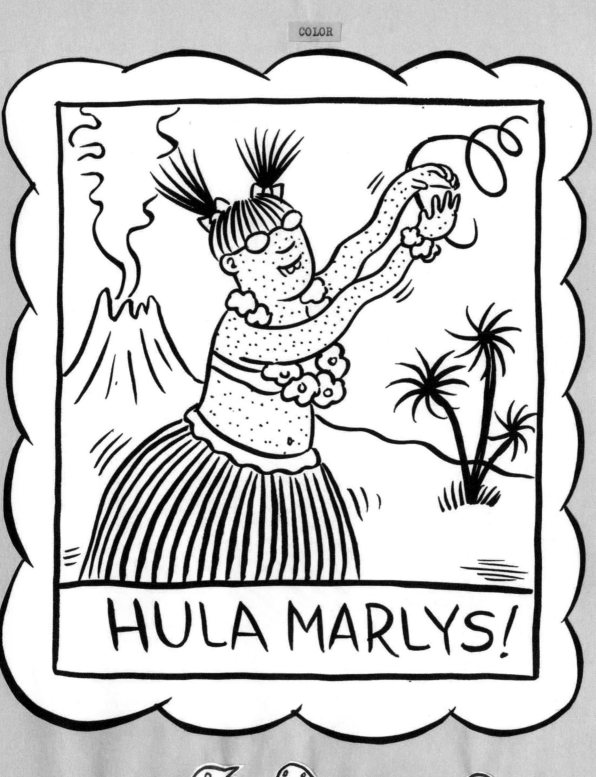

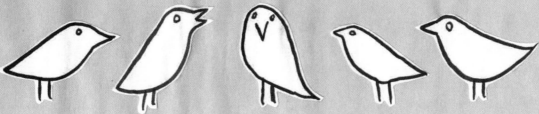

TRACE

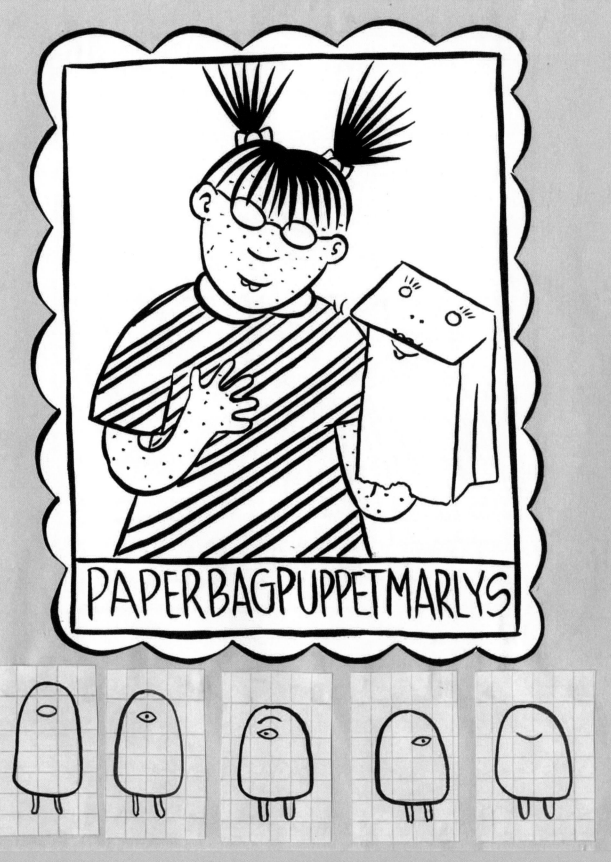

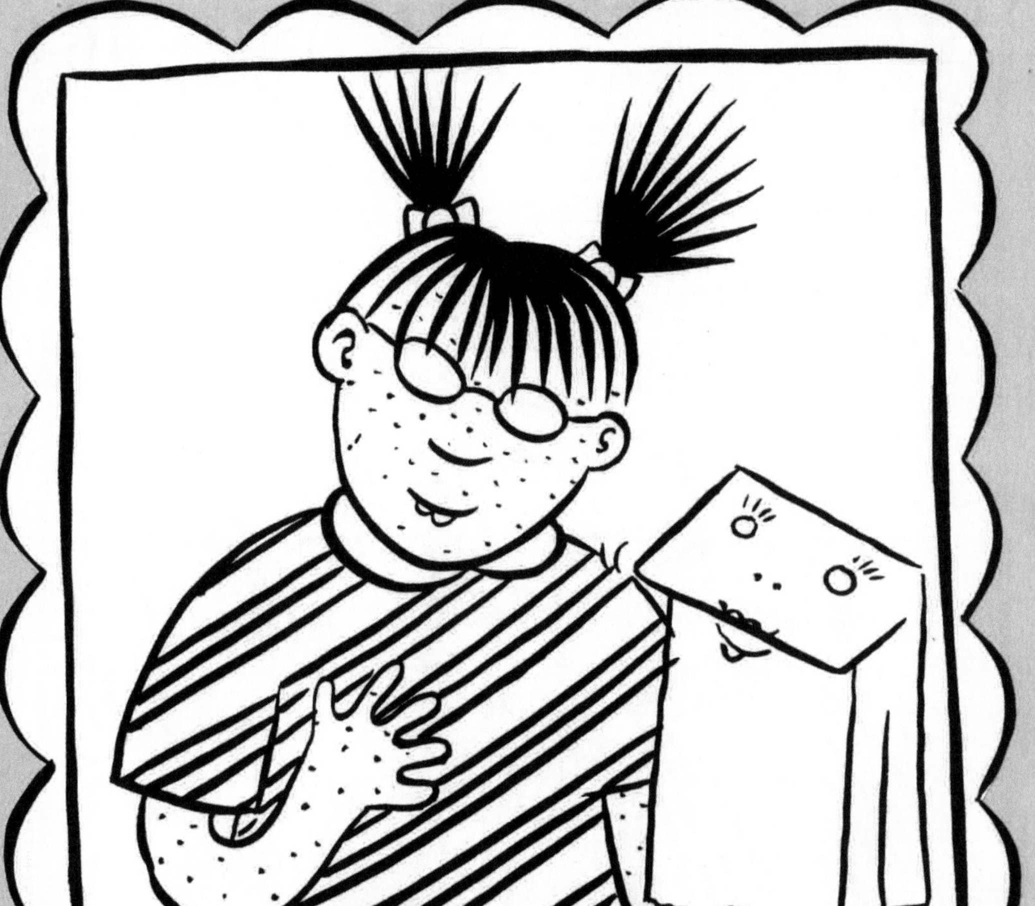
PAPERBAGPUPPETMARLYS

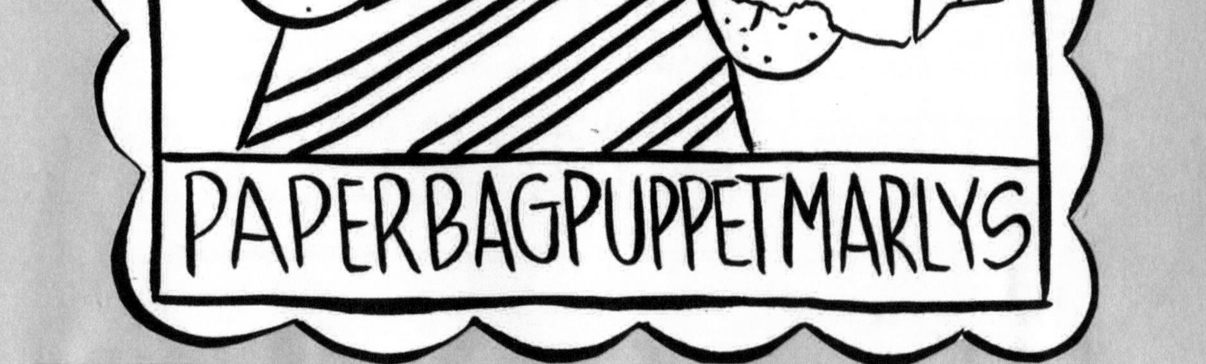

CUT

11
TRAILER PARK MARLYS!

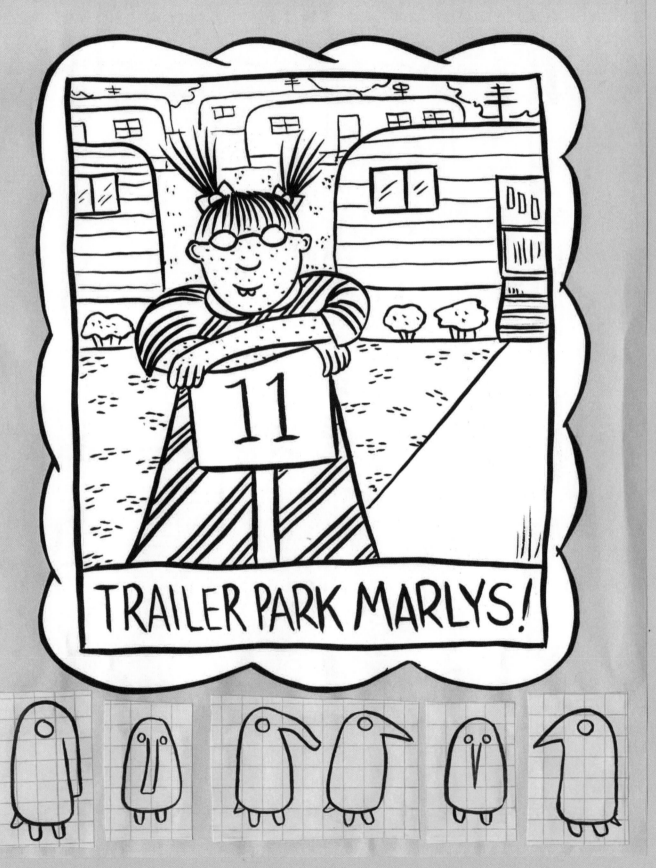

PASTE

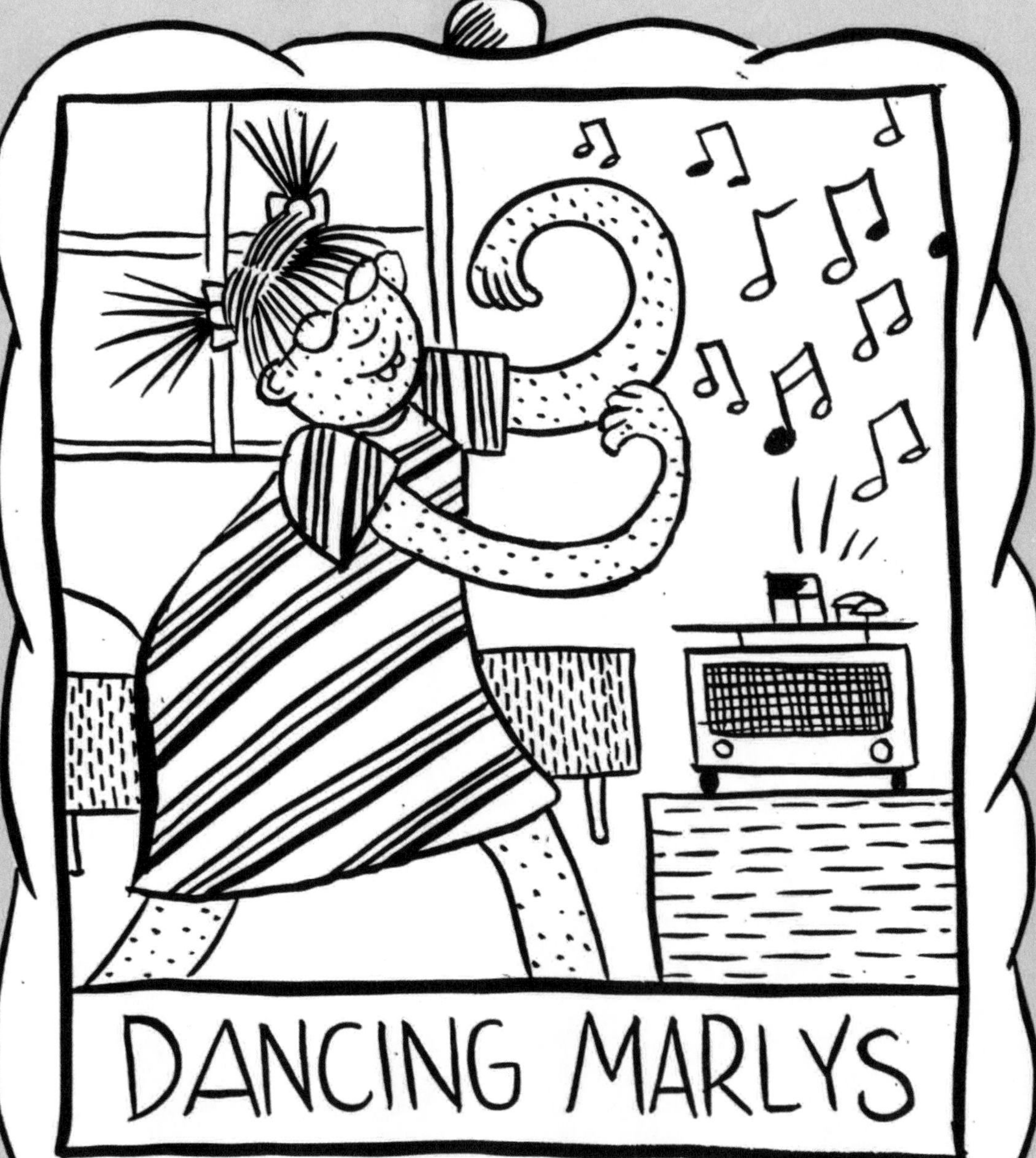
DANCING MARLYS

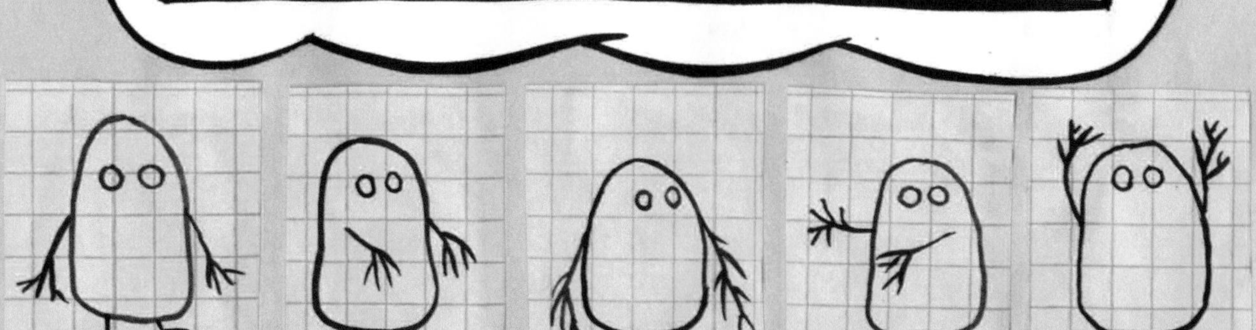

SEAR'S PORTRAIT MARLYS

Cotton swabs and food coloring are art supplies for days when you want to color a picture but don't have regular brushes and paints.

You mix a drop of food coloring with a few drops of water on a plate and mess around. making rows of dots and letting them dry before dotting on another color will give you something to think about. What is it?

This picture was colored in with food coloring and cotton swabs

... take a dance break with "Twirlita" (this is the near-sighted monkey's favorite show)

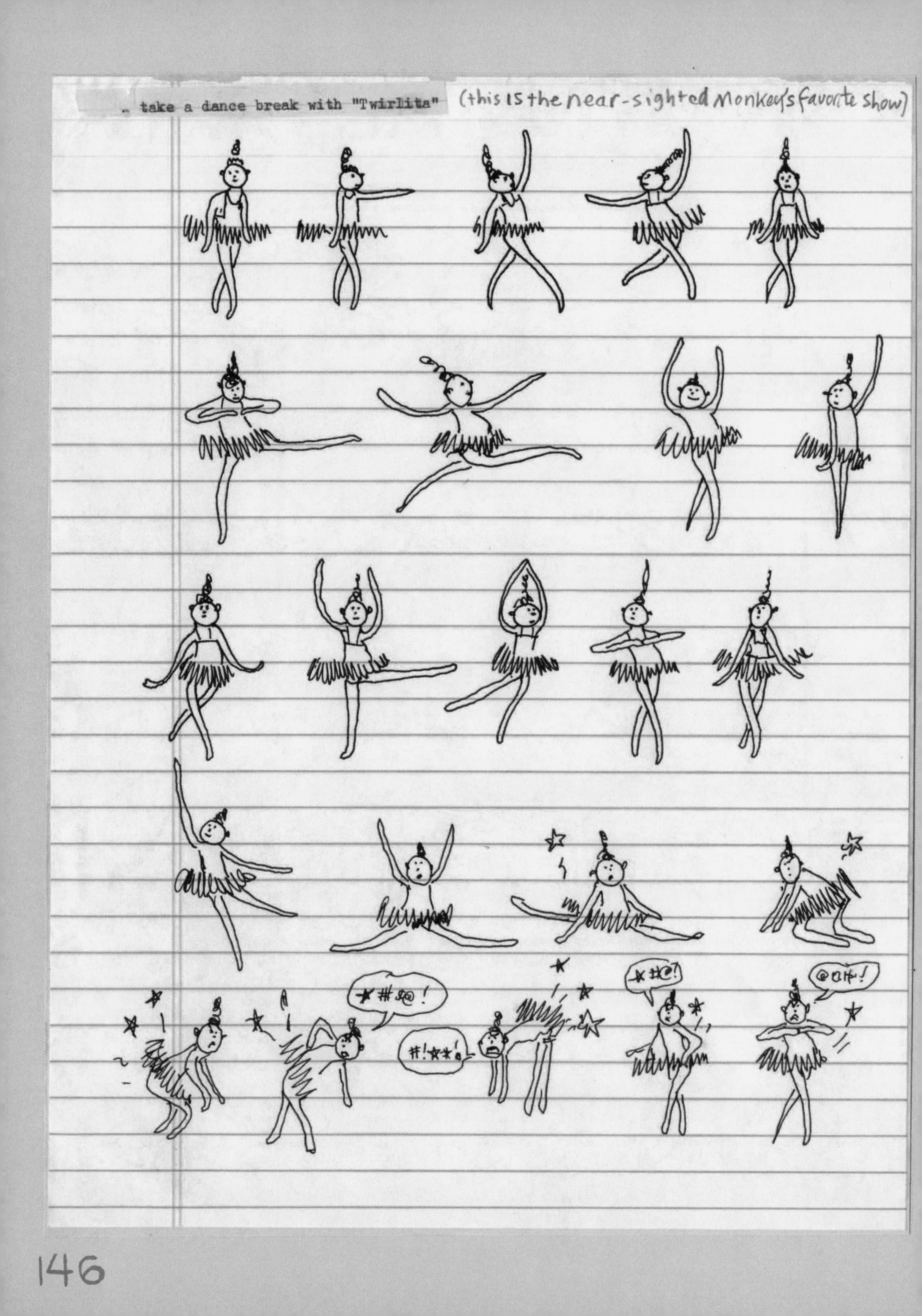

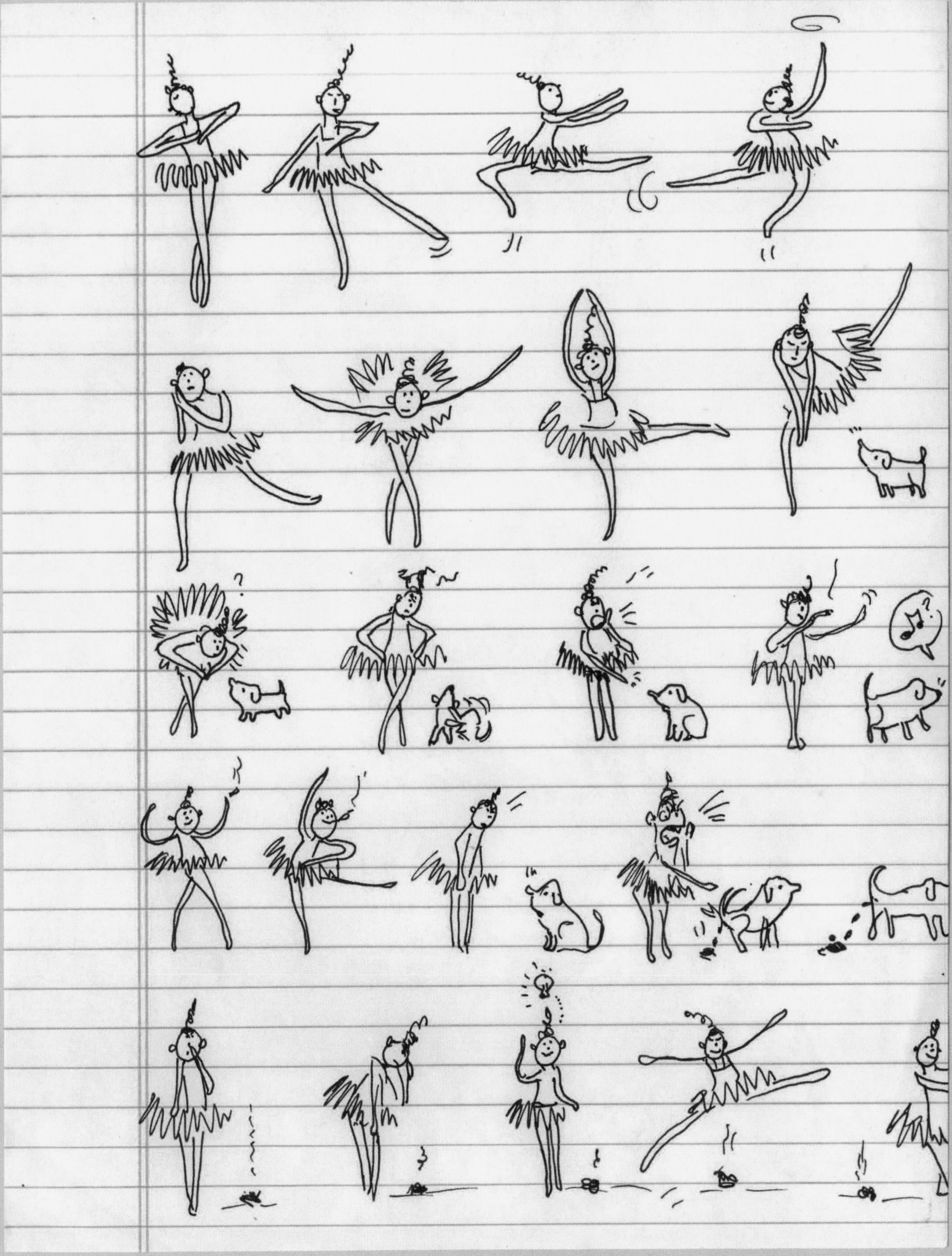

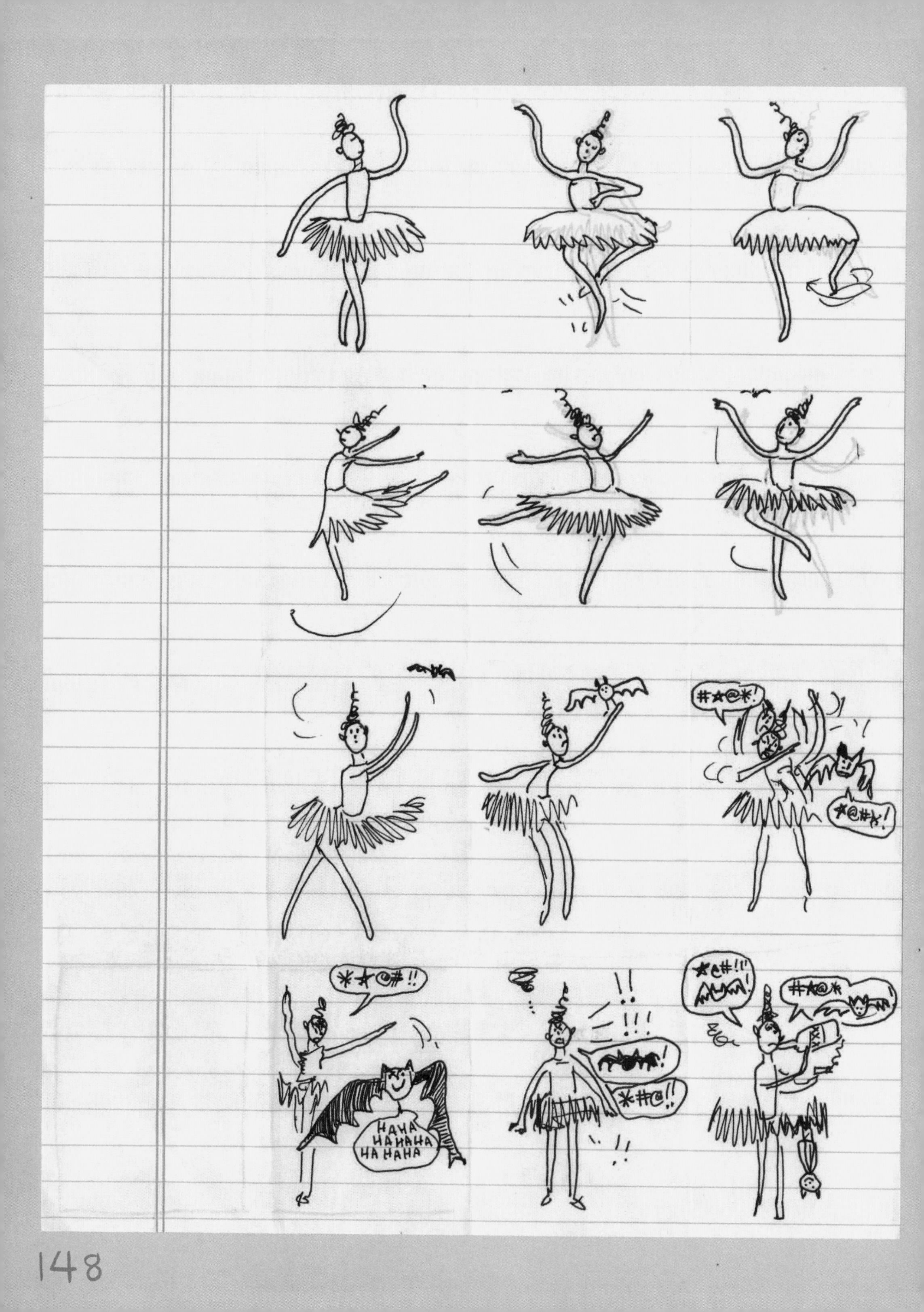

HAHA
HAHAHA
HAHAHA

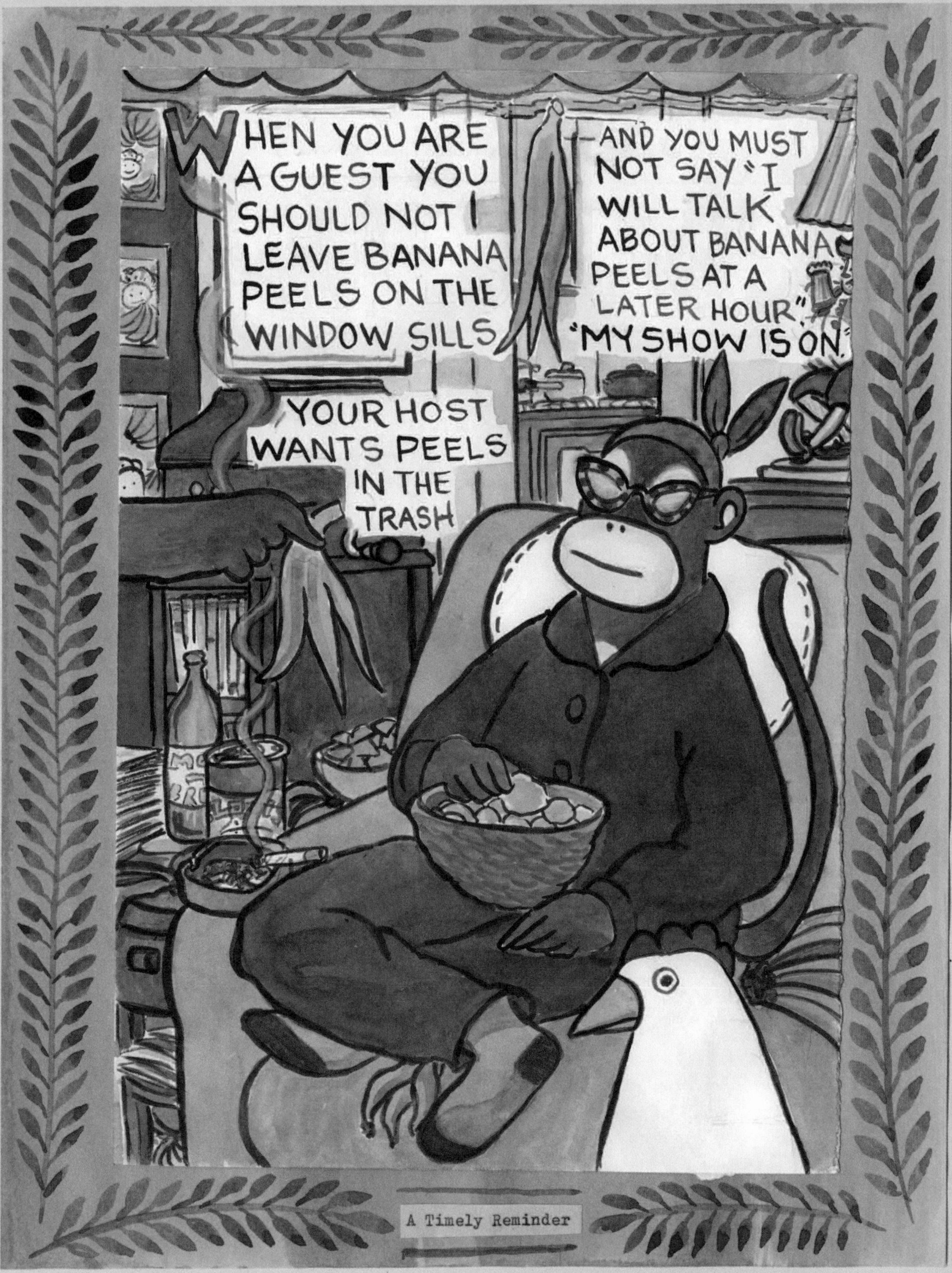
WHEN YOU ARE A GUEST YOU SHOULD NOT LEAVE BANANA PEELS ON THE WINDOW SILLS
YOUR HOST WANTS PEELS IN THE TRASH
-AND YOU MUST NOT SAY "I WILL TALK ABOUT BANANA PEELS AT A LATER HOUR". "MY SHOW IS ON."

A Timely Reminder

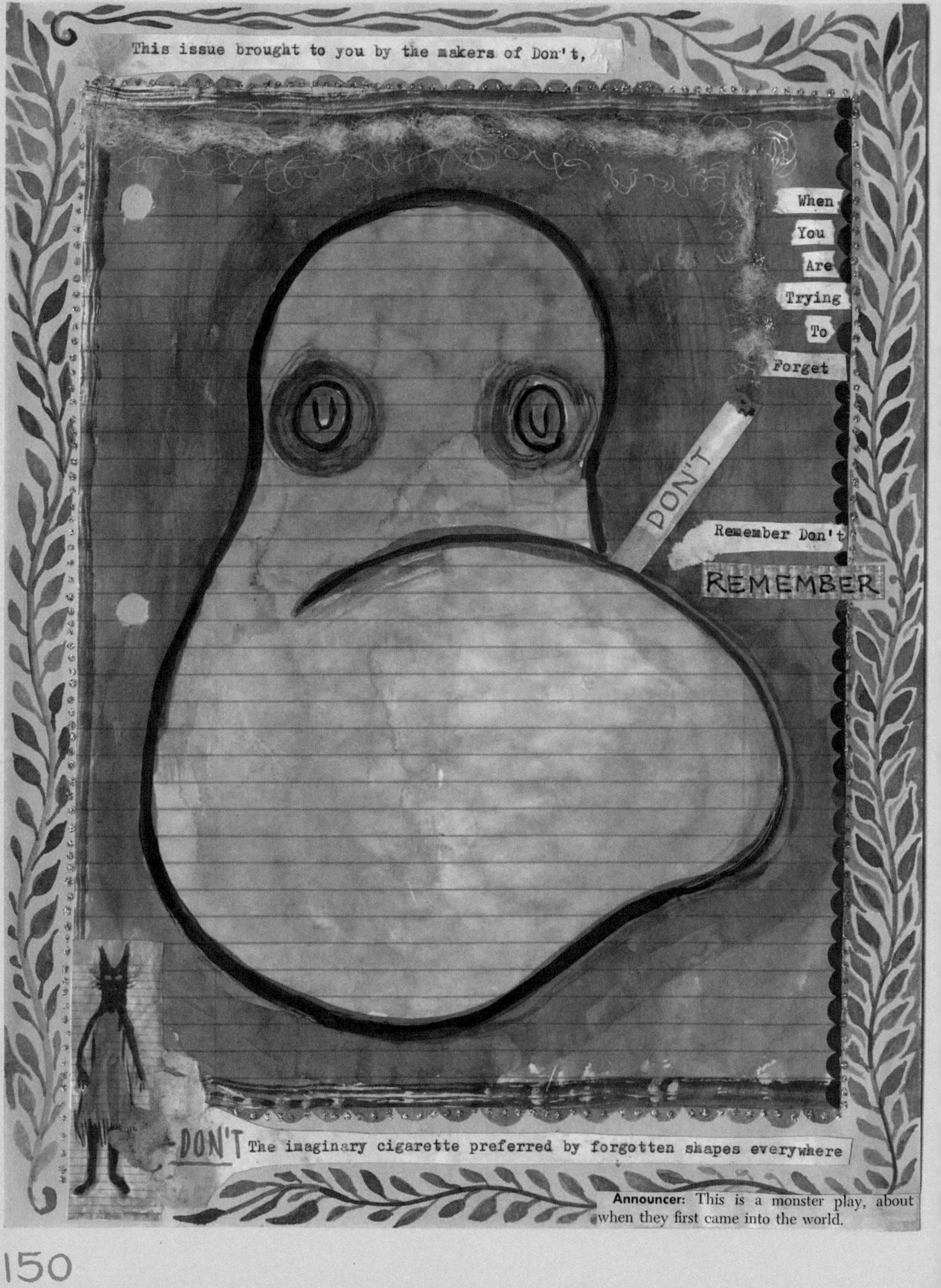
This issue brought to you by the makers of Don't,
When You Are Trying To Forget
DON'T
Remember Don't
REMEMBER
DON'T The imaginary cigarette preferred by forgotten shapes everywhere
Announcer: This is a monster play, about when they first came into the world.

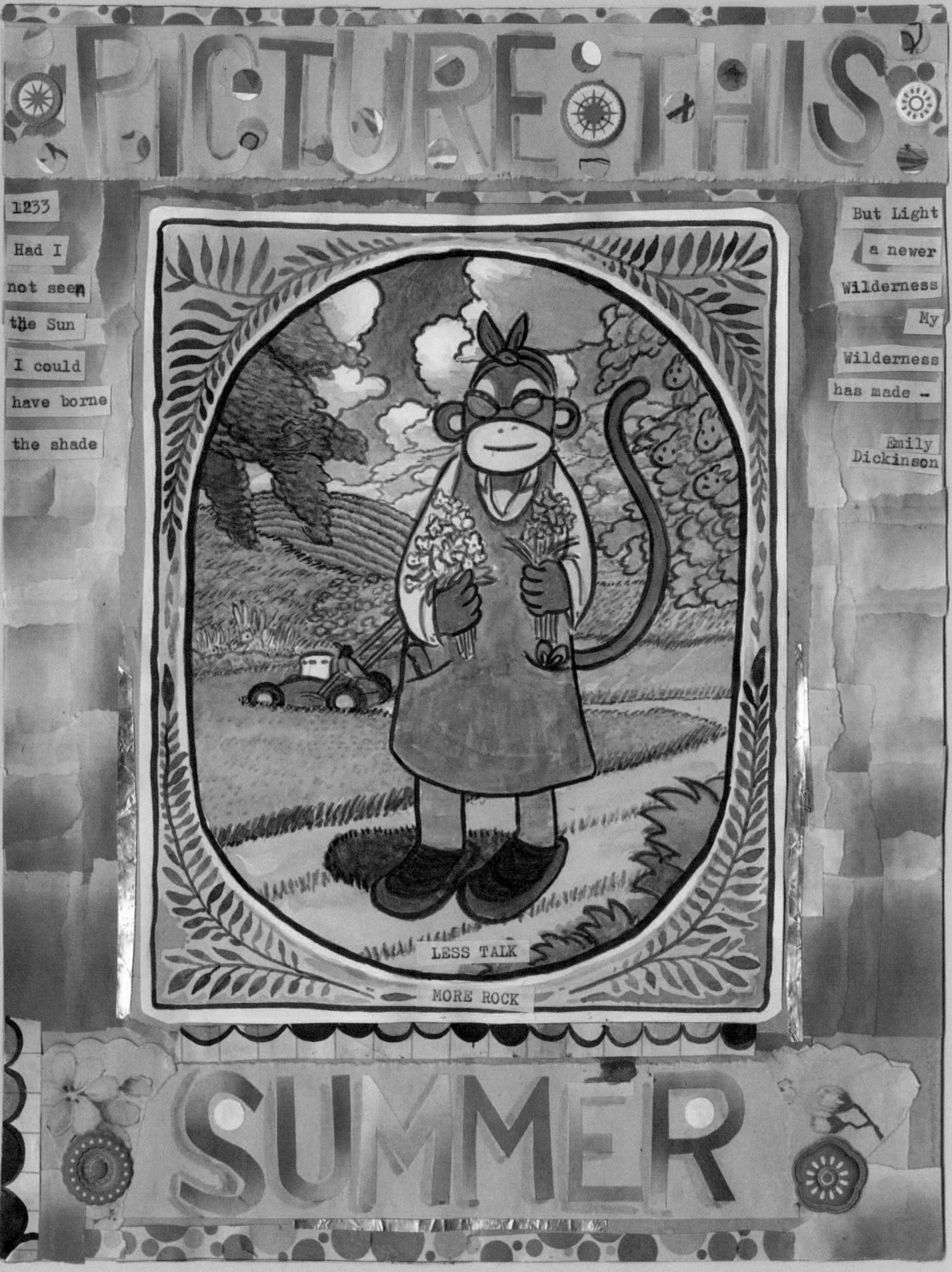
PICTURE THIS
1233
Had I
not seen
the Sun
I could
have borne
the shade
But Light
a newer
Wilderness
My
Wilderness
has made -
Emily
Dickinson
LESS TALK
MORE ROCK
SUMMER

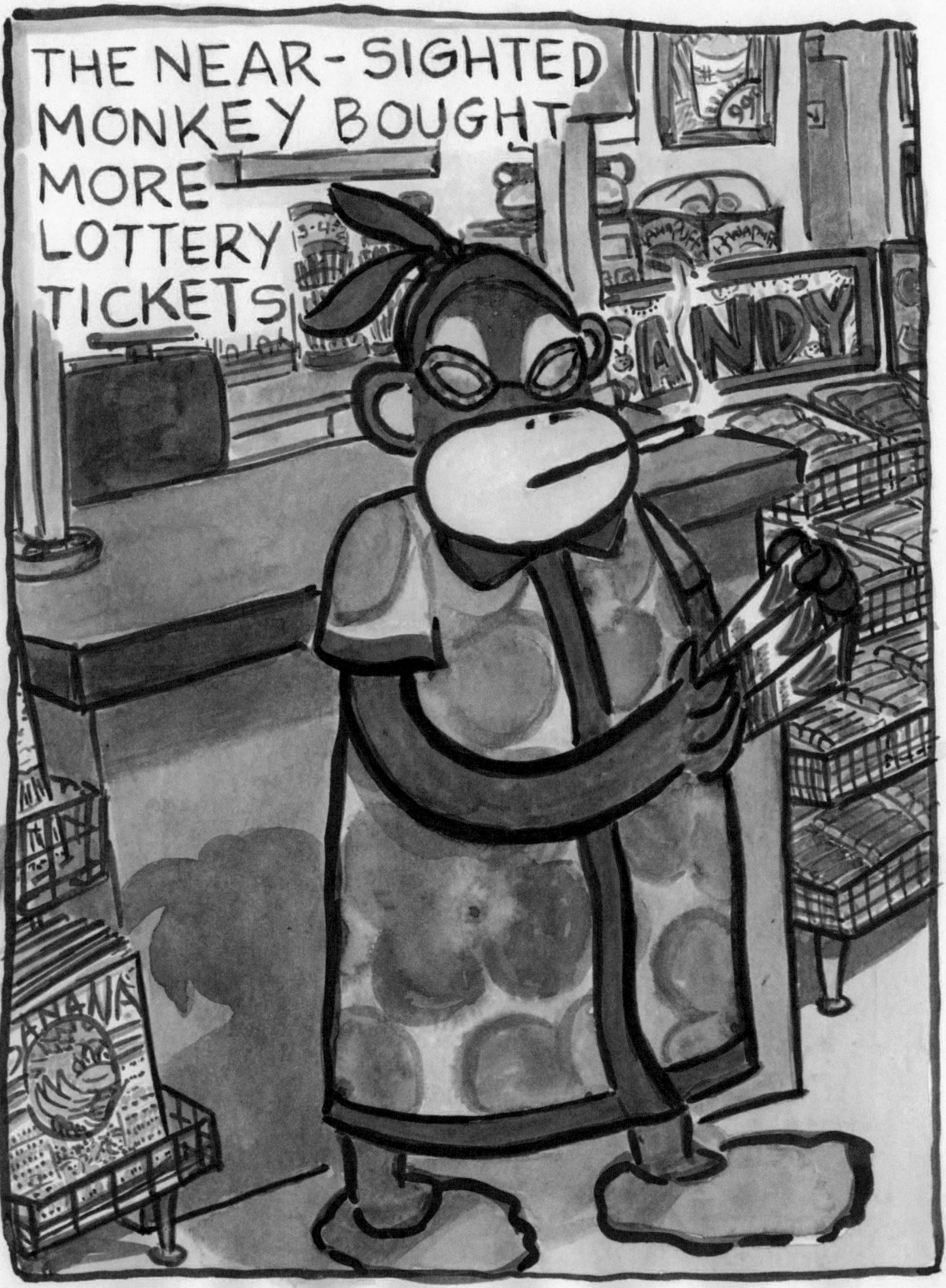
THE NEAR-SIGHTED MONKEY BOUGHT MORE LOTTERY TICKETS
ANDY
BANANA

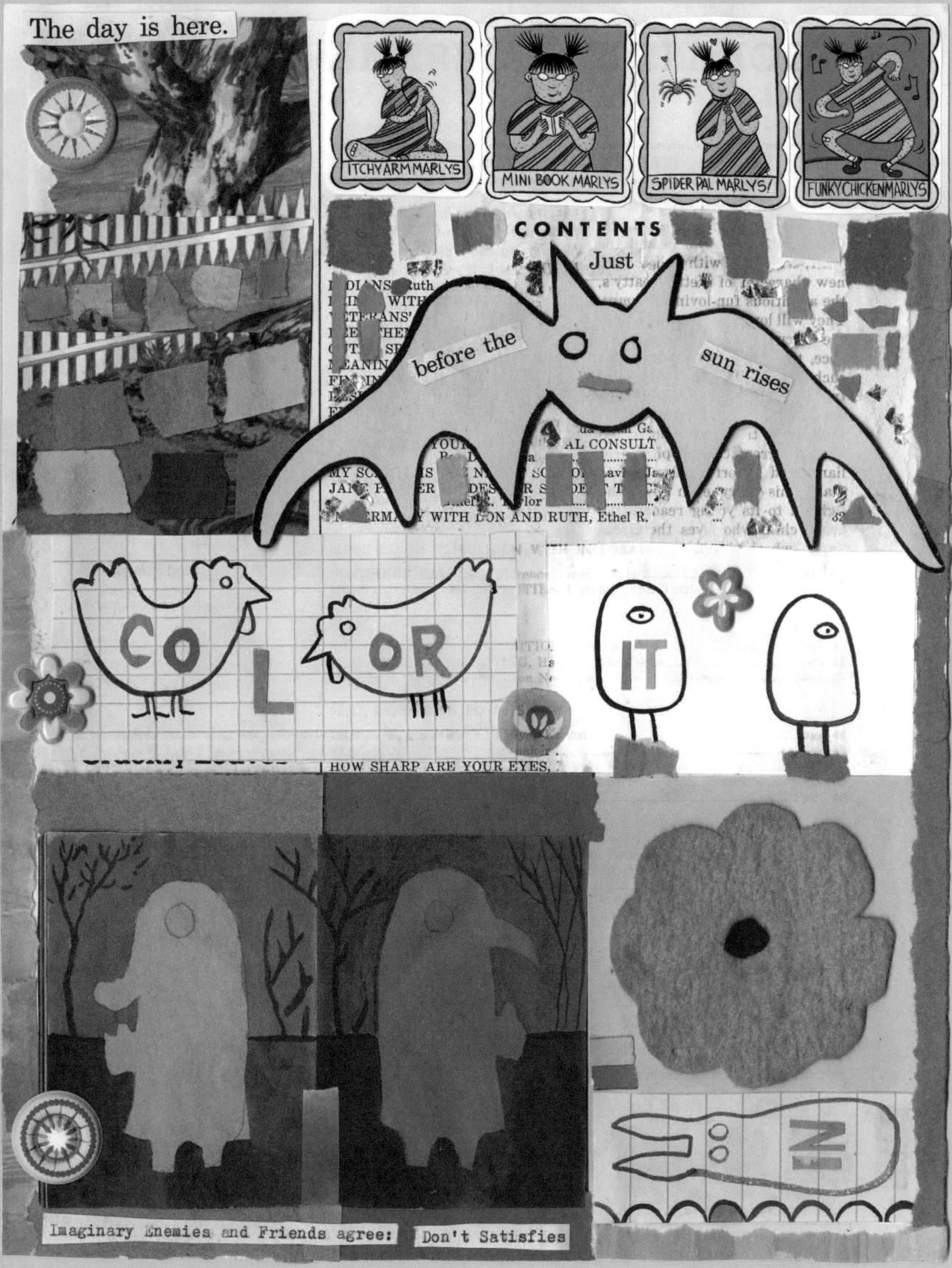

The day is here.
ITCHY ARM MARLYS
MINI BOOK MARLYS
SPIDER PAL MARLYS!
FUNKY CHICKEN MARLYS
CONTENTS
Just
before the
sun rises
CO L OR
IT
HOW SHARP ARE YOUR EYES,
Imaginary Enemies and Friends agree:
Don't Satisfies

If the Sun & Moon should doubt,
FISH STICK MARLYS
BEAN PLANT MARLYS
BIRTHDAY CAKE MARLYS
COIL METHOD MARLYS
DANCING MARLYS!
WHAT HAPPENS WHEN CERTAIN COLORS GET TOGETHER?

Sure was nice to hear from you & I suppose you thought we have forgotten about you but we haven't
BAKERY WINDOW MARLYS
TNT BUNNY
ABC
Drink
MOO Maid MILK
ICE
COFFEE CUP SQUIRREL
ABCDEFGHIJ
KLMNOPQR
STUVWXYZ

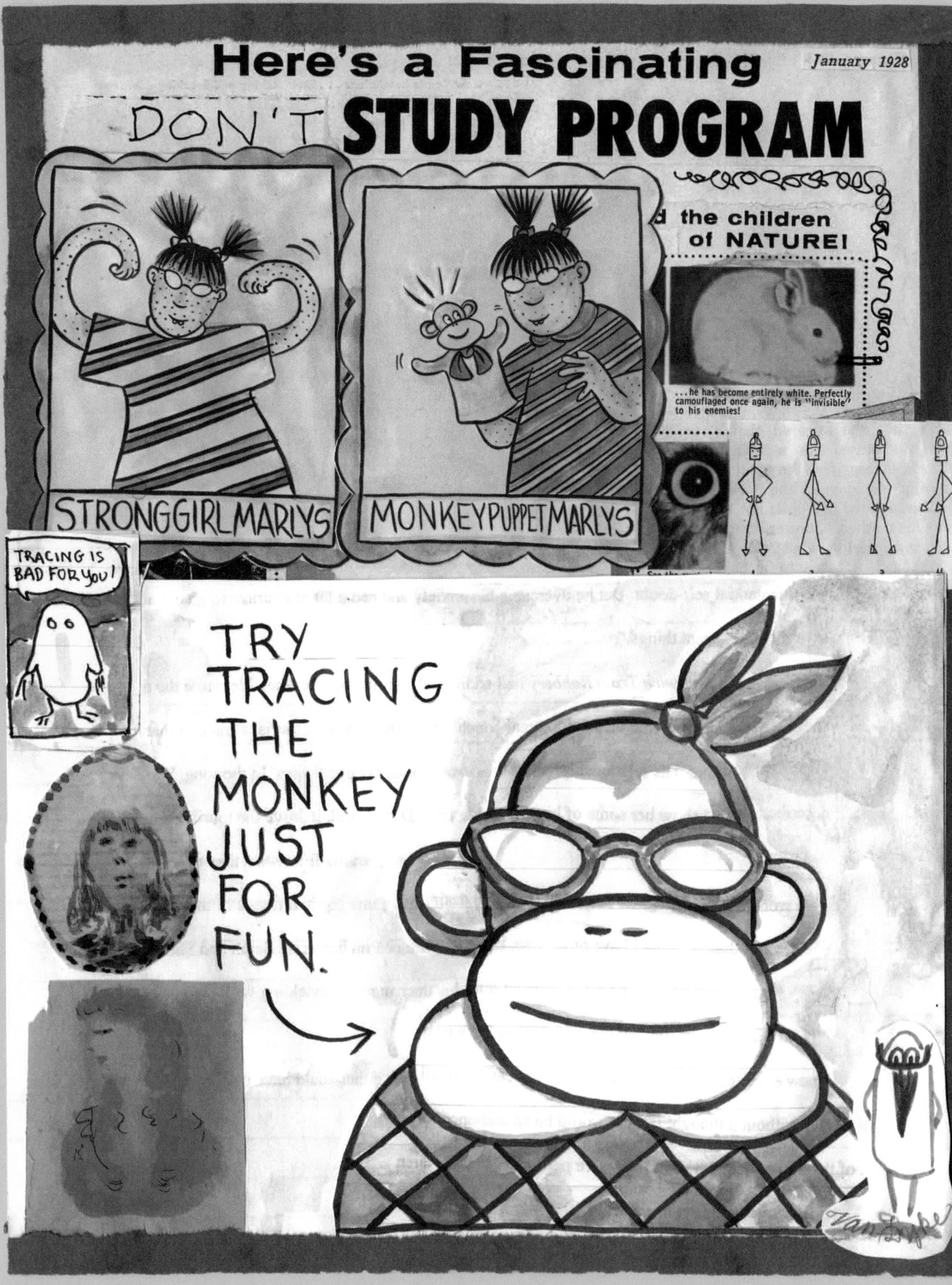
Here's a Fascinating
January 1928
DON'T STUDY PROGRAM
STRONGGIRLMARLYS
MONKEYPUPPETMARLYS
the children
of NATURE!
. . . he has become entirely white. Perfectly camouflaged once again, he is "invisible" to his enemies!
TRACING IS BAD FOR YOU!
TRY TRACING THE MONKEY JUST FOR FUN.
Van Dyke

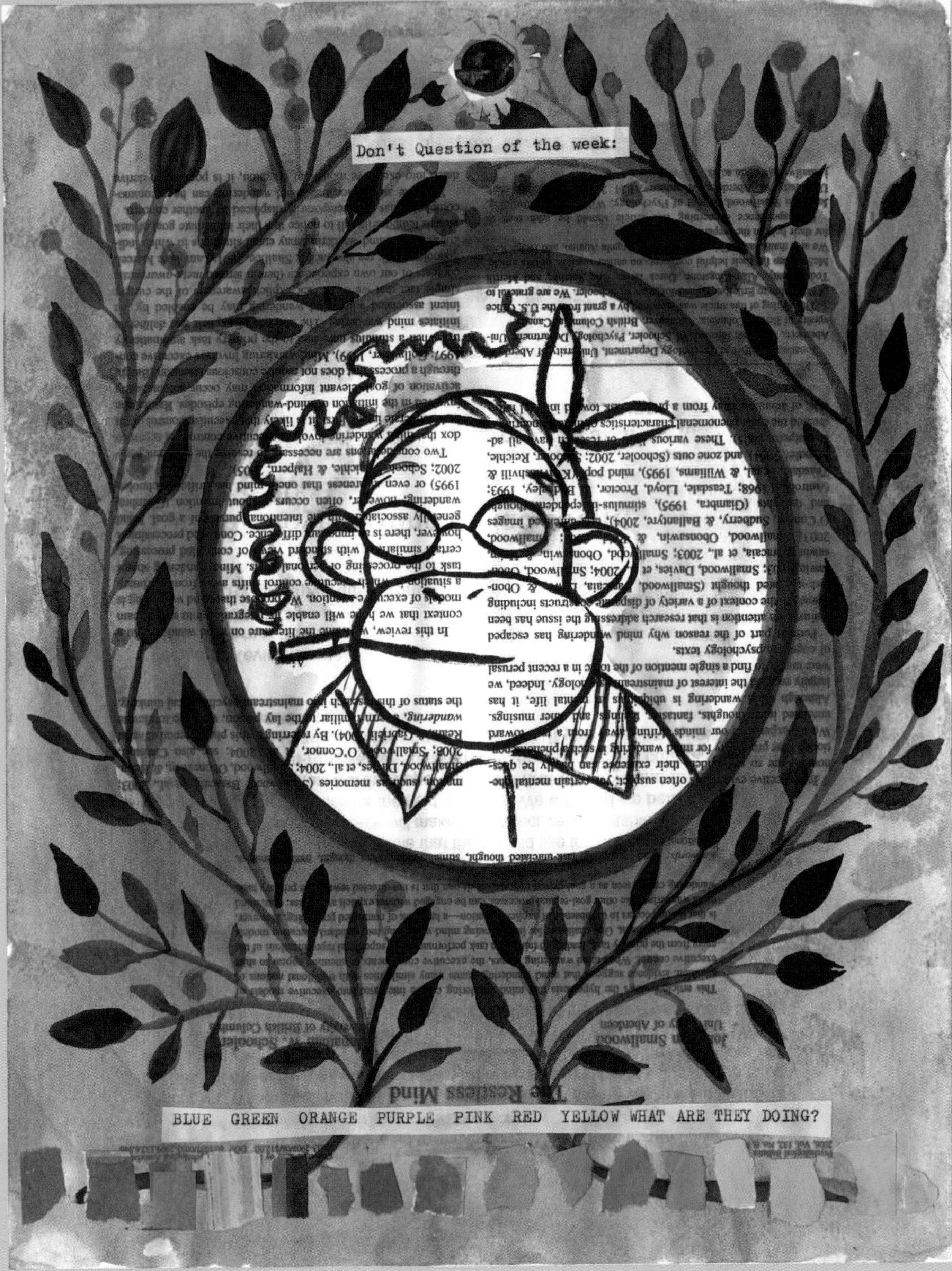
Don't Question of the week:
BLUE GREEN ORANGE PURPLE PINK RED YELLOW WHAT ARE THEY DOING?

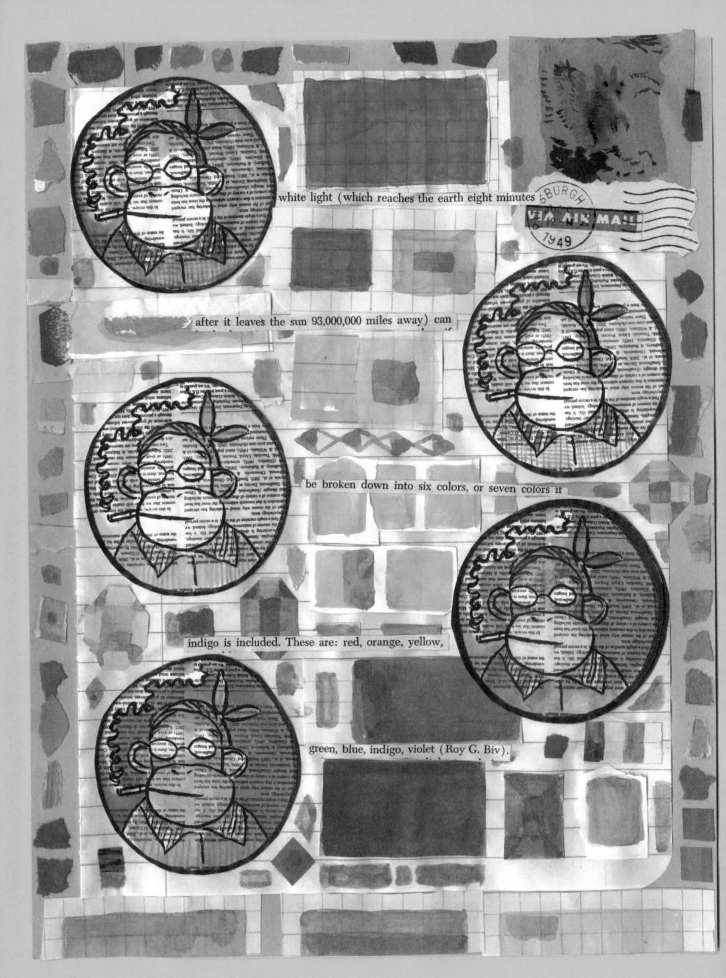

white light (which reaches the earth eight minutes

after it leaves the sun 93,000,000 miles away) can

be broken down into six colors, or seven colors if

indigo is included. These are: red, orange, yellow,

green, blue, indigo, violet (Roy G. Biv).

158

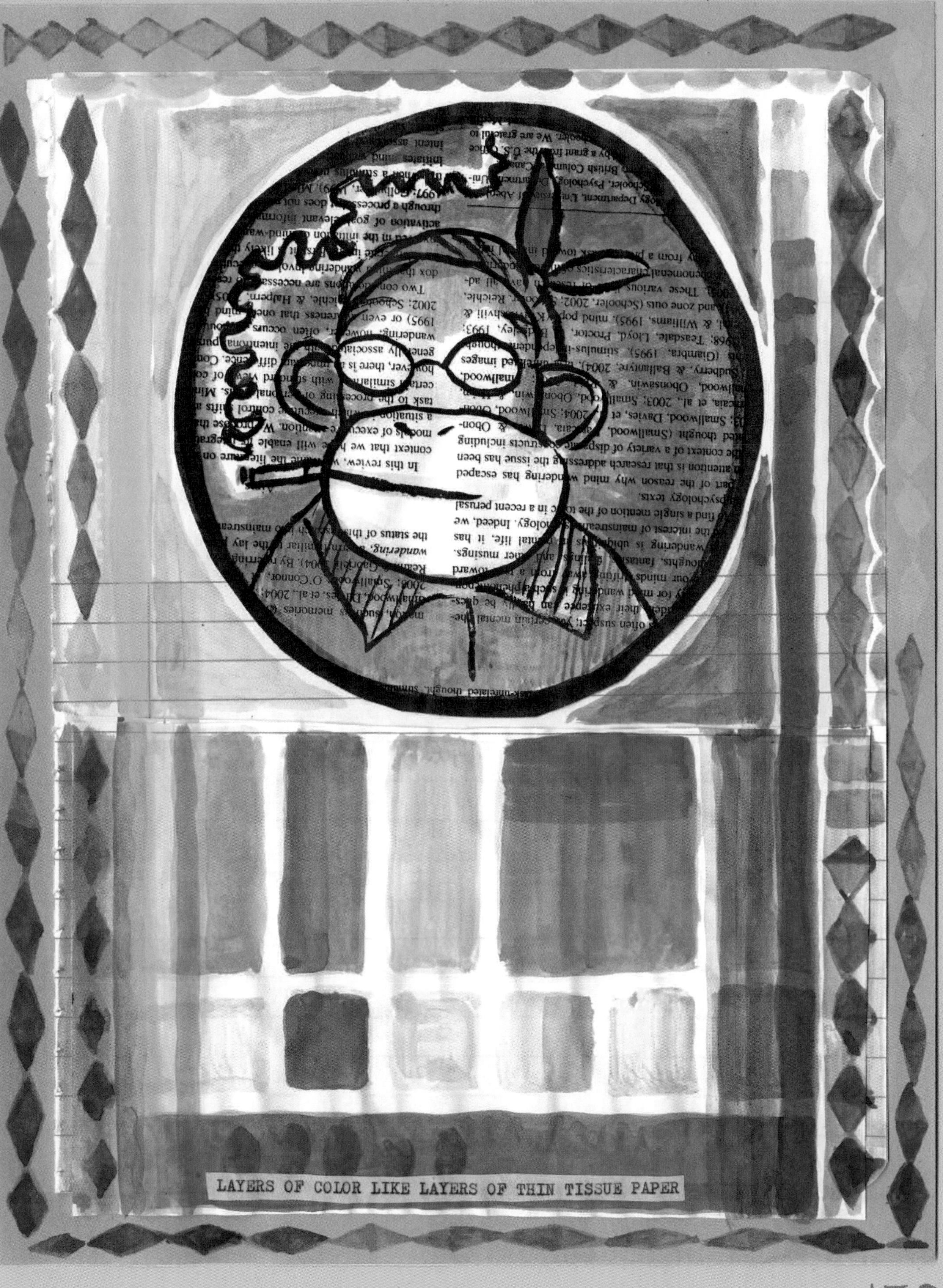
LAYERS OF COLOR LIKE LAYERS OF THIN TISSUE PAPER

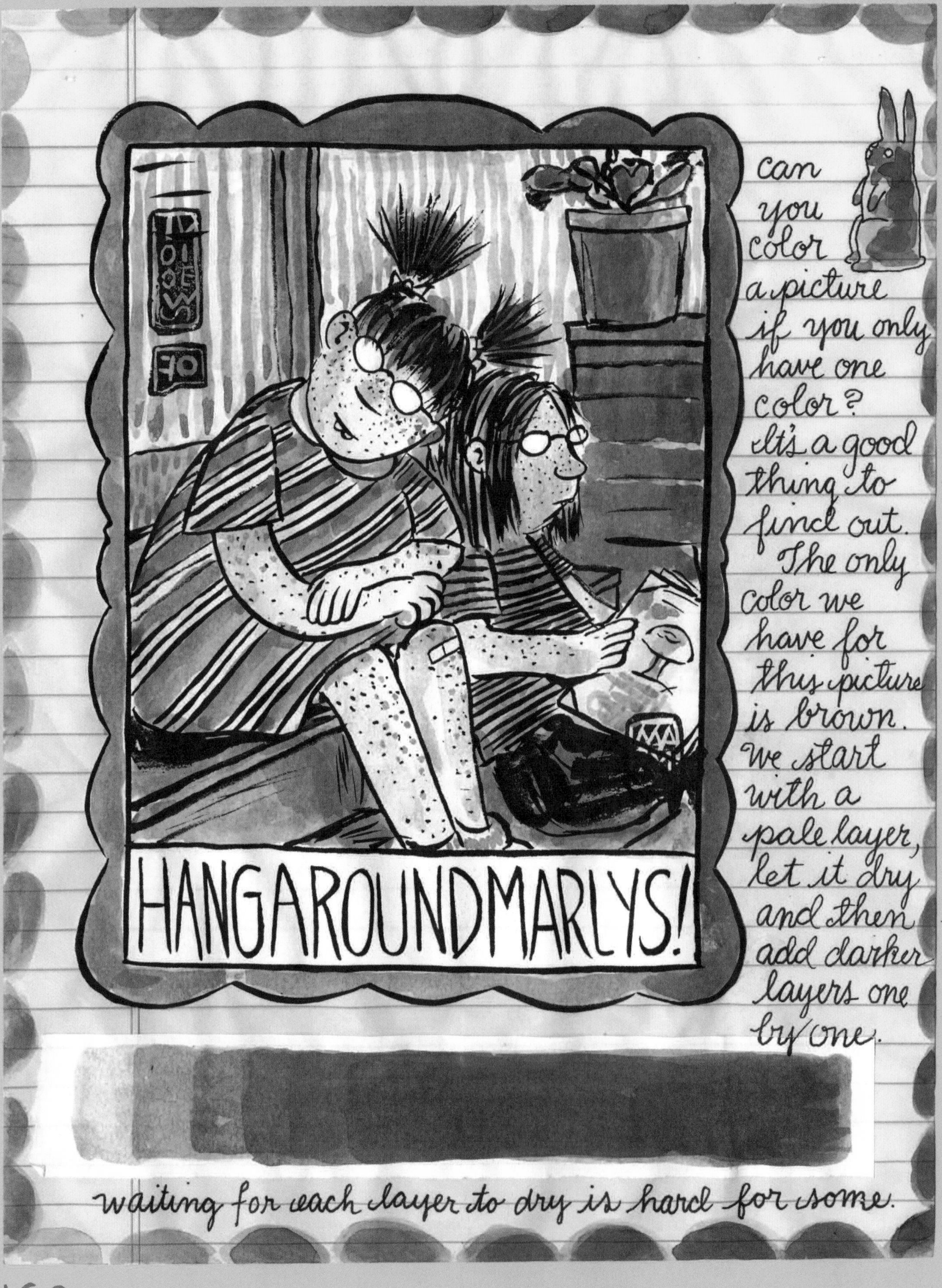
HANGAROUNDMARLYS!
can you color a picture if you only have one color? It's a good thing to find out. The only color we have for this picture is brown. We start with a pale layer, let it dry and then add darker layers one by one.
waiting for each layer to dry is hard for some.

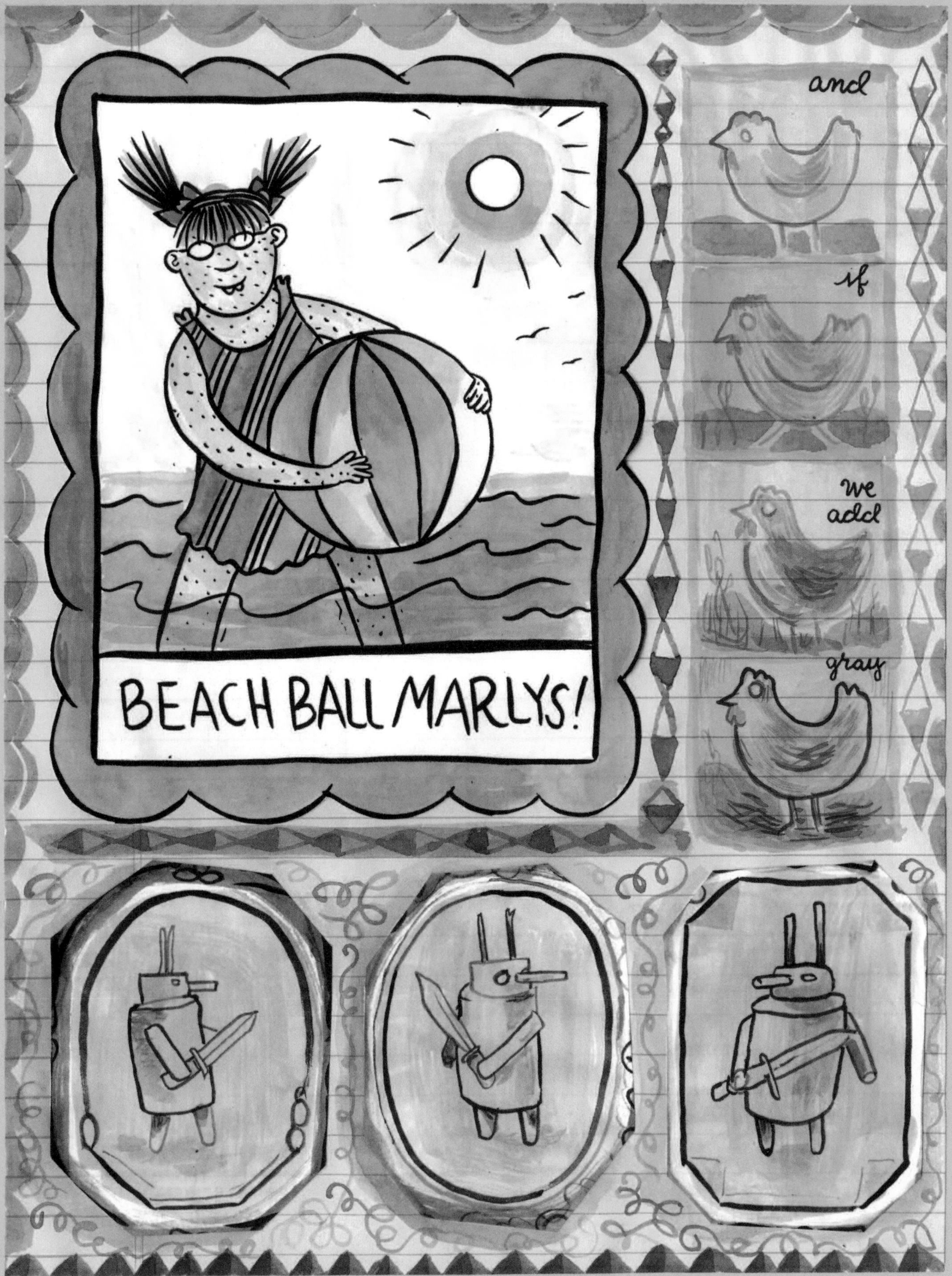
BEACH BALL MARLYS!
and
if
we
add
gray

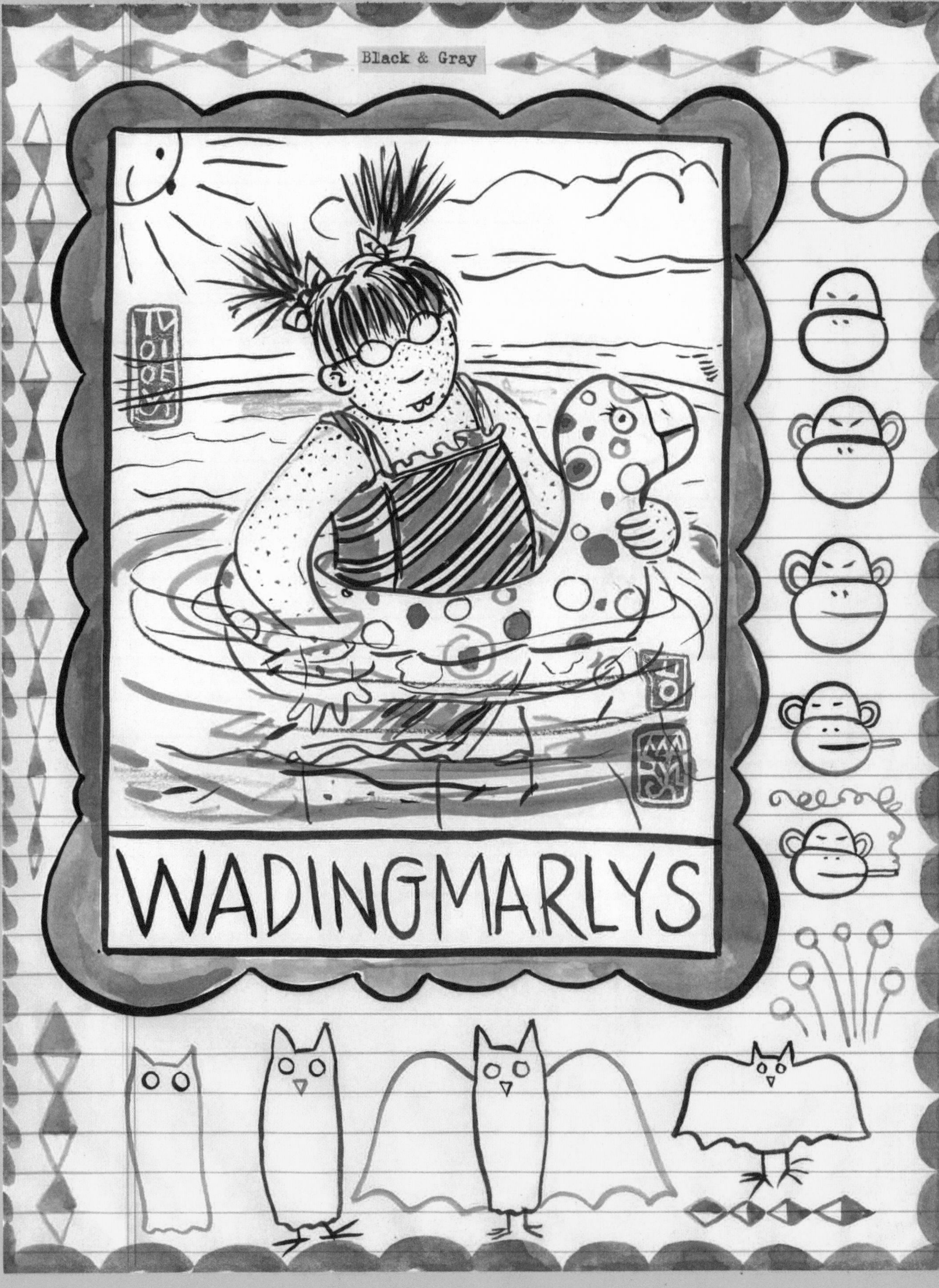
Black & Gray
WADINGMARLYS

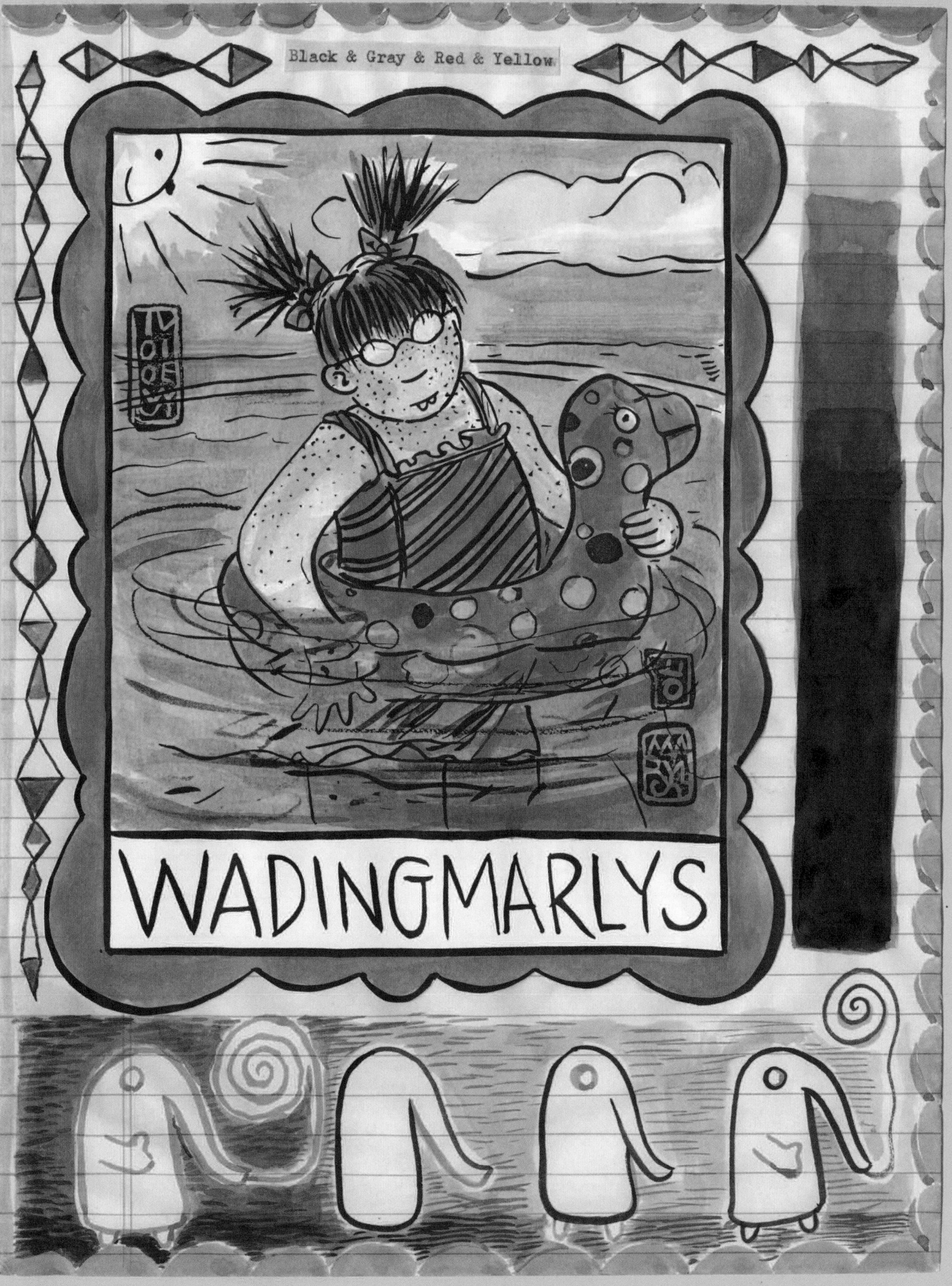
Black & Gray & Red & Yellow
WADINGMARLYS

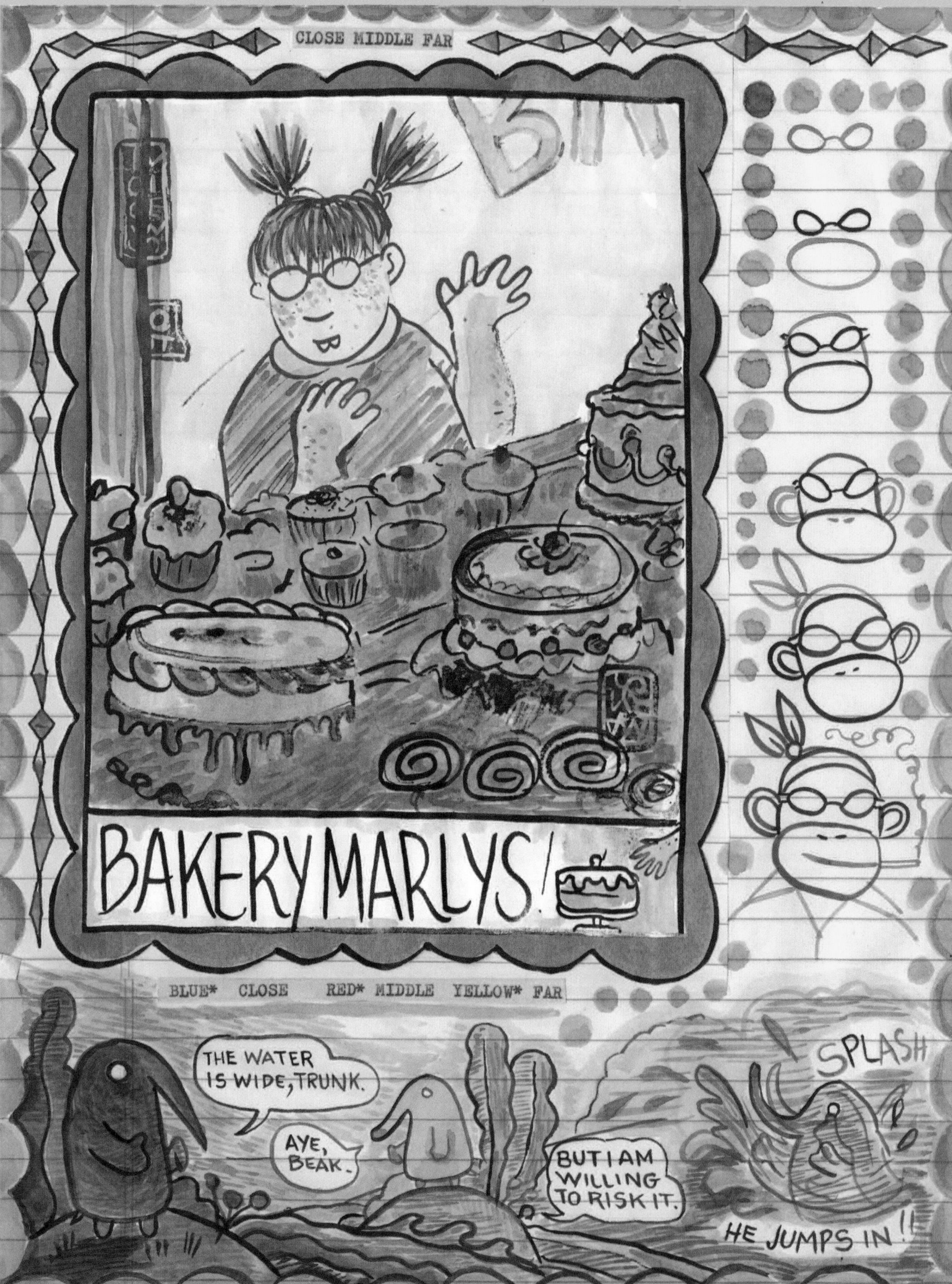
CLOSE MIDDLE FAR
BAKERY MARLYS!
BLUE* CLOSE RED* MIDDLE YELLOW* FAR
THE WATER IS WIDE, TRUNK.
AYE, BEAK.
BUT I AM WILLING TO RISK IT.
SPLASH
HE JUMPS IN!!

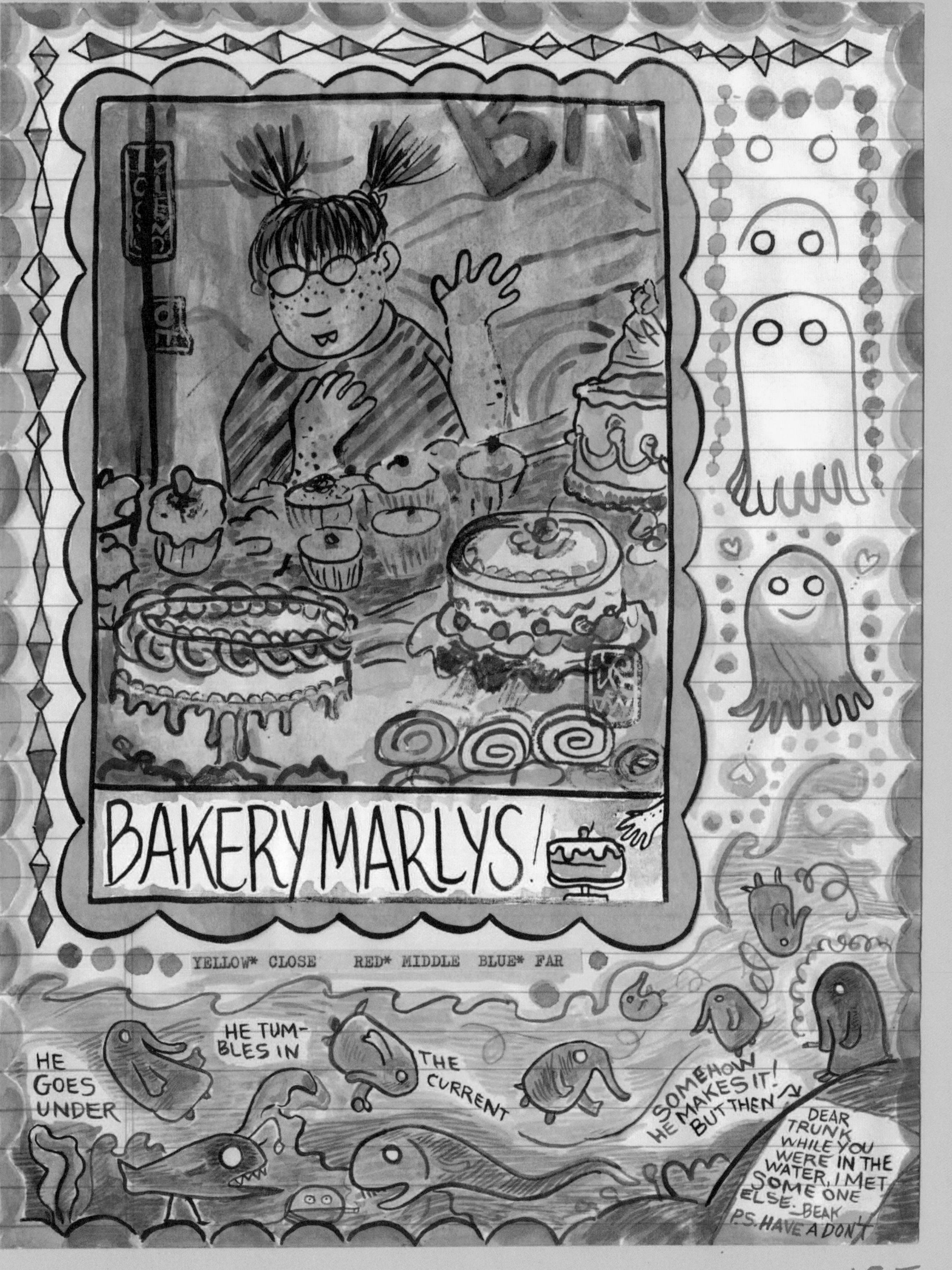
BAKERY MARLYS!
YELLOW* CLOSE RED* MIDDLE BLUE* FAR
HE GOES UNDER
HE TUMBLES IN
THE CURRENT
SOMEHOW HE MAKES IT! BUT THEN→
DEAR TRUNK WHILE YOU WERE IN THE WATER, I MET SOME ONE ELSE. -BEAK
P.S. HAVE A DONUT

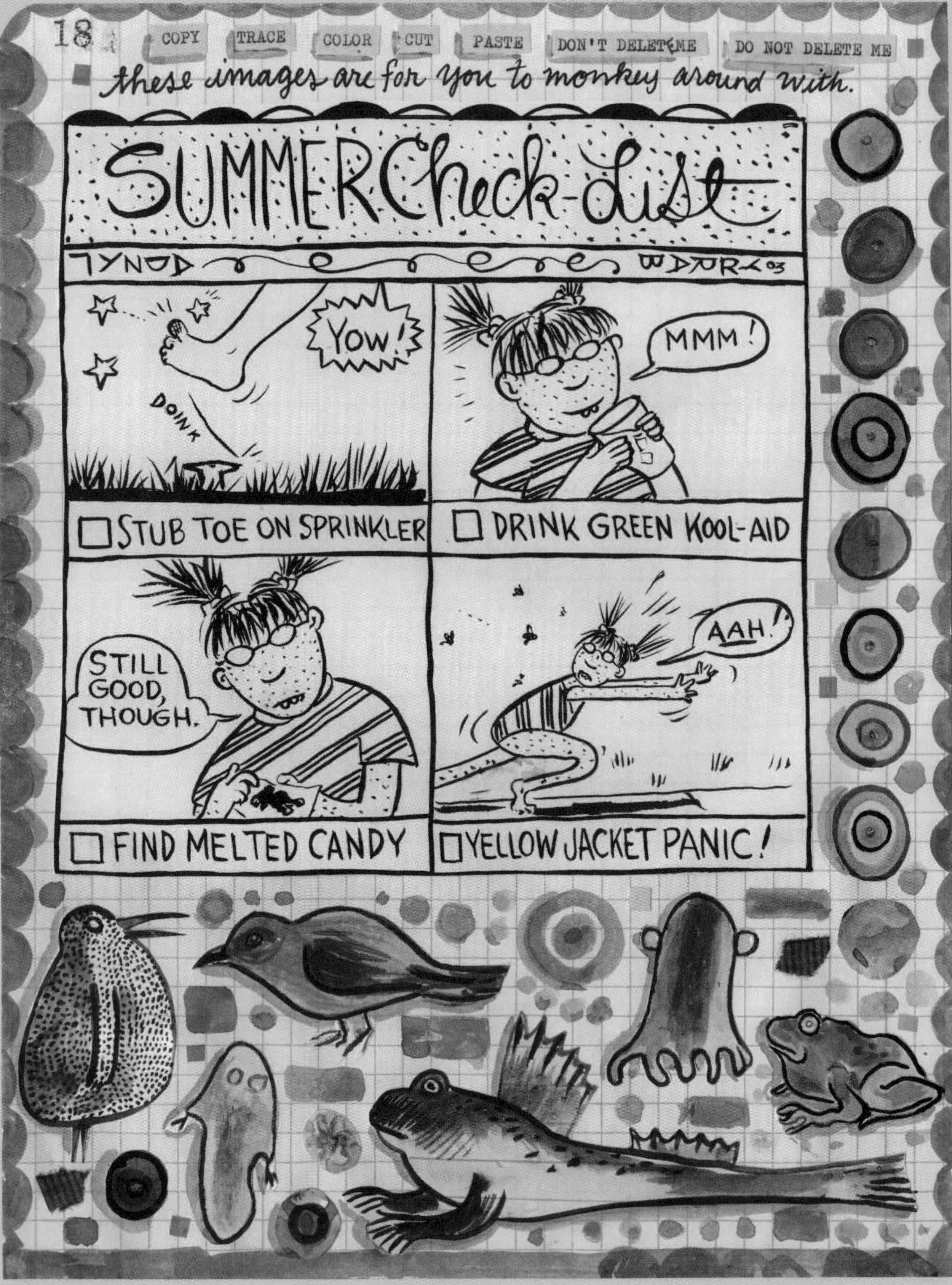
18
COPY
TRACE
COLOR
CUT
PASTE
DON'T DELETE ME
DO NOT DELETE ME
these images are for you to monkey around with.
SUMMER Check-List
YOW!
DOINK
MMM!
☐ STUB TOE ON SPRINKLER
☐ DRINK GREEN KOOL-AID
STILL GOOD, THOUGH.
AAH!
☐ FIND MELTED CANDY
☐ YELLOW JACKET PANIC!

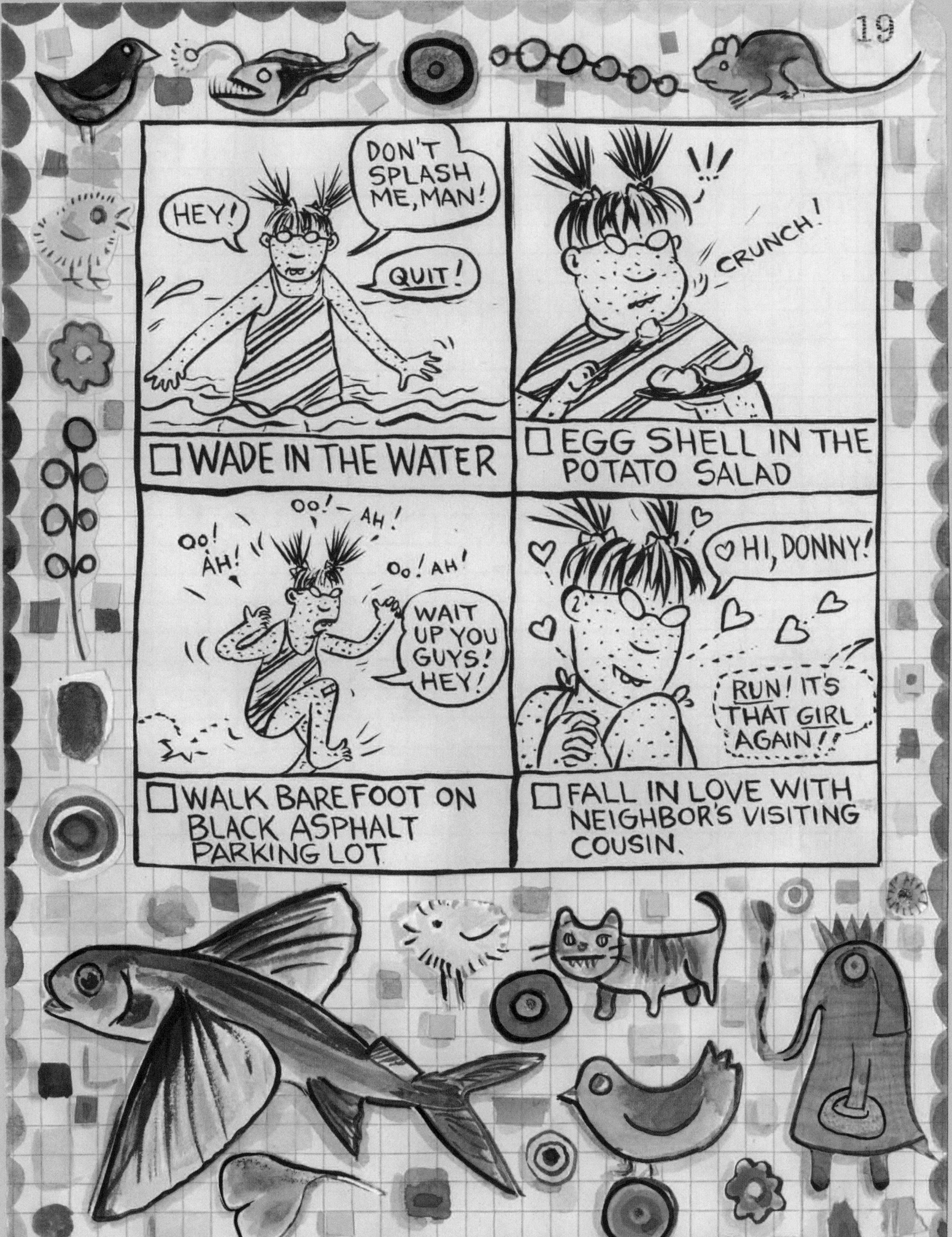
19
HEY!
DON'T SPLASH ME, MAN!
QUIT!
WADE IN THE WATER
!!
CRUNCH!
EGG SHELL IN THE POTATO SALAD
OO! AH!
OO! - AH!
OO! AH!
WAIT UP YOU GUYS! HEY!
WALK BAREFOOT ON BLACK ASPHALT PARKING LOT
HI, DONNY!
RUN! IT'S THAT GIRL AGAIN!!
FALL IN LOVE WITH NEIGHBOR'S VISITING COUSIN.

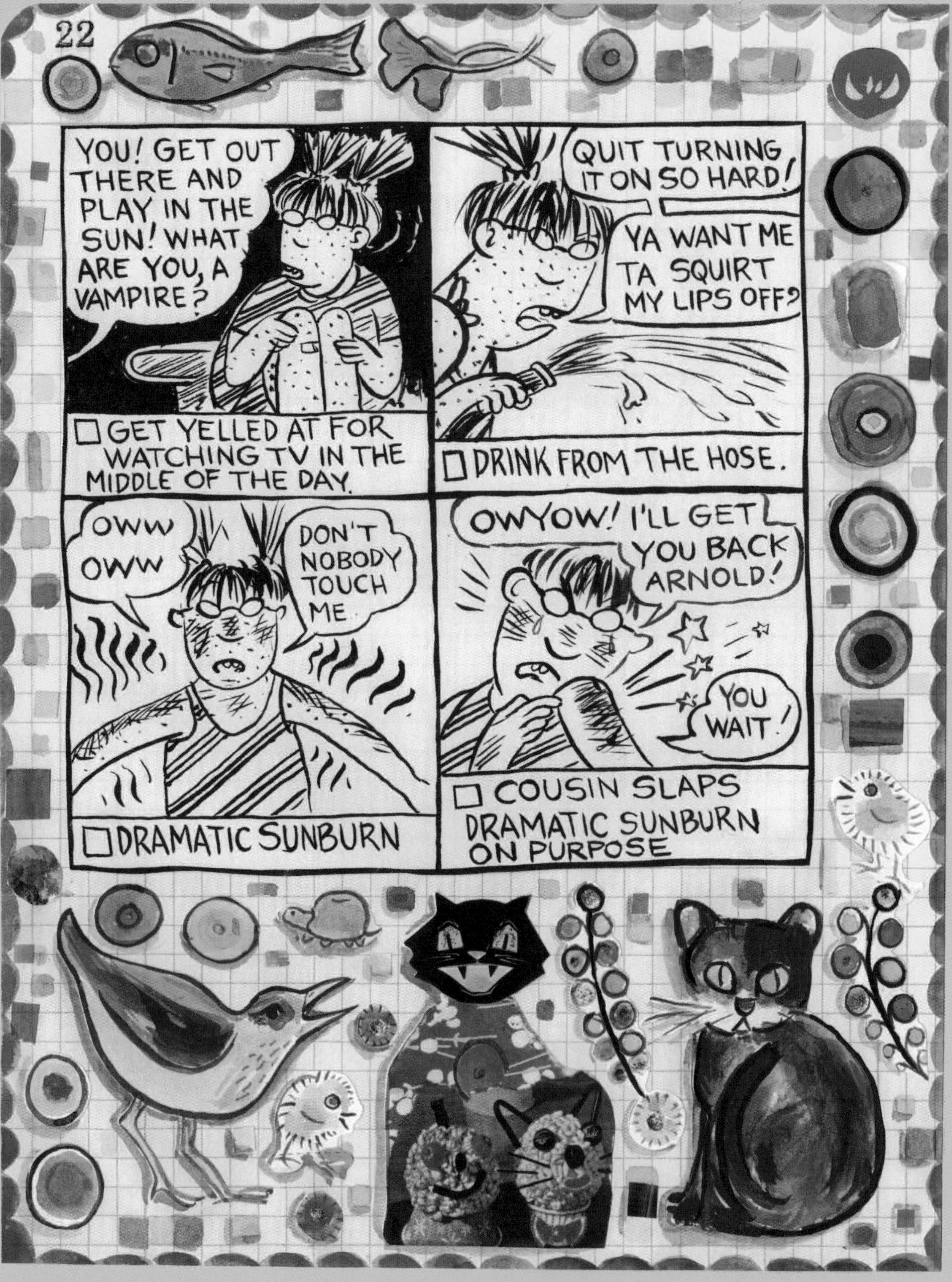
22
YOU! GET OUT THERE AND PLAY IN THE SUN! WHAT ARE YOU, A VAMPIRE?
☐ GET YELLED AT FOR WATCHING TV IN THE MIDDLE OF THE DAY.
QUIT TURNING IT ON SO HARD!
YA WANT ME TA SQUIRT MY LIPS OFF?
☐ DRINK FROM THE HOSE.
OWW OWW
DON'T NOBODY TOUCH ME
☐ DRAMATIC SUNBURN
OWYOW! I'LL GET YOU BACK ARNOLD!
YOU WAIT!
☐ COUSIN SLAPS DRAMATIC SUNBURN ON PURPOSE

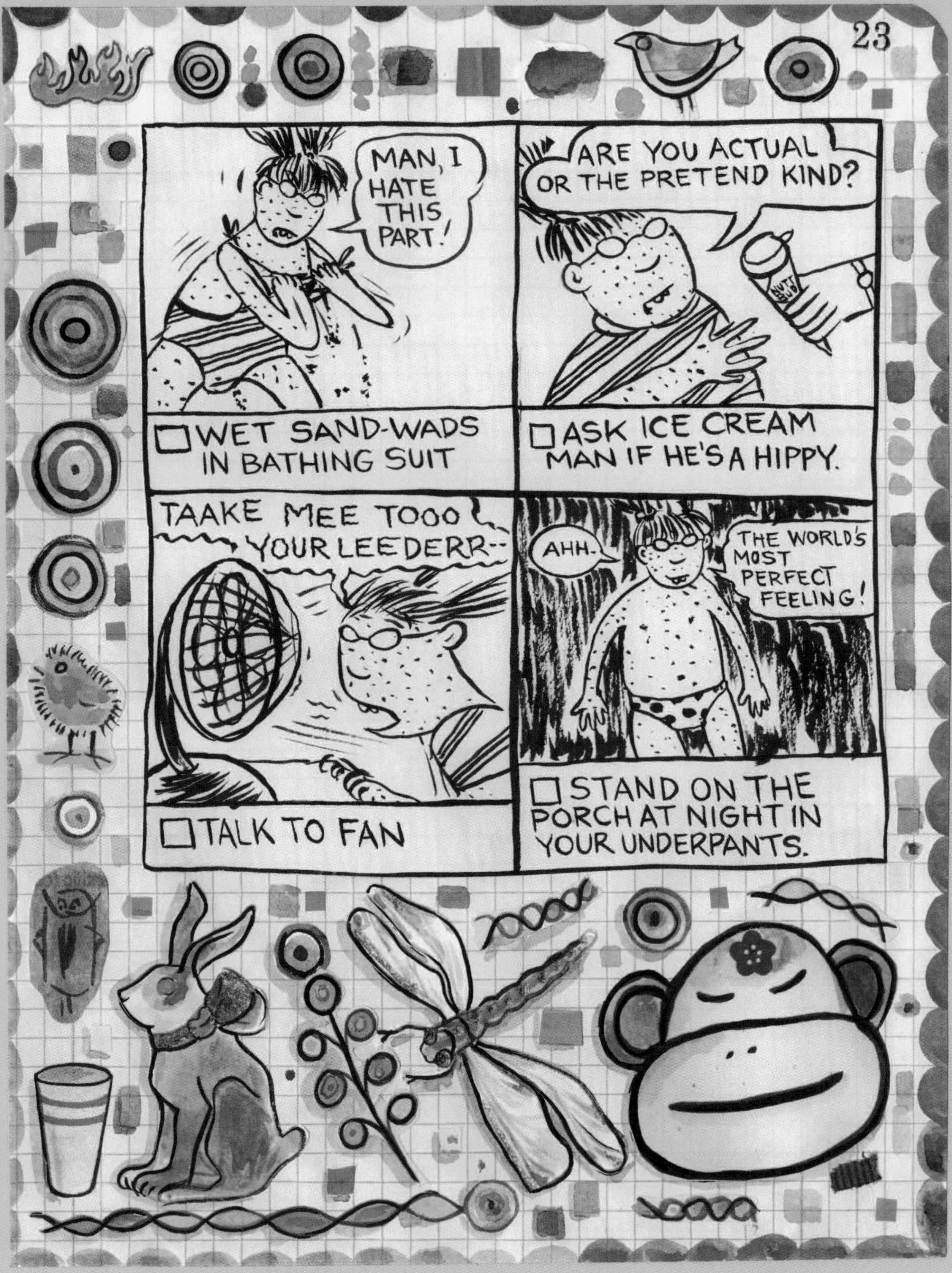
23
MAN, I HATE THIS PART!
WET SAND-WADS IN BATHING SUIT
ARE YOU ACTUAL OR THE PRETEND KIND?
ASK ICE CREAM MAN IF HE'S A HIPPY.
TAAKE MEE TOOO YOUR LEEDERR--
TALK TO FAN
AHH-
THE WORLD'S MOST PERFECT FEELING!
STAND ON THE PORCH AT NIGHT IN YOUR UNDERPANTS.

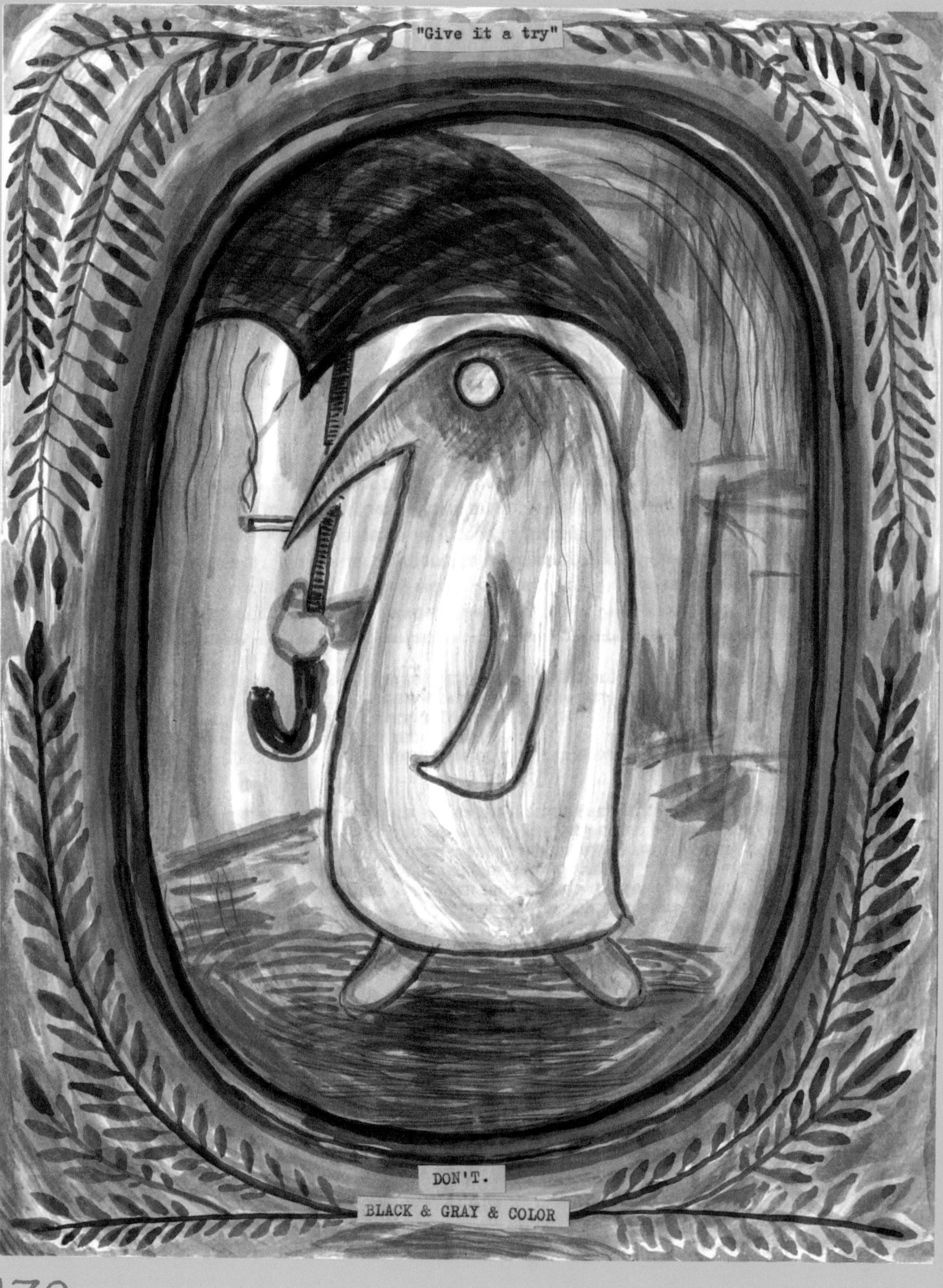
"Give it a try"
DON'T.
BLACK & GRAY & COLOR

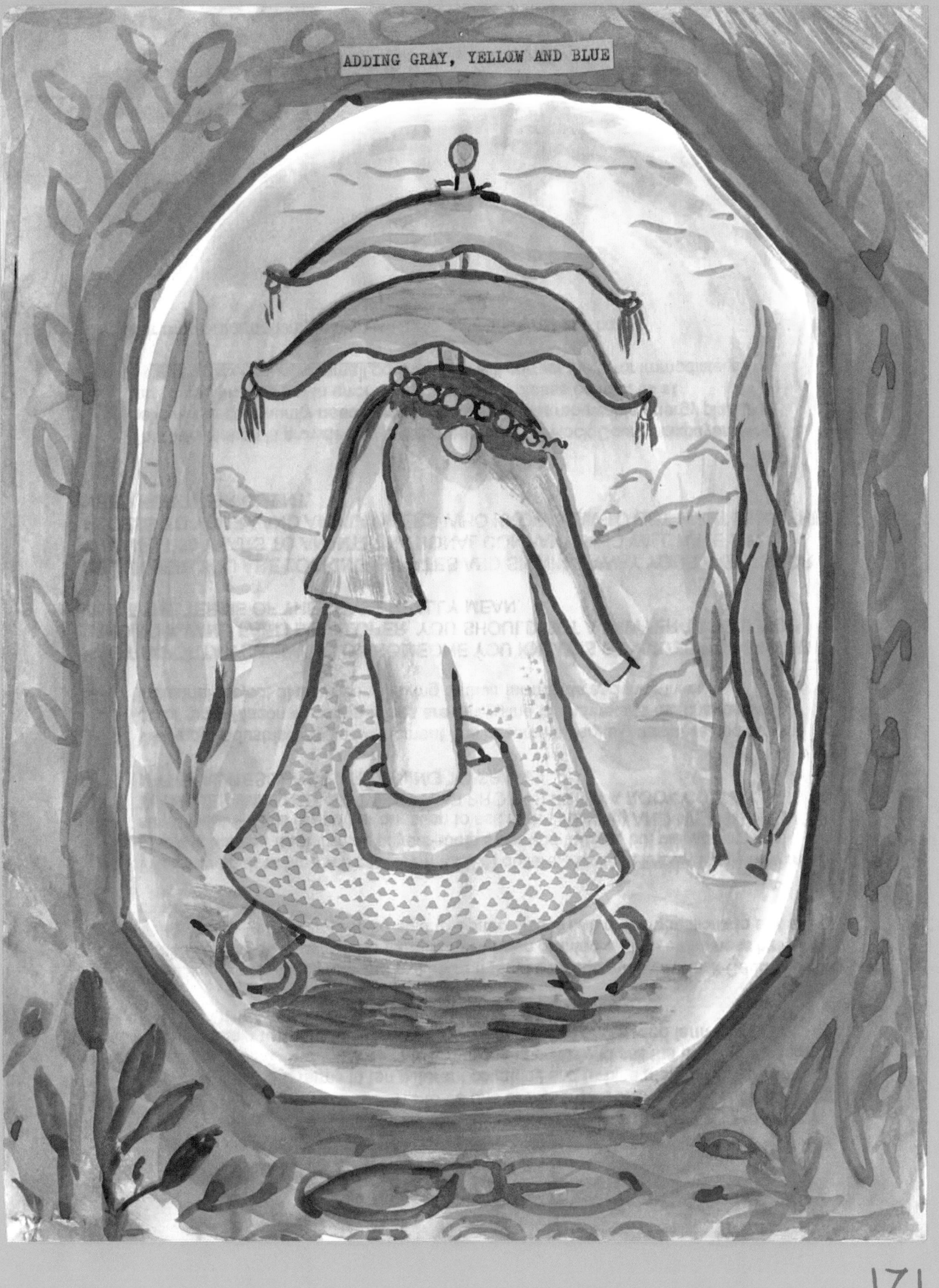
ADDING GRAY, YELLOW AND BLUE

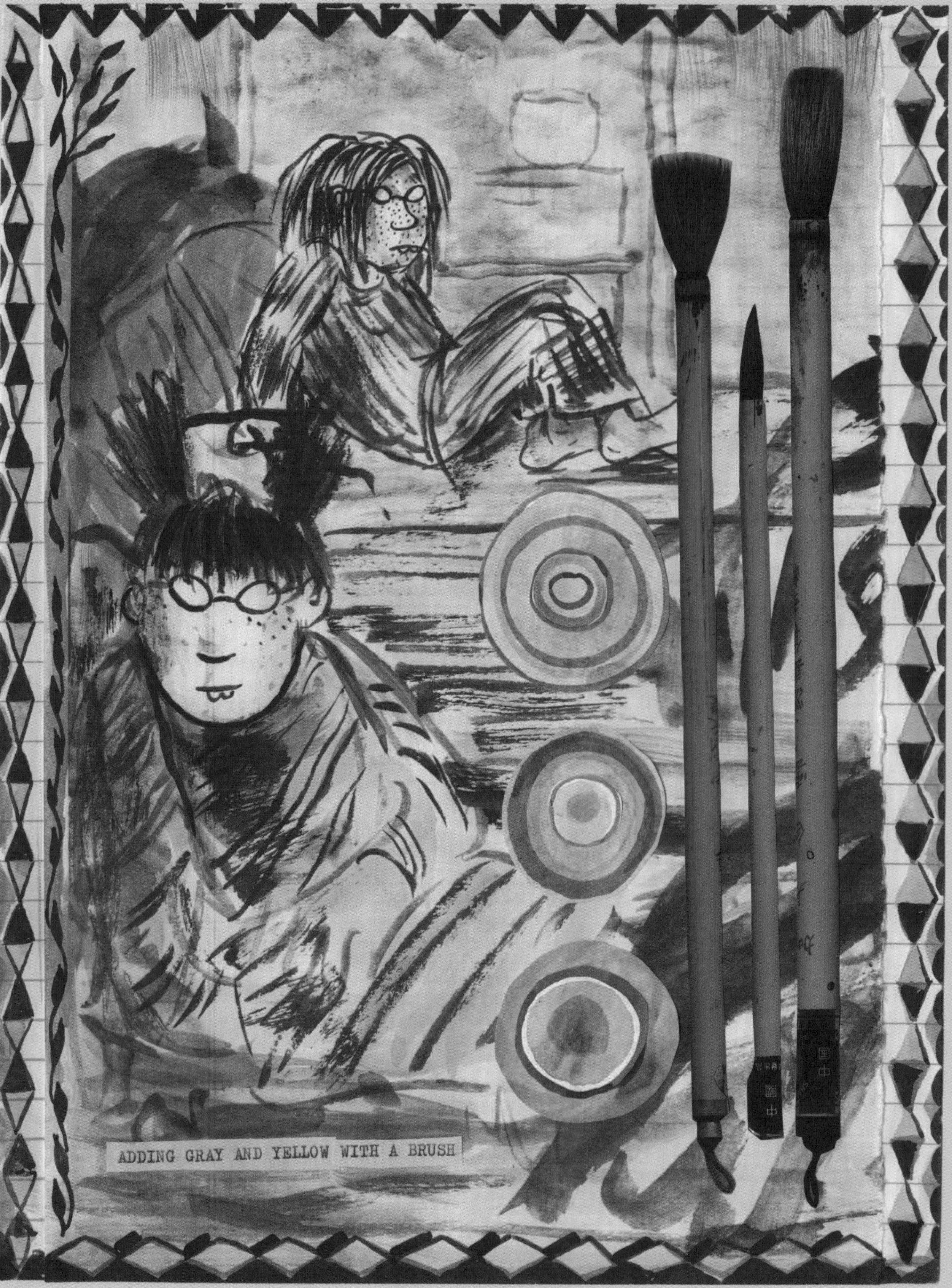
ADDING GRAY AND YELLOW WITH A BRUSH

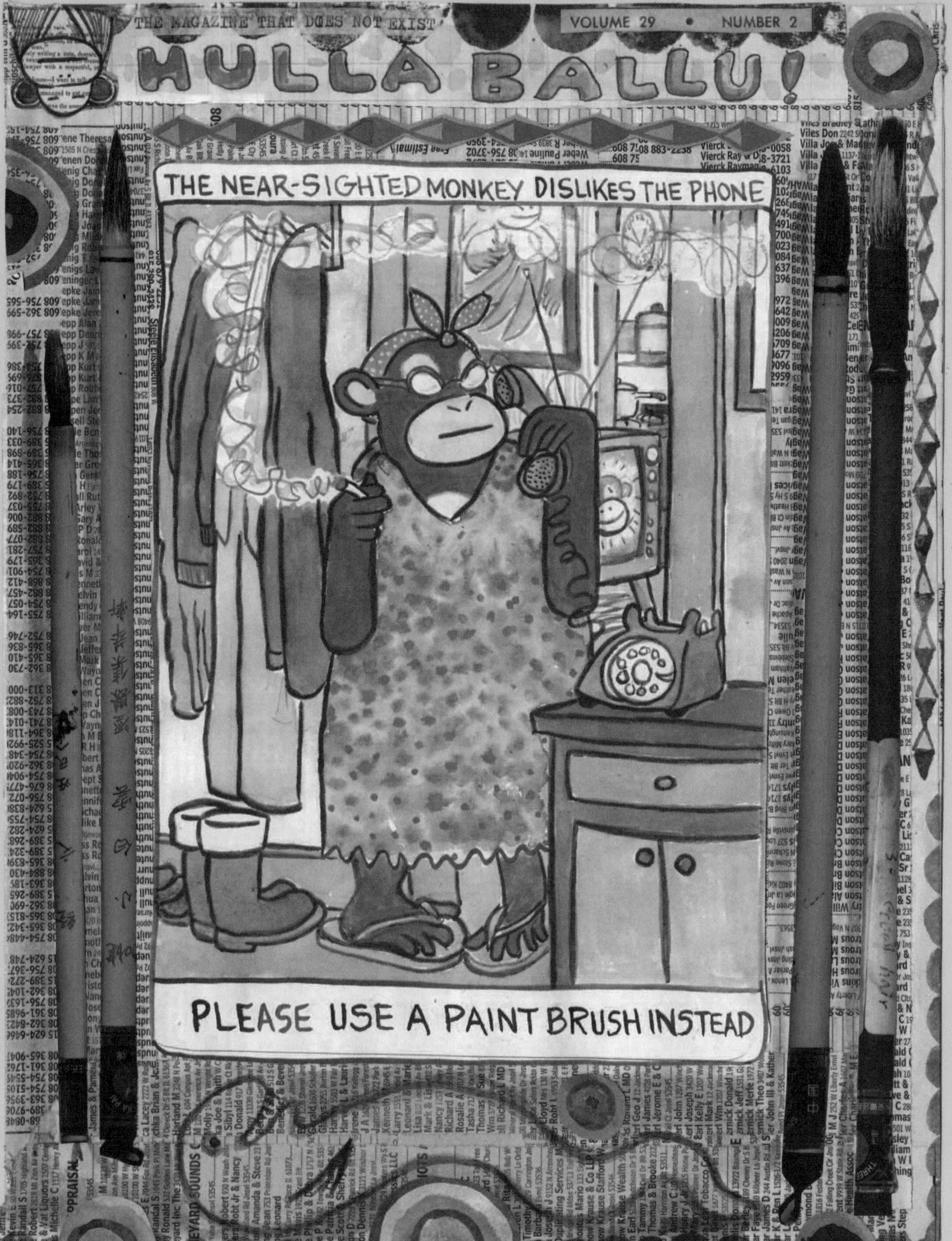
THE MAGAZINE THAT DOES NOT EXIST
VOLUME 29 • NUMBER 2
HULLA BALLU!
THE NEAR-SIGHTED MONKEY DISLIKES THE PHONE
PLEASE USE A PAINT BRUSH INSTEAD

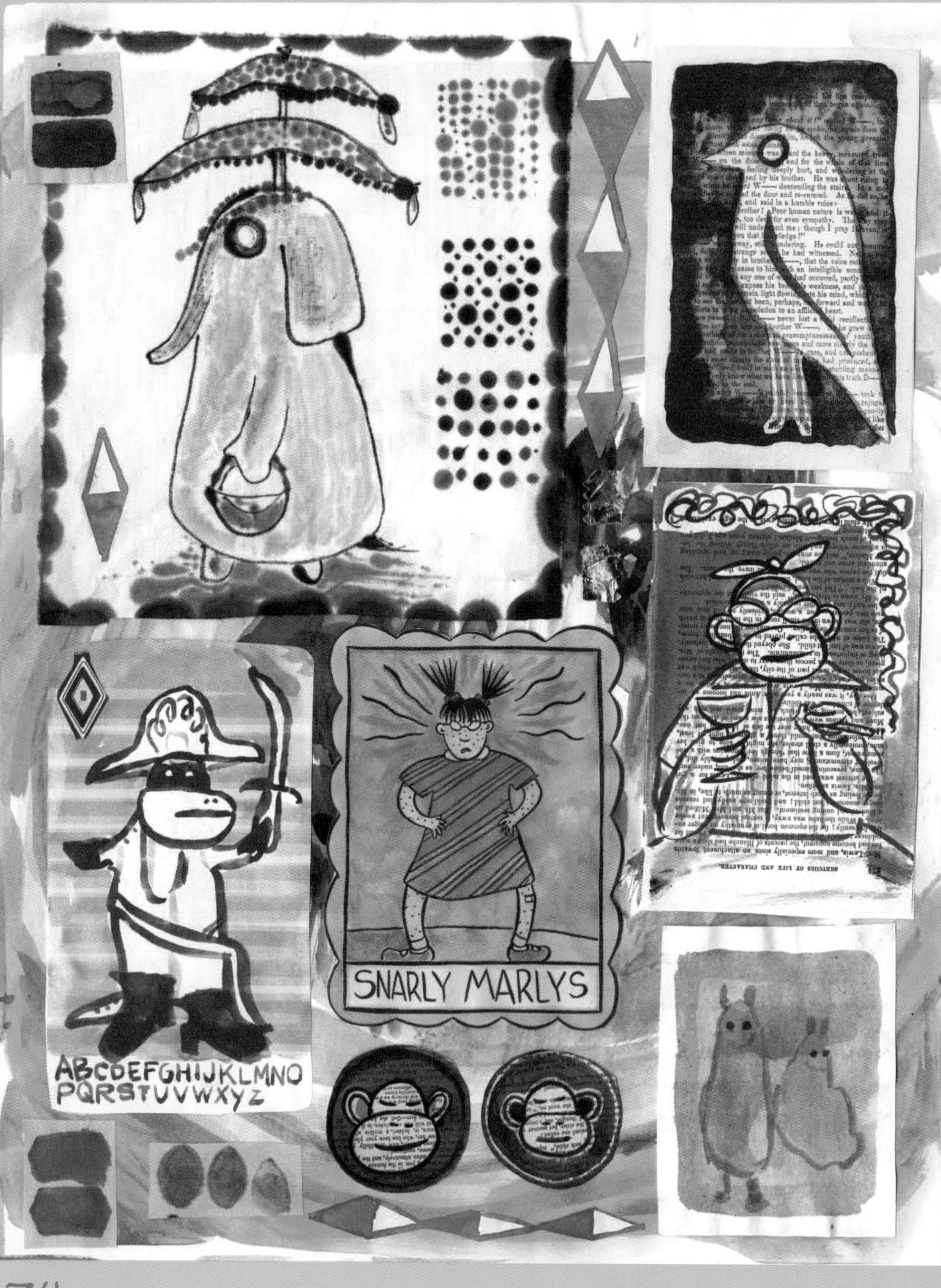
SNARLY MARLYS
ABCDEFGHIJKLMNO
PQRSTUVWXYZ

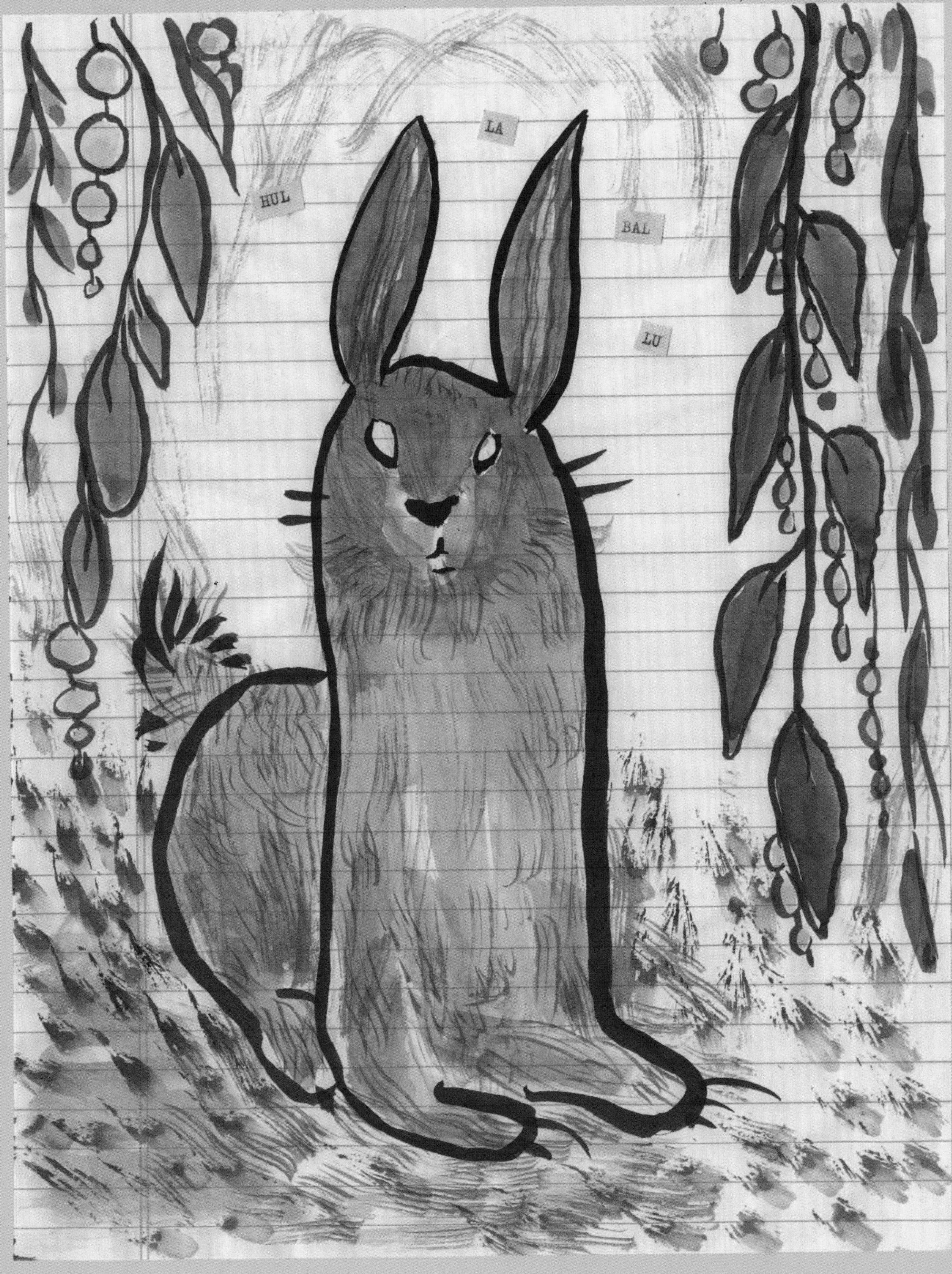
HUL
LA
BAL
LU

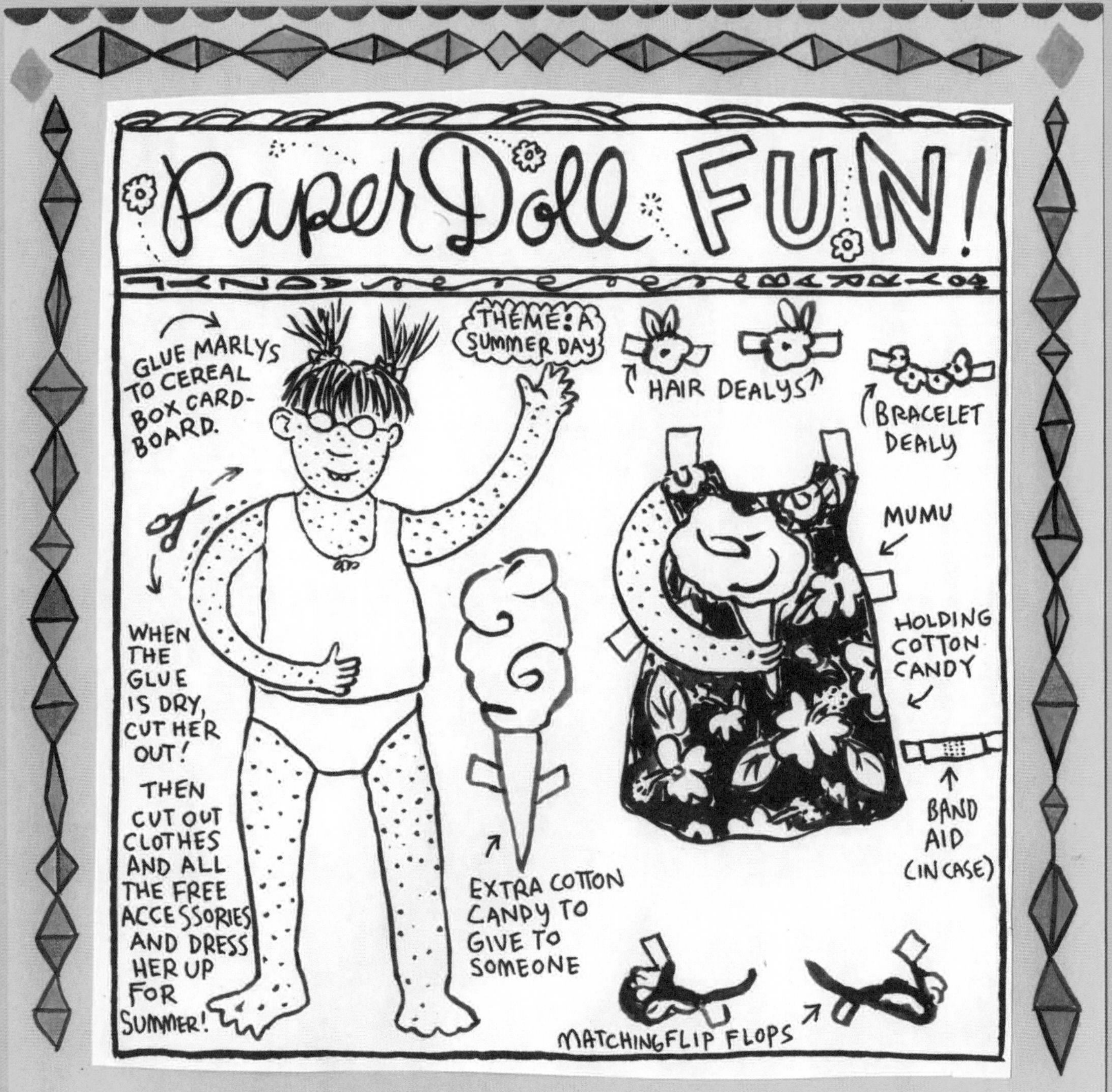
Paper Doll FUN!
GLUE MARLYS TO CEREAL BOX CARD-BOARD.
WHEN THE GLUE IS DRY, CUT HER OUT!
THEN CUT OUT CLOTHES AND ALL THE FREE ACCESSORIES AND DRESS HER UP FOR SUMMER!
THEME: A SUMMER DAY
EXTRA COTTON CANDY TO GIVE TO SOMEONE
HAIR DEALYS
BRACELET DEALY
MUMU
HOLDING COTTON CANDY
BAND AID (IN CASE)
MATCHING FLIP FLOPS

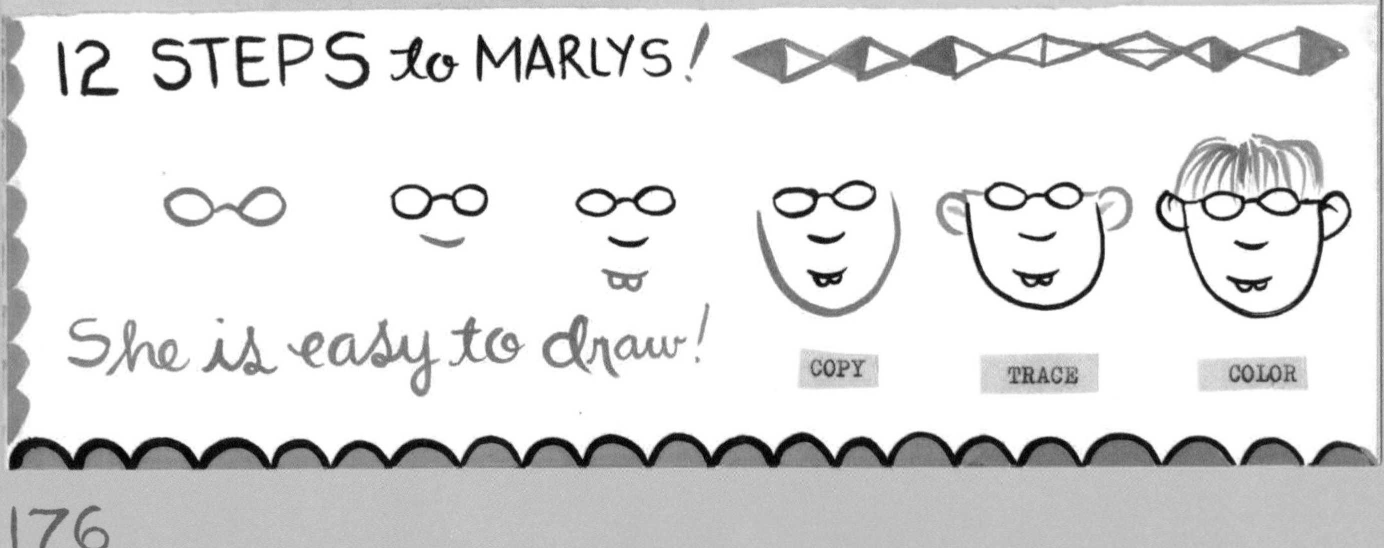
12 STEPS to MARLYS!
She is easy to draw!
COPY
TRACE
COLOR

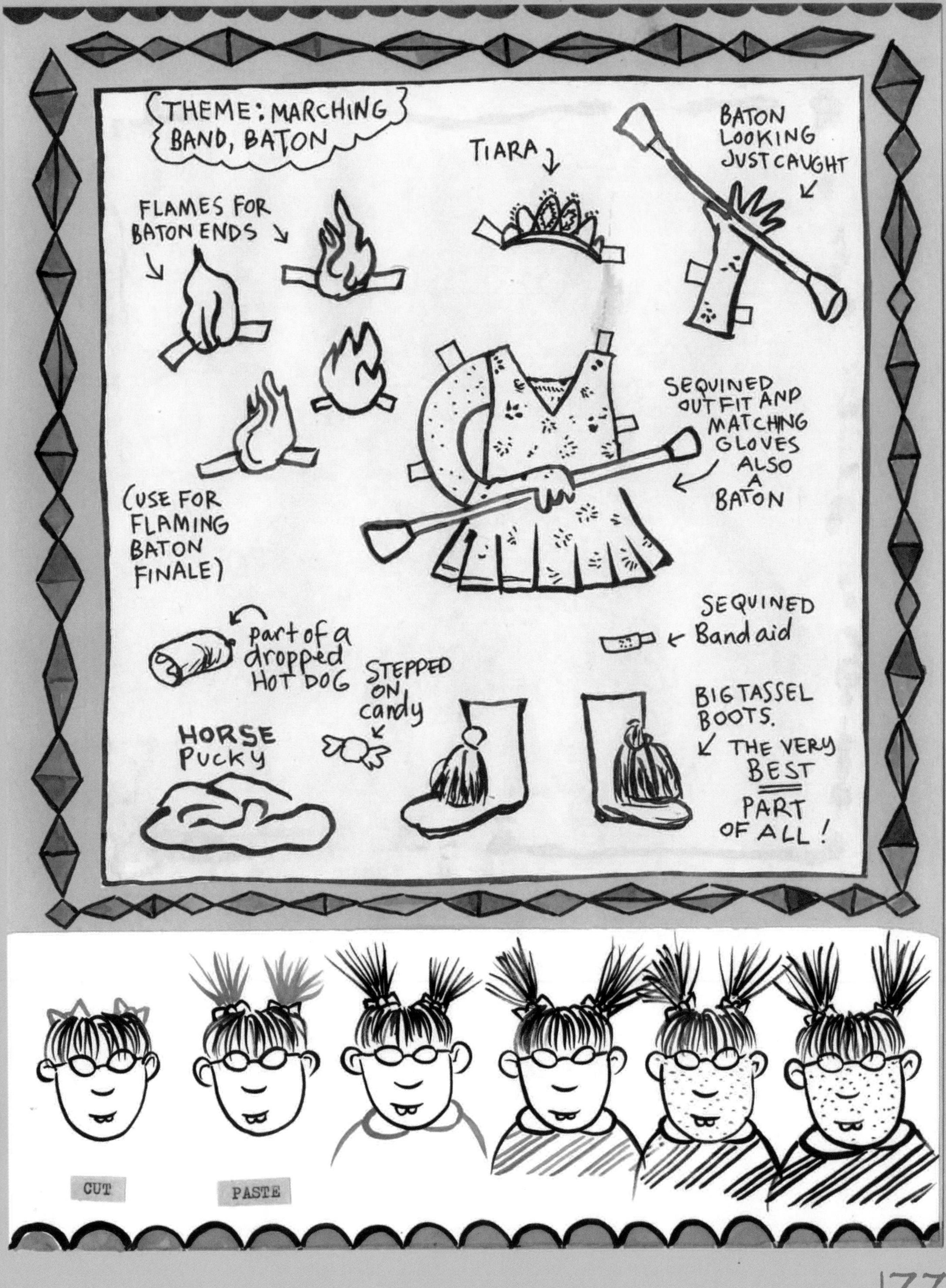
THEME: MARCHING BAND, BATON
TIARA
BATON LOOKING JUST CAUGHT
FLAMES FOR BATON ENDS
SEQUINED OUTFIT AND MATCHING GLOVES ALSO A BATON
(USE FOR FLAMING BATON FINALE)
part of a dropped HOT DOG
SEQUINED Band aid
STEPPED ON candy
HORSE Pucky
BIG TASSEL BOOTS.
THE VERY BEST PART OF ALL!
CUT
PASTE

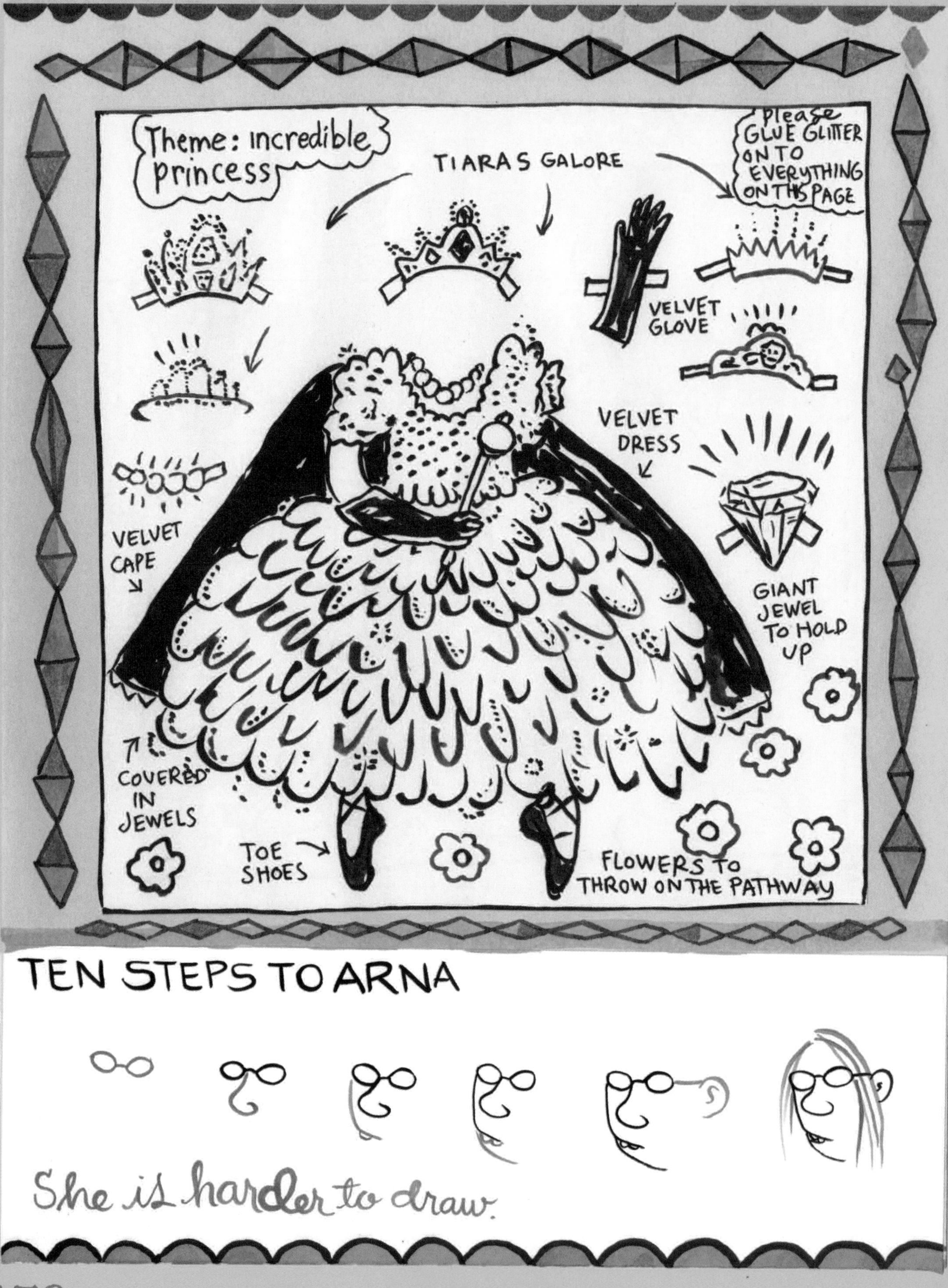

Theme: incredible princess
TIARAS GALORE
please GLUE GLITTER ON TO EVERYTHING ON THIS PAGE
VELVET GLOVE
VELVET DRESS
VELVET CAPE
GIANT JEWEL TO HOLD UP
COVERED IN JEWELS
TOE SHOES
FLOWERS TO THROW ON THE PATHWAY
TEN STEPS TO ARNA
She is harder to draw.

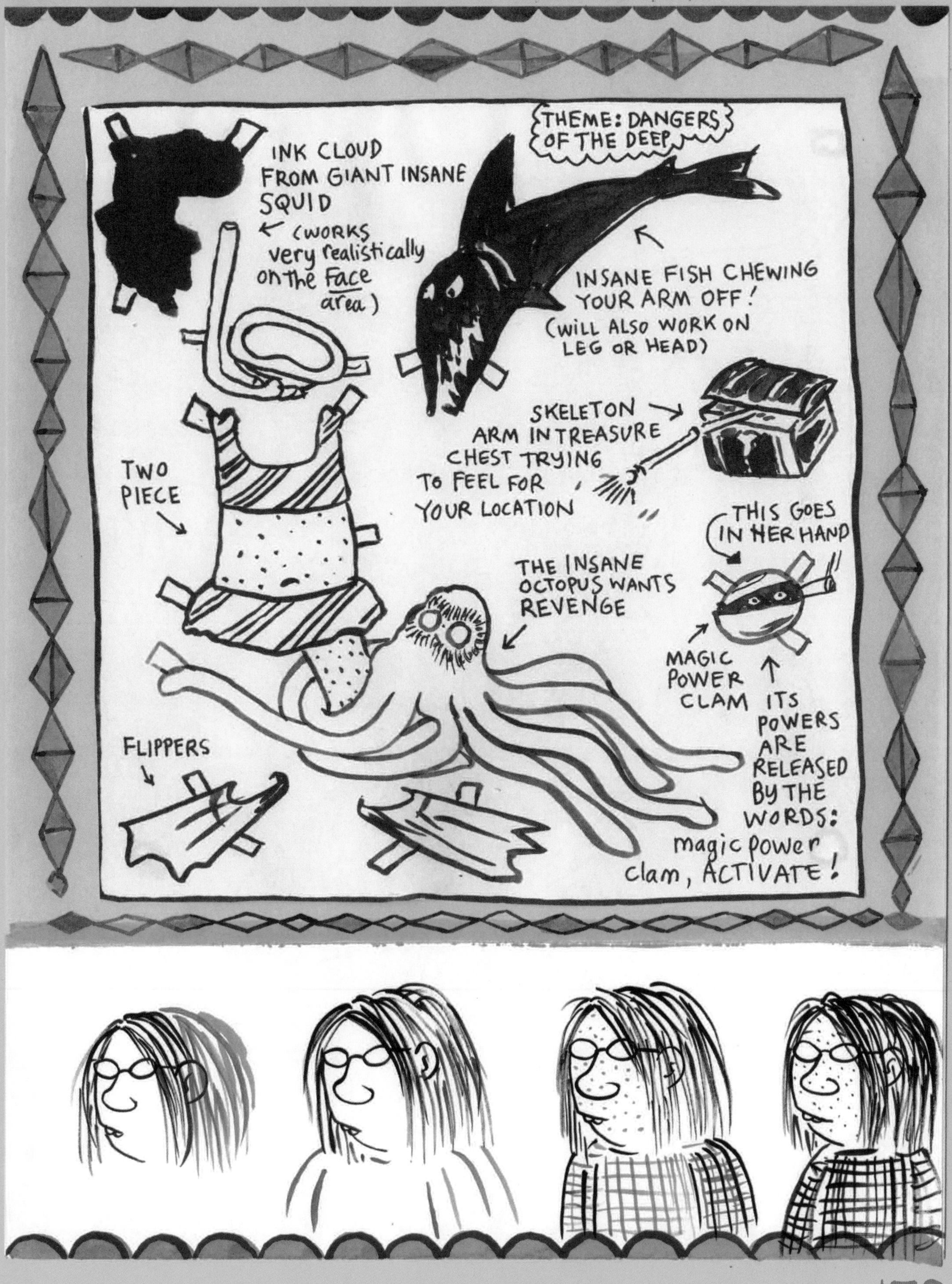

THEME: DANGERS OF THE DEEP
INK CLOUD FROM GIANT INSANE SQUID
(WORKS very realistically on the Face area)
INSANE FISH CHEWING YOUR ARM OFF! (WILL ALSO WORK ON LEG OR HEAD)
SKELETON ARM IN TREASURE CHEST TRYING TO FEEL FOR YOUR LOCATION
TWO PIECE
THIS GOES IN HER HAND
THE INSANE OCTOPUS WANTS REVENGE
MAGIC POWER CLAM
ITS POWERS ARE RELEASED BY THE WORDS: magic power clam, ACTIVATE!
FLIPPERS

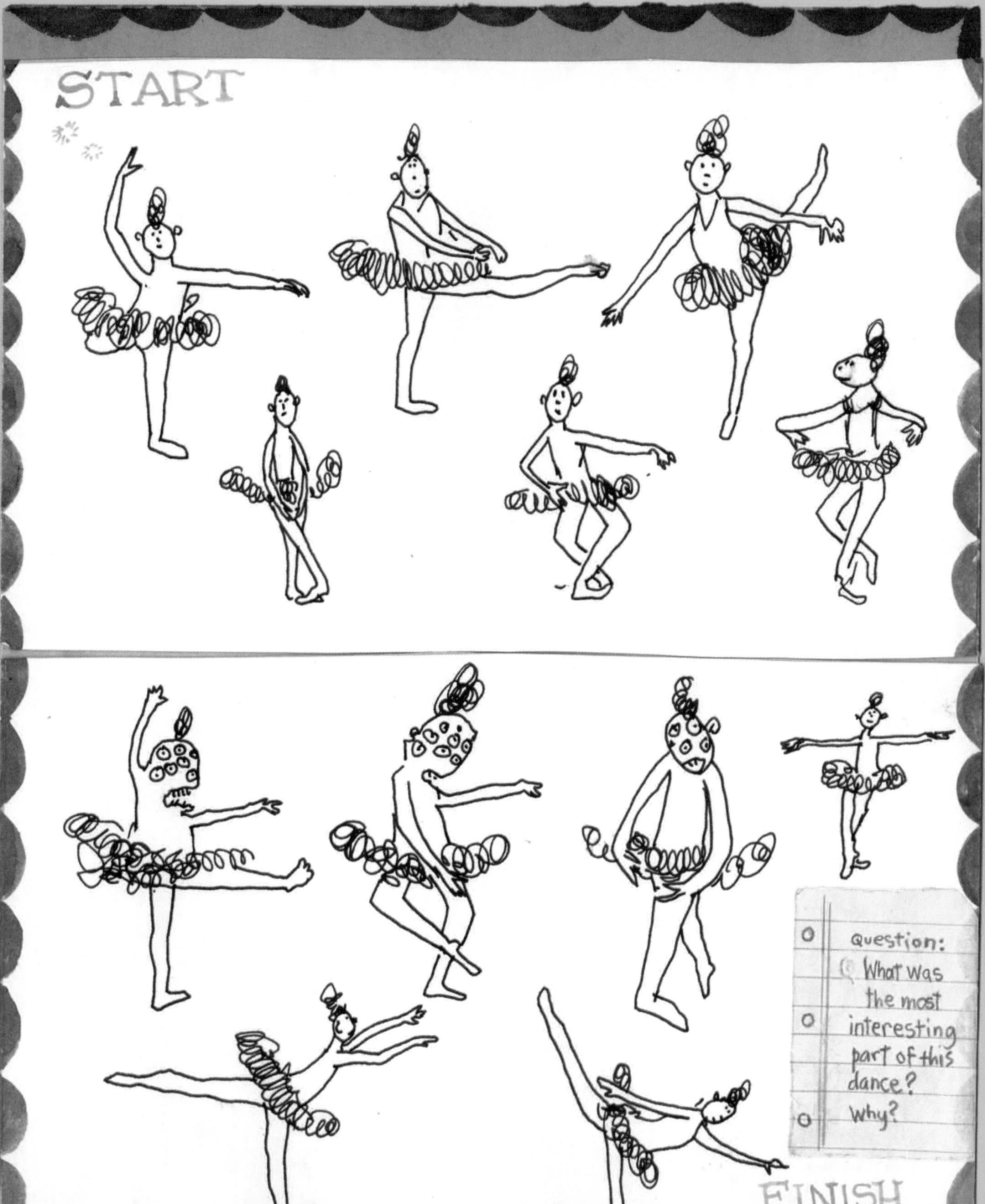
START
Question:
What was the most interesting part of this dance?
Why?
FINISH

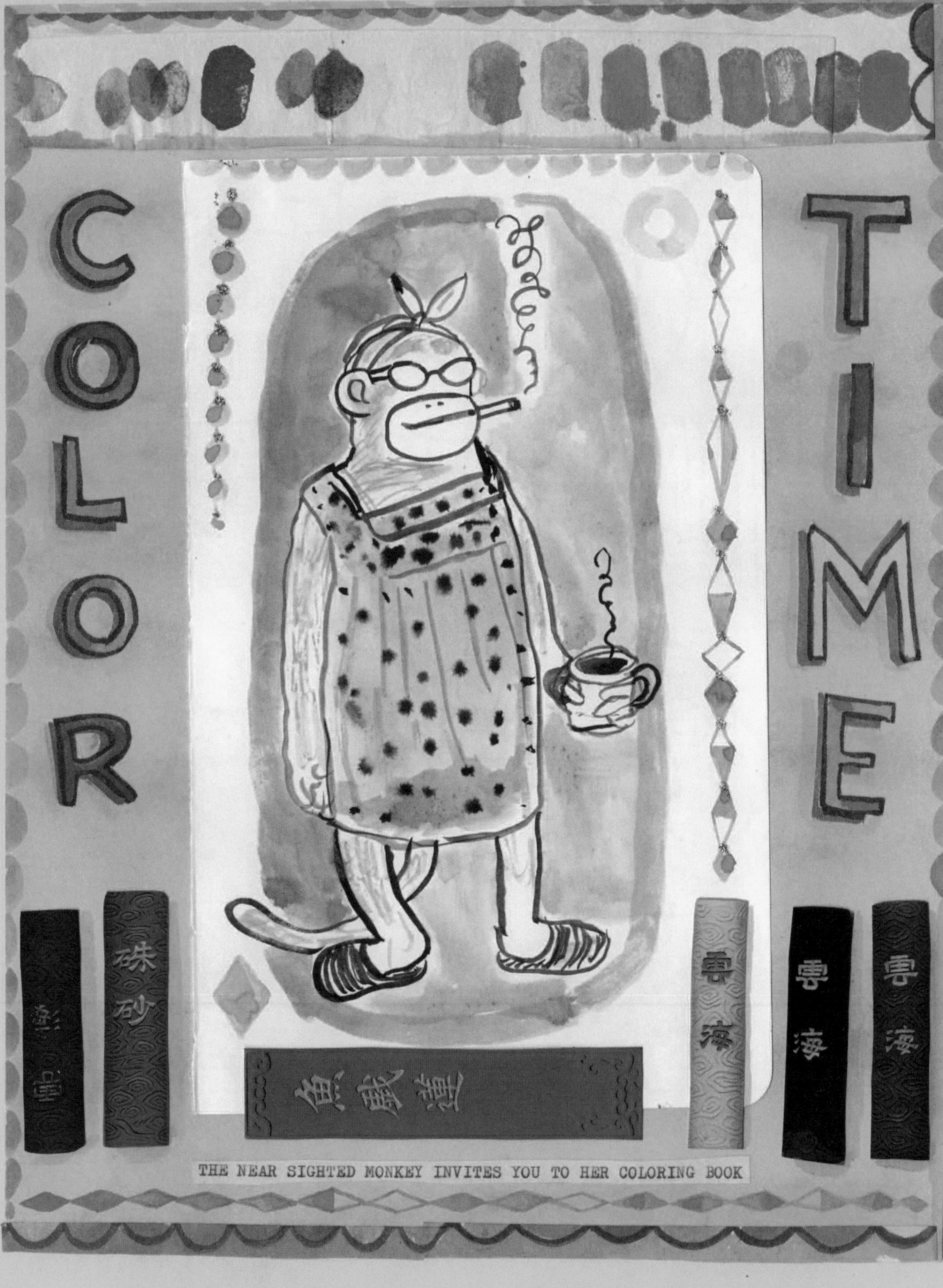
COLOR
TIME
硃砂
雲海
雲海
雲海
THE NEAR SIGHTED MONKEY INVITES YOU TO HER COLORING BOOK

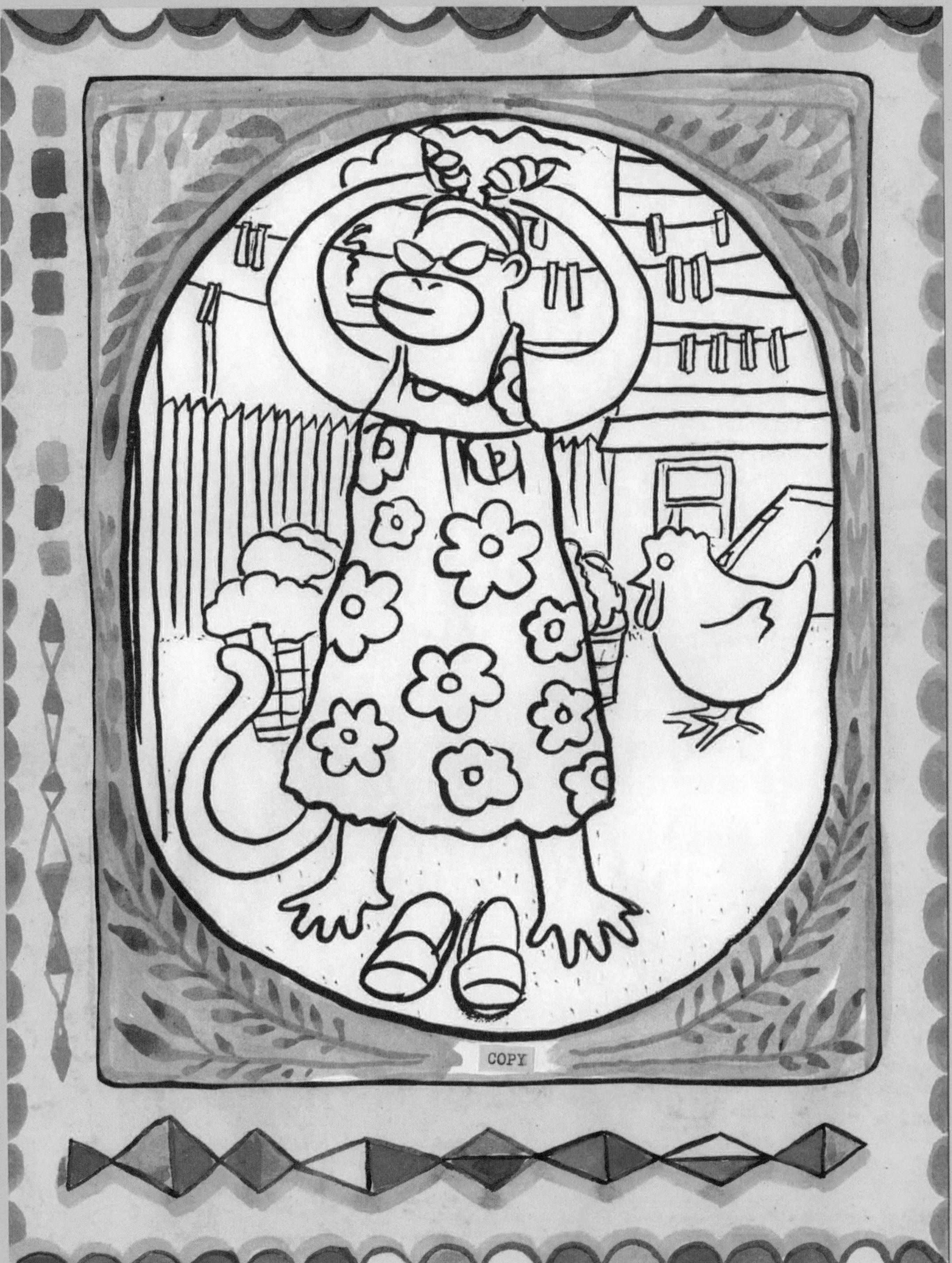
COPY

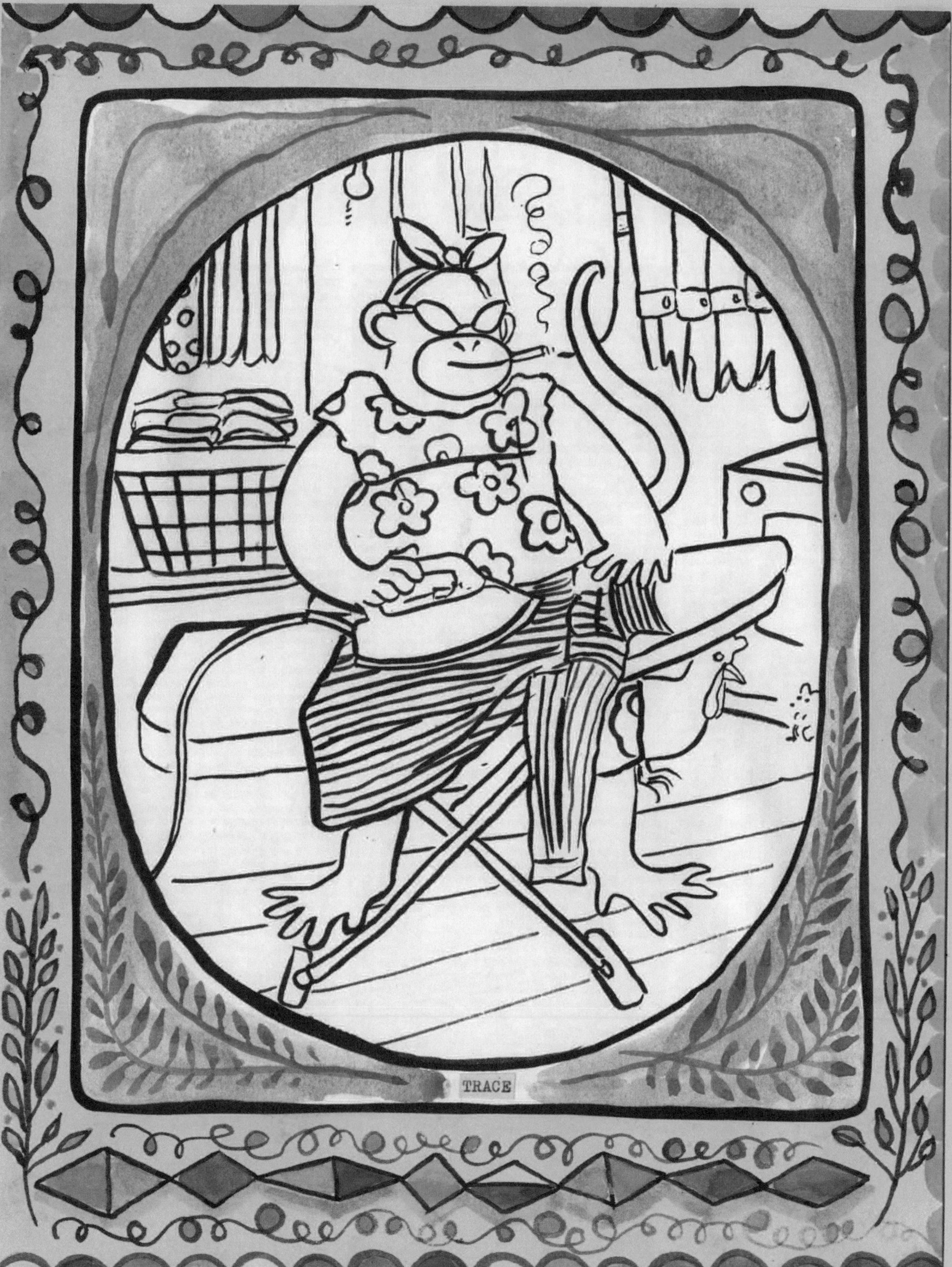
TRACE

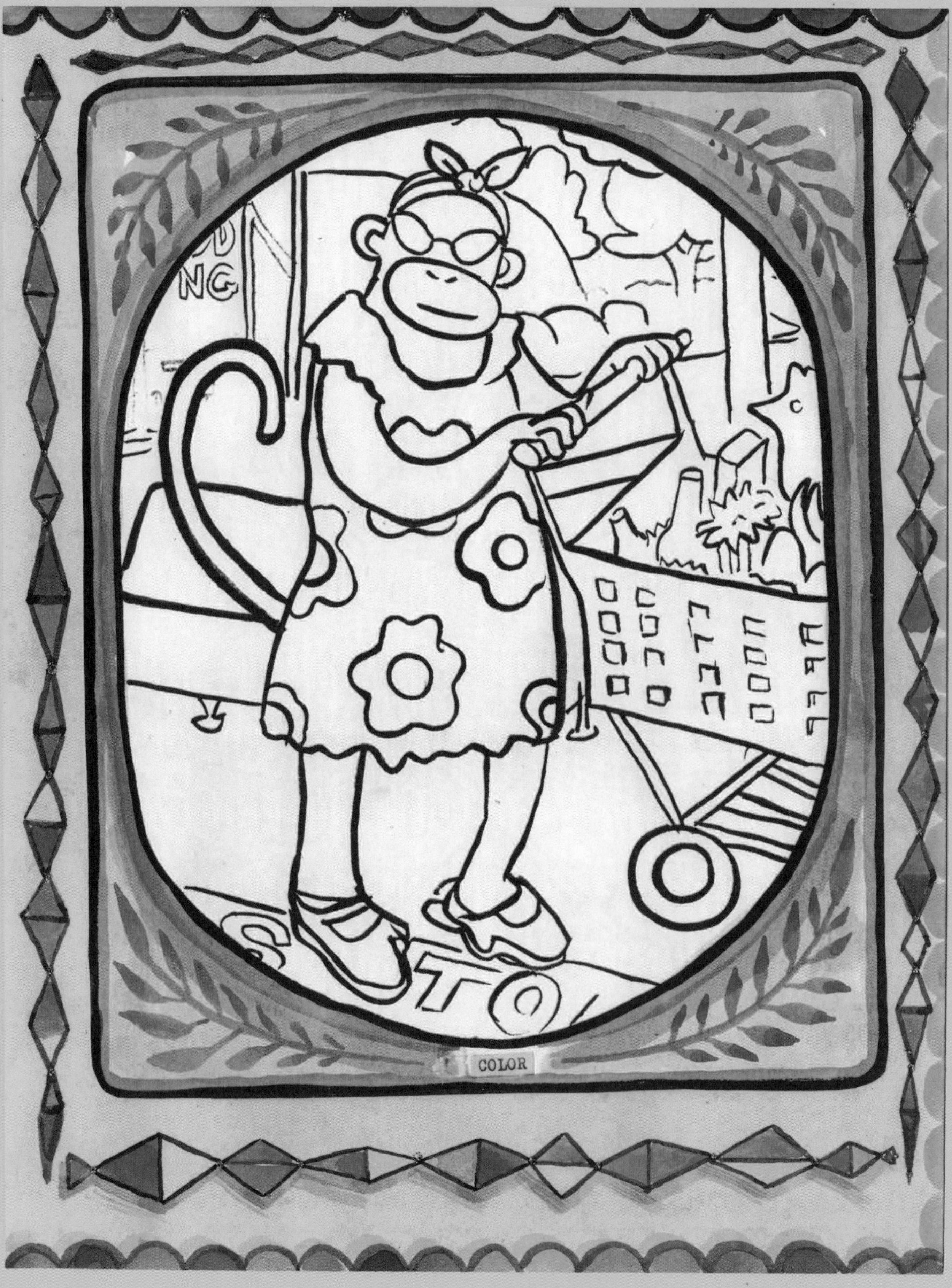
NG
COLOR
STO

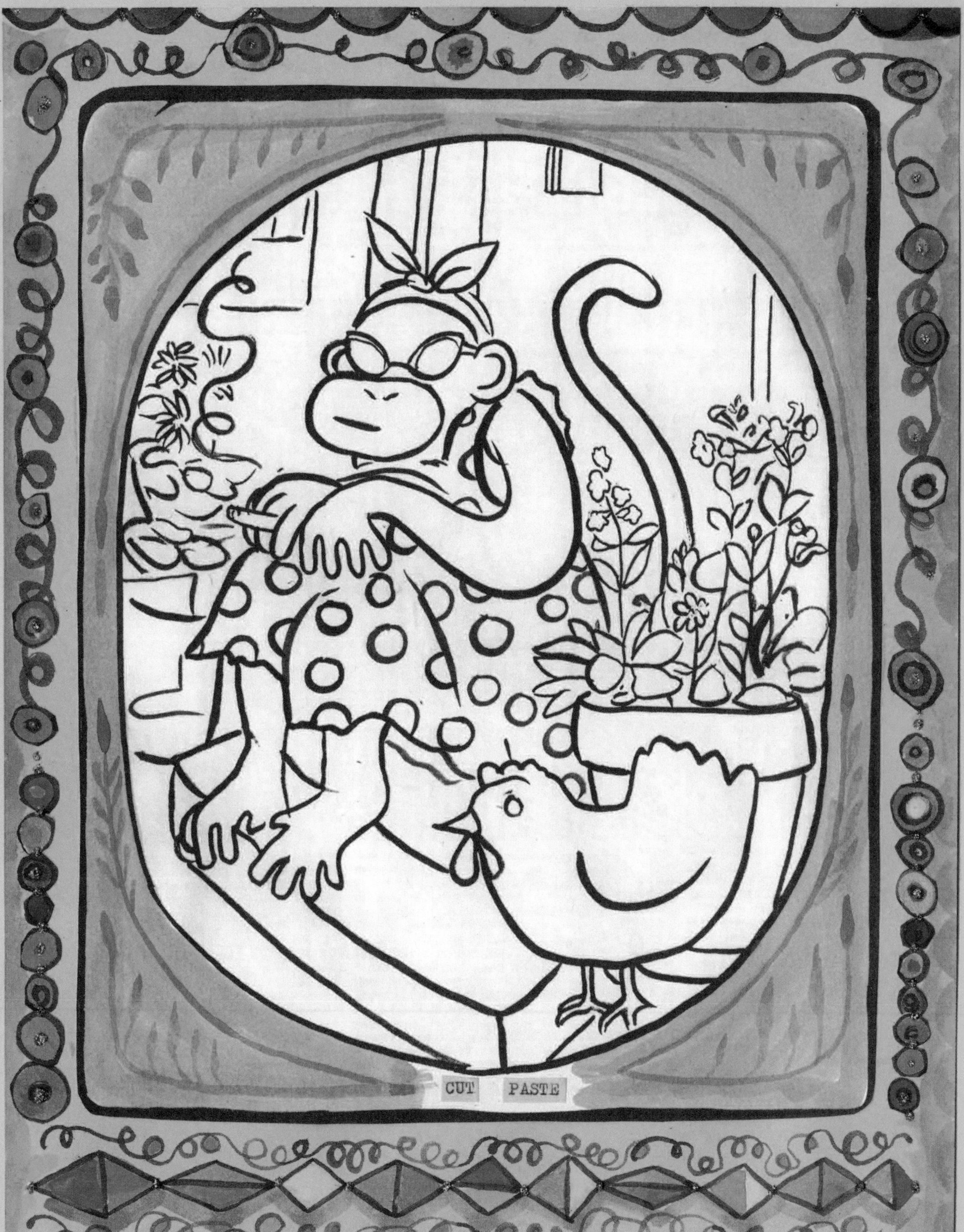
CUT
PASTE

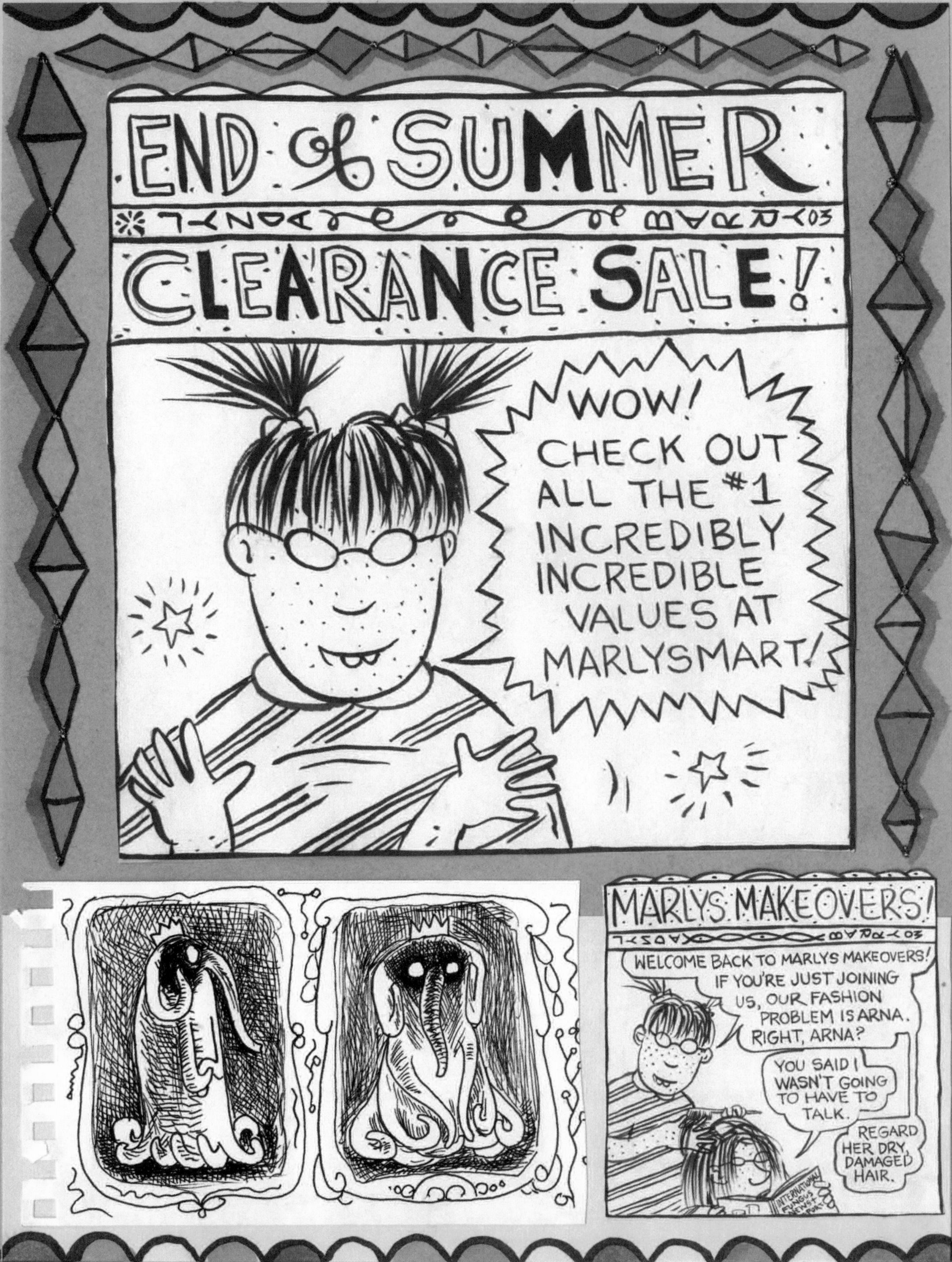
END of SUMMER
CLEARANCE SALE!
WOW! CHECK OUT ALL THE #1 INCREDIBLY INCREDIBLE VALUES AT MARLYSMART!
MARLYS MAKEOVERS!
WELCOME BACK TO MARLYS MAKEOVERS! IF YOU'RE JUST JOINING US, OUR FASHION PROBLEM IS ARNA. RIGHT, ARNA?
YOU SAID I WASN'T GOING TO HAVE TO TALK.
REGARD HER DRY, DAMAGED HAIR.
INTERNATIONAL FUNGUS NEWS REPORT

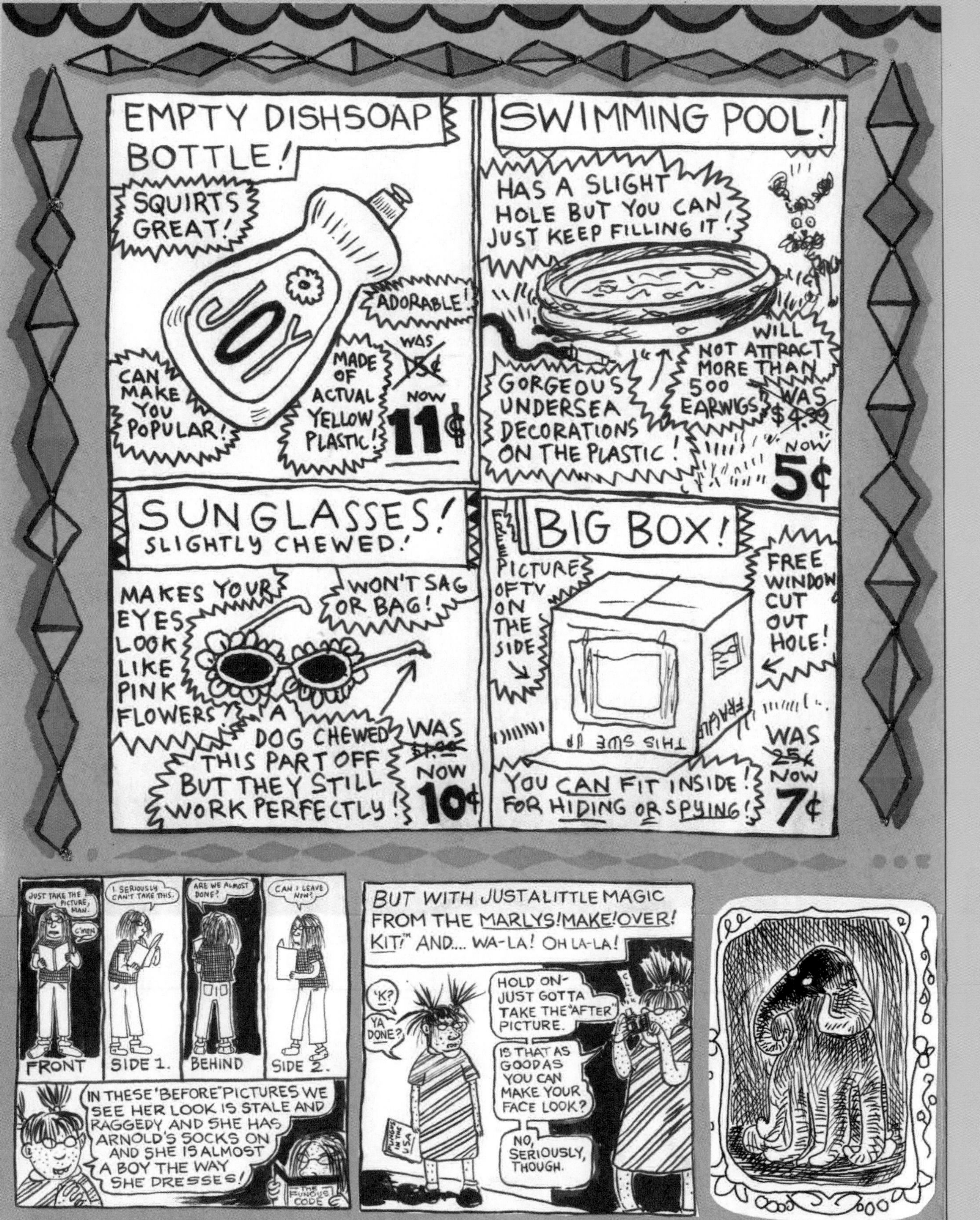
EMPTY DISHSOAP BOTTLE!
SQUIRTS GREAT!
JOY
ADORABLE!
CAN MAKE YOU POPULAR!
MADE OF ACTUAL YELLOW PLASTIC!
WAS 15¢ NOW 11¢
SWIMMING POOL!
HAS A SLIGHT HOLE BUT YOU CAN JUST KEEP FILLING IT!
GORGEOUS UNDERSEA DECORATIONS ON THE PLASTIC!
WILL NOT ATTRACT MORE THAN 500 EARWIGS
WAS $4.99 NOW 5¢
SUNGLASSES! SLIGHTLY CHEWED!
MAKES YOUR EYES LOOK LIKE PINK FLOWERS!
WON'T SAG OR BAG!
A DOG CHEWED THIS PART OFF BUT THEY STILL WORK PERFECTLY!
WAS $1.00 NOW 10¢
BIG BOX!
FREE PICTURE OF TV ON THE SIDE
FREE WINDOW CUT OUT HOLE!
FRAGILE
THIS SIDE UP
YOU CAN FIT INSIDE! FOR HIDING OR SPYING!
WAS 25¢ NOW 7¢
JUST TAKE THE PICTURE, MAN.
C'MON
I SERIOUSLY CAN'T TAKE THIS.
ARE WE ALMOST DONE?
CAN I LEAVE NOW?
FRONT
SIDE 1.
BEHIND
SIDE 2.
IN THESE "BEFORE" PICTURES WE SEE HER LOOK IS STALE AND RAGGEDY, AND SHE HAS ARNOLD'S SOCKS ON AND SHE IS ALMOST A BOY THE WAY SHE DRESSES!
THE FUNGUS CODE
BUT WITH JUST A LITTLE MAGIC FROM THE MARLYS! MAKE! OVER! KIT!™ AND.... WA-LA! OH LA-LA!
'K?
YA DONE?
HOLD ON- JUST GOTTA TAKE THE "AFTER" PICTURE.
CLICK
IS THAT AS GOOD AS YOU CAN MAKE YOUR FACE LOOK?
NO, SERIOUSLY, THOUGH.
FUNGUS IN THE USA

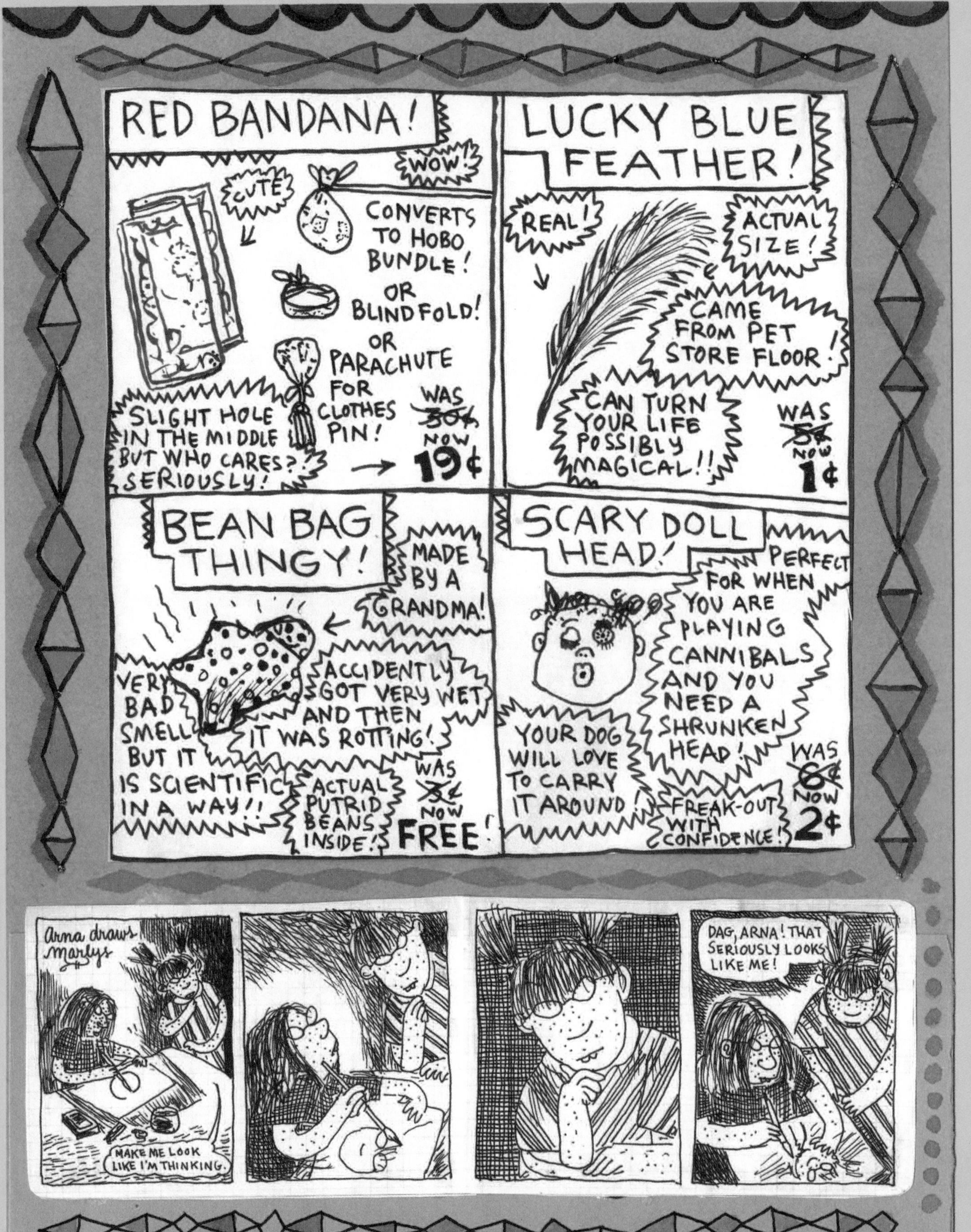

RED BANDANA!
WOW!
CUTE
CONVERTS TO HOBO BUNDLE!
OR BLINDFOLD!
OR PARACHUTE FOR CLOTHES PIN!
SLIGHT HOLE IN THE MIDDLE BUT WHO CARES? SERIOUSLY!
WAS 30¢ NOW 19¢
LUCKY BLUE FEATHER!
REAL!
ACTUAL SIZE!
CAME FROM PET STORE FLOOR!
CAN TURN YOUR LIFE POSSIBLY MAGICAL!!
WAS 5¢ NOW 1¢
BEAN BAG THINGY!
MADE BY A GRANDMA!
VERY BAD SMELL BUT IT IS SCIENTIFIC IN A WAY!!
ACCIDENTLY GOT VERY WET AND THEN IT WAS ROTTING!
ACTUAL PUTRID BEANS INSIDE!
WAS 3¢ NOW FREE!
SCARY DOLL HEAD!
PERFECT FOR WHEN YOU ARE PLAYING CANNIBALS AND YOU NEED A SHRUNKEN HEAD!
YOUR DOG WILL LOVE TO CARRY IT AROUND!
FREAK-OUT WITH CONFIDENCE!
WAS 6¢ NOW 2¢
Arna draws Marlys
MAKE ME LOOK LIKE I'M THINKING.
DAG, ARNA! THAT SERIOUSLY LOOKS LIKE ME!

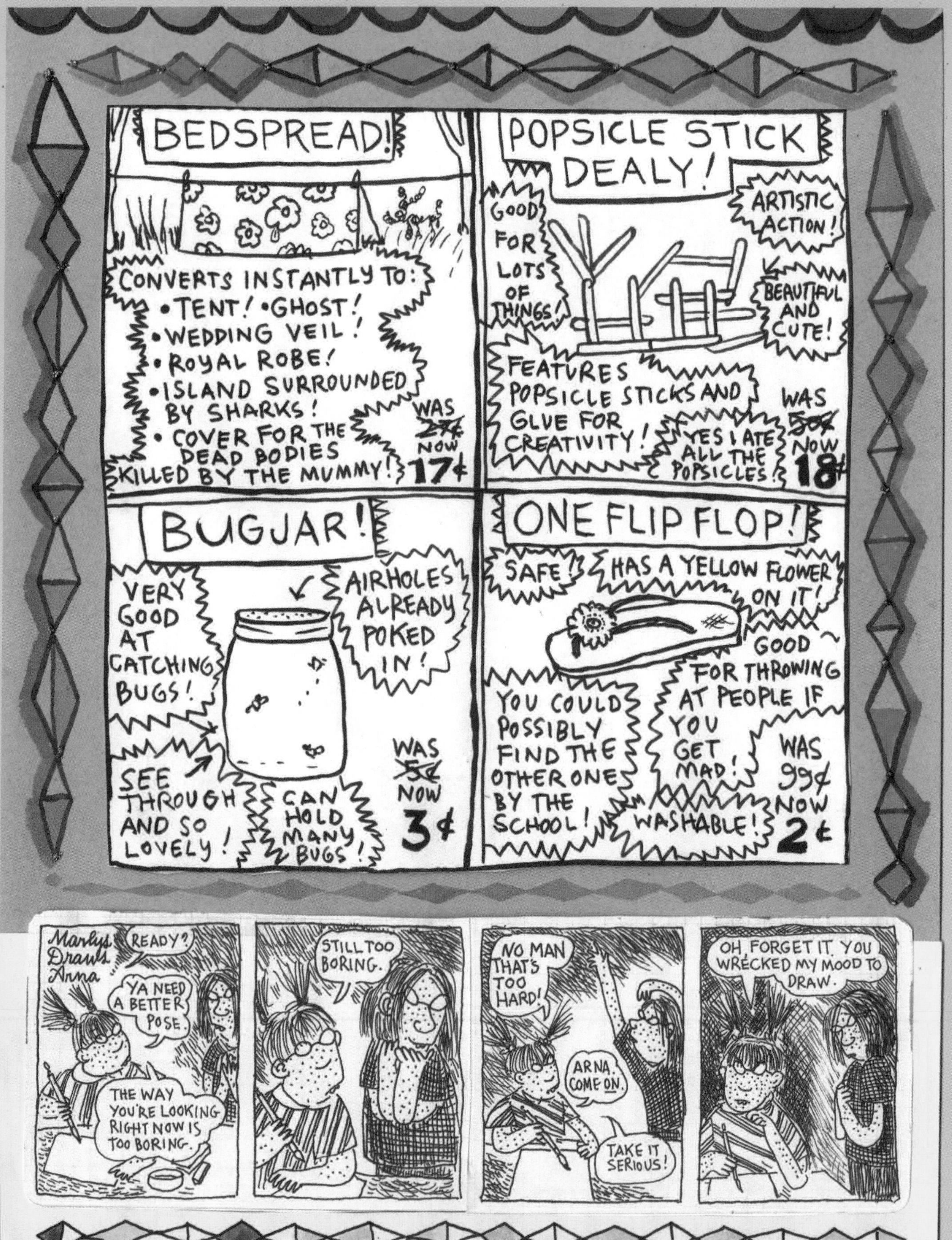
BEDSPREAD!
CONVERTS INSTANTLY TO:
•TENT! •GHOST!
•WEDDING VEIL!
•ROYAL ROBE!
•ISLAND SURROUNDED BY SHARKS!
•COVER FOR THE DEAD BODIES KILLED BY THE MUMMY!
WAS ~~27¢~~ NOW 17¢
POPSICLE STICK DEALY!
GOOD FOR LOTS OF THINGS!
ARTISTIC ACTION!
BEAUTIFUL AND CUTE!
FEATURES POPSICLE STICKS AND GLUE FOR CREATIVITY!
YES I ATE ALL THE POPSICLES!
WAS ~~50¢~~ NOW 18¢
BUGJAR!
VERY GOOD AT CATCHING BUGS!
AIRHOLES ALREADY POKED IN!
SEE THROUGH AND SO LOVELY!
CAN HOLD MANY BUGS!
WAS ~~5¢~~ NOW 3¢
ONE FLIP FLOP!
SAFE!
HAS A YELLOW FLOWER ON IT!
GOOD FOR THROWING AT PEOPLE IF YOU GET MAD!
YOU COULD POSSIBLY FIND THE OTHER ONE BY THE SCHOOL!
WASHABLE!
WAS 99¢ NOW 2¢
Marlys Draws Arna
READY?
YA NEED A BETTER POSE.
THE WAY YOU'RE LOOKING RIGHT NOW IS TOO BORING.
STILL TOO BORING.
NO MAN THAT'S TOO HARD!
ARNA, COME ON.
TAKE IT SERIOUS!
OH, FORGET IT. YOU WRECKED MY MOOD TO DRAW.

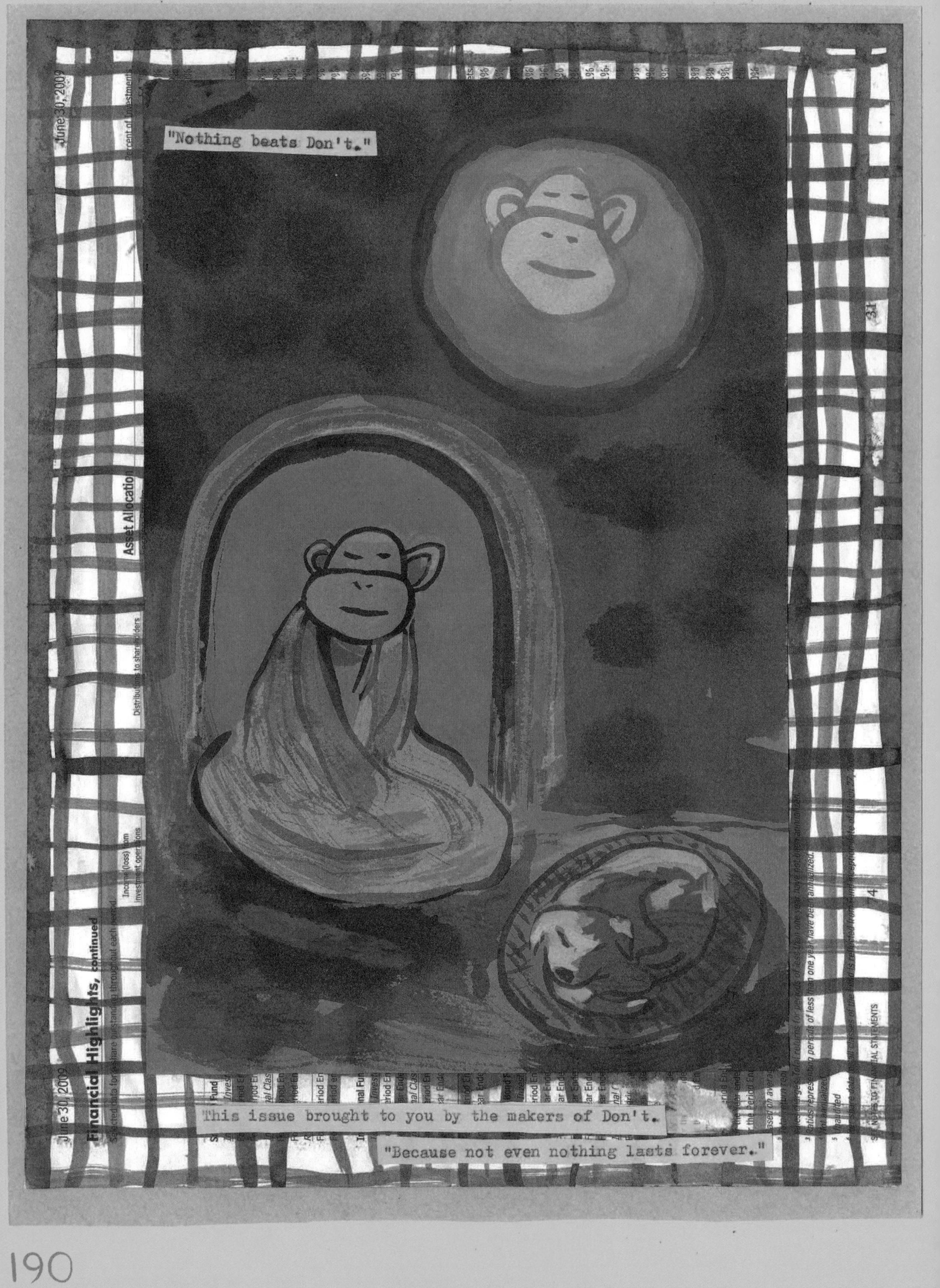
"Nothing beats Don't."
This issue brought to you by the makers of Don't.
"Because not even nothing lasts forever."
June 30, 2009
Financial Highlights, continued
Asset Allocation
Distributions to shareholders
Income (loss) from
investment operations
Percent of Investments
31
74
SEE NOTES TO FINANCIAL STATEMENTS

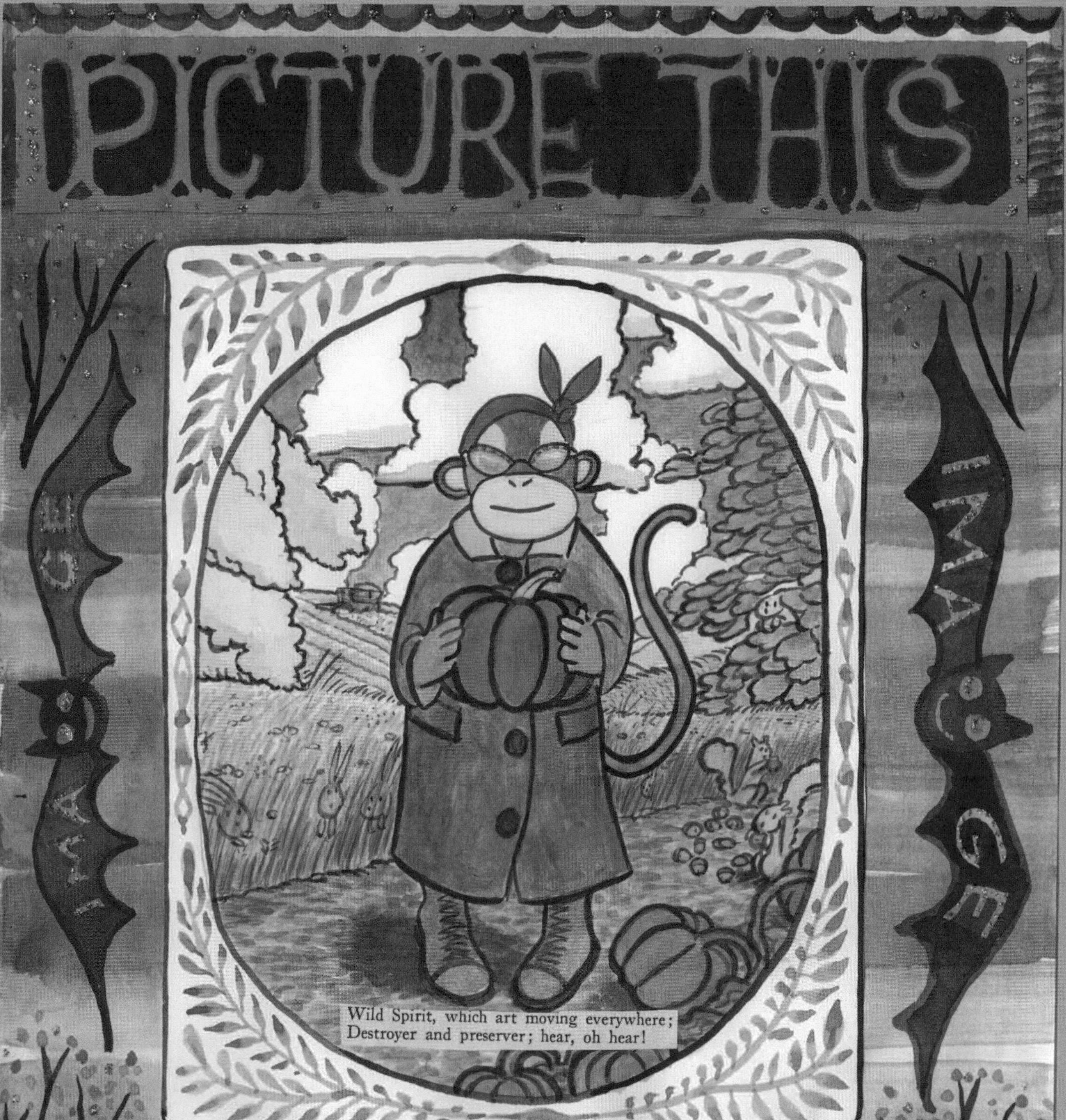
PICTURE THIS
Wild Spirit, which art moving everywhere;
Destroyer and preserver; hear, oh hear!
FALL

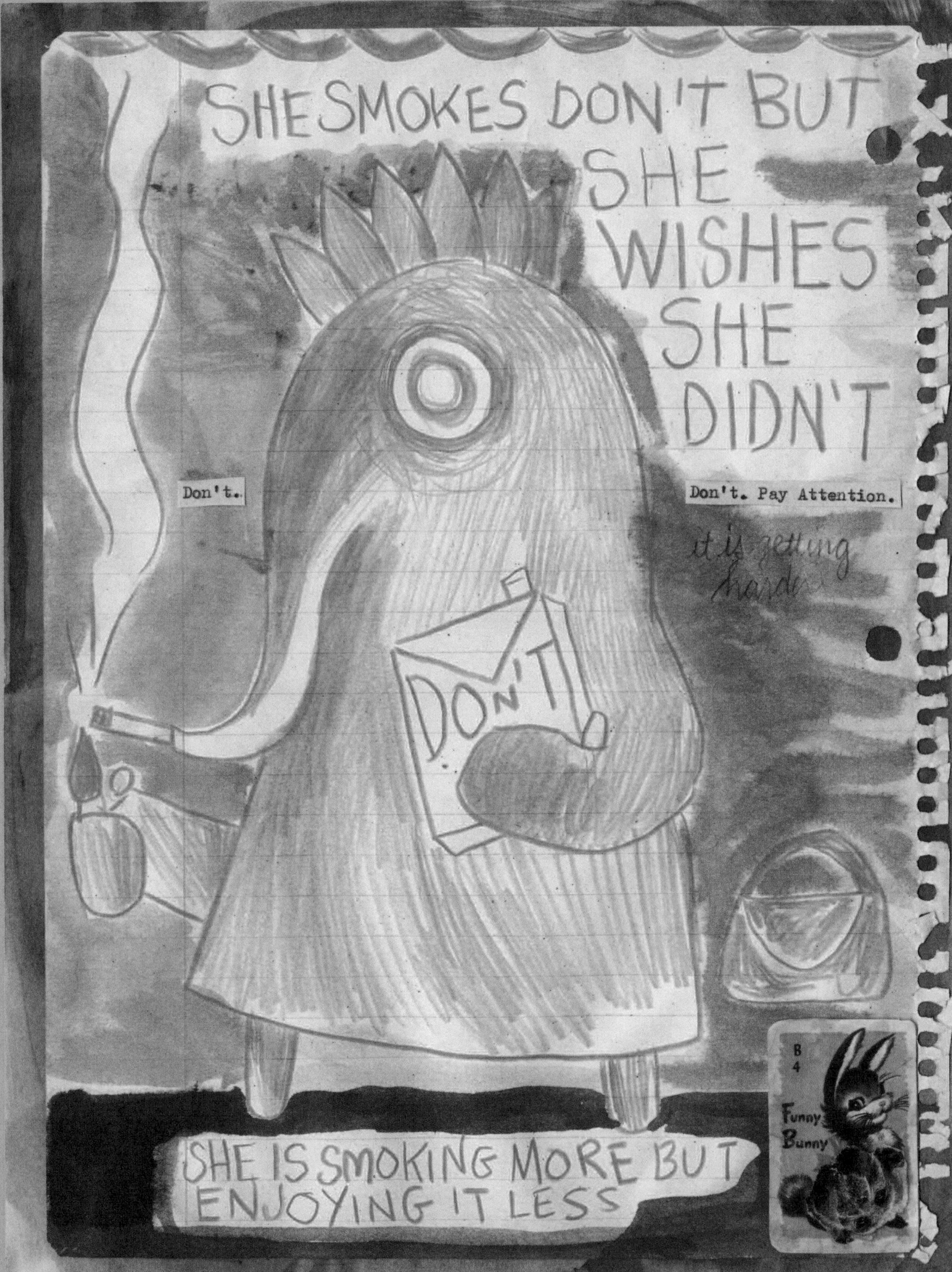
SHE SMOKES DON'T BUT
SHE
WISHES
SHE
DIDN'T
Don't.
Don't. Pay Attention.
it is getting harder
DON'T
B 4
Funny Bunny
SHE IS SMOKING MORE BUT
ENJOYING IT LESS

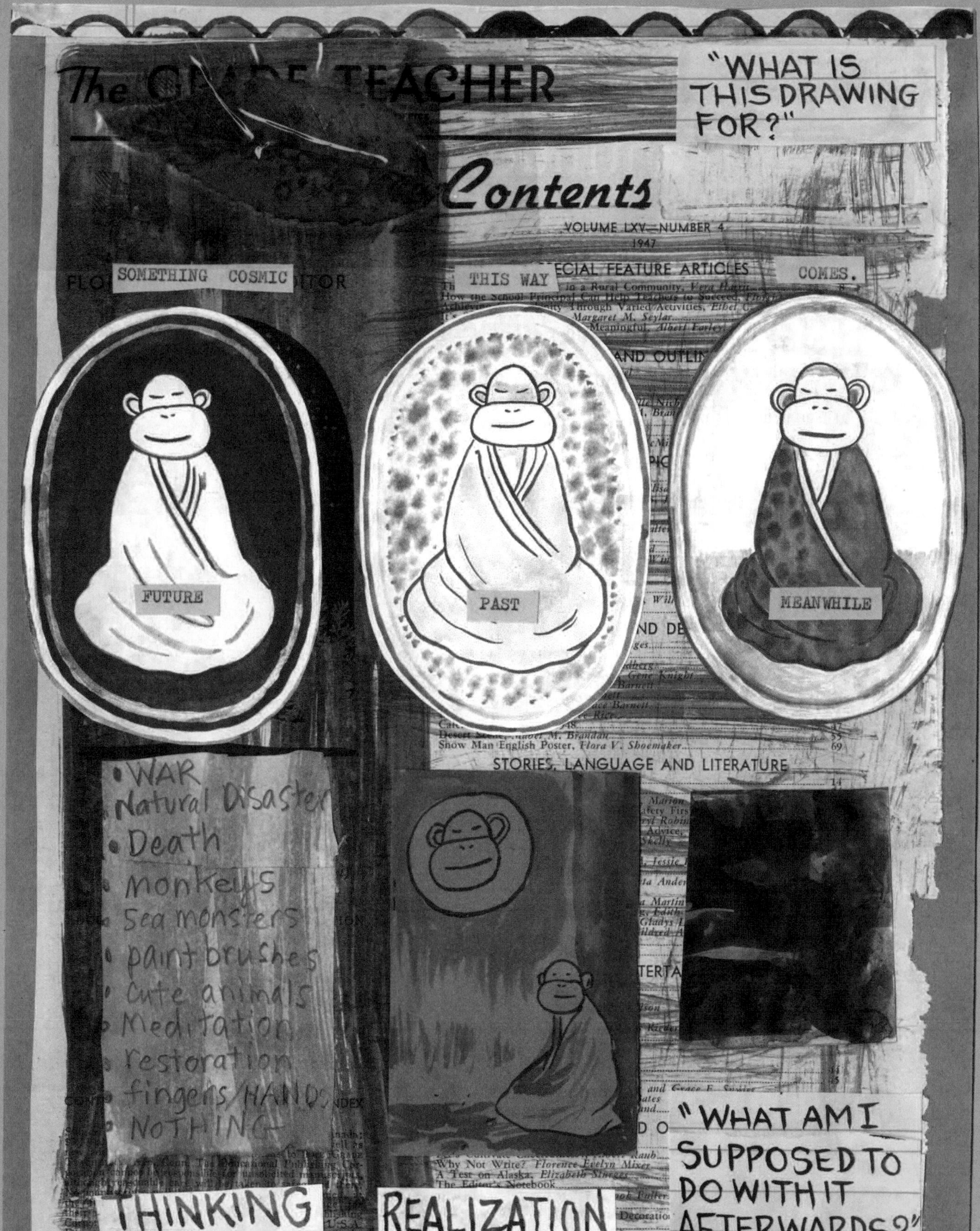

The GRADE TEACHER
"WHAT IS THIS DRAWING FOR?"
Contents
VOLUME LXV—NUMBER 4
1947
SOMETHING COSMIC
THIS WAY
COMES.
FUTURE
PAST
MEANWHILE
STORIES, LANGUAGE AND LITERATURE
• WAR
• Natural Disaster
• Death
• monkeys
• Sea monsters
• paint brushes
• cute animals
• Meditation
• restoration
• fingers/HANDS
• NOTHING
THINKING
REALIZATION
"WHAT AM I SUPPOSED TO DO WITH IT AFTERWARDS?"
PAGE 2
THE GRADE TEACHER

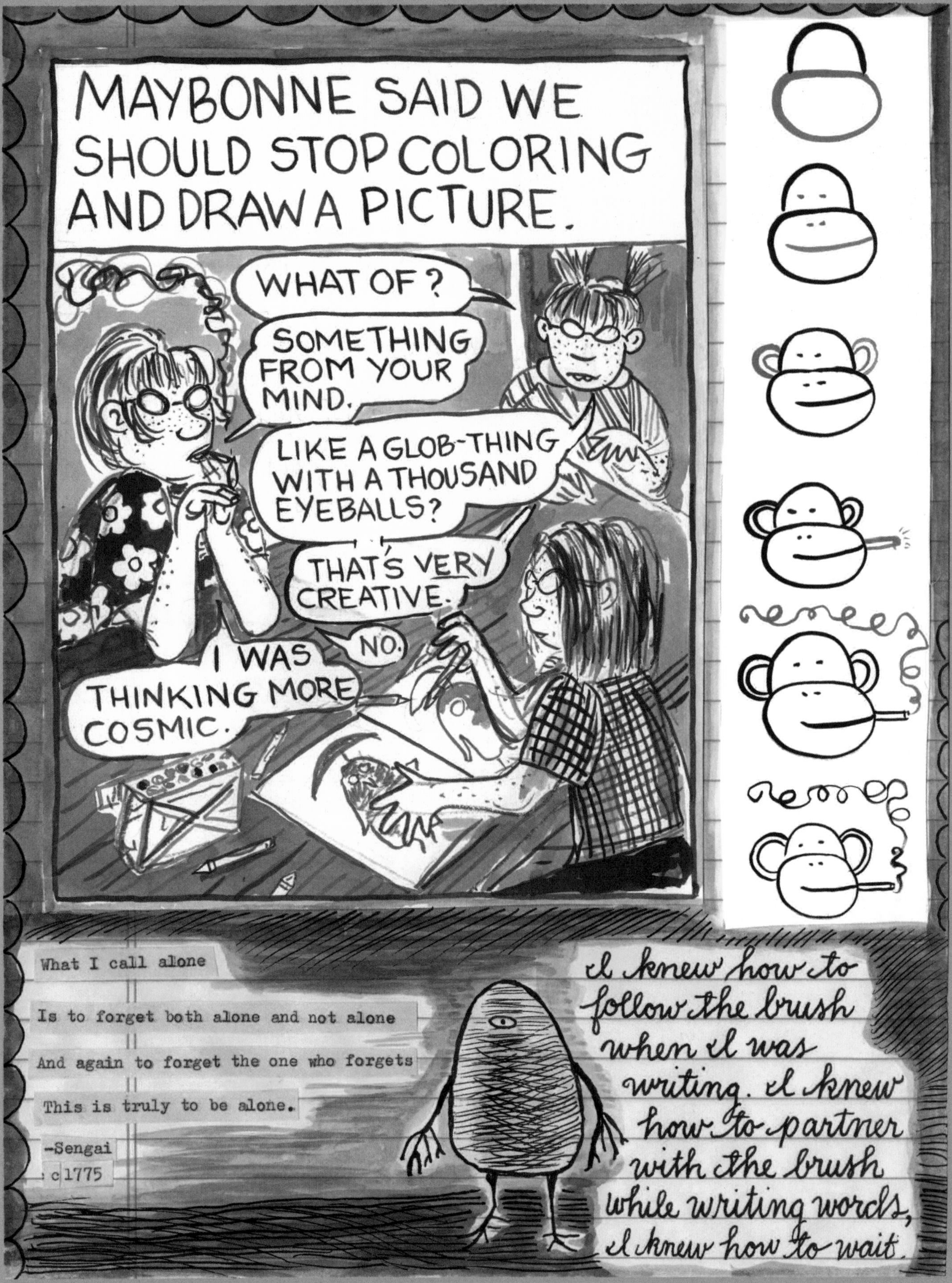
MAYBONNE SAID WE SHOULD STOP COLORING AND DRAW A PICTURE.
WHAT OF?
SOMETHING FROM YOUR MIND.
LIKE A GLOB-THING WITH A THOUSAND EYEBALLS?
THAT'S VERY CREATIVE.
NO.
I WAS THINKING MORE COSMIC.
What I call alone
Is to forget both alone and not alone
And again to forget the one who forgets
This is truly to be alone.
–Sengai
c 1775
I knew how to follow the brush when I was writing. I knew how to partner with the brush while writing words, I knew how to wait.

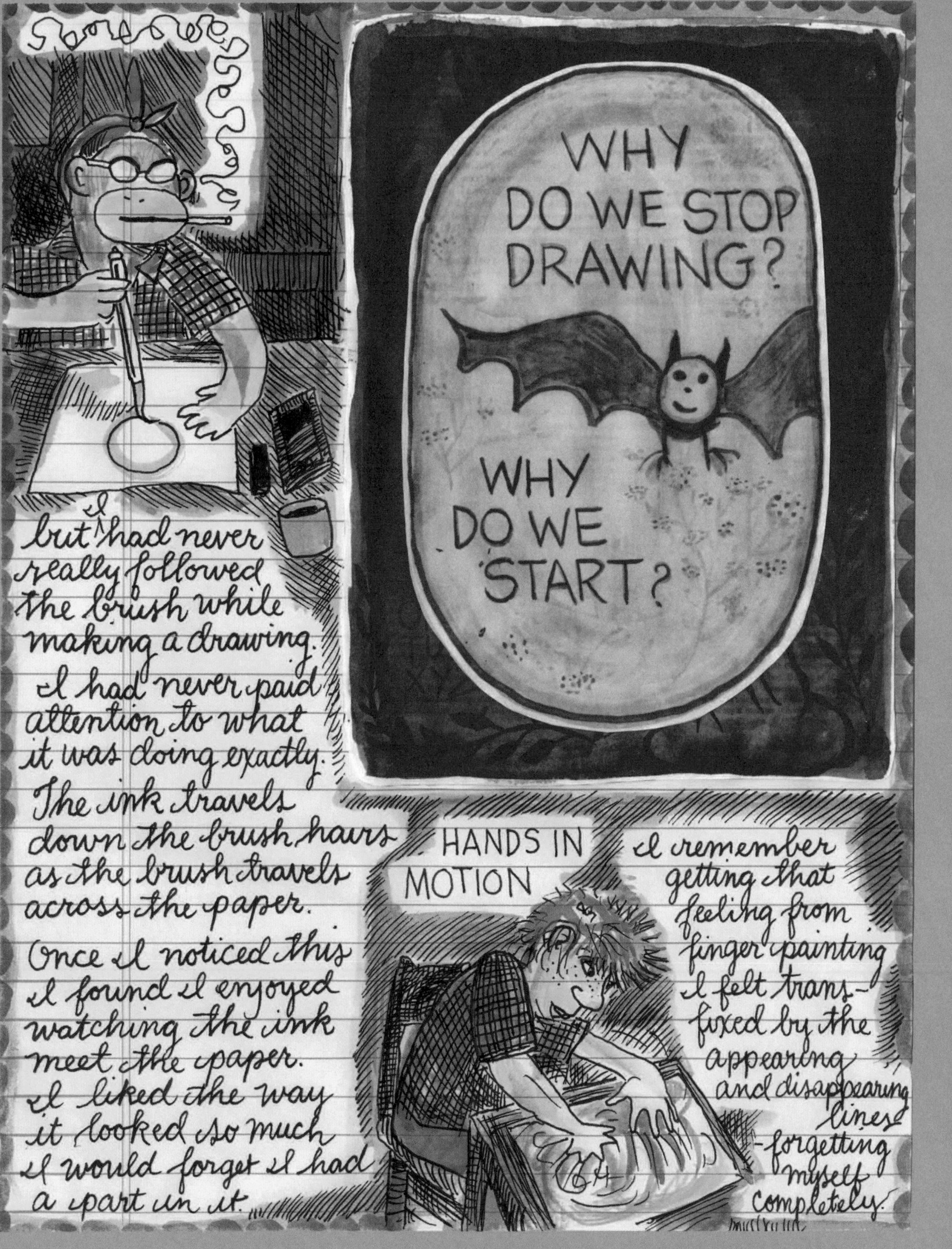
but I had never really followed the brush while making a drawing.
I had never paid attention to what it was doing exactly.
The ink travels down the brush hairs as the brush travels across the paper.
Once I noticed this I found I enjoyed watching the ink meet the paper.
I liked the way it looked so much I would forget I had a part in it.
WHY DO WE STOP DRAWING?
WHY DO WE START?
HANDS IN MOTION
I remember getting that feeling from finger painting
I felt trans-fixed by the appearing and disappearing lines
-forgetting myself completely.

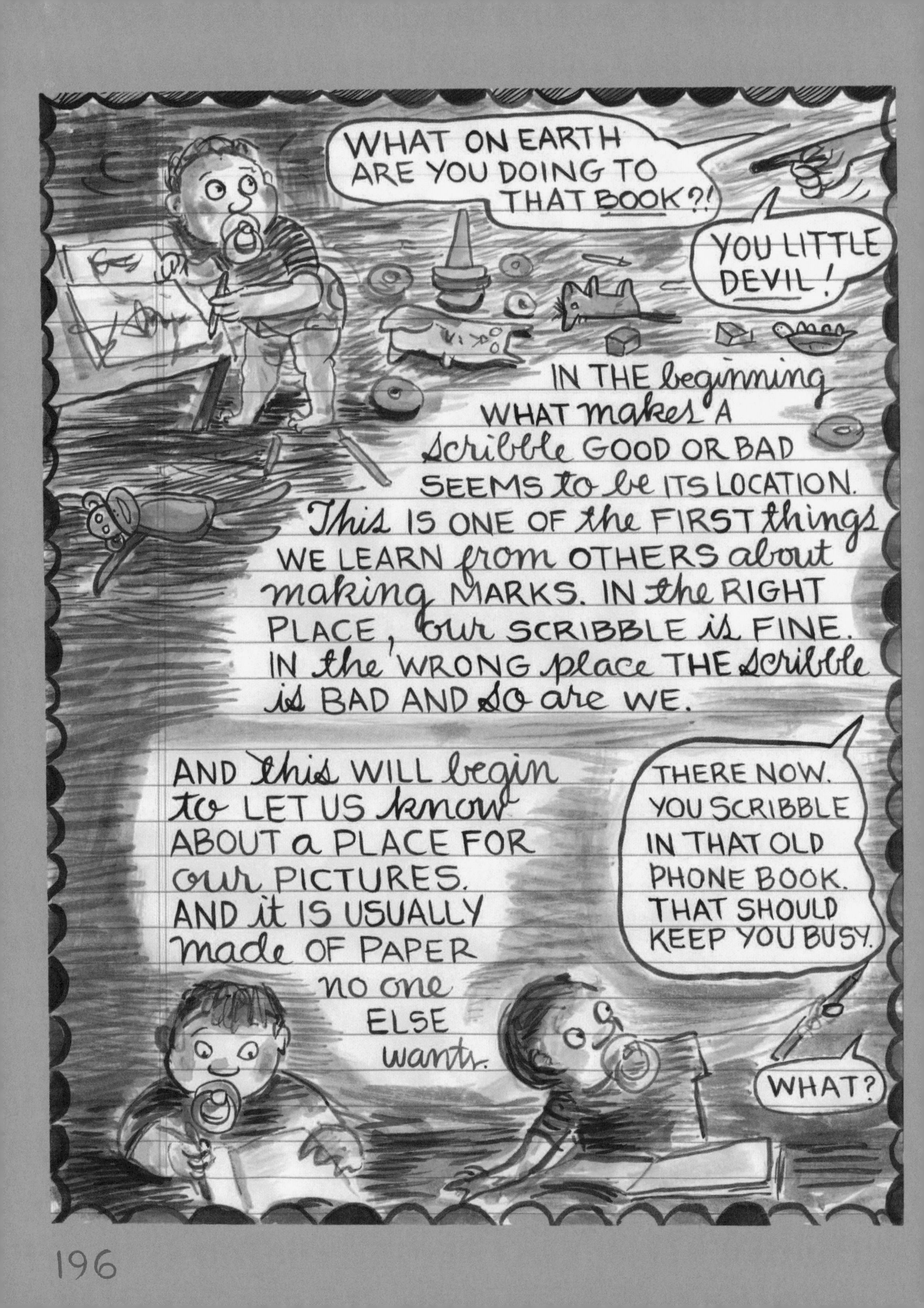
WHAT ON EARTH ARE YOU DOING TO THAT BOOK?!
YOU LITTLE DEVIL!
IN THE beginning WHAT makes A scribble GOOD OR BAD SEEMS to be ITS LOCATION. This IS ONE OF the FIRST things WE LEARN from OTHERS about making MARKS. IN the RIGHT PLACE, our SCRIBBLE is FINE. IN the WRONG place THE scribble is BAD AND SO are WE.
AND this WILL begin to LET US know ABOUT a PLACE FOR our PICTURES. AND it IS USUALLY made OF PAPER no one ELSE wants.
THERE NOW. YOU SCRIBBLE IN THAT OLD PHONE BOOK. THAT SHOULD KEEP YOU BUSY.
WHAT?

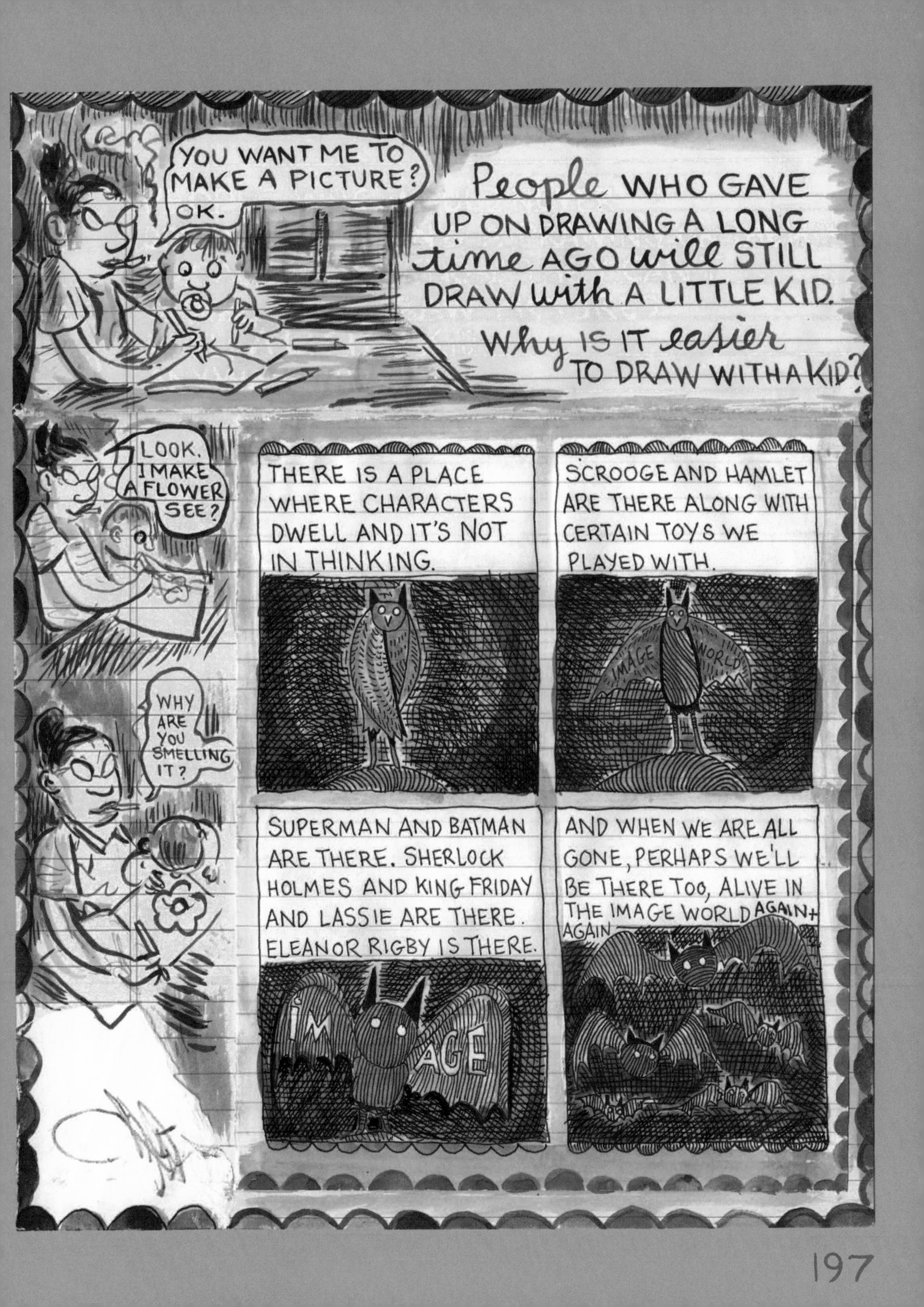
YOU WANT ME TO MAKE A PICTURE? OK.
People WHO GAVE UP ON DRAWING A LONG time AGO will STILL DRAW with A LITTLE KID.
Why IS IT easier TO DRAW WITH A KID?
LOOK. I MAKE A FLOWER SEE?
WHY ARE YOU SMELLING IT?
THERE IS A PLACE WHERE CHARACTERS DWELL AND IT'S NOT IN THINKING.
SCROOGE AND HAMLET ARE THERE ALONG WITH CERTAIN TOYS WE PLAYED WITH.
IMAGE WORLD
SUPERMAN AND BATMAN ARE THERE. SHERLOCK HOLMES AND KING FRIDAY AND LASSIE ARE THERE. ELEANOR RIGBY IS THERE.
IM AGE
AND WHEN WE ARE ALL GONE, PERHAPS WE'LL BE THERE TOO, ALIVE IN THE IMAGE WORLD AGAIN + AGAIN

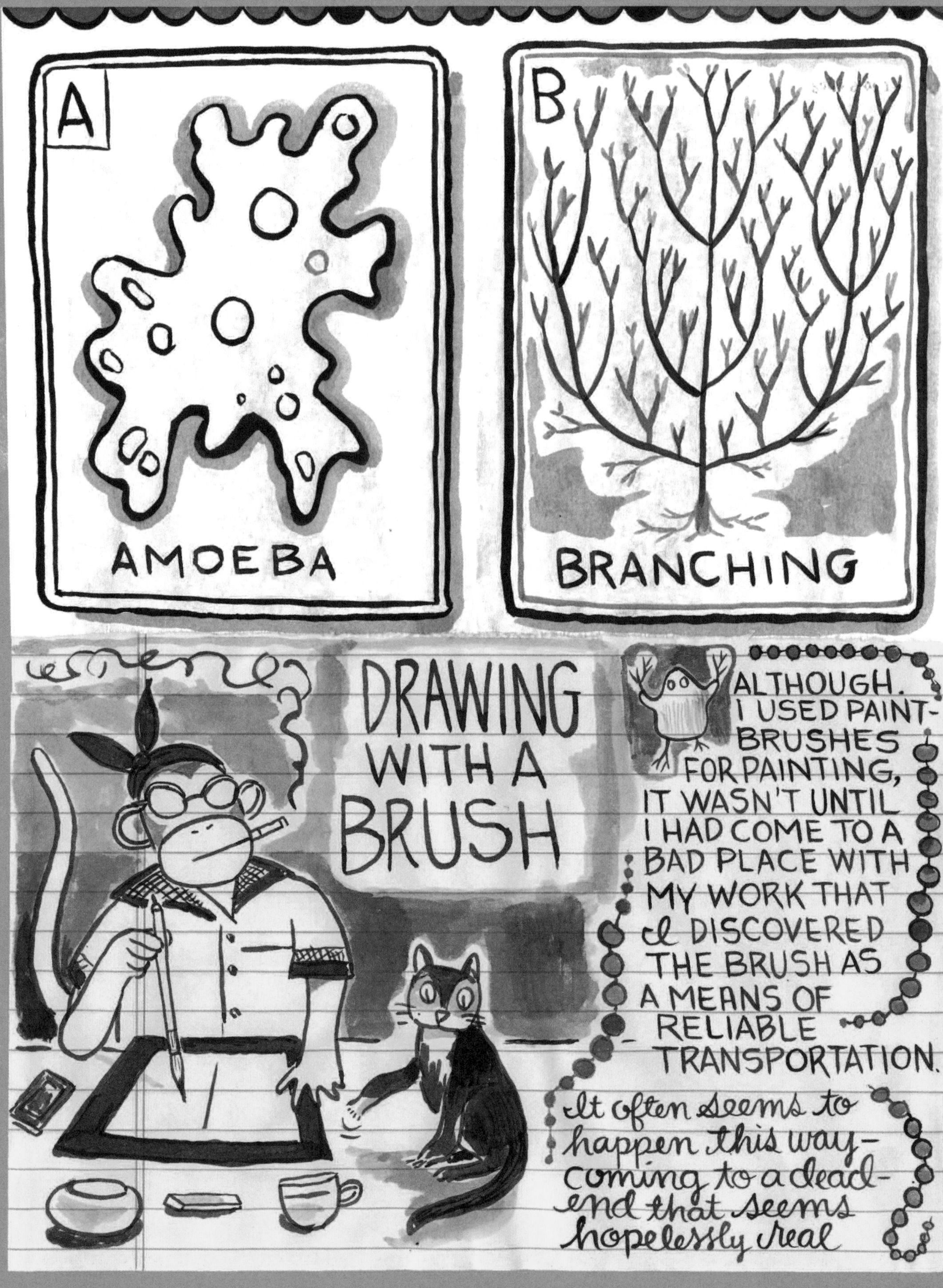
A
AMOEBA
B
BRANCHING
DRAWING WITH A BRUSH
ALTHOUGH. I USED PAINT-BRUSHES FOR PAINTING, IT WASN'T UNTIL I HAD COME TO A BAD PLACE WITH MY WORK THAT I DISCOVERED THE BRUSH AS A MEANS OF RELIABLE TRANSPORTATION.
It often seems to happen this way- coming to a dead-end that seems hopelessly real

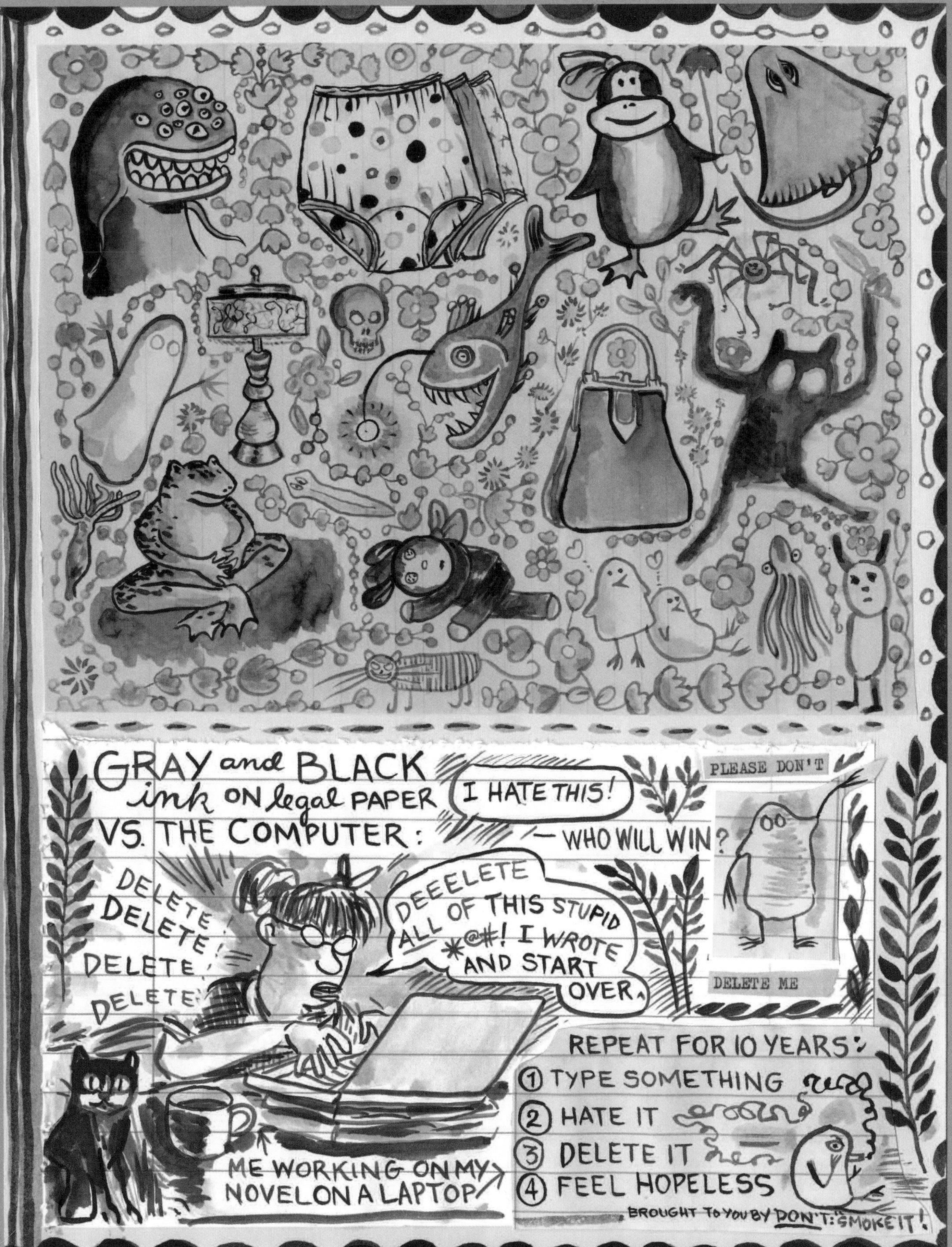

GRAY and BLACK ink ON legal PAPER VS. THE COMPUTER:
I HATE THIS!
— WHO WILL WIN?
PLEASE DON'T
DELETE ME
DELETE DELETE DELETE DELETE
DEEELETE ALL OF THIS STUPID *@#! I WROTE AND START OVER.
REPEAT FOR 10 YEARS:
① TYPE SOMETHING
② HATE IT
③ DELETE IT
④ FEEL HOPELESS
ME WORKING ON MY NOVEL ON A LAPTOP
BROUGHT TO YOU BY DON'T: SMOKE IT!

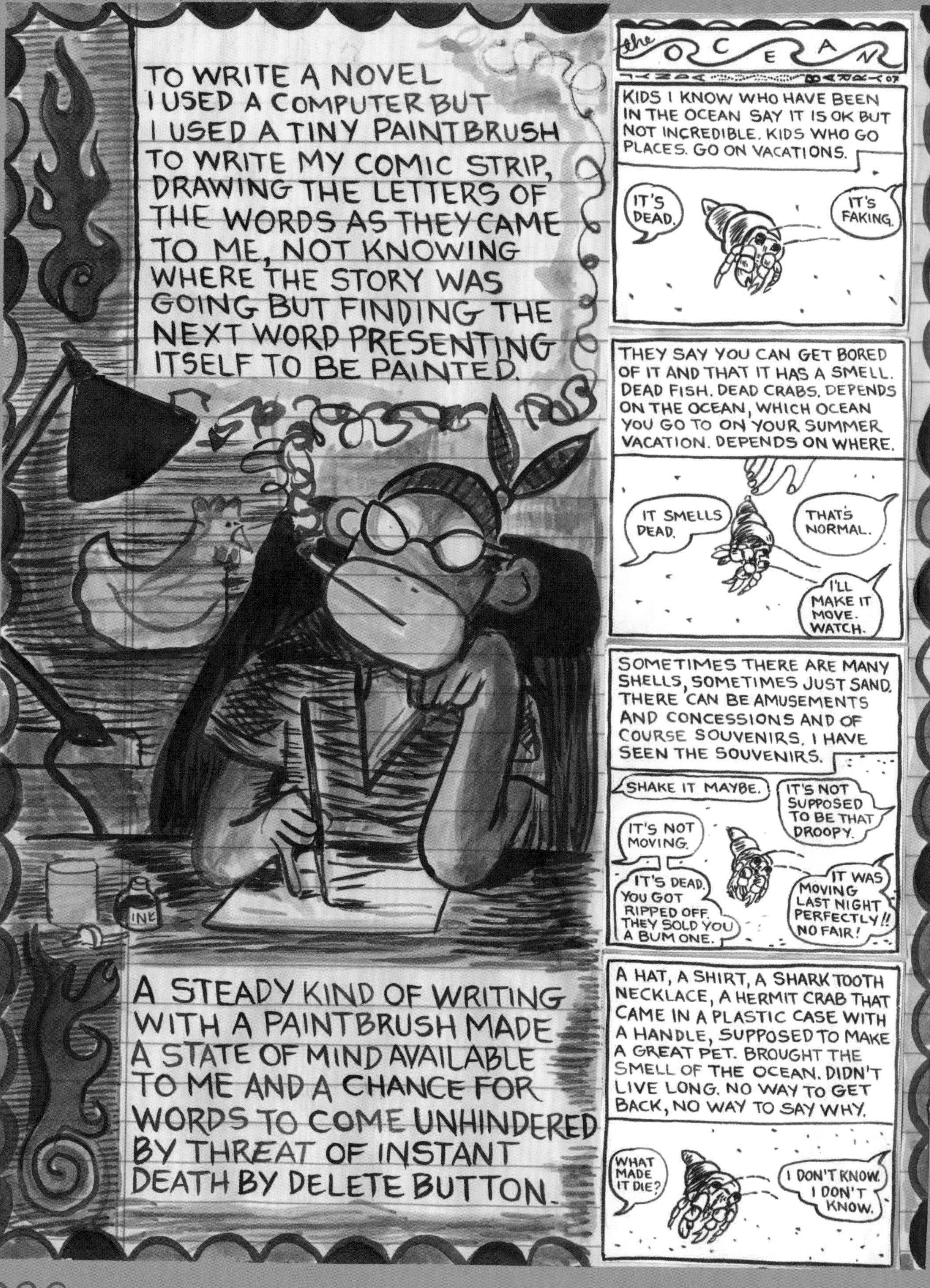
TO WRITE A NOVEL I USED A COMPUTER BUT I USED A TINY PAINTBRUSH TO WRITE MY COMIC STRIP, DRAWING THE LETTERS OF THE WORDS AS THEY CAME TO ME, NOT KNOWING WHERE THE STORY WAS GOING BUT FINDING THE NEXT WORD PRESENTING ITSELF TO BE PAINTED.
INK
A STEADY KIND OF WRITING WITH A PAINTBRUSH MADE A STATE OF MIND AVAILABLE TO ME AND A CHANCE FOR WORDS TO COME UNHINDERED BY THREAT OF INSTANT DEATH BY DELETE BUTTON.
the OCEAN
KIDS I KNOW WHO HAVE BEEN IN THE OCEAN SAY IT IS OK BUT NOT INCREDIBLE. KIDS WHO GO PLACES. GO ON VACATIONS.
IT'S DEAD.
IT'S FAKING.
THEY SAY YOU CAN GET BORED OF IT AND THAT IT HAS A SMELL. DEAD FISH. DEAD CRABS. DEPENDS ON THE OCEAN, WHICH OCEAN YOU GO TO ON YOUR SUMMER VACATION. DEPENDS ON WHERE.
IT SMELLS DEAD.
THAT'S NORMAL.
I'LL MAKE IT MOVE. WATCH.
SOMETIMES THERE ARE MANY SHELLS, SOMETIMES JUST SAND. THERE CAN BE AMUSEMENTS AND CONCESSIONS AND OF COURSE SOUVENIRS. I HAVE SEEN THE SOUVENIRS.
SHAKE IT MAYBE.
IT'S NOT SUPPOSED TO BE THAT DROOPY.
IT'S NOT MOVING.
IT'S DEAD. YOU GOT RIPPED OFF. THEY SOLD YOU A BUM ONE.
IT WAS MOVING LAST NIGHT PERFECTLY!! NO FAIR!
A HAT, A SHIRT, A SHARK TOOTH NECKLACE, A HERMIT CRAB THAT CAME IN A PLASTIC CASE WITH A HANDLE, SUPPOSED TO MAKE A GREAT PET. BROUGHT THE SMELL OF THE OCEAN. DIDN'T LIVE LONG. NO WAY TO GET BACK, NO WAY TO SAY WHY.
WHAT MADE IT DIE?
I DON'T KNOW. I DON'T KNOW.

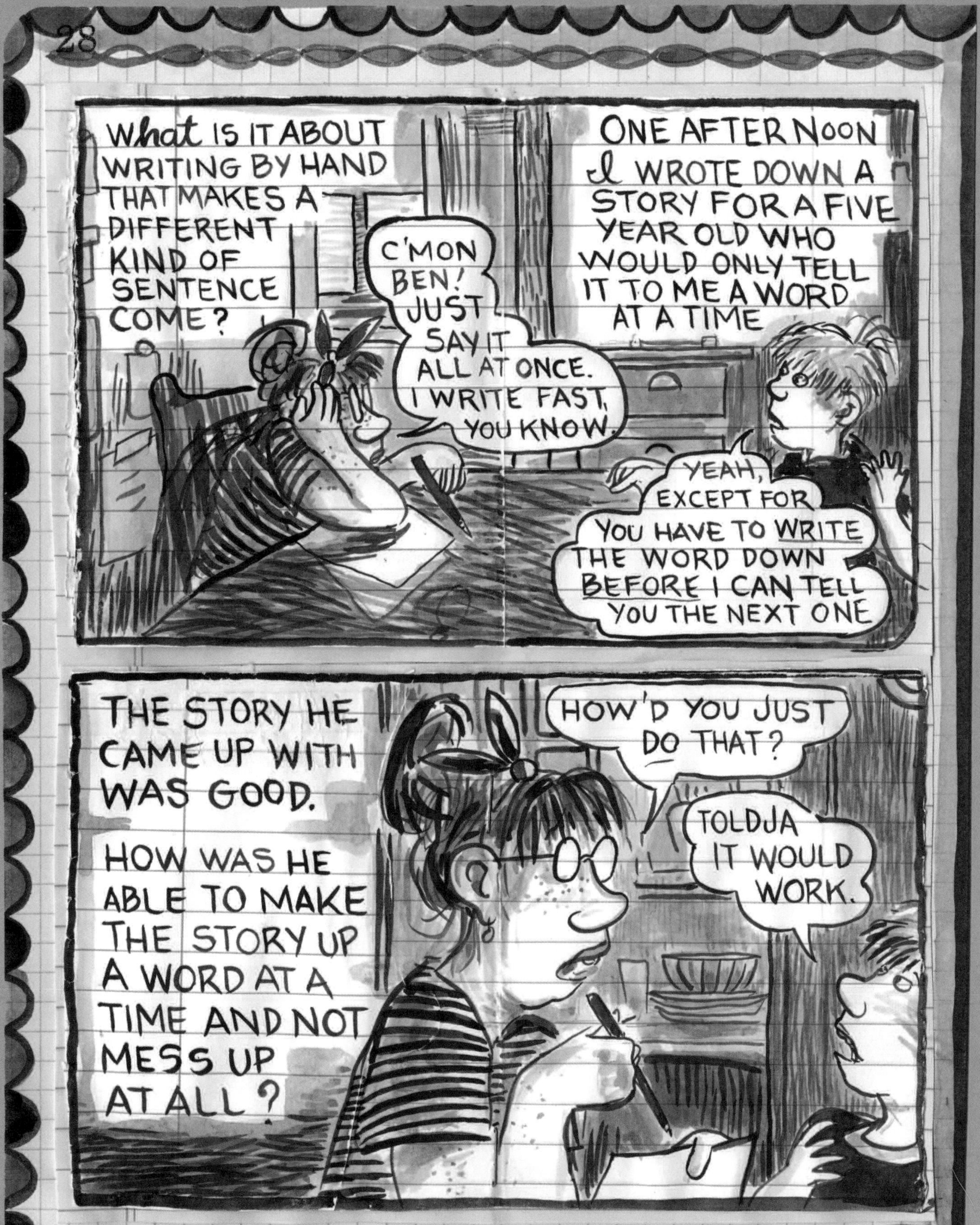
28
WHAT IS IT ABOUT WRITING BY HAND THAT MAKES A DIFFERENT KIND OF SENTENCE COME?
C'MON BEN! JUST SAY IT ALL AT ONCE. I WRITE FAST, YOU KNOW.
ONE AFTERNOON I WROTE DOWN A STORY FOR A FIVE YEAR OLD WHO WOULD ONLY TELL IT TO ME A WORD AT A TIME
YEAH, EXCEPT FOR YOU HAVE TO WRITE THE WORD DOWN BEFORE I CAN TELL YOU THE NEXT ONE
THE STORY HE CAME UP WITH WAS GOOD.
HOW WAS HE ABLE TO MAKE THE STORY UP A WORD AT A TIME AND NOT MESS UP AT ALL?
HOW'D YOU JUST DO THAT?
TOLDJA IT WOULD WORK.

Water color applied with sign-painter's brush.

Construction paper staples and legal paper.

When you come across the scrubland in a hillbilly vehical in the middle of the night on un-detectable side roads on very rough roads releasing so much chiocking dust, satisfies.

COULD I WRITE A NOVEL THE SAME WAY? COULD I WRITE A NOVEL WITH A PAINTBRUSH?

IT TURNS OUT THAT WRITING IT WITH A PAINT-BRUSH WAS WHAT FINALLY BROUGHT THE BOOK TO LIFE.

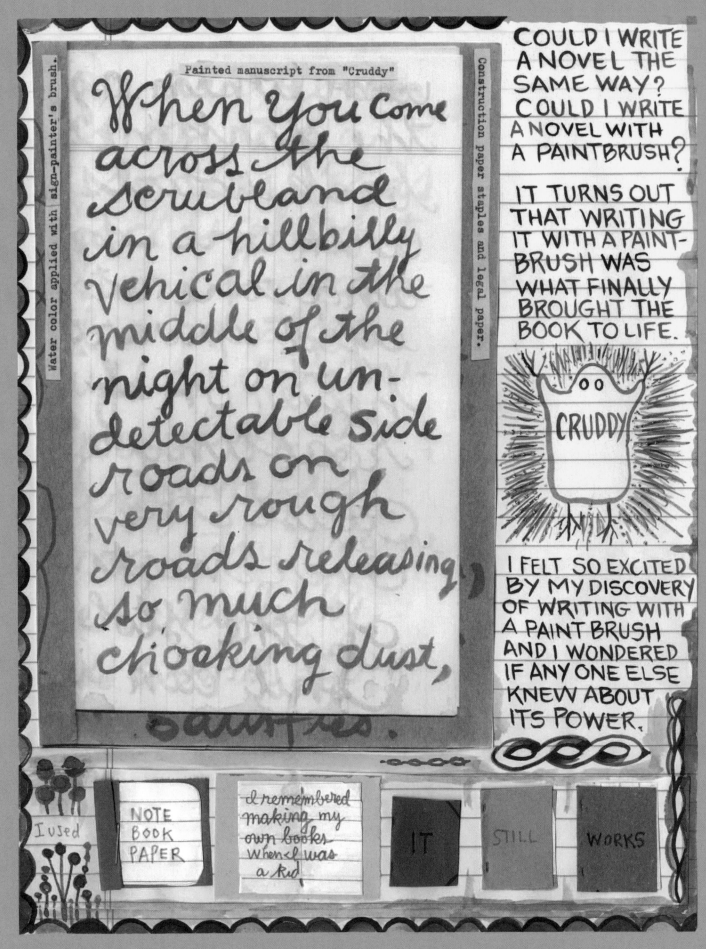

CRUDDY

I FELT SO EXCITED BY MY DISCOVERY OF WRITING WITH A PAINT BRUSH AND I WONDERED IF ANY ONE ELSE KNEW ABOUT ITS POWER.

I used

NOTE BOOK PAPER

I remembered making my own books when I was a kid

IT

STILL

WORKS

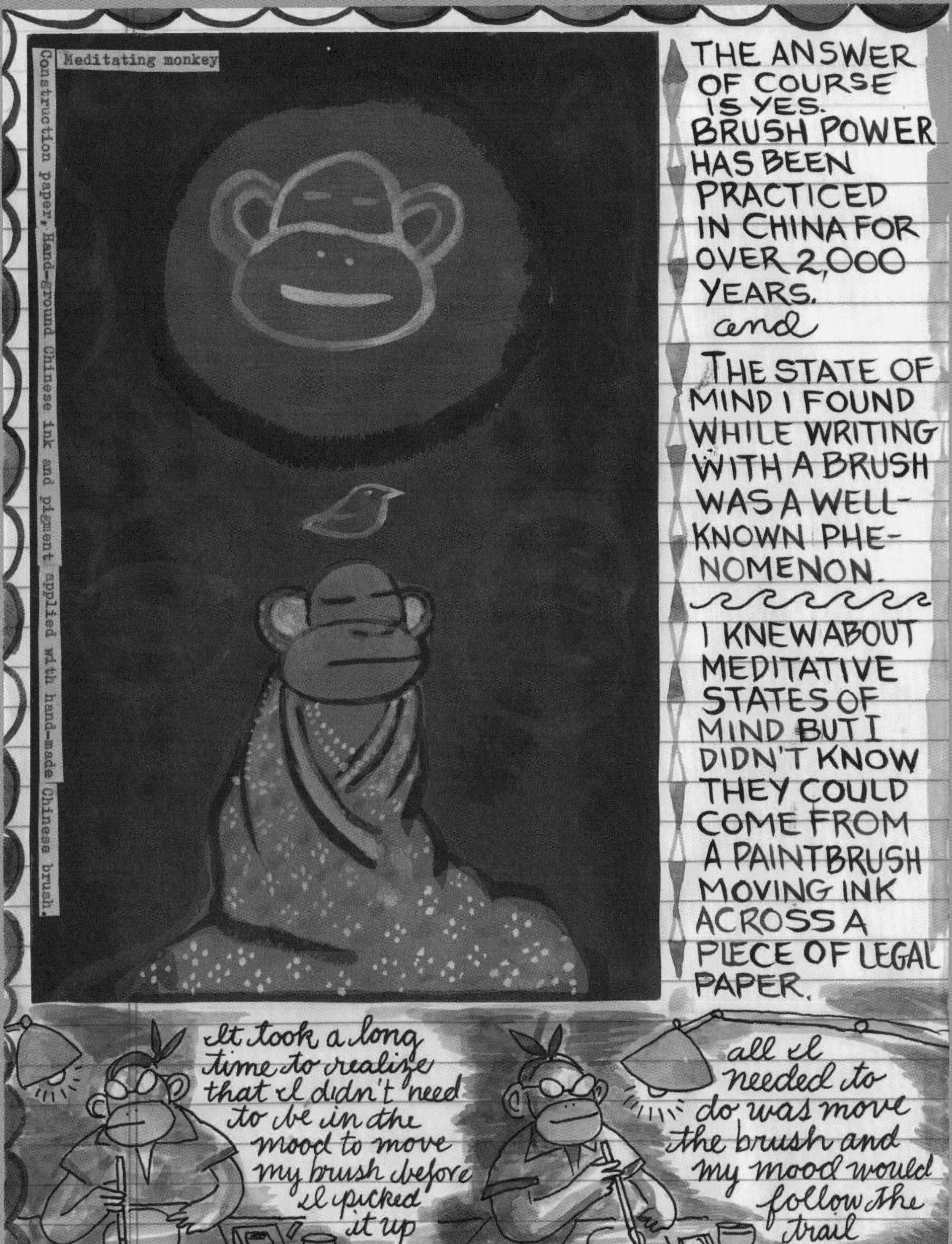
THE ANSWER OF COURSE IS YES. BRUSH POWER HAS BEEN PRACTICED IN CHINA FOR OVER 2,000 YEARS.
and
THE STATE OF MIND I FOUND WHILE WRITING WITH A BRUSH WAS A WELL-KNOWN PHENOMENON.
I KNEW ABOUT MEDITATIVE STATES OF MIND BUT I DIDN'T KNOW THEY COULD COME FROM A PAINTBRUSH MOVING INK ACROSS A PIECE OF LEGAL PAPER.
It took a long time to realize that I didn't need to be in the mood to move my brush before I picked it up
all I needed to do was move the brush and my mood would follow the trail

Meditating monkey

Construction paper, Hand-ground Chinese ink and pigment applied with hand-made Chinese brush.

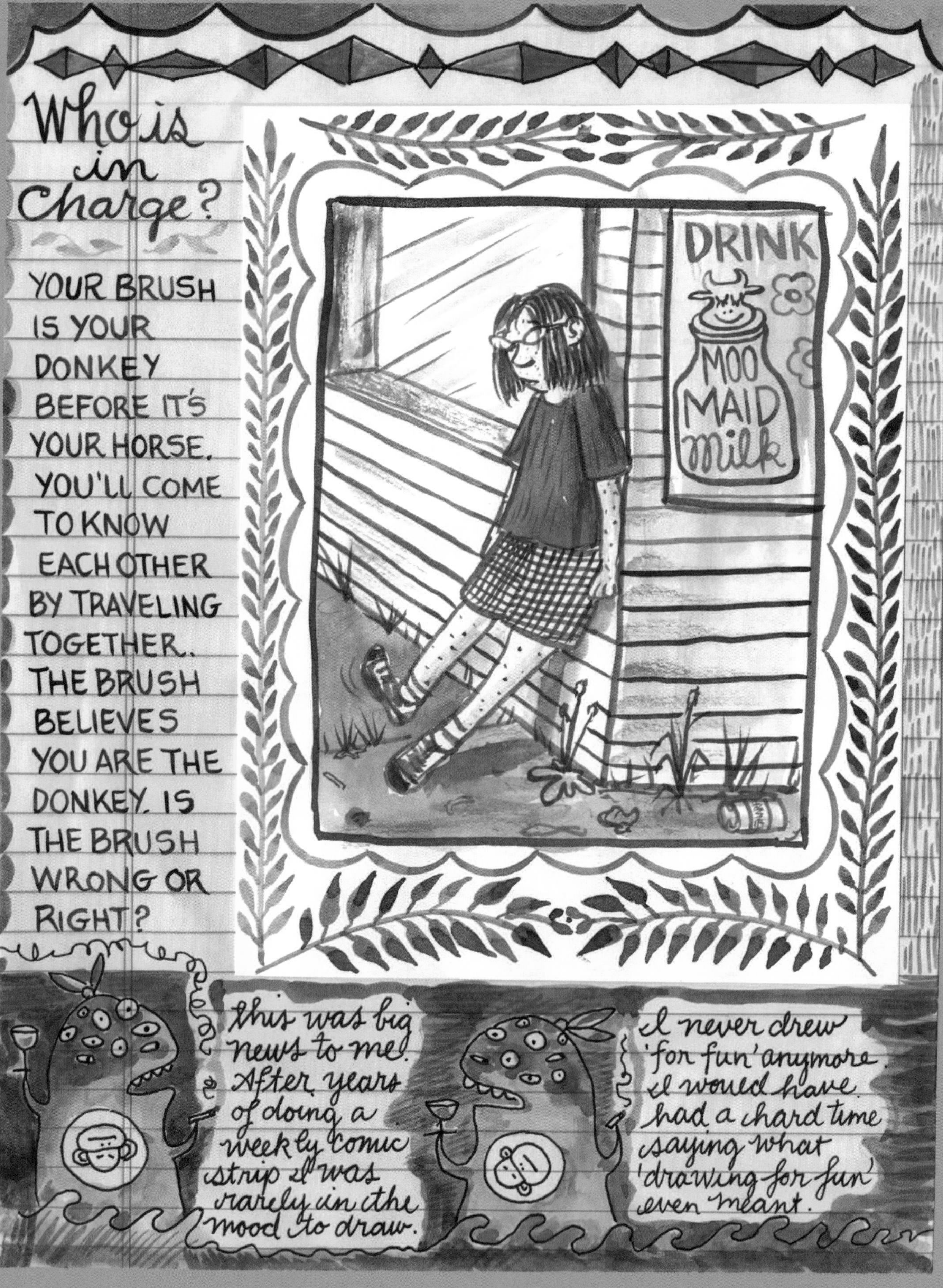
Who is in Charge?
YOUR BRUSH IS YOUR DONKEY BEFORE IT'S YOUR HORSE. YOU'LL COME TO KNOW EACH OTHER BY TRAVELING TOGETHER. THE BRUSH BELIEVES YOU ARE THE DONKEY. IS THE BRUSH WRONG OR RIGHT?
DRINK
MOO MAID milk
this was big news to me. After years of doing a weekly comic strip I was rarely in the mood to draw.
I never drew 'for fun' anymore. I would have had a hard time saying what 'drawing for fun' even meant.

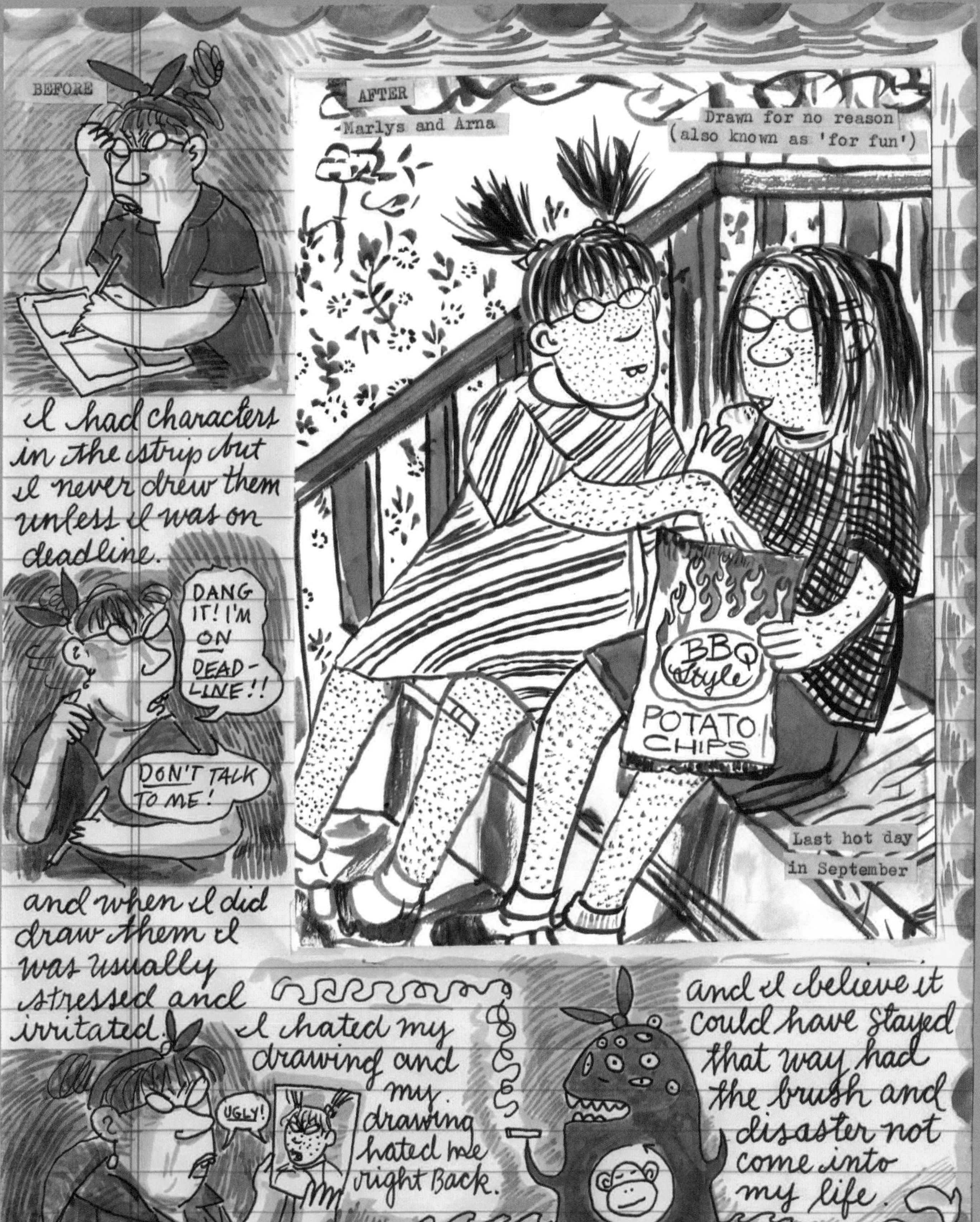
BEFORE
AFTER
Marlys and Arna
Drawn for no reason (also known as 'for fun')
I had characters in the strip but I never drew them unless I was on deadline.
DANG IT! I'M ON DEAD-LINE!!
DON'T TALK TO ME!
BBQ Style POTATO CHIPS
Last hot day in September
and when I did draw them I was usually stressed and irritated.
UGLY!
I hated my drawing and my drawing hated me right back.
and I believe it could have stayed that way had the brush and disaster not come into my life.

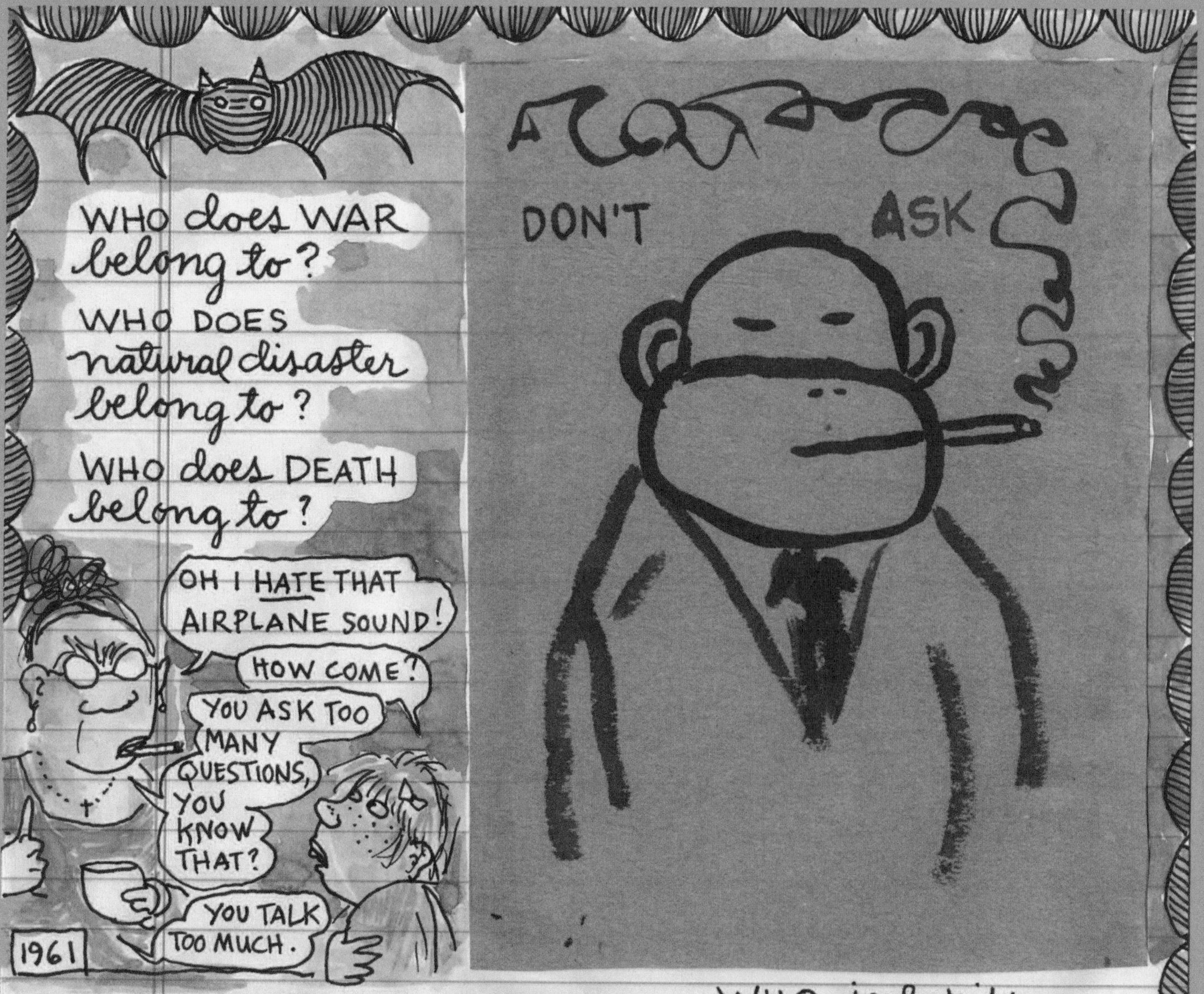
WHO does WAR belong to?
WHO DOES natural disaster belong to?
WHO does DEATH belong to?
OH I HATE THAT AIRPLANE SOUND!
HOW COME?
YOU ASK TOO MANY QUESTIONS, YOU KNOW THAT?
YOU TALK TOO MUCH.
1961
A
DON'T
ASK

My mother was a kid in a village just outside of Manila when the bombing raids begain on December 7, 1941.

WHO inherits these things?

Kevin's painting of the bombing of the Philippines. Watercolor on notebook paper.

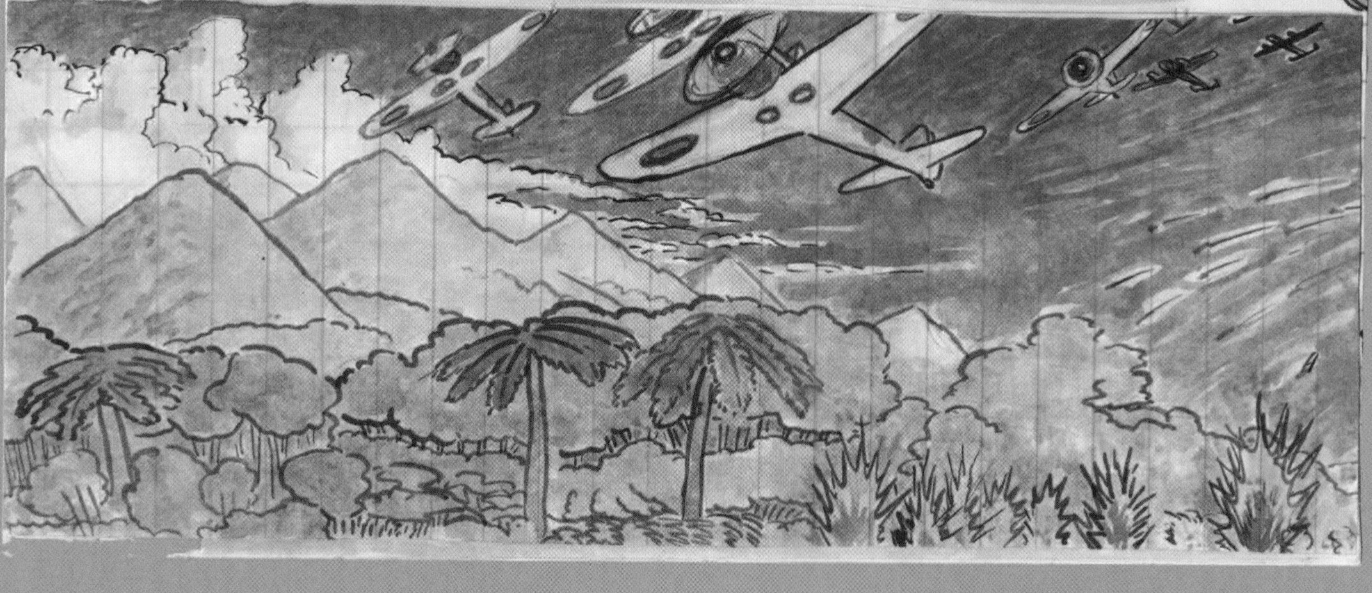

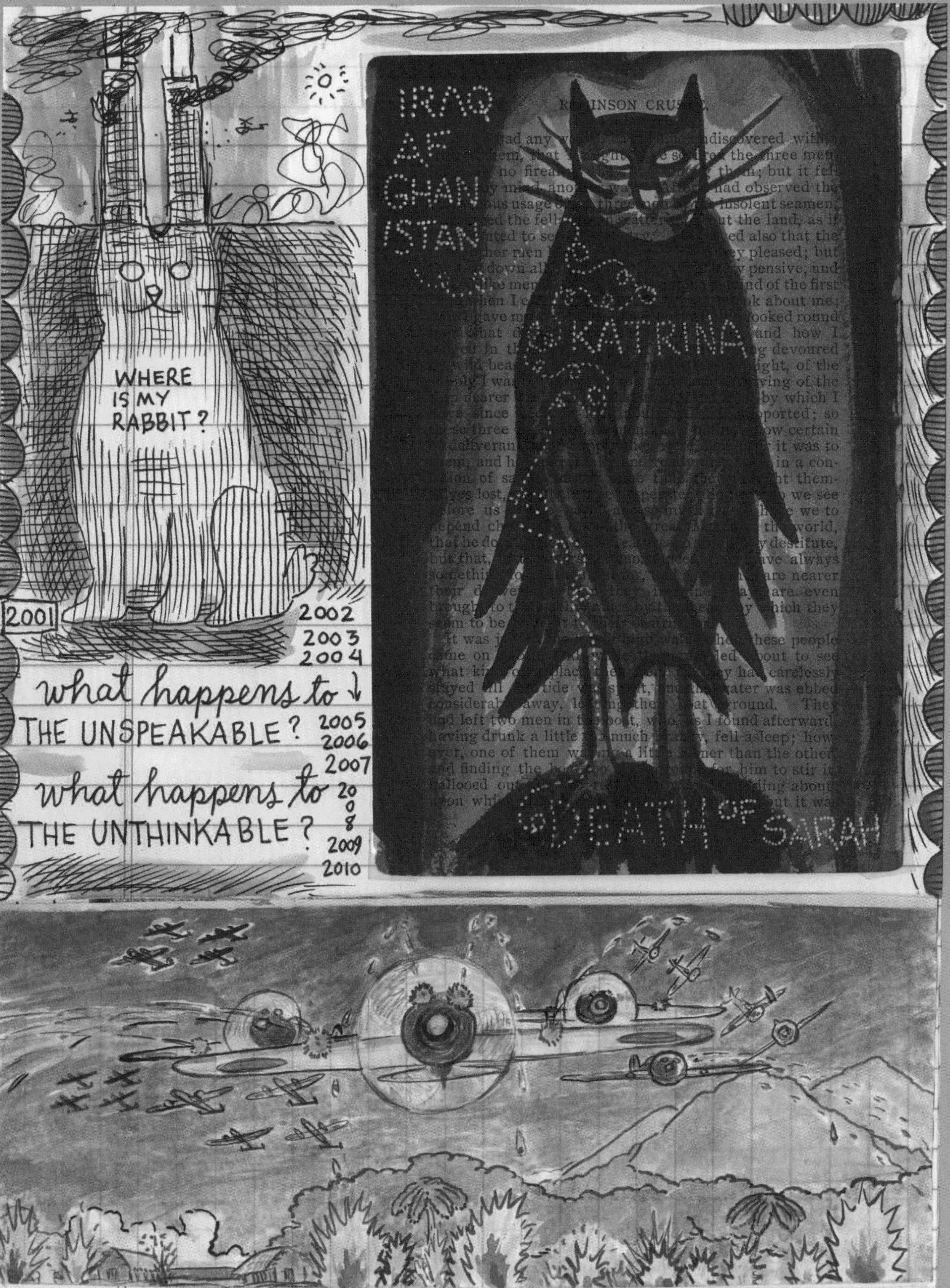
WHERE IS MY RABBIT?
2001
2002
2003
2004
what happens to ↓
THE UNSPEAKABLE?
2005
2006
2007
what happens to
2008
THE UNTHINKABLE?
2009
2010
IRAQ
AFGHANISTAN
KATRINA
DEATH OF SARAH

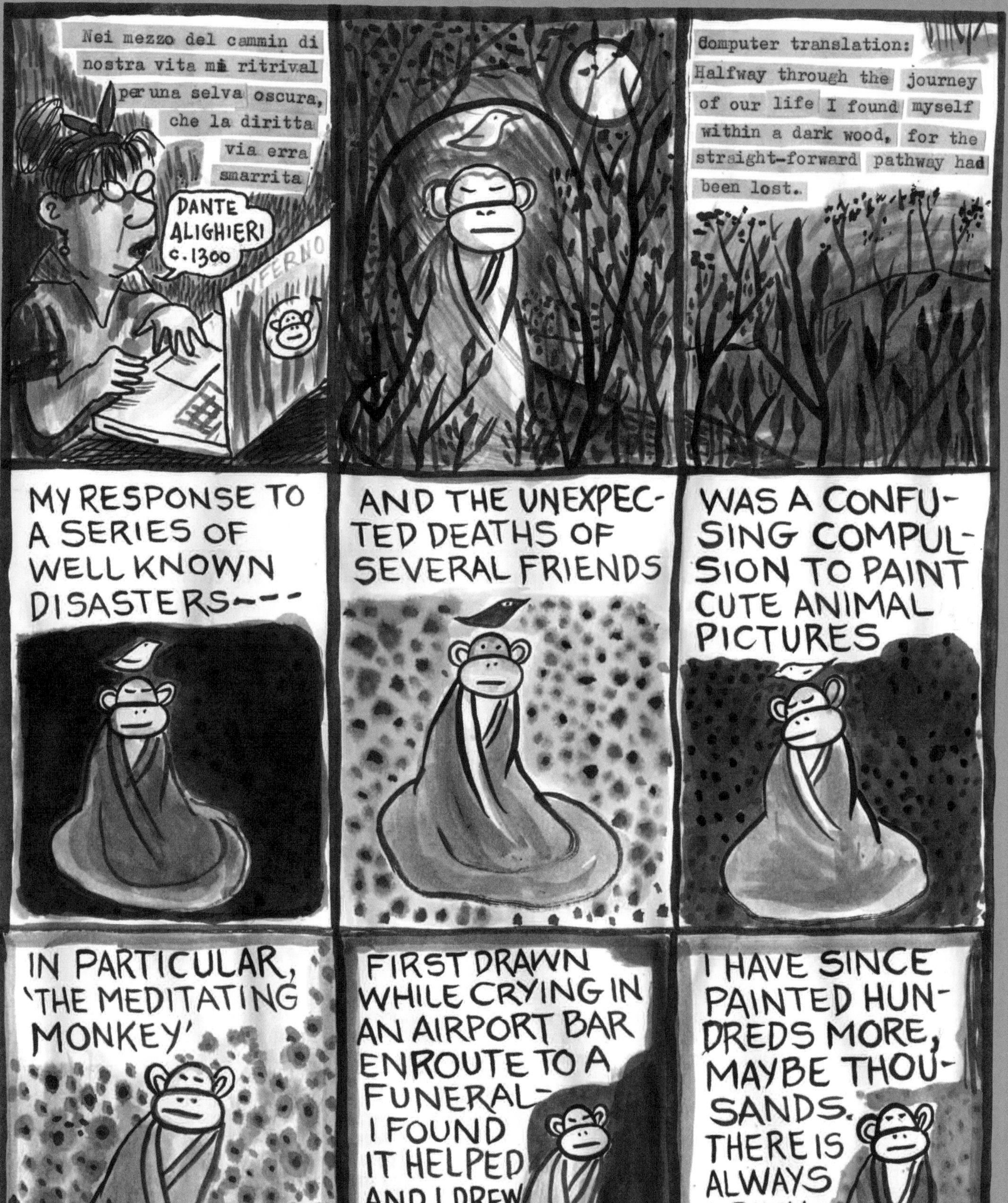
Nei mezzo del cammin di nostra vita mi ritrival per una selva oscura, che la diritta via erra smarrita
DANTE ALIGHIERI c.1300
INFERNO
Computer translation: Halfway through the journey of our life I found myself within a dark wood, for the straight-forward pathway had been lost.
MY RESPONSE TO A SERIES OF WELL KNOWN DISASTERS---
AND THE UNEXPECTED DEATHS OF SEVERAL FRIENDS
WAS A CONFUSING COMPULSION TO PAINT CUTE ANIMAL PICTURES
IN PARTICULAR, 'THE MEDITATING MONKEY'
FIRST DRAWN WHILE CRYING IN AN AIRPORT BAR ENROUTE TO A FUNERAL- I FOUND IT HELPED AND I DREW IT AGAIN AND AGAIN
I HAVE SINCE PAINTED HUNDREDS MORE, MAYBE THOUSANDS. THERE IS ALWAYS A PATH THAT IS LOST.

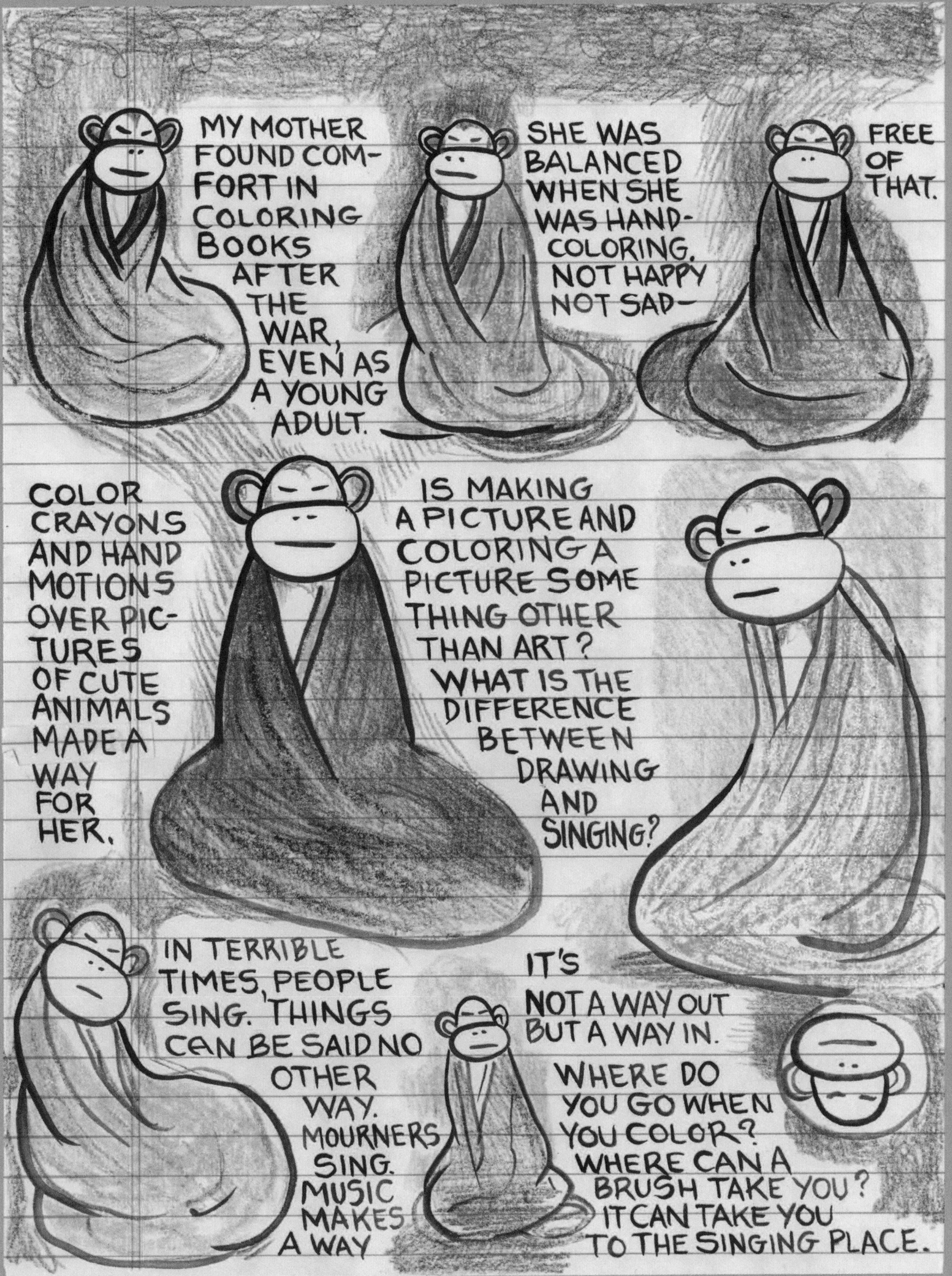
MY MOTHER FOUND COMFORT IN COLORING BOOKS AFTER THE WAR, EVEN AS A YOUNG ADULT.
SHE WAS BALANCED WHEN SHE WAS HAND-COLORING. NOT HAPPY NOT SAD—
FREE OF THAT.
COLOR CRAYONS AND HAND MOTIONS OVER PICTURES OF CUTE ANIMALS MADE A WAY FOR HER.
IS MAKING A PICTURE AND COLORING A PICTURE SOMETHING OTHER THAN ART? WHAT IS THE DIFFERENCE BETWEEN DRAWING AND SINGING?
IN TERRIBLE TIMES, PEOPLE SING. THINGS CAN BE SAID NO OTHER WAY. MOURNERS SING. MUSIC MAKES A WAY
IT'S NOT A WAY OUT BUT A WAY IN.
WHERE DO YOU GO WHEN YOU COLOR? WHERE CAN A BRUSH TAKE YOU? IT CAN TAKE YOU TO THE SINGING PLACE.

ure, and the squire's pleasure was like law among them all. N... ... old Redruth would have dared so much as even to grumble.

The next morning he and I set out on foot for the *Ad...* there I found my mother in good health and spirits. The... long been the cause of so much discomfort was... ...ease from... ...ling. The squire had had everything re... ...rooms and the sign repainted, and had added some furniture—above all, a beautiful arm-chair for mother at the bar. He had found her a boy as an apprentice also, so that she should not want help while...

It was on seeing that boy that I understood, for the first time, my situation. I had thought up to that time of the adventures before me... ...ll of the home I was leaving. Now at the sight of this clumsy stranger... ...to stay here in my place beside my mother, I had my first attack... ...was afraid I led the... ...a dog's life; for as he was new to the work... ...and oppor-tunity of... ...ing him right and putting him down... ...profit by...

...next day, after di... ...and I set out again upon the road. I said good-bye to mother and the cove where I had lived... ...and the dear old Admiral Benbow—since... ...remained... ...were of the ocean, with his cocked hat, his saber-cut... and his old brass telescope. Next moment we had turned the corner, and... ...was out of sight.

The mail picked us up about dusk at the *Royal George* on the heath. I was wedged in between Redruth and a stout old gentleman, and in spite of... ...motion and the cold night air, I must have slept a great deal from the very... and then... ...log up hill and down... ...through stage to stage; for when I was... ...it was by a pull in the ribs, and I opened my eyes... ...in a city street, and that the day had already...

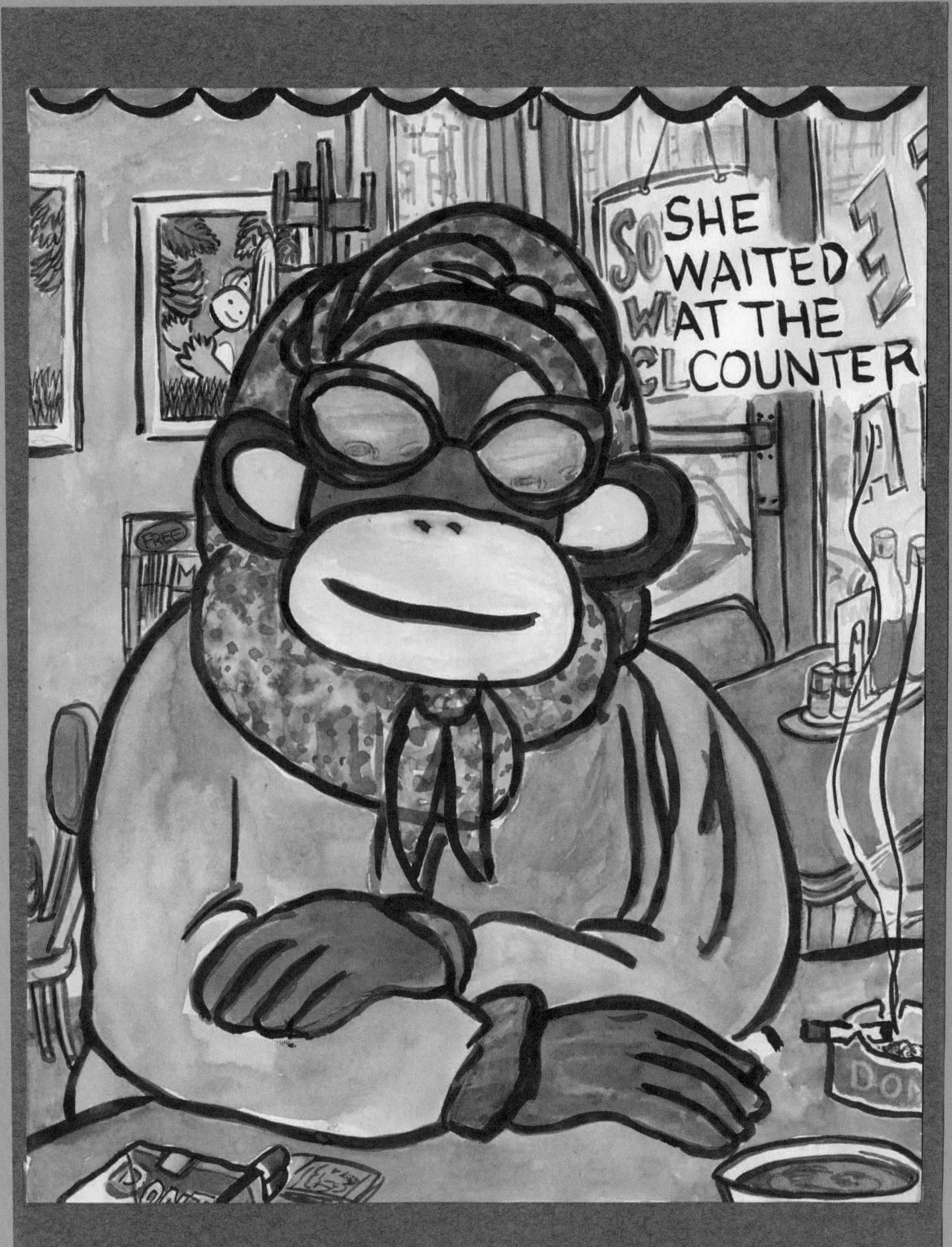
SHE WAITED AT THE COUNTER

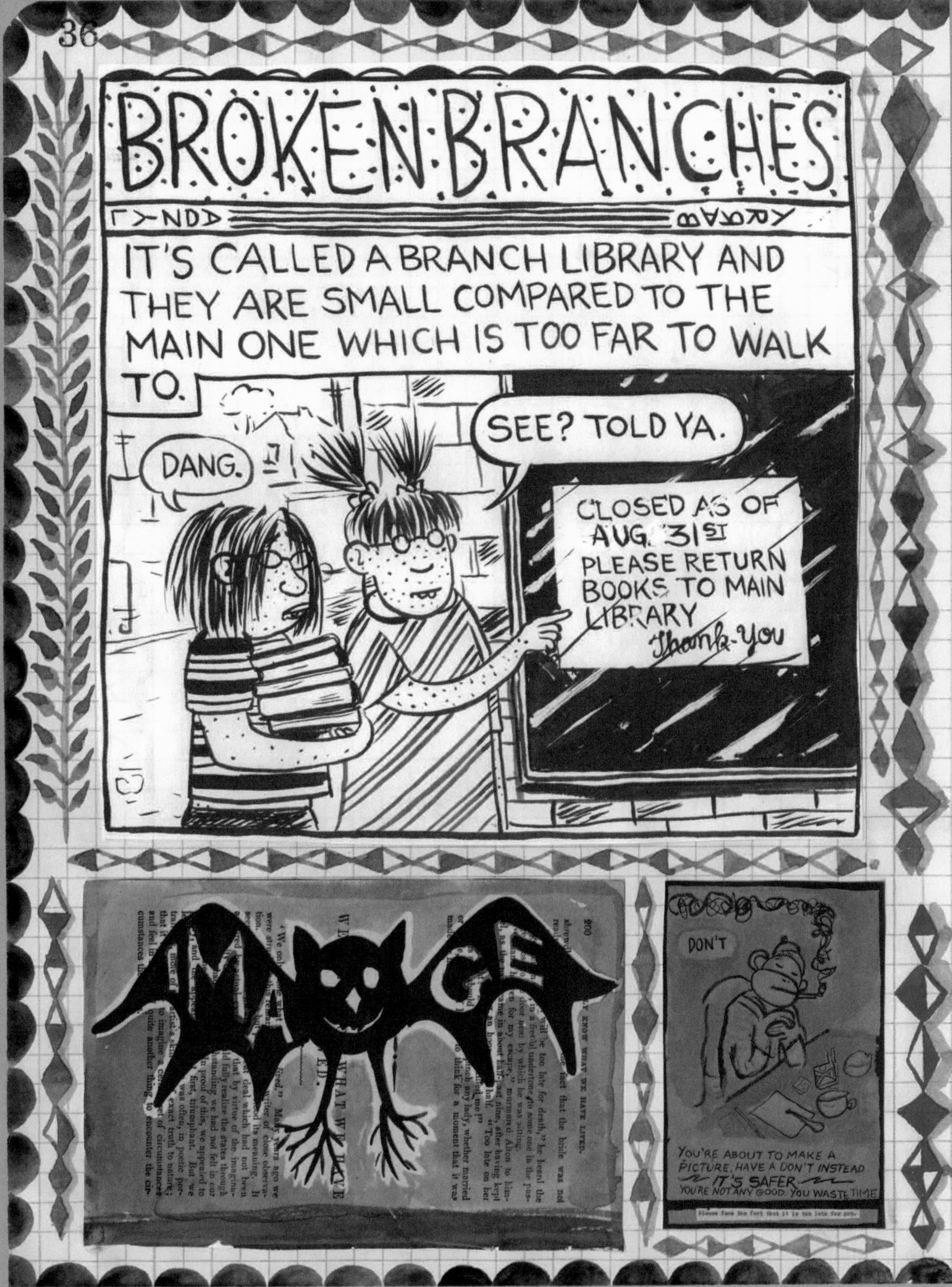
36
BROKEN BRANCHES
IT'S CALLED A BRANCH LIBRARY AND THEY ARE SMALL COMPARED TO THE MAIN ONE WHICH IS TOO FAR TO WALK TO.
DANG.
SEE? TOLD YA.
CLOSED AS OF AUG. 31ST PLEASE RETURN BOOKS TO MAIN LIBRARY Thank-you
DON'T
YOU'RE ABOUT TO MAKE A PICTURE, HAVE A DON'T INSTEAD
IT'S SAFER
YOU'RE NOT ANY GOOD. YOU WASTE TIME

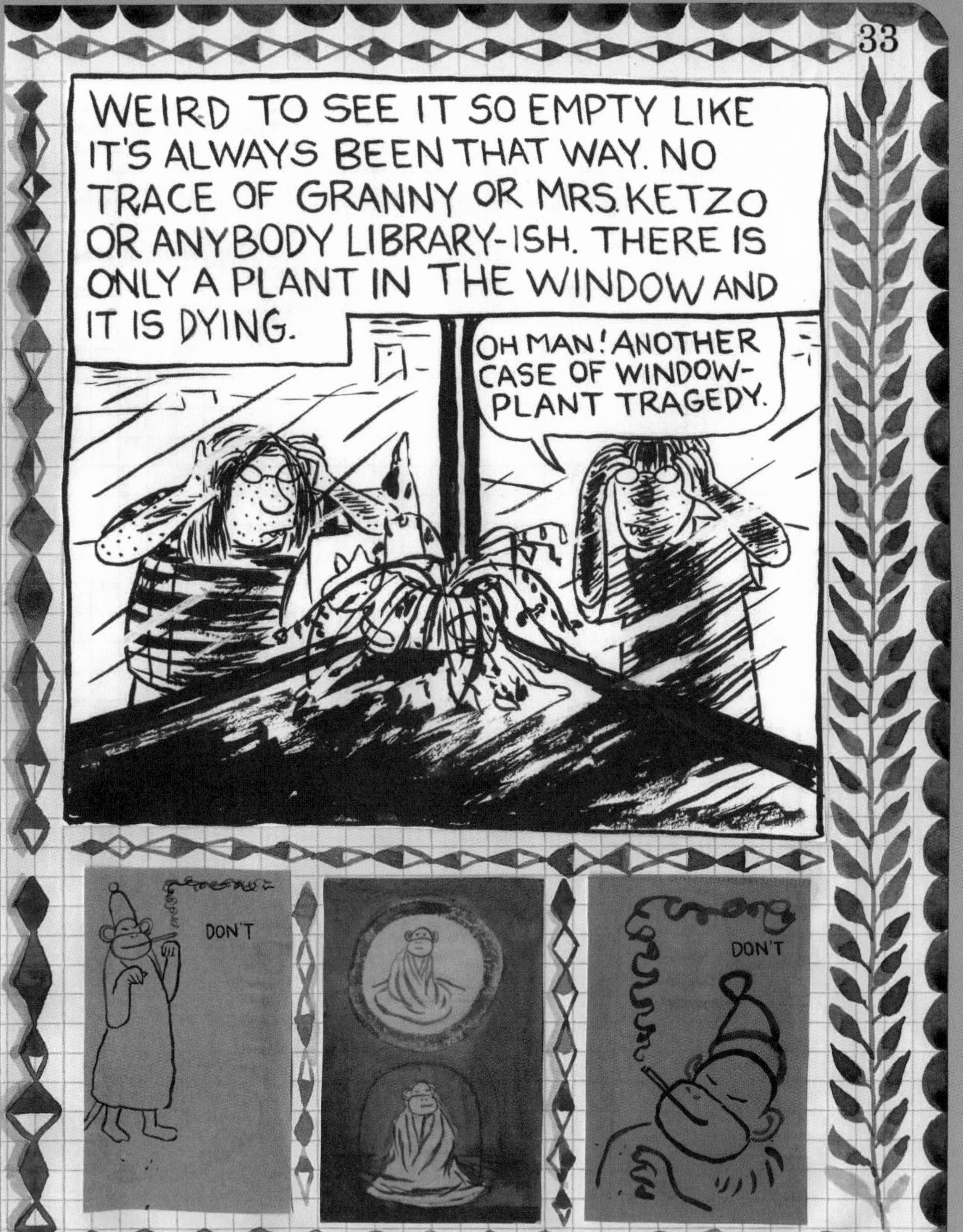
33
WEIRD TO SEE IT SO EMPTY LIKE IT'S ALWAYS BEEN THAT WAY. NO TRACE OF GRANNY OR MRS. KETZO OR ANYBODY LIBRARY-ISH. THERE IS ONLY A PLANT IN THE WINDOW AND IT IS DYING.
OH MAN! ANOTHER CASE OF WINDOW-PLANT TRAGEDY.
DON'T
DON'T

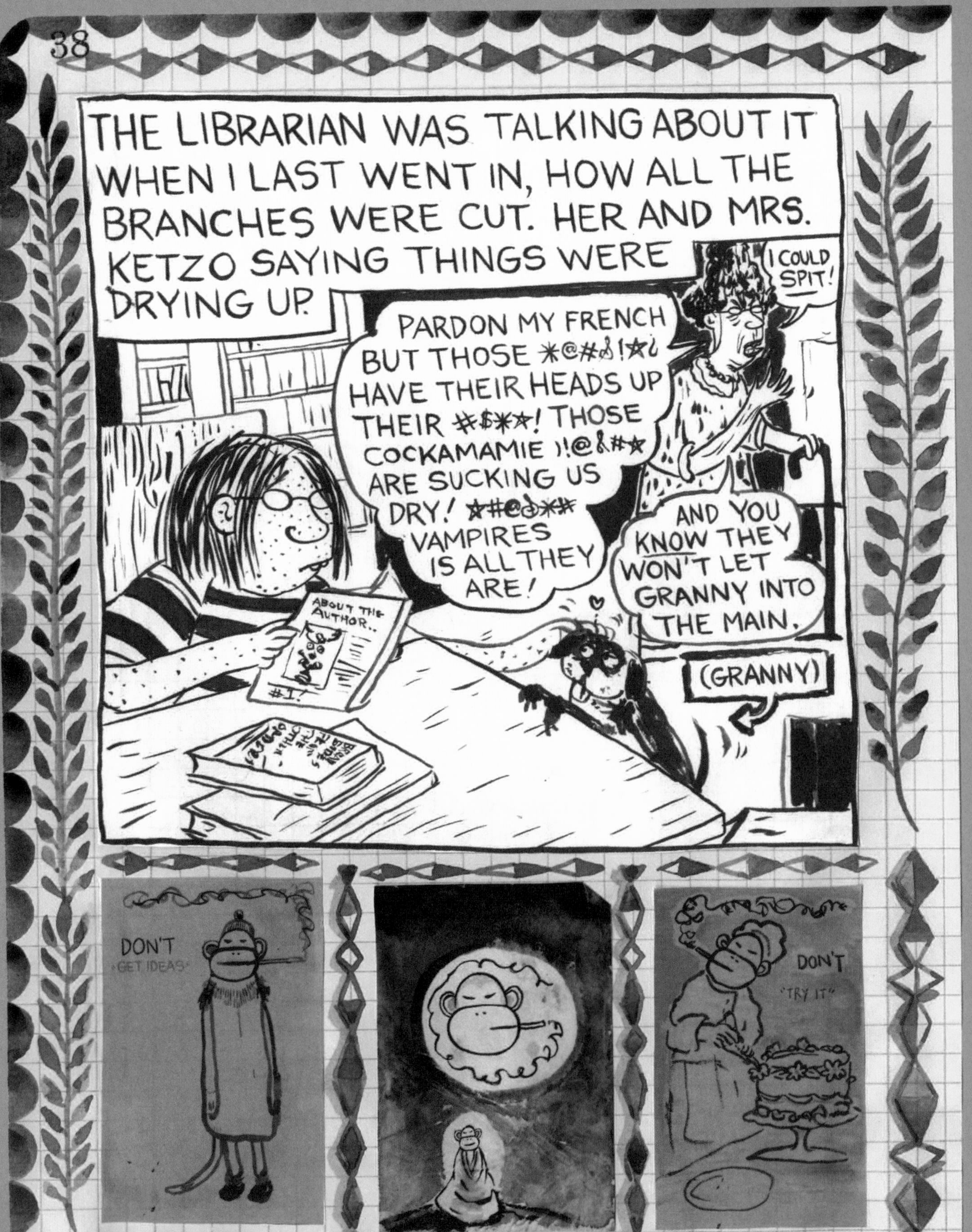

38
THE LIBRARIAN WAS TALKING ABOUT IT WHEN I LAST WENT IN, HOW ALL THE BRANCHES WERE CUT. HER AND MRS. KETZO SAYING THINGS WERE DRYING UP.
I COULD SPIT!
PARDON MY FRENCH BUT THOSE *@#&!*¿ HAVE THEIR HEADS UP THEIR #$**! THOSE COCKAMAMIE)!@&#* ARE SUCKING US DRY! *#@&** VAMPIRES IS ALL THEY ARE!
AND YOU KNOW THEY WON'T LET GRANNY INTO THE MAIN.
(GRANNY)
ABOUT THE AUTHOR..
#1!
DON'T
GET IDEAS
DON'T
TRY IT

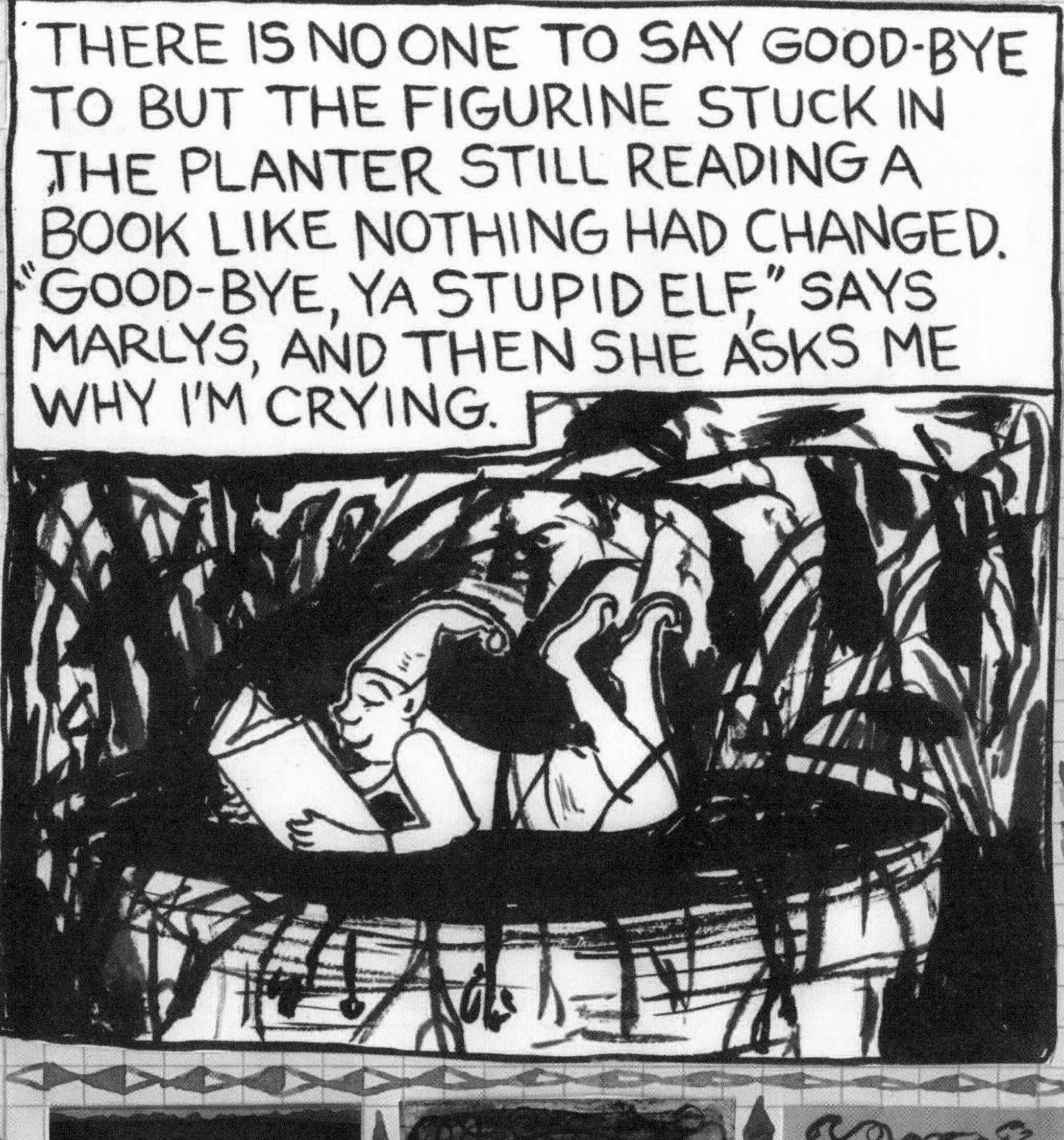
THERE IS NO ONE TO SAY GOOD-BYE TO BUT THE FIGURINE STUCK IN THE PLANTER STILL READING A BOOK LIKE NOTHING HAD CHANGED. "GOOD-BYE, YA STUPID ELF," SAYS MARLYS, AND THEN SHE ASKS ME WHY I'M CRYING.

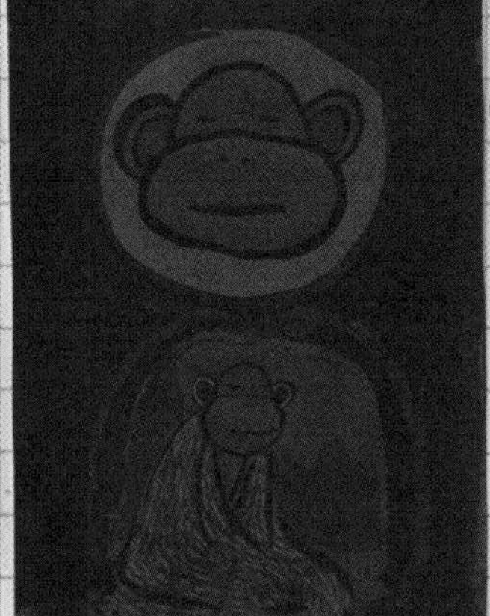

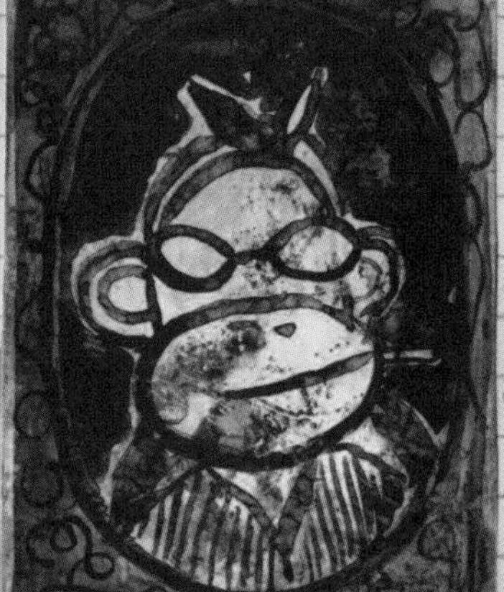

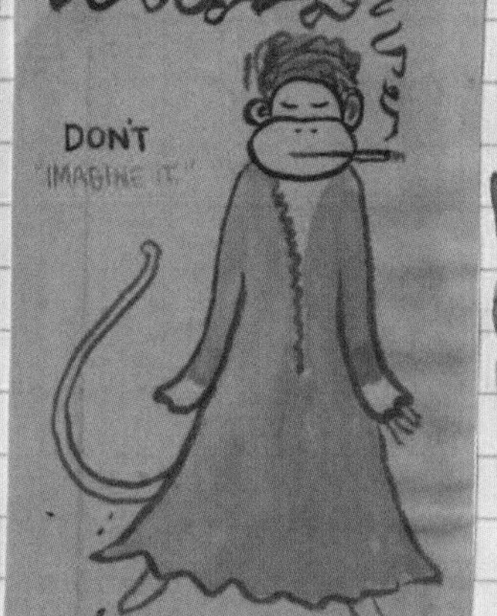
DON'T
"IMAGINE IT."

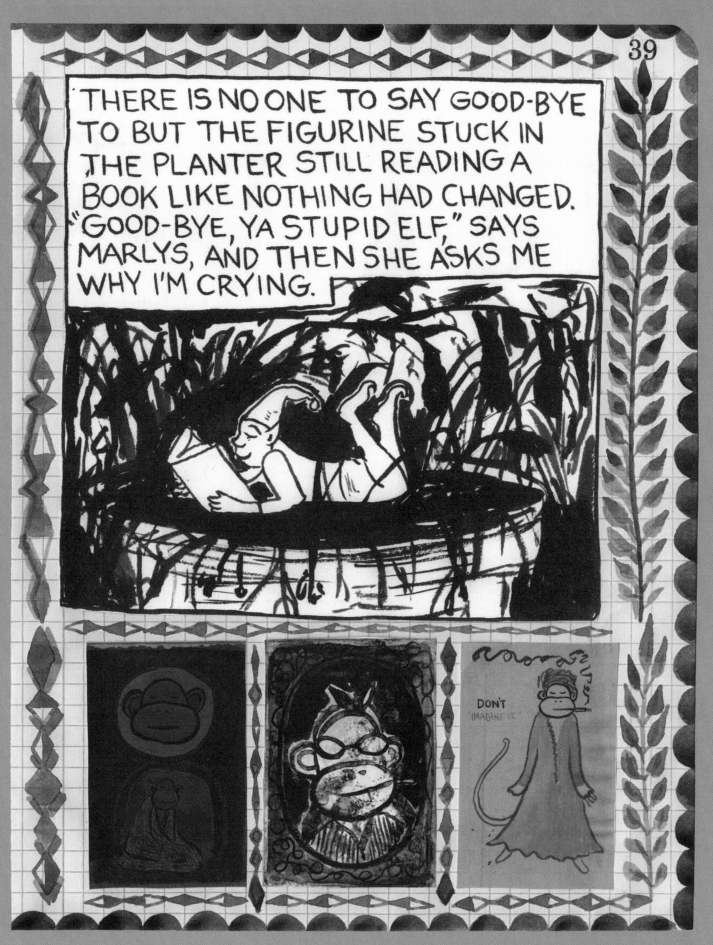

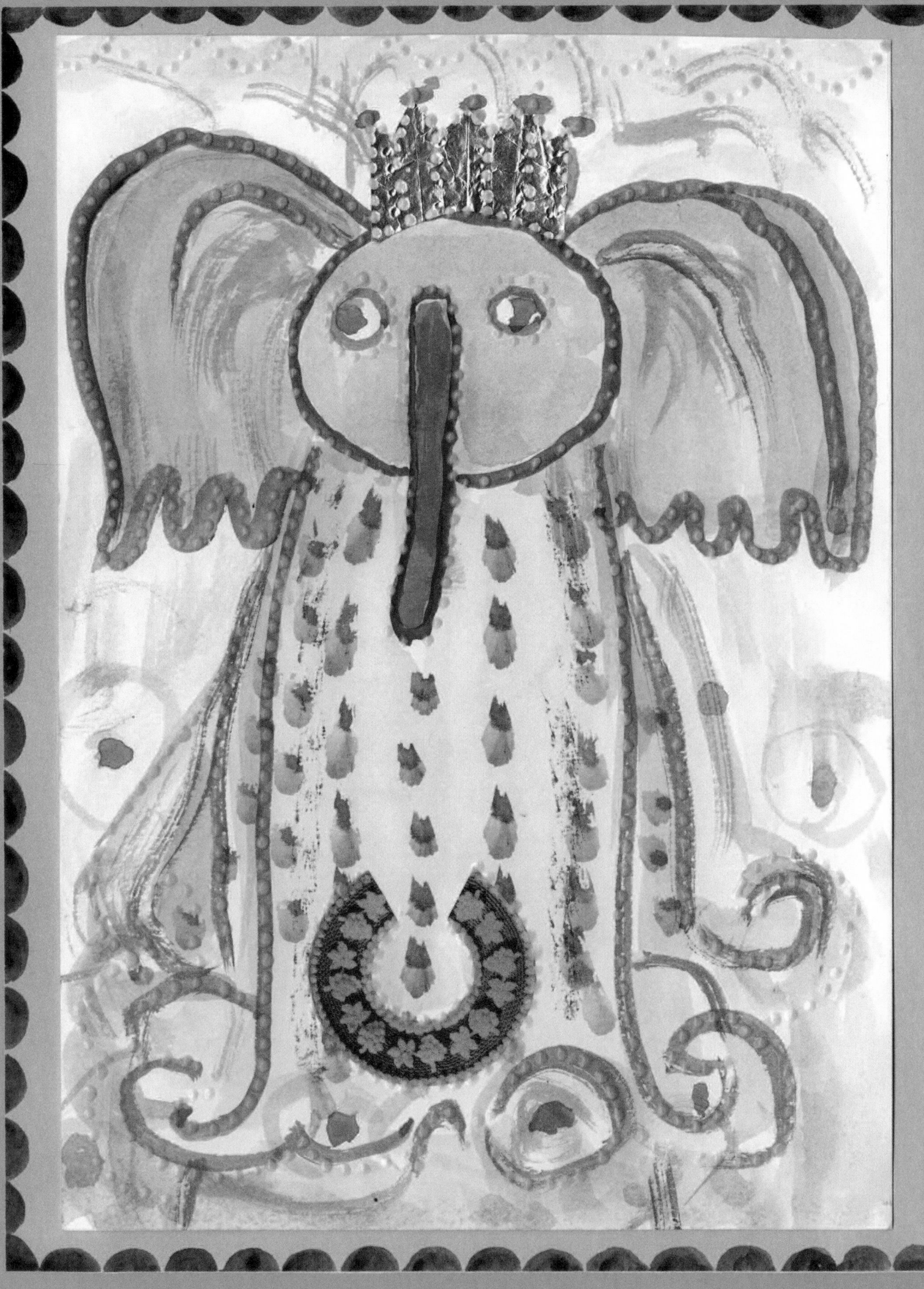

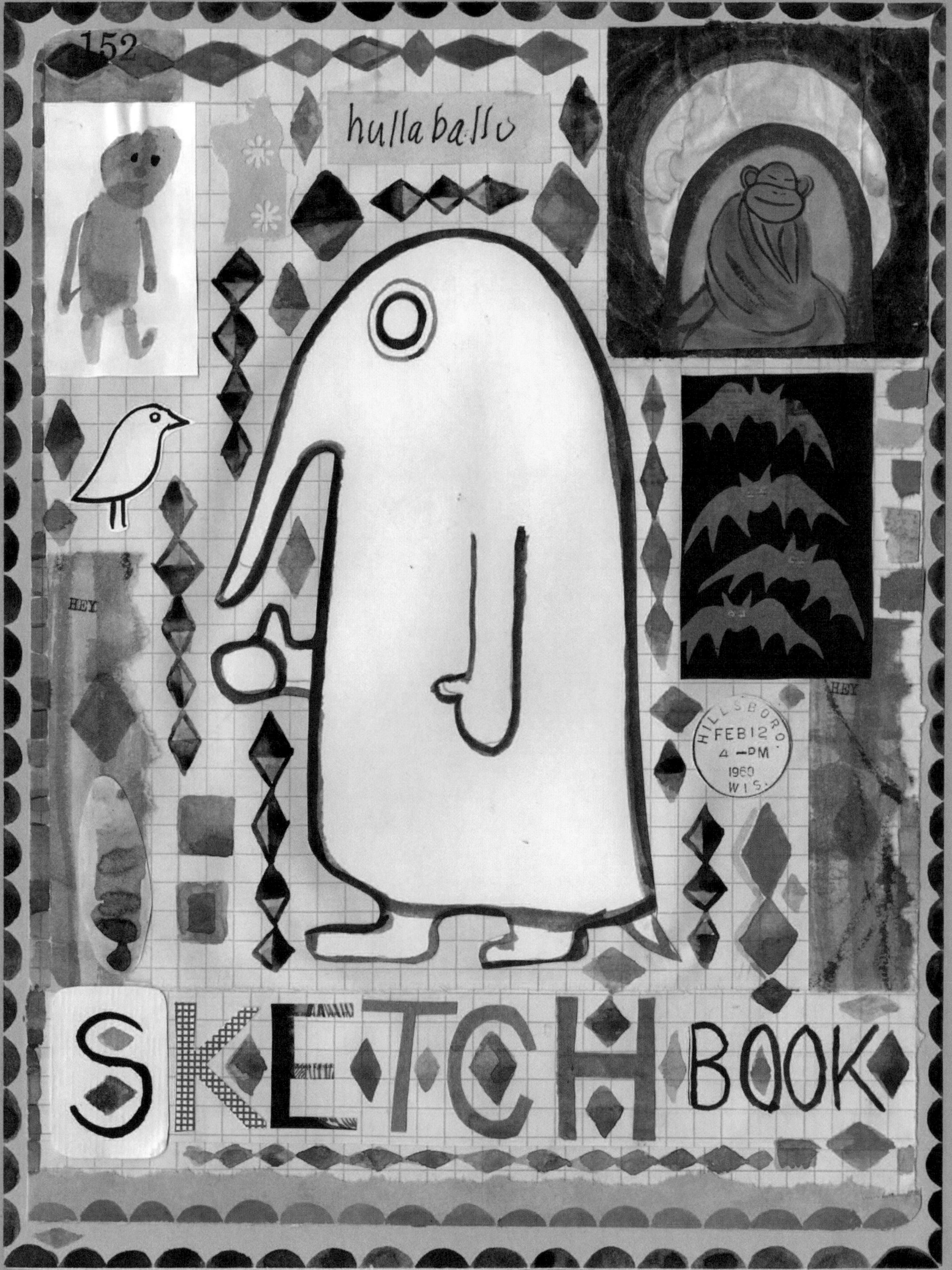
152
hulla ballu
HEY
HEY
HILLSBORO FEB 12 4 PM 1960 WIS.
SKETCH BOOK

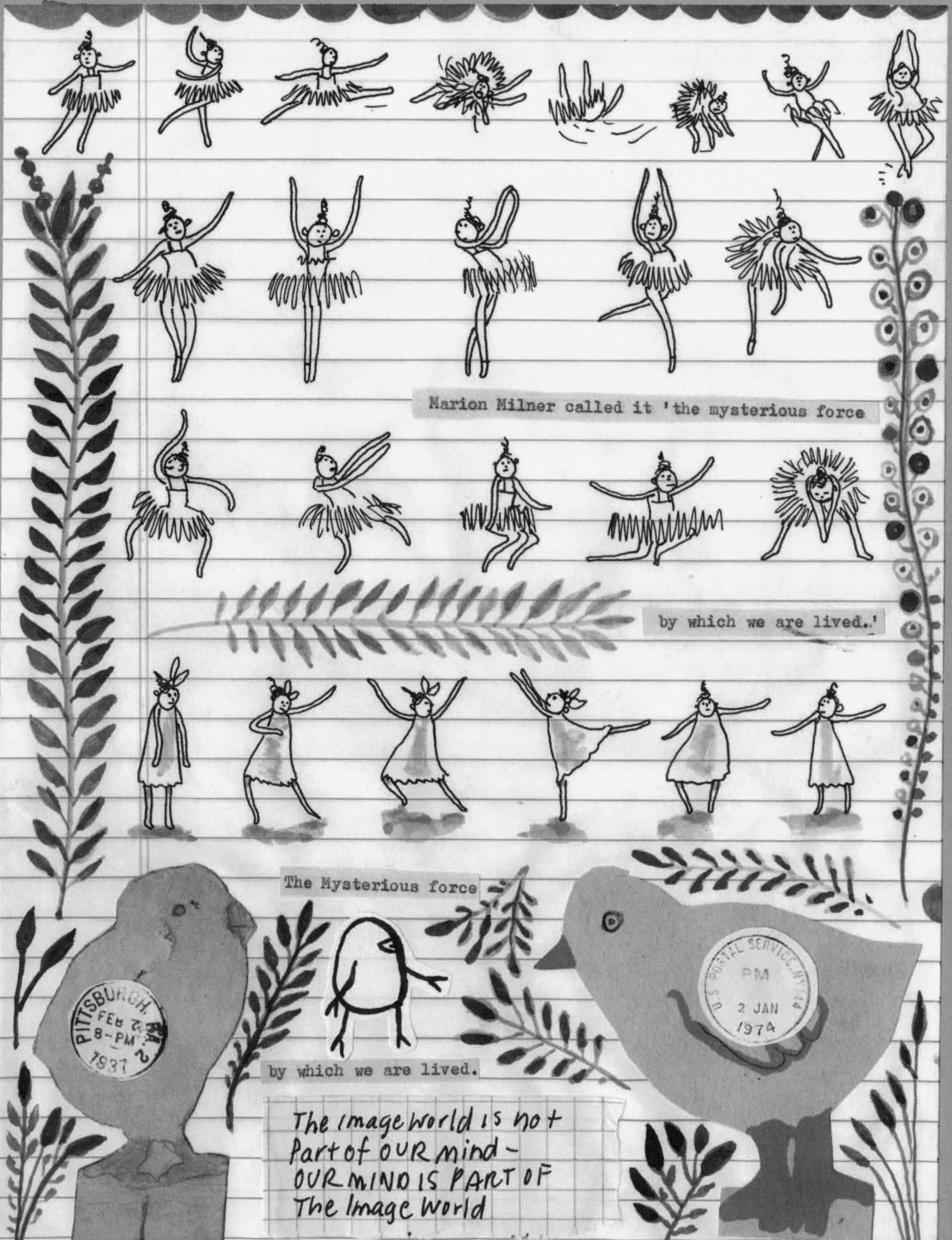
Marion Milner called it 'the mysterious force
by which we are lived.'
The Mysterious force
by which we are lived.
PITTSBURGH, PA. FEB 2 8-PM 1937
U.S. POSTAL SERVICE NY 14 PM 2 JAN 1974
The image world is not
Part of OUR mind –
OUR MIND IS PART OF
The Image world

by Lynda Barry

with guest artist Kevin Kawula   with Kevin Kawula

with watercolor guest Kevin Kawula

with guest watercolorist, Guest artist:

MAKING PICTURES
WITHOUT A LOT OF TALKING
ABOUT IT WHILE WE
WE'RE DOING IT

IN THIS BOOK

This is a picture of Kevin and I made by Scrounge Rocheleau
It is accurate. That is exactly what Kevin looks like.
"SPRING PRAIRIE BURN AT MILTONIA"
Also that is exactly what I look like

KEVIN and I PAINTED
THE NEAR-SIGHTED MONKEY
PICTURES TOGETHER. I LIKE
TO DRAW THINGS THAT ARE
CLOSE UP, HE LIKES TO
DRAW THINGS THAT ARE
FAR AWAY. HE ALSO LIKES
TO WATERCOLOR AND SO
I WOULD HAND HIM A
MONKEY PICTURE
DRAWN IN INK AND A
FEW DAYS LATER HE
WOULD HAND IT BACK
PAINTED IN. WE HARDLY
TALKED ABOUT THE PIC-
TURES BEYOND SAYING "I
DIG THAT, MAN!" AND THE
PICTURES HAPPENED ANYWAY.

COLORING BOOKS

You are invited
to a Drawing
party.

Draw for X min
straight - music
none / NO TALKING
ABOUT THE PICTURES.

You CAN TALK ABOUT ANYTHING EXCEPT THE PAINTINGS

TRANSLATION IS POSSIBLE BECAUSE

I had an idea for
a party where
people made pictures
together and the
rule is you can talk
about anything except
the pictures.

What happens when
we make pictures
without talking
about them?

Why would we not
talk about a picture?
what does not talking
give us?

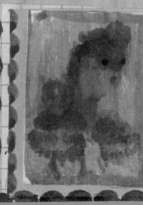

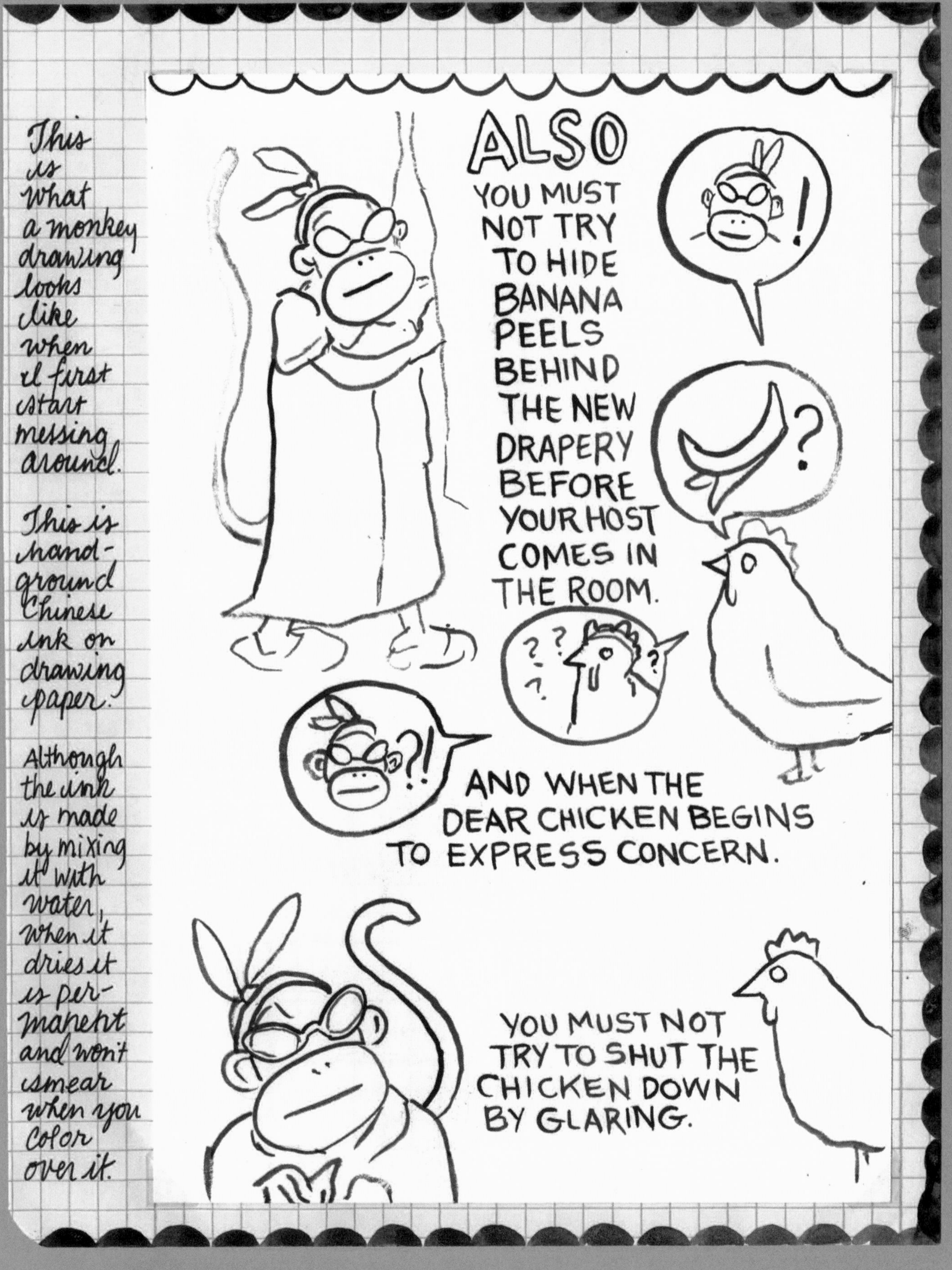
This is what a monkey drawing looks like when I first start messing around.
This is hand-ground Chinese ink on drawing paper.
Although the ink is made by mixing it with water, when it dries it is permanent and won't smear when you color over it.
ALSO
YOU MUST NOT TRY TO HIDE BANANA PEELS BEHIND THE NEW DRAPERY BEFORE YOUR HOST COMES IN THE ROOM.
!
?
?!
AND WHEN THE DEAR CHICKEN BEGINS TO EXPRESS CONCERN.
YOU MUST NOT TRY TO SHUT THE CHICKEN DOWN BY GLARING.

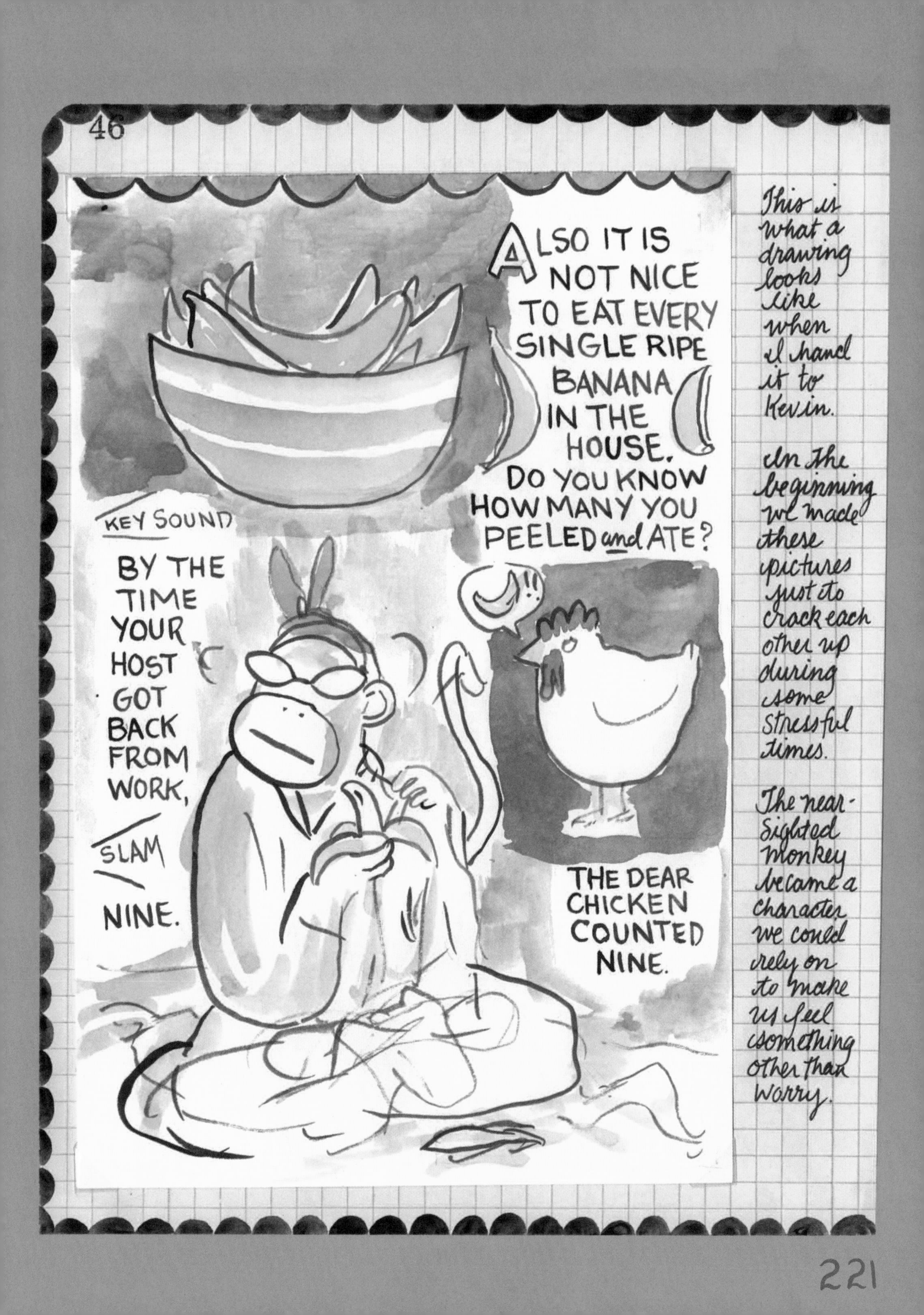
46
ALSO IT IS NOT NICE TO EAT EVERY SINGLE RIPE BANANA IN THE HOUSE. DO YOU KNOW HOW MANY YOU PEELED and ATE?
KEY SOUND
BY THE TIME YOUR HOST GOT BACK FROM WORK,
SLAM
NINE.
!!
THE DEAR CHICKEN COUNTED NINE.
This is what a drawing looks like when I hand it to Kevin.
In the beginning we made these pictures just to crack each other up during some stressful times.
The near-sighted Monkey became a character we could rely on to make us feel something other than worry.

41

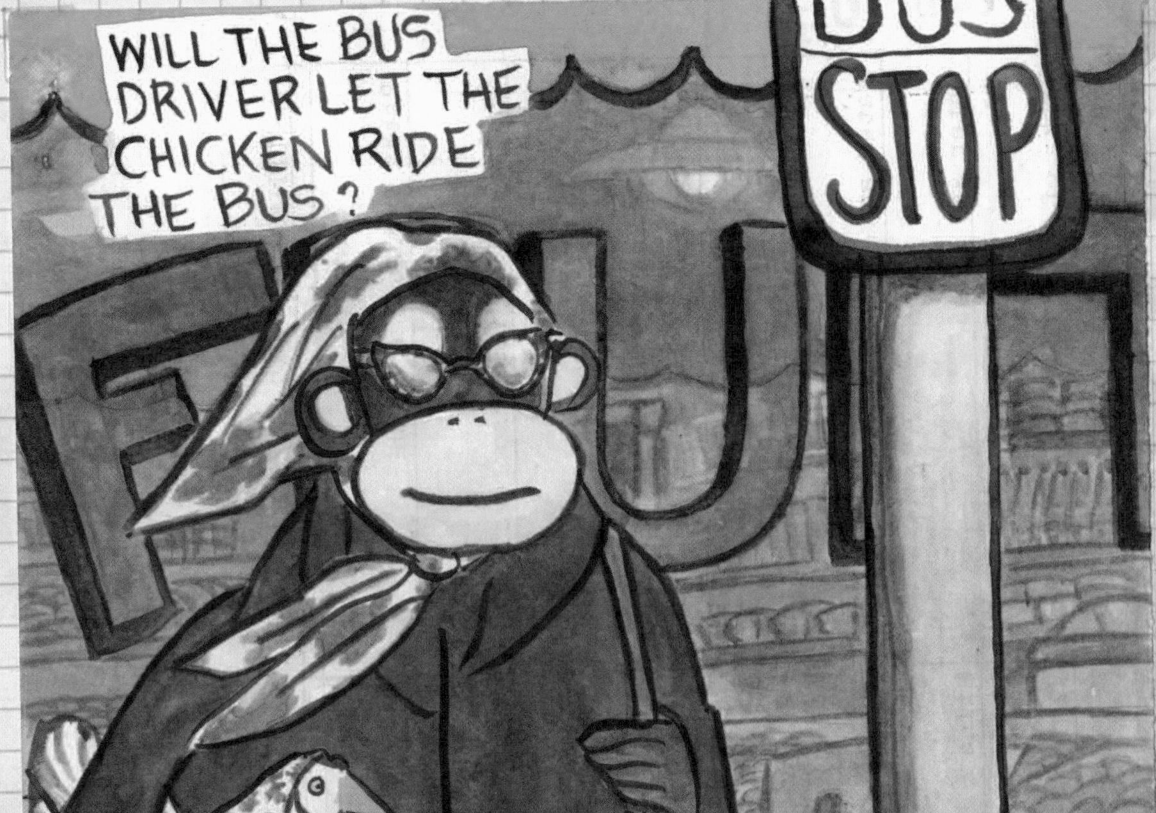
WILL THE BUS DRIVER LET THE CHICKEN RIDE THE BUS?
STOP
THE NEAR SIGHTED MONKEY MUST PAY 10¢ EXTRA

This is what it looks like when Kevin hands it back. often we can't remember who drew what. I thought he put the scarf on the dear chicken. He says I did it. I really don't know who put the scarf on the chicken

THE NEAR-SIGHTED MONKEY DRANK ALL YOUR WINE AND READ ALL YOUR TABLOIDS AGAIN

BANANA SLIMS

YOU'VE SWUNG A LONG WAY, MONKEY

we made alot of these pictures over the last three years and they began to change my ideas about drawing as something to struggle with.

what if drawing could be something else?

what if drawing could be about being a being in motion — like a skater leaving a line by velocity and balance?

What if drawing was a way to get to a certain state of mind that was very good for us? And what if this certain state of mind was more important than the drawing itself?

I believe making lines and shapes and coloring them in can still help us in the way it helped us when we were kids. when we used paper as if it were a place rather than a thing. A place where something alive can happen through motion. The motion of our bare hands — the original digital devices; wireless, biofueled, completely ours. Drawing is one of our oldest ways of working things out.

There is a letter in your mailbox. When you see it, you say, "Oh no!"

BUT SHE IS ON HER WAY NOW

The Near-Sighted Monkey is coming to visit.

WHY NOT SAY "HECK YES!"

YOU CAN DO IT TOO!

I taught myself how to use Chinese brush and ink by going to the library and looking through books such as

• BRUSH STROKES IN SUMI-E PAINTING by MOTOI OI (1963)

• THE WAY OF THE BRUSH by FRITZ VAN BRIESSEN (1962)

• CHINESE PAINTING IN FOUR SEASONS (1981) by LESLIE TSENG-TSENG YU

• ORIENTAL PAINTING COURSE: A PRACTICAL GUIDE TO PAINTING SKILLS AND TECHNIQUES OF CHINA AND THE FAR EAST by WANG Jianan + CAI Xiali (2001)

I also like the videos on YOUTUBE by YANG HAI YING – "DEMYSTIFY CHINESE PAINTING"
"CHI OF YOUR HAND"
"HOW ABOUT DANCE LIKE EVERYBODY IS WATCHING"
"BLA·BLA·BLA – IDEA GROWS FROM PRACTICE"

ALSO "ON NOT BEING ABLE TO PAINT" by MARION MILNER has been a BIG HELP TO ME when I get stuck

SEAMA

I get my Chinese Art supplies from YING XING WANG at ACORNPLANET.COM She has wonderful ink stones, ink - sticks, color pigment sticks and brushes. I love everything I've gotten from her.

MASH NOTE TO EVERYONE AT DRAWN AND QUARTERLY This book, like "WHAT IT IS" would not exist without you. The playfield you've given me has allowed a new way of making books to happen and I LOVE YOU for this chance to follow my inclination as I go. XXOOX!!

TRUE
LB + D+Q
LOVE

JUST REMEMBER TO MONKEY AROUND AND YOU'LL BE OK!

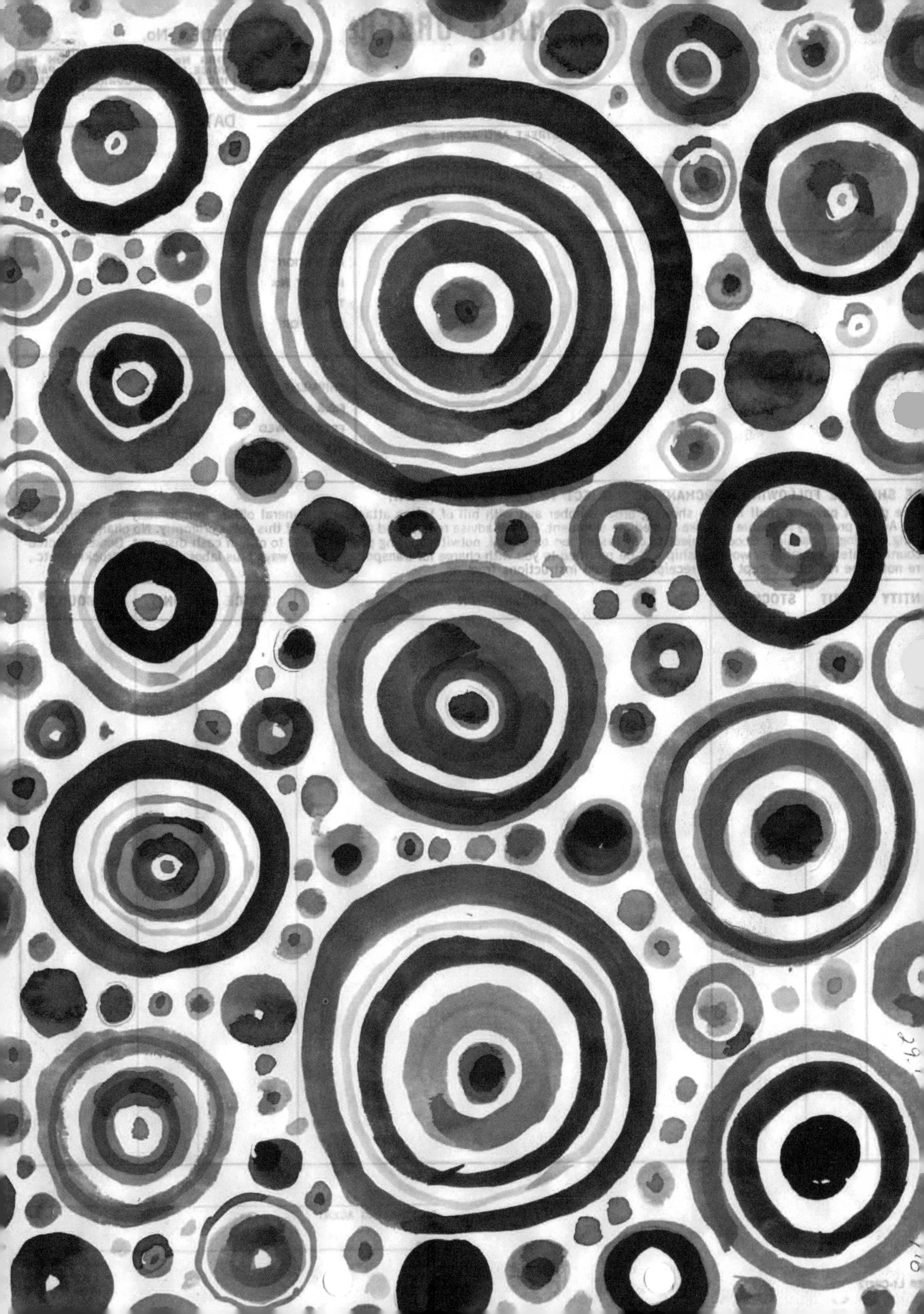